Optional Instruments of the European Union

A Definitional, Normative and Explanatory Study

William A. Bull

Optional Instruments of the European Union

A Definitional, Normative and Explanatory Study

intersentia

METRO

Ius Commune Europaeum

Intersentia Ltd
Sheraton House | Castle Park
Cambridge | CB3 0AX | United Kingdom
Tel.: +44 1223 370 170 | Fax: +44 1223 370 169
Email: mail@intersentia.co.uk
www.intersentia.com | www.intersentia.co.uk

Distribution for the UK and Ireland:
NBN International
Airport Business Centre, 10 Thornbury Road
Plymouth, PL6 7PP
United Kingdom
Tel.: +44 1752 202 301 | Fax: +44 1752 202 331
Email: orders@nbninternational.com

Distribution for Europe and all other countries:
Intersentia Publishing nv
Groenstraat 31
2640 Mortsel
Belgium
Tel.: +32 3 680 15 50 | Fax: 32 3 658 71 21
Email: mail@intersentia.be

Distribution for the USA and Canada:
International Specialized Book Services
920 NE 58th Ave. Suite 300
Portland, OR 97213
USA
Tel.: +1 800 944 6190 (toll free) | Fax: + 1 503 280 8832
Email: info@isbs.com

Optional Instruments of the European Union: A Definitional, Normative and Explanatory Study

ISBN 978-1-78068-410-9
D/2016/7849/83
NUR 822

British Library Cataloguing in Publication Data. A catalogue record for this book is available from the British Library.

ACKNOWLEDGEMENTS

So many esteemed colleagues and friends have provided me with inspiration, advice and support in the researching and writing of this thesis (including experts and participants in the various seminars and workshops at which I have discussed parts of it) that I could not possibly provide an exhaustive list of them here, and I owe each and every one of them a debt of gratitude.

Naturally deep appreciation is first and foremost owed to my supervisor and promotor *Jan Smits*, who has followed my work most closely over the past four years. Jan has helped me infinitely every step of the way with his insightful comments, challenging questions and passion for the subject of this thesis, and in so doing has made a huge contribution to the positions and line of argumentation I have developed in this book. I have very much enjoyed all of the inspiring and thought-provoking discussions we have had during the process, as much as I have appreciated Jan's clear guidance and direction in the more testing of times.

I would also like to give special thanks to the assessment committee for taking the time to read and evaluate the book. *Jaap Hage* has been an enthusiastic and committed committee chair, not to mention the best sounding board for my philosophical ideas and dilemmas that I could have wished for, and I am very grateful to *Bram Akkermans, Hector MacQueen, Mieke Olaerts* and *Alex Wulf* for their willingness to participate in the assessment committee.

I am equally grateful to my close colleagues *Bram Akkermans, Anna Beckers, Anna Berlee, Caroline Cauffman, Catalina Goanta, Jiangqiu Ge, Mark Kawakami, Nicole Kornet, Adela Ognean, Mieke Olaerts* and *Daniel On* for all the support, both substantive and moral, that they have given me throughout this process. *Mark Kawakami* and *Jiangqiu Ge* deserve a particular word of thanks in this respect for their support as paranymphs, friends and fellow Leicester City fans, as do *Marjo* Mullers and *Benedikt Schmitz* for doing an excellent job in helping me to finalize the manuscript for submission in an extraordinarily short space of time. Last but not least, there are no words with which I can adequately express my appreciation to my family (my brothers *Gregory* and *Thomas*, my father *David* and particularly my mother *Anna*) for their eternal encouragement, understanding and patience: *Non so come fate, ma so che senza di voi io non ce la farei.*

This research is part of the project on transnational societal constitutionalism that was funded by the *Hague Institute for the Internationalisation of Law* (HiiL) as part of the UM-HiiL-Chair on the Internationalisation of Law.

The manuscript was completed in November 2015. Later developments in legislation and case law have not been taken into account. They are, however, occasionally reported in footnotes. All websites and hyperlinks were last visited at the time of completion of the manuscript.

CONTENTS

ABBREVIATIONS

Art(s).	Article(s)
B2B	business-to-business
B2C	business-to-consumer
CD	Community Design
CESL	Common European Sales Law
CISG	Contracts for the International Sale of Goods
CJEU	Court of Justice of the European Union
CPC	Community Patent Convention of 1975
CPVO	Community Plant Variety Office
CPVR	Community Plant Variety Right
CTM	Community Trade Mark
DCFR	Draft Common Frame of Reference
ECG	European Cooperation Grouping
ECJ	European Court of Justice
EEA	European Economic Area
EEC	European Economic Community
EEIG	European Economic Interest Grouping
EEO	European Enforcement Order
EESC	European Economic and Social Committee
EOP	European Order for Payment Procedure
EPC	European Patent Convention
EPO	European Patent Office
ESCP	European Small Claims Procedure
EU	European Union
FE	European Foundation (*Fundatio Europaea*)
GIE	Groupement d'Intérêt Economique
IP	Intellectual Property
IPR	Intellectual Property Right
JCCM	Judicial Cooperation in Civil Matters
LLC	Limited Liability Company
OHIM	Office for Harmonisation in the Internal Market
OIs	Optional Instruments
OJ	Official Journal

OMC	Open Method of Coordination
Para(s).	paragraph(s)
PBR	Plant Breeders' Rights
PECL	Principles of European Contract Law
PETL	Principles of European Tort Law
PVR	Plant Variety Rights
RCD	Registered Community Design
SCE	European Cooperative Society (*Societas Cooperativa Europaea*)
SE	European Company (*Societas Europaea*)
SME	small and medium-sized enterprise
SPE	European Private Company (*Societas Privata Europaea*)
SUP	European single-member private limited liability company (*Societas Unius Personae*)
TEC	Treaty establishing the European Community
TFEU	Treaty on the Functioning of the European Union
TRIPS	Trade-Related Aspects of Intellectual Property Rights
UCD	Unregistered Community Design
UK	United Kingdom
UP	Unitary Patent
UPC	Unified Patent Court
UPOV Convention	Convention for the Protection of New Varieties of Plants
US	United States
WIPO	World Intellectual Property Organization

Chapter 1

INTRODUCTION

1. *Background*

(a) EU Legislation

Since the turn of the Millennium, a form of European Union legislation known as the 'optional instrument' has been on the rise.[1] Although this kind of legislative instrument was actually first contemplated just a few years after the inception of the European project itself, and the first official proposal for such an instrument was put forth back in 1970,[2] by the end of the twentieth century only three such instruments had seen the light of day, in two areas of European law (namely company law and intellectual property law). Since then, however, this particular legislative approach of the EU has increased both in prevalence and in reach. The EU legislator[3] has introduced more optional instruments in the fields of company and intellectual property law, as well as in other areas, such as procedural law, and it has also made formal proposals for various others.

Optional Instruments (OIs) of the European Union are legislative instruments that create legal regimes available throughout the EU for private actors (i.e. natural and/or legal persons)[4] to make use of *if they so choose*.[5] Their existence is not new. The first such Optional Instrument, the Regulation on the European Economic

1 The term 'optional instrument' was first used explicitly in the context of EU lawmaking by the European Commission in its 2010 Green Paper on European Contract Law (COM(2010) 348 final; on this see further Chapter 3, CESL description, and it is the express use of the term in this area of law that has awakened the discussion of optional instruments in European law more generally. Examples of European Union optional instruments will be given in what follows.

2 Proposal for a Council Regulation Embodying a Statute for the European Company, COM(70) 600 final.

3 In this thesis the term 'EU legislator' (or 'European legislator') will be used to refer either to the EU legislative institutions (i.e. the European Commission, the European Parliament and the Council of Ministers) collectively, or more particularly to the Commission, as appropriate.

4 See further Chapter 2.

5 The question of what exactly defines EU OIs is examined in detail in Chapter 2.

Interest Grouping (EEIG), was adopted back in 1985.[6] This established a new European corporate entity in the company law of the Member States, which private actors could form, and which would be applicable only (or at least primarily) to those private actors that opted to do so. Then, just under a decade later, the EEIG was followed by the adoption of the Regulation on the Community Trade Mark (CTM) at the end of 1993,[7] and the Regulation on the Community Plant Variety Right (CPVR) in 1994,[8] each of which introduced a new European intellectual property right recognized in all of the Member States that private actors can obtain. Yet, although the European Commission had put forward a number of other proposals for legislation creating OIs in that time, by the year 2000 these remained the only Community OIs that had been enacted.

In the course of recent years, however, this legislative landscape has changed quite drastically. First of all, the 2000s saw the creation of a further six EU OIs. These included two more in the area of European company law - the European Company (SE) in 2001[9] and the European Cooperative Society (SCE) in 2003[10] - and one additional OI in the field of European intellectual property (IP) law, i.e. the Community Design (CD), also in 2001.[11] But these also included three OIs that were introduced in a 'new' field where none had been hitherto, namely that of civil procedure (or, more accurately, judicial cooperation in civil matters). They are the European Enforcement Order (EEO) of 2004,[12] the European Order for Payment Procedure (EOP) of 2006[13] and the European Small Claims Procedure of 2007,[14] all of which provide for common procedures for cross-border debt recovery that private actors can initiate if they wish.[15] Furthermore, yet another OI in the area of IP law

6 Council Regulation 2137/85 of 25 July 1985 on the European Economic Interest Grouping. See further Chapter 3, EEIG description.

7 Council Regulation 40/94 of 20 December 1993 on the Community trade mark. See further Chapter 3, CTM description.

8 Council Regulation 2100/94 of 27 July 1994 on Community plant variety rights. See further Ch. 3, CPVR description.

9 Council Regulation 2157/2001 of 8 October 2001 on the Statute for a European company (SE) and Council Directive 2001/86/EC of 8 October 2001 supplementing the Statute for a European company with regard to the involvement of employees. See further Chapter 3, SE description.

10 Council Regulation 1435/2003 of 22 July 2003 on the Statute for a European Cooperative Society (SCE) and Council Directive 2003/72/EC of 22 July 2003 supplementing the Statute for a European Cooperative Society with regard to the involvement of employees. See further Chapter 3, SCE description.

11 Council Regulation 6/2002 of 12 December 2001 on Community designs. See further Chapter 3, CD description.

12 Regulation 805/2004 of the European Parliament and of the Council of 21 April 2004 creating a European Enforcement Order for uncontested claims. See further Chapter 3, EEO description.

13 Regulation 1896/2006 of the European Parliament and of the Council of 12 December 2006 creating a European order for payment procedure. See further Chapter 3, EOP description.

14 Regulation 861/2007 of the European Parliament and of the Council of 11 July 2007 establishing a European Small Claims Procedure. See further Chapter 3, ESCP description.

15 Being of a procedural nature, these OIs are quite a different variety to the substantive OIs in the areas of European company and intellectual property law. Nevertheless they are included →

was adopted in 2012, namely the so-called Unitary Patent (UP);[16] and, in the same year, this kind of legislative instrument was introduced into yet another area of law (the law of succession, or more precisely succession procedures), with the adoption of the Regulation creating the European Certificate of Succession.[17] And most recently, in 2014, the EU enacted another OI still in the field of procedural law relating to the cross-border enforcement of debts, called the European Account Preservation Order Procedure.[18]

Secondly, the European Commission has submitted a series of other proposals for OIs in recent years that have not yet been adopted at the time of writing, or that have since been withdrawn.[19] As regards the former category, one notable proposal for an OI that is currently being debated by the EU institutions is the European single-member private limited liability company (SUP),[20] which, if adopted, would create another corporate form in European company law. In fact, this was proposed in place of a proposal that now falls in the latter category, namely the European Private Company (SPE) proposal of 2008,[21] this having been withdrawn in 2014.[22] And the Commission has now withdrawn its proposal for a Regulation establishing a European Foundation (FE)[23] in the area of company law too, which it had

in our discussion of EU OIs for the simple reason that they fall within the definition thereof elaborated in this study (see further Chapter 2).

16 Regulation 1257/2012 of the European Parliament and of the Council of 17 December 2012 implementing enhanced cooperation in the area of the creation of unitary patent protection and Regulation 1260/2012 of 17 December 2012 implementing enhanced cooperation in the area of the creation of unitary patent protection with regard to the applicable translation arrangements. See further Chapter 3, UP description.

17 Regulation 650/2012 of the European Parliament and of the Council of 4 July 2012 on jurisdiction, applicable law, recognition and enforcement of decisions and acceptance and enforcement of authentic instruments in matters of succession and on the creation of a European Certificate of Succession. The European Certificate of Succession is not covered in this study; on this instrument see e.g. Hertel 2014.

18 Regulation 655/2014 of the European Parliament and of the Council of 15 May 2014 establishing a European Account Preservation Order procedure to facilitate cross-border debt recovery in civil and commercial matters. The European Account Preservation Order is not covered in this study.

19 Not to mention the fact that the Commission has also made informal suggestions for other OIs: See further Chapter 4, section D.2.

20 Proposal for a Directive of the European Parliament and of the Council on single-member private limited liability companies, COM(2014) 212 final. See further Chapter 3, SUP description.

21 Proposal for a Council Regulation on the Statute for a European private company, COM(2008) 396/3. See further Chapter 3, SUP description.

22 See Official Journal C 153 Volume 57 of 21 May 2014. The Commission announced its intention to withdraw the SPE proposal in late 2013; see Annex to the Communication from the Commission to the European Parliament, the Council, the European Economic and Social Committee and the Committee of the Regions 'Regulatory Fitness and Performance (REFIT): Results and Next Steps', COM(2013)685, p. 9.

23 Proposal for a Council Regulation on the Statute for a European Foundation (FE), COM(2012) 35 final. The proposal for a European Foundation is not covered in this study.

presented in 2012.[24] Then, in addition, another important OI that was formally proposed but has since been withdrawn is the Common European Sales Law (CESL) proposal of 2011,[25] in the area of contract law, which was also retracted by the Commission in 2014.[26]

All of these developments lay the foundation for the finding of a novel legislative trend occurring in the European Union. That is, it can be observed that the EU legislator is increasingly looking to legislation establishing optional instruments as an alternative means of regulating different areas of (private) law falling within its competence.[27] Indeed, this appears to coincide with the strive for better EU lawmaking initiated by the European Commission's White Paper on European Governance of 2001.[28] In this Paper, the Commission announced (among other things) its intention to consider the use of 'different policy tools', stressing that the principles of proportionality and subsidiarity entail that '... the selection of the instruments used must be in proportion to the objectives pursued'.[29] And, as we shall see, optional instruments are considered by the EU legislator (not to mention others) as an alternative method of lawmaking to more traditional measures, such as 'approximating' (or 'harmonizing') measures,[30] that is (more) consistent with these principles. In fact, the connection between optional regimes and better regulation (or 'less lawmaking') in respect of EU legislation aimed at the completion of the Single Market has already been noted explicitly by the European Economic and Social Committee (EESC) in an own-initiative opinion of 2011 on the very subject.[31] In this opinion the EESC discusses specifically 'the question as to whether an optional regime could be adopted as an alternative to the traditional way of harmonising legislation in specific areas ...',[32] and expresses the view that '[a]n optional instrument would strongly support the functioning of the Single Market, and represents the most perfect form of voluntary harmonisation in line with the principle of subsidiarity'.[33]

24 See Annex to the Communication from the Commission to the European Parliament, the Council, the European Economic and Social Committee and the Committee of the Regions 'Commission Work Programme 2015: A New Start', COM(2014) 910 final, Annex 2, p. 12, item 61.

25 Proposal for a Regulation of the European Parliament and of the Council on a Common European Sales Law, COM(2011) 635 final. See further Chapter 3, CESL description.

26 See *supra* note 24, item 60.

27 On this 'increasing importance of optional law' see notably Smits 2010b.

28 COM(2001) 428 final.

29 *Ibid.*, p. 8.

30 On the meaning of the terms 'approximation' and 'harmonization see further Chapter 2.

31 Opinion of the European Economic and Social Committee on 'The 28th regime – an alternative allowing less lawmaking at Community level' (own-initiative opinion) CESE 758/ 2010, available at: <www.eesc.europa.eu/?i=portal.en.int-opinions.10007>. On this opinion see further Chapter 4, section A.2(a).

32 Opinion of the European Economic and Social Committee on 'The 28th regime – an alternative allowing less lawmaking at Community level' (own-initiative opinion) CESE 758/2010, para. 1.1.

33 *Ibid.*, para. 4.1.1.

Thus, the EU legislator's increasing use of the optional instrument method represents a shift in its approach to lawmaking that should be viewed against the backdrop of wider initiatives towards new governance in the process of European integration.[34]

(b) State of the Art

Given that the trend of the EU legislator legislating by means of optional instruments is a recent one (even if the history of optional instruments in European law is not), it is perhaps unsurprising that there is a conspicuous paucity of academic literature on the subject of Optional Instruments of the European Union taken as a whole. It is true that, as with virtually any piece of EU legislation, one can find numerous commentaries on specific EU OIs in particular areas of European law (like the SE in the area of company law, or the CTM in the area of IP law, etc.). Without too much difficulty one can also find literature on optional instruments as a distinct form of legislation in particular fields of law (like the area of European contract law, for example).[35] However, a *general* account of EU OIs as a distinct kind of EU legislative method, which transcends individual policy areas, is much harder to come by. In fact, until a few years ago not a single academic contribution of any great length had been written on this significant legislative trend happening within the European Union. This situation changed in 2012, however, with the publication of a study commissioned by the Legal Affairs Committee of the European Parliament and produced by Fauvarque-Cosson & Behar-Touchais on the 'implementation of optional instruments within European civil law'.[36] This is a study of almost 400 pages covering a range of optional instruments (predominantly, though not only, of the European Union) in various areas of law, which, according to the abstract, 'provides a comprehensive analysis of this innovative method' and, in particular, 'identifies the strengths and weaknesses of this method and poses thought-provoking questions for the future'.[37] Hence, the *Fauvarque-Cosson* study addresses different aspects of European optional instruments as a general legislative method, and also includes extensive empirical data drawn from field surveys conducted in the Member States. In fact, summaries and analyses of the country-by-country responses to the questionnaire on optional instruments prepared by the authors make up a large part of the study.

Of course, bearing in mind the absence of academic discussion of EU OIs in general, the value of this contribution cannot be understated. Indeed the *Fauvarque-Cosson* study is of huge importance for (and referred to frequently in) the present

34 On the emergence of new governance in the European Union see e.g. Dawson 2011 and, comparing the EU and the US, Trubek & Trubek 2006.

35 See, e.g., Wulf 2014.

36 Fauvarque-Cosson & Behar-Touchais 2012. Although this is not to say that the phenomenon of EU OIs had not been discussed at all in the academic literature before the publication of this study: See for example the editorial by Smits 2010b. Also in 2012 a book by Basedow containing a chapter dedicated to European Union Optional Instruments was published; Basedow 2012, Chapter IV ('Optional Law in Europe').

37 Fauvarque-Cosson & Behar-Touchais 2012, abstract.

study. Nevertheless, while this study of European optional instruments is no doubt substantial, the general analysis offered by the authors lacks theoretical underpinnings. Naturally this is understandable given the rather practical purpose of the study, as a report to a Committee of the European Parliament, but the point remains that the more academic aspects of the subject are not elaborated upon in detail therein. So, a comprehensive study of the phenomenon of EU OIs at a more theoretical level still has not been produced.

In summary, the state of the art in terms of the academic discussion of EU OIs as a distinct legislative method is at an early stage of development, and the existing literature addressing the topic is therefore minimal. In particular, as the EESC has remarked, there has been a lack of 'in-depth discussion on the nature, object, areas of application, advantages and difficulties of such an instrument and its possible contribution to the completion of the Single Market'.[38]

2. *Research*

(a) Research Questions

The rise of legislation introducing optional instruments in the European Union gives rise to a wide array of intriguing questions, and many of these are addressed in the present study. Ultimately, though, this thesis seeks to tackle three major research questions, from which many others then logically follow.

Firstly, there is the fundamental question of what defines Optional Instruments of the European Union, and what distinguishes EU OIs from other kinds of EU legislation (such as EU 'approximating' legislation). That is, on what basis can the various pieces of legislation in different fields of European law outlined above be characterized as 'EU Optional Instruments', and how do such instruments compare to other legislative measures of the EU? For the time being the brief definition given at the outset of this chapter will suffice, but it will be necessary to define EU OIs more precisely. In addition, it will also be necessary in this regard to place EU OIs in the wider context of optional instruments, by first considering the more abstract question of what constitutes an 'optional regime' in the law, and how EU Optional Instruments relate to this. Furthermore, the question of whether there exist different types of EU OIs will be addressed in this connection, focusing in particular on the idea of a dichotomy between '28th regimes' and '2nd national regimes'.[39]

Secondly, the thesis discusses at length the key normative question of whether this alternative EU legislative approach based on OIs is desirable,[40] and for what reasons. In particular, what are the motivations for the use of OIs put forward by the EU legislator, and, more generally, what are the arguments (political, social, economic, etc.) in favour of and against OIs as an alternative method of EU

38 Opinion of the European Economic and Social Committee on 'The 28th regime – an alternative allowing less lawmaking at Community level' (own-initiative opinion) CESE 758/2010, 1.5.

39 See Chapter 2.

40 Of course, this depends on how 'desirability' is assessed; see further next section.

lawmaking? Are OIs preferable to 'approximating measures', and if so is this only from the European perspective, or also from the perspective of Member States and private actors? Does the effectiveness of EU OIs depend on their being 'opted into' by private actors? And, in any case, does their effectiveness vary depending on the specific OI and EU policy area in question? Are OIs even practicable in all EU policy areas, and if not, why not? All of these issues and more will need to be examined as part of this normative discussion.[41]

Last but not least, in connection with the previous question, and departing from the premise that some EU OIs have apparently been opted into by a larger proportion of private actors than others (relatively speaking), the question is posed as to why the popularity of EU OIs seems to diverge considerably. More precisely, what are the factors driving the popularity (or unpopularity) of EU OIs with private actors, and do these factors vary depending on the OI in question, or are they common to different OIs? And if they are common to different EU OIs, could this lead to certain lessons for the EU legislator when promulgating OIs in future?[42]

The aims behind the discussion of each of these main research questions are as follows. The objective of addressing the first question is to determine whether and why the various legislative measures in diverse policy areas mentioned above should be understood and studied as a distinct group or category of EU instruments. Only once this has been established can the research proceed to consider the other questions. As for the second key question, the aim behind this is ultimately to evaluate whether and why the EU legislator's increasing use of optional instruments should be welcomed. In examining a range of arguments and perspectives for this purpose, however, the aim is first and foremost to identify possible criteria that could be employed to assess the desirability of this growing tendency in EU lawmaking.[43] Finally, as regards the third question, the objective is to identify factors that could have an influence on the popularity of any EU OI, and particularly factors that are related to the design of Union optional regimes.

(b) Research Method

In the last few decades, legal research has increasingly adopted novel approaches and pluralist research methods, often drawing upon the social sciences. Traditionally, legal research has relied upon the doctrinal approach, which privileges description and systematization and treats the law as a self-contained system. However, this approach has been criticized for being too narrow, on the basis that a) it takes a legal system by and large as given (or 'static') and b) it mainly adopts an internal perspective, without concerning itself with comparative issues, or with the relationship between legal systems, on the one hand, and economic, social and political systems, on the other. Furthermore, the doctrinal approach leaves out considerations of the practical effects of the law, and focuses purely on so-called 'black letter law'.

41 See Chapter 4.
42 See Chapter 5.
43 This is also explained in the next section on the research method.

For these reasons, the doctrinal approach has been increasingly supplemented by a variety of other approaches to legal research, most notably the comparative, the functionalist, the empirical, as well as the sociological and historical.[44] Recently, Smits put forward an innovative approach to legal research, arguing that 'the core of legal science is formed by the normative question of what the law ought to be': From this perspective, 'the legal discipline reflects upon what it is that individuals, firms, states and other organisations ought to do or ought to refrain from'.[45] Specifically, a normative approach requires the researcher to adopt an argumentative methodology, in the sense that s/he needs to take into account, analyse and assess the law as it ought to be from the perspective of different and often contrasting normative positions. Hence legal research does not aim at providing clear-cut answers and legal certainty, but rather at raising doubts and reflecting on conflicting arguments.

It follows from the above that legal researchers nowadays have at their disposal an array of research approaches and methods to choose from. In fact, many scholars even advocate a 'pluralist' approach, which does not limit itself to just one method but makes use of a variety of angles and perspectives. And so, given these various possibilities, this entails that legal researchers need to both clarify and justify the method(s) they have chosen to employ in order to tackle the research questions they have posed, while at the same time accepting that such questions may not yield precise answers (or indeed that this may not be a desirable goal in itself). This therefore raises the issue of which methods have been used to conduct the present study, and for what reasons.

The present study deals with the subject of Optional Instruments of the EU (in general), which is, as was indicated already, an under-researched phenomenon in European legal studies. Therefore this has actually necessitated, to begin with, the adoption of certain methods traditionally linked to the doctrinal approach, including some degree of description and systematization of EU OIs in diverse areas of law. I would argue that this is an important and relevant task in the light of the fact that most EU legal instruments have been studied individually and separately, and have not been systematized so as to allow us to view them as a distinct legislative method. As the title of an article by Dutch legal academic Schoordijk states: 'We should not View the Law as a System, before Systematising it.'[46] Furthermore, this type of descriptive analysis has gone hand in hand with the development of appropriate new definitions for this legal phenomenon, as I have found that there is considerable confusion over the terms used to describe its various aspects.

Yet, even though it does engage at the outset with a descriptive account of the EU legislation introducing the optional instruments under examination, this thesis does not concern legal codes per se. Instead, the primary research question concerns the desirability of EU OIs, and this is the question that is addressed in the central part of this thesis. That is to say, the nucleus of the research is the inquiry into the

44 See further, e.g., McConville & Chui 2007; Murray & DeSanctis 2009; Watkins & Burton 2013.

45 Smits 2012a, p. 41.

46 Schoordijk 2008.

merits of OIs as an alternative method of EU lawmaking. Now, for this purpose, primarily a normative-analytical approach is followed, meaning the focus will be on analysing and assessing contrasting arguments in this respect, and from a variety of perspectives. The reasoning behind this plan to examine these instruments from a range of often contrasting perspectives follows Smits' point regarding the need for academic legal research to concentrate on 'the identification and rethinking of the relevant argument'. More particularly, I would maintain that in any normative legal analysis, there is a need to consider the perspectives of stakeholders as well as the views of legal experts, as this way it is possible to not only identify but also rethink a range of relevant arguments - because what is desirable can depend on the perspective one takes. In the case of EU optional instruments, therefore, I have taken into consideration and assessed the perspectives of the EU legislator, the Member States, and also private actors, and at all levels I have fed in the insights of academics from different disciplines and standpoints. This means that I have endeavoured not to treat EU OIs as insulated from social, economic and political systems. It is equally not my aim to critique this kind of EU legislation purely in the light of its relation to socio-economic or political considerations, but such arguments do feature prominently alongside legal arguments in my normative analysis. Indeed this is another reason why I believe it is important to consider this variety of viewpoints for the present study, as this could point to different possible criteria according to which the desirability of EU OIs should be assessed. In the end, though, my analysis leads me to propose a general criterion for assessing the desirability of EU OIs as an alternate legislative method, based on the optimal mix between legal uniformity and legal diversity, which takes into account the perspectives of the European legislator, national legislators and private actors.[47]

Finally, the last core chapter of the thesis, which addresses the related question of the 'popularity' of EU OIs (in the sense of the degree of take-up among eligible private actors),[48] adopts a comparative research method, although not in the classic comparative law sense. For, rather than comparing the laws of different national jurisdictions, this more explanatory part looks at different EU Optional Instruments, in order to identify and compare features that are common to all such instruments, and how these particular features have affected their uptake, with reference to empirical data.[49] This is done with a view to assessing the impact these features can have on the popularity of EU OIs among private actors. In terms of the precise methodology adopted for this purpose, this will be explained in Chapter 5.

47 See Chapter 4, section D.3(a).

48 See Chapter 5, section B.1.

49 Still, in comparing these different EU OIs, there are certain issues that arise which are also faced by comparative law researchers, such as the issue of how to weigh similarities as opposed to differences.

3. *Outline and Structure of Thesis*

The thesis is structured as follows.

The first part of the thesis begins by looking at optional regimes in general, before defining the fundamental nature and essential character of Optional Instruments of the European Union. In this regard, the thesis identifies certain core elements of EU Optional Instruments, and contrasts such instruments with EU 'approximation', both in a conceptual sense and in a technical, legal sense. Furthermore, in connection with the latter, the question of whether there exist different types of EU OIs is discussed at length (Chapter 2). It then goes on to describe in detail a variety of existing and proposed EU OIs[50] in diverse areas of European law, noting some pertinent similarities and differences between them, albeit without comparing them directly at that stage (Chapter 3).

In the second (and main) part of the thesis, a framework for the normative evaluation of EU OIs is developed, through an examination of the overall case for and against the use of such instruments. This framework takes into account a range of arguments and perspectives, including those of the EU legislator, the Member States and private actors, and also considers the extent to which the strength of the case for EU OIs varies according to the OI and EU policy area in question (Chapter 4). This is then followed by a (connected) assessment of the (un)popularity of different EU OIs, based on a novel explanatory framework that distinguishes and investigates various factors which potentially play a role in this respect, through a comparison of distinct EU OIs and with reference to existing empirical data (Chapter 5).

Lastly, the third and final part of the thesis discusses the main outcomes of the study, which are of relevance both to academics and policymakers. It also offers some future perspectives on EU OIs, both in terms of future research on the subject and of future optional legislative instruments of the European Union, before concluding (Chapter 6).

4. *Relevance of Thesis*

(a) Academic Relevance

It was explained previously that there is a lack of academic literature on Optional Instruments of the European Union as a general legislative method. Yet, the need for an innovative and profound inquiry into the phenomenon of EU OIs is indubitable, and clearly felt. Indeed, even the EESC 'has expressed its support in several opinions for an in-depth study of this mechanism and its possible application in specific domains'.[51] Therefore, the present study should be of great relevance to an academic discussion that is still in its infancy. By defining, mapping

[50] The phrase 'existing and proposed EU OIs' is used in this thesis to denote also proposals for EU OIs that have been withdrawn, including notably the CESL proposal.

[51] Opinion of the European Economic and Social Committee on 'The 28th regime - an alternative allowing less lawmaking at Community level' (own-initiative opinion) CESE 758/2010, 1.3.

and analysing in detail existing and proposed optional instruments in the EU, as well as identifying pertinent similarities and differences between them, the research will serve to advance knowledge of this novel legislative trend in academia. In particular, the study's analysis and evaluation of the normative issues surrounding EU OIs is of especial academic relevance, as this is intended not only to provoke but also to provide a framework for further academic debate on the subject of OIs, primarily (though not necessarily only) in the field of European private law. Hence, it is expected that the results of the research could both inspire and serve as the basis for further exploration into the topic.

As for the topic itself, the phenomenon of EU OIs is linked with a number of highly relevant issues in current legal research. One was already indicated; namely the new governance debate and the exploration of alternative ways of lawmaking in the Europeanization process. But there are also various others, such as the question of how to find solutions for problems that cannot be solved at the national level while at the same time seeking to preserve the sovereignty of member states; or whether to encourage the transnational application and enforcement of law amidst fears of 'forum-shopping' and a 'race to the bottom'; or how to reconcile pleas for greater choice of law for individuals with concerns of social justice. All of these issues constitute central themes in the academic discussion of EU Optional Instruments.

(b) Societal and Practical Relevance

Alongside its academic relevance, the present study also has a strong societal and practical relevance. First and foremost, the research is able to promote greater awareness and understanding of EU OIs in wider society as well, and particularly among actual and potential 'users' of these optional instruments (i.e. eligible natural and legal persons). Bearing in mind the proliferation of existing and proposed optional instruments of the EU in recent years, the importance of informing private actors about them should not be underestimated. Furthermore, by individuating and comparing certain common provisions of different EU OIs with a view to assessing the influence such provisions (can) have on the 'popularity' of a Union optional instrument with end users, it is also envisaged that the research will have a valuable practical relevance for policymakers. Most notably, this will be of relevance to the EU legislator, insofar as it could help to inform the design of future EU OIs. But this aspect of the research could also be relevant for national policymakers, insofar as it could help to guide their input on Commission proposals for Union optional instruments.

(c) Limits of Research

The scope of the present study is confined in certain noteworthy respects.

Firstly, in terms of the breadth of the inquiry (i.e. the subject matter), the research is limited to optional instruments *of the European Union*. Although it does also touch upon optional instruments established through international conventions (such as the United Nations Convention on Contracts for the International Sale of

Goods), as well as 'optional law' (or 'choice of law') more generally, the focus of the study is on optional instruments created by EU legislation.[52] And even when it comes to such EU optional instruments the research is not exhaustive, as it does not cover all OIs that have been adopted or proposed by the EU legislator to date, nor does it deal with all aspects of those EU OIs that it does cover. This is partly because, as we will see, this is not needed for the attainment of the specific aims of the research, but it is also because this would not be realistic. Depending on one's interests, there is a vast array of pertinent legal issues one could discuss in relation to each and every one of the existing and proposed EU OIs, of which there are also many, and to attempt to address them all would be over-ambitious to say the least. Moreover, this would require a high level of expertise in each of the diverse areas of European law in which EU OIs have been adopted and/or proposed, and to be specialized in all of these different fields is almost an oxymoron. Clearly, it is possible to have extensive knowledge and an advanced understanding of these different areas of law - and indeed this is necessary in order to carry out a study like the present one. However, I certainly do not profess to be an expert in each of the fields covered in this study: Rather, my specialization lies in EU OIs as a distinct kind of EU legislative method.

Secondly, as regards the depth of the analysis, even many of the issues that *are* discussed in detail in this study could (and should) undoubtedly be researched and developed still further. Indeed, the complexity of these issues is such that there is a great deal more that needs to be said about them. However, for the purposes of concision - and in order to ensure that the wider picture is not lost on the reader - it has been necessary to draw a line under the various discussions at a certain point. While it would have been interesting to delve more deeply still into many issues, this carried with it the risk of introducing unnecessary levels of complexity into the study. Therefore, the study leaves open various avenues for possible future research on the topic. That is, it is foreseen that the results of the study could subsequently be explored in more depth, as well as in relation to other optional instruments.[53]

Last but not least, following on from the aforementioned limitations, it is also important to recognize that there are limits in terms of how far the aims and objectives of the research can be achieved. This is true of the first objective, because while it may be possible to provide a workable definition of Optional Instruments of the European Union as a distinct category of EU legislation, it is just as difficult to truly define such legal instruments as it is law itself. Therefore it must be accepted that any definition provided will inevitably be incomprehensive and incomplete. But this is especially true of the other aims of the research. As far as the normative aims are concerned, it is of course hard to say whether the EU legislator's use of optional instruments is desirable, or even what the criteria for assessing desirability should be. To be sure, one could arrive at a reasoned conclusion on the matter - and this is precisely what this study seeks to do - but, as is the case with any normative evaluation, one cannot expect to deliver definitive conclusions. And when it comes

52 Hence the present study does not look in detail at the matter of optional regimes at national level either.

53 See further Chapter 6.

to the explanatory objective of identifying factors that may affect the popularity of EU OIs, it will be seen that, while it is possible to distinguish a number of potential factors and to form an impression of their effects, demonstrating this with precision presents a far greater challenge.

PART 1

EU OPTIONAL INSTRUMENTS: DEFINITION AND DESCRIPTION

Chapter 2

NATURE AND TYPE(S) OF EU OPTIONAL INSTRUMENTS

INTRODUCTION

Before proceeding to examine and analyse Optional Instruments (OIs) of the European Union, it is first necessary to define them.[1] That is, it must be laid out precisely on what grounds the various legislative measures in diverse European policy areas outlined in the preceding introductory chapter can be grouped together under the single heading of 'EU Optional Instruments'. This is of course essential to understand exactly what we are referring to, and because the very idea of studying these different measures as a distinct kind of EU legislative method rests on the premise that they can all be said to conform to a basic definition, in the sense that they all share certain core elements, which other kinds of EU legislative measures do not. But the question of what defines EU OIs is an important one to address also because it gives rise to a number of other, related questions. Foremost among these is the question of how EU OIs compare to other types of EU legislation, and particularly where EU OIs stand in relation to European 'approximation'. Furthermore, there is also the question of whether there are actually different types of EU OIs and, in particular, whether a distinction should be drawn between a '28th regime', on the one hand, and a '2nd national regime', on the other. In addition, prior to these, there is even the more abstract issue of what constitutes 'an optional regime' in the law, and how EU Optional Instruments relate to this. For these reasons, the present chapter is entirely dedicated to the definition of EU OIs, before we move to describe the specific legislative measures under examination in this study in the next chapter.

Accordingly, this chapter starts with a discussion of optional legal regimes in general, and of the place of EU OIs within this broader context (section A), before zooming in more concretely to the matter of Optional Instruments of the European Union (section B). In this regard, the aim is first and foremost to identify the basic

1 Being a relatively novel trend, a detailed definition of EU legislation establishing OIs has not yet been provided in the literature. On the other hand, a short definition has been proposed by Fauvarque-Cosson & Behar-Touchais 2012, p. 22; see further below. Also see e.g. Basedow 2015, p. 283 *et seq.*

elements that may be said to 'make up' a European Union OI, and to consider to what extent existing and proposed 'EU OIs' adhere to this definition. Then, in addition, we will also seek to juxtapose EU Optional Instruments with other kinds of EU legislation, as well as with each other, with a view to elaborating further on the fundamental nature of EU OIs.

A. Optional Regimes in General

1. *Law, Legal Systems and Legal Regimes*

At the outset, it must be stressed that the question of what constitutes an optional legal regime per se is, from a theoretical perspective, a highly complicated one; since - even leaving aside the aspect of 'optionality' - the matters of what is a legal regime, or even what is (a) law, are issues that are so complex they form the basis for an entire academic discipline, known as jurisprudence (or 'philosophy of law'). So, with this in mind, it should be clear that the intention behind discussing optional regimes in general here is certainly not to enter into the long-standing debate on the nature of law, or anything of that sort. Indeed, not only would this be well beyond the scope of the present study, it is also unnecessary. The aim of this preliminary discussion is the much more modest one of looking at EU OIs against the backdrop of existing legal regimes or instruments in the law that may similarly be described as 'optional', and for this purpose it will therefore suffice to defer to existing schools of thought on the wider question of how to define law and legal systems.[2]

Having said that, it is necessary to provide at least a rudimentary explanation of the meaning of such terms as they are used in this study, before we can begin to contemplate the concept of optional regimes in the law, and, in turn, the conception of EU OIs as a form of optional regime. Thus, first of all, the term 'law' is used here to refer loosely to any rule or principle (or collection thereof) that has binding force on those whom it concerns, which means it can potentially be enforced by competent authorities, and particularly judicial authorities. Secondly, the term 'legal system' is employed to denote any jurisdiction (and particularly national jurisdictions) in the territory of which an array of interconnected and coordinated laws covering various areas (both public and private, substantive and procedural, etc.) is applicable and enforceable by competent authorities established on that territory for that purpose. Thirdly, 'field of law' or 'area of law' will be used to indicate simply a grouping of laws within a legal system (or legal systems) according to their subject matter. This could be a rather broad demarcation like criminal law, or contract law, or company law, etc., or it may be more defined, such as consumer contract law, or the law on the public limited liability company form, for example. Finally, this is to be contrasted with a 'legal regime', which in the present context is intended to signify a *sub-system of laws pertaining to a certain field of*

[2] Equally, for the same reason, the intention here is not to discuss how optional legal regimes could affect conventional understandings of what law is.

law within a legal system.[3] In other words, legal regimes equate to systems of law that are part of (and therefore cannot be separated from) an overarching legal system (or systems), but that can be (and indeed normally are) regarded as 'distinct' insofar as they each encompass a paradigmatic set or body of closely interrelated rules of law within that overarching system. Again, this may be intended in a broad sense, as a sub-system covering most if not all of a given field of law, or in a more restricted way, as a sub-system governing only some (or even or few) aspects of a certain area of law. Hence unlike legal systems, systems of law characterized as legal regimes do not need to be (more or less) 'complete' in order to qualify as legal regimes. A legal regime is necessarily systematized, but not self-contained.

2. *Optional Legal Regimes*

This then brings us to the question of what is meant by an *optional* legal regime; and this is by no means a straightforward one either. For one thing, there are many regimes in a legal system that may be described as 'optional' in the sense that they do not apply to all individuals in an obligatory fashion, but rather enable individuals to execute a certain legal act, or achieve a certain legal result, prescribing rules that are applicable only (or at least primarily) to those who elect to do so. For instance, unlike criminal law, which is applicable independently of one's own will, contract law is in principle applicable only to individuals who elect to make a contract, while company law is applicable predominantly to those who choose to form a company. Understood in this way, optional regimes could thus simply be taken to be synonymous with so-called 'facultative rules' of law. This, however, is not what is intended in the present study. It is true that optional regimes as they are interpreted here are optional for private actors (i.e. natural and/or legal persons), and they are found in the realm of private law[4] rather than public law, but it is not the fact that they are facultative in nature that makes them optional. Instead, an optional legal regime for our purposes is one that individuals can use as an *alternative body of rules of law* under which to execute the *equivalent legal act* (be it making an enforceable contract, or forming a recognized company, or registering an intellectual property right, or initiating a civil procedure, etc.) in the *same jurisdiction*. In other words, the aspect of 'optionality' refers not to the fact that individuals have a choice as to whether to perform the legal act (and thereby fall under a legal regime that would otherwise be inapplicable to them) or not, but rather to those situations where individuals who do elect to perform a given legal act in a certain territory have a further choice as to the legal regime under which to do so. More precisely, optional regimes are legal regimes that private actors who wish to execute a legal act in a certain jurisdiction can choose as an applicable

3 On the notion of law as a system see notably MacCormick 2008; Luhmann 2004; Teubner 1987.

4 The term 'private law' is used in a broad sense in this thesis, comprising not only the law of obligations and property law but also intellectual property law, company law, the law of civil procedure, etc.

regime, as an alternative to the legal regime (or possibly regimes)[5] provided by the (pre-existing) domestic law of that jurisdiction.[6] This initial observation still requires further elaboration though: for what is meant exactly by a legal regime that private actors can 'choose', and in what sense are these legal regimes 'alternatives' to existing legal regimes?

As regards the former, it is important to specify that private actors can 'choose' an optional legal regime by means of either a positive or a negative manifestation of will. That is, optional legal regimes can take the form of either 'opt in' or 'opt out' regimes. When it comes to optional regimes of the European Union, we shall see that all existing and proposed EU OIs that have been introduced to date are in fact opt-in regimes.[7] But this is not to say that a Union optional regime could not be an opt-out instrument. There already exists one notable international optional regime that is 'chosen' (implicitly) by parties in accordance with an opt-out method, namely the United Nations Convention on Contracts for the International Sale of Goods (CISG) of 1980. The CISG is a treaty embodying an international sales law regime that is applicable to transactions in goods between professional parties (i.e. businesses) from different Contracting States in lieu of the otherwise applicable domestic regimes, unless its applicability is expressly and explicitly excluded by the parties in their contract.[8] So a legal regime certainly need not be chosen explicitly in order for it to be optional. What is essential, however, is that the applicability of the legal regime is excluded in its entirety unless private actors choose to opt into it (or, in the case of opt-out regimes, its application can be entirely excluded if private actors choose to opt out of it).[9] And, as we shall see shortly, EU Optional Instruments do constitute optional regimes so defined.

As for optional legal regimes being 'alternatives' to existing legal regimes, this fundamentally entails that in areas of law where optional legal regimes exist, there will (almost always) be a corresponding or comparable legal regime (or regimes)[10] available for private actors to use in the national jurisdiction (or rather, jurisdictions) in which the optional regimes apply: In this sense, optional regimes offer such actors an alternative. Admittedly, this may not be completely true of all jurisdictions (as we will see), but it is typically the case. And if an individual in one of these jurisdictions chooses to execute a legal act under an optional regime instead

5 In some cases a jurisdiction may provide more than one legal regime governing similar subject matter (think, for instance, of different national company forms).

6 In this sense, it is arguable that the term 'alternative regimes' would be more apt than 'optional regimes'. However, we will stick to the latter in this study, for the simple reason that this is the term of art.

7 See *infra* section B.1(b). On this point see also Fauvarque-Cosson & Behar-Touchais 2012, p. 29.

8 Cf. United Nations Convention on Contracts for the International Sale of Goods, Art. 6.

9 In principle the reverse is also true, i.e. the legal regime will be applicable in its entirety if private actors opt into it. However it must be borne in mind that optional legal regimes can contain not only mandatory but also default rules of law, which may eventually be deviated from after opting in to the regime. This is the case notably with optional regimes in the area of contact law, for example. See further description of CESL in Chapter 3.

10 On the meaning of 'corresponding legal regime' as it is used here see further *infra* section B.1(c).

of under a domestic regime provided by the legal system of the jurisdiction, the optional regime is applicable to that legal act rather than the regime of the national legal system (or at least in the first instance).[11] This does not mean, however, that for a legal regime to be optional it must necessarily exclude the possibility of pre-existing regimes also being *used* by private actors simultaneously with the optional regime. It will often be that by choosing an optional legal regime to execute a given legal act, private actors effectively eliminate the possibility of using other legal regimes to perform the equivalent act at the same time, but some optional legal regimes can potentially be used concurrently with pre-existing legal regimes. For example, we will see that some EU optional regimes, such as the Regulations creating the Community Trade Mark and the Community Design, do not exclude the possibility of registering a national IP right in one or more of the Member States for the same intellectual property that is protected in the Member States under a Community IP right. Conversely, the Community Plant Variety Right Regulation, for instance, does expressly prohibit the protection of plant varieties by national plant variety rights simultaneously with the Community right.

It is true that some domestic legal regimes could also be described as optional legal regimes in the sense of 'alternative regimes', insofar as they too could be 'chosen' by private actors as alternatives to legal regimes available in different national jurisdictions. In particular, domestic contract law regimes could be seen as optional regimes on this view, to the extent that they can be chosen as the applicable legal regime by parties contracting between different jurisdictions through so-called 'choice of law' clauses.[12] In addition, national company forms could also be considered as optional regimes in this sense, inasmuch as operators can choose the applicable company law by choosing the state of incorporation. Indeed, as we will see later, the choice that an individual makes for a Union OI is very much comparable to such choices of law, and can even be considered as another kind of choice of law.[13] However, domestic legal regimes that can be used via a choice of law are distinguishable from optional legal regimes because, if private actors in a given jurisdiction choose to execute a legal act using the domestic legal regime of another jurisdiction - in which case they at the same time 'choose not to' use the legal regime(s) of the jurisdiction in which they are based to execute that legal act - the applicability of the legal regime(s) of their *own* jurisdiction is still not necessarily excluded entirely. In particular, certain essential rules in their 'home' jurisdiction can still be of application to the legal act in question, even if (or rather as far as)

11 See further Chapter 5, section A.2(b).

12 On these clauses see further Chapter 3, CESL Description and Chapter 4, section A.2(b). In fact, even the contract itself could be said to be an optional regime in the sense of an 'alternative set of rules', insofar as parties may deviate from default rules of national contract law regimes in their contractual agreements. However, for the purposes of this thesis a contract constitutes a legal act that may be executed under an optional regime - even if a contract could itself be seen as a form of (private) rule-making.

13 This choice has been referred to as a 'supra-national choice of law'. See further Chapter 4, section A.2(b).

these differ to those in the legal regime chosen.[14] By contrast, if private actors choose not to use an optional legal regime (either implicitly or explicitly) in preference for the domestic legal regime of a certain jurisdiction, the optional regime is (again in principle) not applicable to their legal act in any way. Therefore, unlike optional legal regimes, domestic legal regimes may be applicable to the legal acts of private actors even if they are not 'chosen'. Furthermore, there is also the more conceptual point that, unlike domestic legal regimes, optional legal regimes are created specifically with a view to their being chosen by private actors in different jurisdictions. That is, optional regimes are conceived of as such, whereas national legal regimes are not.[15]

In summary, then, the term 'optional regime' in law could be used to describe any number of different kinds of legal regime, and there is no doubt good reason to view EU OIs as falling within this broader context. Still, with this being the case, it is necessary to define EU optional regimes more specifically, also to see precisely what distinguishes EU OIs from other optional legal regimes (among other things).

B. Optional Instruments of the European Union

1. *The Core Elements of EU OIs*

Focusing now on Optional Instruments of the European Union in particular, the first (and primary) question to be addressed in this regard is: What are the basic elements that define EU OIs as a specific form of optional legal regime?[16] We shall see that there are essentially three core elements that are common to all EU OIs (at least for the most part): the element of EU legislation, the element of 'selection' and the element of 'choice'. In what follows, each of these core elements will be elaborated in turn.

14 National rules that are still applicable even in the event of a choice of (foreign) law are sometimes called 'super-mandatory' rules; see e.g. O'Hara & Ribstein 2009, p. 219. On such rules see further Chapter 4, section A.3(b)(ii). In the European context another example of domestic rules that could still be applicable even in the event of a choice of foreign law would be the mandatory consumer protection rules that can apply in the case of choice of (business-to-consumer) contract law; see further Chapter 3, CESL Description.

15 And this could also mean something for the content of the rules these legal regimes provide; see further Chapter 5.

16 It should be noted that the concept of a European Union legal regime is even more indefinite than the concept of a legal regime per se, since it gives rise to the additional question of what the nature of the EU legal system actually is, as compared to national legal systems, on the one hand, and the international legal system, on the other; and this is a question that has been discussed extensively in the literature. Still for present purposes it will suffice to observe that, conceptually-speaking, EU legal regimes are essentially like any other legal regimes that form part of national legal systems, except that they are derived from EU legislation.

(a) The Element of EU Legislation

The first core element of Optional Instruments of the EU is that, as already mentioned, they are all optional regimes established by European Union legislation. More precisely, EU OIs are created by binding 'legal acts of the Union' within the meaning of the Treaty on the Functioning of the European Union (TFEU).[17] In fact, all currently existing EU optional regimes are embodied (at least principally) in regulations, this being the Union legal act that has 'general application' and is 'binding in its entirety and directly applicable in all Member States',[18] and there are arguably good reasons for this.[19] Admittedly, as we will see later, in the case of certain EU OIs (namely the European Company[20] and European Cooperative Society[21]), the optional regime has been supplemented by an accompanying European Union directive, which is 'binding, as to the result to be achieved' while leaving to the Member State authorities 'the choice of form and methods'.[22] However, even in these cases, the EU OIs in question are still incorporated primarily in regulations. This is not necessarily to say that it would not be possible for a Union OI to be created solely by means of a directive, though. On the contrary, this is a theoretical possibility,[23] and actually the Commission has submitted a proposal for an OI embodied in a directive, in the form of the European single-member private limited liability company (SUP).[24] At any rate, what is certain is that, whether it is by regulations, regulations supplemented by directives, or even directives alone, EU OIs are established by binding EU legal acts.

Still, there are two further caveats or qualifications that must be added to this statement. Firstly, while all EU OIs are created by binding legal acts of the Union, it is not necessarily the case that the institutions or bodies competent to administer the OI[25] or indeed adjudicate upon the instrument (where these are different) will also have been created by EU legislation. As we shall see, in some cases this is true, but in others the relevant bodies are pre-existing domestic institutions such as national registries or courts, and in the case of one OI in the area of IP law, namely the Unitary Patent, they are (or rather will be) international bodies set up by intergovernmental agreement. Secondly, it is also not necessarily true that EU OIs are binding on *all* Member States. Rather, it will be seen that, while this is usually the case, there are a few exceptions. For one thing, there is the example of the OIs in

17 See in particular Part Six, Title 1, Chapter 2, section 1 of the Treaty on the Functioning of the European Union, and notably Art. 288.
18 Art. 288 TFEU.
19 See further Chapter 4, section A.3(a)(i).
20 Council Regulation 2157/2001 of 8 October 2001 on the Statute for a European Company (SE). See description of SE in Chapter 3.
21 Council Regulation 1435/2003 of 22 July 2003 on the Statute for a European Cooperative Society (SCE). See description of SCE in Chapter 3.
22 Art. 288 TFEU.
23 Cf. Fauvarque-Cosson & Behar-Touchais 2012, p. 29.
24 Proposal for a Directive of the European Parliament and of the Council on single-member private limited liability companies, COM(2014) 212 final. See description of SUP in Chapter 3.
25 See next section.

the area of procedural law, which are not applicable in all Member States due to the fact that not all Member States participate in EU measures in this area.[26] But there is also the example of (again) the Unitary Patent Regulation, which was eventually adopted through the enhanced cooperation procedure, without the participation of two Member States.

So, with this in mind, it can be stated more accurately that EU OIs themselves (if not also the institutions responsible for their application) are established by EU legislation that is binding on (at least some if not all) Member States. Thus, EU OIs are not 'optional' for Member States (or at least not for the Member States that participate in them).[27]

(b) The Element of Selection

The second core element of EU Optional Instruments is what will be termed the element of 'selection'. That is to say, all EU OIs constitute legal regimes that are available for private actors to select; or, more precisely, EU OIs are pieces of EU legislation that in principle are applicable to private activities only if they are selected by individuals (who, depending on the EU optional regime in question, may be one or more natural and/or legal persons, 'based'[28] only in the EU or also third countries) in the manner that the legislation prescribes. In fact, as was mentioned previously, all existing and proposed EU OIs that have so far been introduced have taken the form of opt-in regimes, meaning private actors must positively select these optional regimes in order for them to apply. But the element of selection would also be present in the case of an opt-out regime of the EU, as the selection need not necessarily take the form of a positive manifestation of will. What is crucial is that the applicability of the EU regime is subject to its being selected (be it expressly or by implication) by private actors.

In the case of nearly all existing and proposed EU OIs, the 'opt-in' is (or would be) made through an application to a competent institution (or institutions).[29] Again, the particular mode of application will depend on the EU OI in question: Thus, we will see that in the case of some EU OIs (such as those in the area of European company law), private actors wishing to opt in must undergo a registration procedure that is administered by (pre-existing) domestic bodies of the Member States; while in the case of others (notably EU OIs in the area of intellectual property law) there is a registration procedure overseen by a (newly-created)

26 Specifically, Denmark did not participate in the adoption of the Regulations establishing these OIs.

27 EU OIs should also not be confused with the notion of EU legislation according discretion to Member States in the implementation process (i.e. what some have termed 'optional harmonization'; see for Barnard 2007, p. 599, and also previously Currall 1984); although, as we shall see, EU legislation establishing OIs may also accord Member States such discretion on certain points.

28 This term is used loosely here, for what it means exactly to say that an individual is 'based' in a Member State or third country depends not only on whether the individual is a natural or legal person, but also on the EU OI in question: See further Chapter 3.

29 On this see further Chapter 5, section A.2(a).

European Union body; and in the case of others still (for instance those in the area of European procedural law), the application takes the form of a request before a national court in the context of legal proceedings. But, in any event, a (successful) application of some form or another to one institution or another is invariably required in order for individuals to select EU OIs. Having said that, when it comes to the now-withdrawn proposal for a Common European Sales Law (CESL) in the area of contract law, on the other hand, it will be seen that this proposed EU OI did not actually foresee any form of application procedure for the purpose of opting into the regime.[30] Nevertheless, even in this anomalous case, a positive selection by contracting parties would still have been necessary in order for the CESL to become applicable; it is just that this would have been done simply by way of inclusion of a provision to that effect in the parties' agreement.[31]

In short, then, the element of selection by private parties is one that is essential to the nature of all EU OIs, without exception. If the applicability of a piece of EU legislation is not subject to a requirement for individuals to select it (either by opting in or not opting out), it cannot possibly be an optional instrument of EU law.

(c) The Element of Choice

The third and final basic element of EU OIs we shall call the element of 'choice'. This refers to the fact that, like any optional regime, EU optional regimes are available to private actors as an alternative to existing domestic regimes available within the legal systems of the Member States.[32] Accordingly, EU OIs leave individuals with a choice (or at least an additional choice) between the optional EU regime and corresponding regimes provided by domestic legal orders. By 'corresponding' it is not necessarily meant that the domestic legal regime will be a *direct* equivalent to the Union optional regime; for example, we will see that at the time of adoption of the European Economic Interest Grouping, most of the then Member States did not offer a business form directly comparable with the EEIG.[33] But Member State legal systems will typically offer at least a similar regime (or regimes) to private actors. Sticking with the example of the EEIG, the kind of economic cooperation between private actors in different Member States that the EEIG allows for could still take the form of a national company or a temporary grouping in one of the Member States, for instance. Although, even in this broader sense, the element of choice may not always be present in the case of all EU OIs with respect to all Member States. For example, the Community Plant Variety

30 See Chapter 3, CESL Description and Chapter 5, section A.2(a).

31 Another anomalous case in this regard is the Community Design, or more precisely the Unregistered Community Design (see Chapter 3, CD Description). As the name implies, there is no requirement to register such a design right, and therefore no need to apply to an institution in order to obtain UCD protection. Rather, in the case of the UCD, the 'selection' essentially corresponds to the moment at which the design protection is claimed.

32 See further Chapter 4.

33 See further description of EEIG in Chapter 3. Other examples that could be mentioned here are the European Order for Payment and European Small Claims Procedures; see further description of EOP in Chapter 3.

Right[34] is rather anomalous in this respect, since at the time the CPVR Regulation entered into force, the legal systems of a few of the then Member States offered no regime of plant variety protection whatsoever.[35] Therefore, as far as these Member States were concerned, the CPVR was actually the *only* regime of its kind available for private actors to use. Still, as we shall see, even in this case the vast majority of Member States did provide a legal regime for the protection of plant varieties.

So it is fair to say that EU optional regimes invariably do constitute an alternative to pre-existing regimes at national level. Like the element of selection, this element of choice is innate in Union optional regimes (as indeed it is in other optional regimes).

2. *EU OIs and Approximation: Affiliation versus Similarization*

Having set out the fundamental elements that define EU OIs, it is useful to expand on this definition further by discussing certain related issues; the first of these being the question of how EU legislation establishing OIs compares to other types of EU legislation, and especially 'approximation' (or 'harmonization').[36]

In response to this question, it is necessary to begin by clarifying what is (or can be) meant by the term 'approximation' (or 'harmonization') in the context of EU law - and the first point to be noted in this respect is that this terminology is itself ambiguous. This is partly because it is used both in a conceptual way and in a technical legal way within the meaning of the EU treaties (and particularly the TFEU); but it is also because, whether used conceptually or technically, the words 'approximation' and 'harmonization' can be - and have been - interpreted in a variety of different ways, by commentators and EU institutions alike.

In general terms, the concept of approximation in this context may be understood as the idea of 'bringing Member State legal systems closer together' (or, in the case of harmonization, that of 'making Member State legal systems more consistent') through the reduction or elimination of legal disparities between these systems. Commonly, this refers to legislative measures of the EU that are designed to engender convergence between Member State legal systems.[37] And, most commonly, this denotes binding EU legislation (especially directives, but also regulations) that seeks to attain such convergence by replacing and/or amending divergent national rules of law with uniform (or at least more uniform) European

34 Council Regulation of 27 July 1994 on Community plant variety rights. See description of CPVR in Chapter 3.

35 See further description of CPVR in Chapter 3.

36 The present study treats these terms as synonymous because they tend to be used interchangeably both in literature and in the EU treaties, even if some may draw a distinction between them.

37 Although some actually use 'approximation' to refer to the *effect* of EU legislation on the different national legal systems, in a similar way to that in which 'convergence' is used in this sentence (see, for example, Kamba 1974), while others have used 'harmonization' also to refer to convergence engendered not by legislation but through case law (see, for example, Colombi Ciacchi 2005). Nevertheless, these terms are not used in either of these senses in the present study.

rules or standards.[38] Certainly, the European legislator frequently employs the language of approximation or harmonization to describe this type of EU legislation. For example, in the preamble to the SE Regulation, it mentions '[t]he approximation of Member States' company law by means of Directives ...',[39] and in the preamble to the Regulation establishing the Community Design, it discusses '[t]he effect of design protection being limited to the territory of the individual Member States whether or not their laws are approximated ...';[40] while, in the recitals to the Directive on the legal protection of biotechnological inventions, the legislator speaks of the need for 'effective and harmonized protection throughout the Member States ...'.[41]

However, this is not always the case. For one thing, this terminology has also been used by some commentators in connection with non- (or at least less) binding 'soft law' measures[42] adopted by the European legislator, such as those taken through the Open Method of Coordination (OMC).[43] Moreover, the European legislator has also used the language of approximation/harmonization in a wider sense, to describe not soft law measures, but Optional Instruments of the European

38 Cf. e.g. Craig & De Búrca 2015. Of course, depending on the EU legislation in question, the degree of uniformity aimed at can and does vary (see further Chapter 4, section A.2(c), and in any event total uniformity is not realistic (see further Chapter 4, section A.3(a)(i)). In fact, a distinction is often made between approximation or harmonization (particularly by Directives) and 'unification' (particularly by Regulations), on the basis that some European measures seek to establish more uniform rules than other (cf. Lilleholt 2011). For present purposes, however, a distinction will not be drawn between EU measures that are aimed at achieving more or less uniformity in national laws, and the terms 'approximation' and 'harmonization' (or, as will be seen, 'similarization') will be used generally to refer to all such measures. This is not intended to imply, however, that distinctions such as the one just mentioned are in some way not useful or valid.

39 Regulation 2157/2001 of 8 October 2001 on the Statute for a European company (SE), consideration 3. See also Regulation 1435/2003 of 22 July 2003 on the Statute for a European Cooperative Society (SCE), consideration 18.

40 Regulation 6/2002 of 12 December 2001 on Community designs, consideration 4. See also Regulation 207/2009 of 26 February 2009 on the Community trade mark, consideration 4, not to mention the preamble to Directive 98/71 of 13 October 1998 on the legal protection of designs.

41 Directive 98/44 of 6 July 1998 on the legal protection of biotechnological inventions, consideration 3. See also consideration 9.

42 Although so-called soft law measures are often characterized simply as non-binding, it should be recognized that soft law may have different levels of 'bindingness'. See further e.g. Senden 2012. Still, for present purposes an understanding of soft law as non- or at least less binding legislative or non-legislative measures will suffice. And, in addition, it should also be noted that the term soft law is used in this thesis purely because this is the term of art. It is not intended as an implicit acknowledgement that such measures do actually constitute *law*, which may or may not be true (in whole or in part). Indeed, apart from the fact that this notion is very much disputed, many such measures would most likely not fall within the rudimentary definition of law put forward at the outset of this chapter.

43 See, for example, Ashiagbor 2004. Again, though, this terminology is not used in this sense in the present study. That is, for the purposes of this study, the terms approximation and harmonization are considered to equate to binding Union legal acts within the meaning of Art. 288 TFEU.

Union.[44] Even though in many instances the legislator distinguishes between EU legislation establishing OIs and approximation/harmonization in the narrow sense outlined above,[45] in other cases it appears to conflate the two. Take, for example, the Commission Green Paper on a European order for payment procedure and on measures to simplify and speed up small claims litigation of 2002. In this Green Paper, the Commission describes the European Enforcement Order, a Union OI in the area of procedural law,[46] as 'a specific, uniform or *harmonised* procedure laid down within the Community',[47] and the creation of a European order for payment procedure (another EU OI)[48] as 'an endeavour of *harmonisation*'.[49] And, as we shall soon see, these conflicting interpretations (narrow versus wide) have arisen in the technical application of this terminology too.[50]

Of course, in general terms, it is understandable why EU legislation creating OIs could be classed *within* the concepts of approximation and harmonization, since undeniably such legislation can also be said to bring Member State legal systems 'closer together', or to make them 'more consistent.' However, this obscures the fact that there are certain important differences between EU OIs and approximation/harmonization in the narrow sense.[51] Most notably, unlike Optional Instruments of the European Union, EU approximating legislation does not create alternative legal regimes that are only applicable when selected by private individuals.[52] Instead, as already indicated, EU harmonizing instruments 'modify' (i.e. amend and/or replace) existing national rules in some way (or, as the Commission sometimes puts it, 'require an adaptation of national legislation to the standards set in that instrument ...'),[53] and the applicability of these rules is not (or at least not necessarily) subject to any requirement for individuals to first opt into them. Admittedly, it would be inaccurate to say that EU OIs do not also 'modify' the laws of the Member States, as clearly the introduction of alternative legal regimes in each of their respective legal systems does change these systems, by adding to them potentially applicable legal regimes that previously did not exist.[54] But the point is

44 On the distinction between EU soft law and EU OIs see further below. Also it should be noted that the terminology of harmonization has been used in this way in academic literature too. In a recent piece on the CESL proposal, for example, van Schagen uses the phrase 'optional harmonization' (see Van Schagen 2012).

45 Again, see for example the preambles to the SE Regulation, the CD Regulation, and also the CTM Regulation. See also further Chapter 4, section A.1.

46 See further description of EEO in Chapter 3.

47 Green Paper on a European order for payment procedure and on measures to simplify and speed up small claims litigation, COM(2002) 746 final, p. 14 (italics added).

48 See further description of EOP in Chapter 3.

49 Green Paper on a European order for payment procedure and on measures to simplify and speed up small claims litigation, COM(2002) 746 final, p. 11 (italics added).

50 See *infra*, section B.3.

51 Unless stated otherwise, the terms 'approximation' and 'harmonization' will henceforth be used in this narrow sense.

52 See further Chapter 4.

53 Proposal for a Regulation creating a European order for payment procedure, COM(2004)173 final, p. 8.

54 See also further Chapter 4 and in particular sections A.1(b) and B.1(a).

that EU OIs are fundamentally different, insofar as, being alternative options, they do not in principle require *any amendment to or replacement of existing provisions* within the legal orders of the Member States.[55] In this sense, EU legislation establishing OIs may be considered as a kind of 'soft hard law', because although it is binding on the Member States[56] in the same way as traditional 'hard law' approximating measures[57] (and unlike soft law measures), it leaves Member States free to maintain their own legal regimes, and private actors with the choice as to whether to become subject to its application or not.[58] In the words of Fauvarque-Cosson & Behar-Touchais, 'the optional instrument is a solution that combines effectiveness and freedom, freedom of the State to retain its national law and freedom for the operator to choose its law'.[59]

For this reason alone, it can be argued that the labelling of EU OIs as 'approximation' or 'harmonization' is confusing - and that the European legislator would do well not to blur the conceptual distinction between EU legislation creating OIs and approximating legislation that it has often drawn - as approximating measures do not share all of the core elements of EU OIs laid out in the preceding section.[60] Yet the difference between EU OIs and EU harmonizing law goes deeper than the fact that the latter does not possess the essential features that define the former (and particularly that approximating legislation replaces and/or amends existing national law whereas legislation creating OIs introduces alternative legal regimes into national law). For it is also the legal outcome or 'result' of each of these types of EU legislation that fundamentally differs. In the case of approximating law, as was already mentioned, the expected result is national legal convergence, in the sense that existing domestic regimes (or more precisely the rules thereof) within the legal systems of the Member States are *made more similar*, while at the same time remaining separate and distinct legal regimes, with no (or at least no especial) connection between each other. By contrast, in the case of legislation establishing OIs, the Member State legal systems are *affiliated* to the same 'European' legal regime, which takes effect within - and is therefore recognized in unison by - each of these systems. This has the consequence that a new legal form (or right, or title, etc., as the case may be) is introduced into each of the Member States in addition to

55 Cf. Fauvarque-Cosson & Behar-Touchais 2012, p. 384 (section entitled 'Has the optional instrument replaced the national standard?').

56 See *supra* section B.1(a).

57 Approximating legislation is characterized here as 'traditional' simply on the basis that the European legislator has frequently and consistently enacted legislation of this kind ever since the creation of the European Economic Community. It does not mean to say, however, that approximating measures of the Community have not developed over time, or indeed that there are not actually different varieties of approximation (as mentioned also above): See, for example, Trubek & Trubek 2006, and also *infra*, section B.3(b). Nor does it mean to say that approximation constitutes the 'standard' EU legislative approach, for that matter.

58 See further Chapter 4.

59 Fauvarque-Cosson & Behar-Touchais 2012, p. 385.

60 *Supra* section B.1. Specifically, approximating measures do not share the second and third basic elements of EU OIs, i.e. the element of selection and the element of choice.

the pre-existing domestic regimes of those States - and each of these new legal forms is connected with one another, under the umbrella of the European regime.

The best illustration of this difference is provided by the field of European intellectual property law, and specifically European trade mark law.[61] As we shall see, in this field the European legislator has adopted both a Directive approximating the national trade mark laws of the Member States,[62] as well as (shortly thereafter) a Regulation establishing a Community trade mark (CTM), which is an optional instrument.[63] As regards the former, the result of this measure was that the (main) rules and requirements governing the various national trade mark rights became more consistent, so that private actors looking to obtain trade mark protection in another Member State were confronted with fewer disparities between the domestic trade mark regimes. However, these existing trade mark regimes remained un-associated, meaning they are still recognized and applicable only in the legal system to which they pertain. Hence a German trade mark is recognized as an intellectual property right and protected as such in the German jurisdiction, but not in the French, just as a French trade mark is recognized in France but not in Germany, or any other state for that matter. On the other hand, when it comes to the CTM Regulation, the outcome was the creation of an additional trade mark right of European origin available in each of the national jurisdictions that is *recognized by all of them as one and the same*, with the result that it is effectively a single right that provides protection in France just as (and in the same way) it does in Germany, and indeed all of the other Member States.[64] Thus, under the umbrella of the Community trade mark, the trade mark protection systems of the Member States have been linked together in a way that they have not been before.

So, with this in mind, I propose that EU legislation approximating national laws would better be described as 'similarization', while EU legislation creating OIs should rather be called 'affiliation', in order to reflect the differences between the two. That is, I maintain that a new lexicon is needed to ensure a better conceptual understanding and greater transparency of such EU legislation, as the term approximation is ambiguous, and fails to capture the differences between the various legislative measures to which it may be (and has been) applied. Accordingly, the present study will make use of this alternative terminology where appropriate, and particularly the term 'similarization' to denote approximation/harmonization in the narrow sense.

61 Although the field of European design law would serve equally well as an example, as the statements made in what follows are also true of this field.

62 Directive 98/71 of 13 October 1998 on the legal protection of designs.

63 Regulation 207/2009 of 26 February 2009 on the Community trade mark, See further description of CTM in Chapter 3.

64 In this respect, there is a noteworthy link between the affiliating nature of EU OIs and their added value; see Chapter 5, particularly section A.2(c).

3. *EU OIs and Approximation within the Meaning of the EU Treaties*

Following directly on from the previous discussion, it was mentioned that there have also been conflicting interpretations as to the technical meaning of the terms 'approximation' and 'harmonization' for the purpose of the EU treaties. Now, for reasons that will become apparent, this will lead us to a second issue related to the fundamental nature of EU OIs, which is the question of whether there are actually different types of Union Optional Instruments.

The words 'approximation' and 'harmonization' are used throughout the EU treaties, and especially in various articles of the TFEU laying out the legal bases for Union legislative action in different policy areas.[65] In many of these legal bases, harmonizing measures are actually cited as legislation that is excluded from the ambit of the legal base, meaning it cannot be used to adopt these kinds of measures. For example, Article 149 TFEU empowers the EU legislator to 'adopt incentive measures designed to encourage cooperation between Member States and to support their action in the field of employment ...', but then states that '[t]hose measures shall not include harmonization of the laws and regulations of the Member States'.[66] This is also confirmed in general by Title I on 'Categories and Areas of Union Competence', and specifically Article 2(5) TFEU. Conversely, in other instances, the legal base expressly provides *for* the possibility of enacting harmonizing/approximating measures. The most noteworthy example of this for our purposes is Article 114 TFEU, which, ('[s]ave where otherwise provided in the Treaties') allows the European legislator to 'adopt the measures for the approximation of the provisions laid down by law, regulation or administrative action in Member States which have as their object the establishment and functioning of the internal market'.[67] This therefore raises the question of how the terms 'harmonization' and 'approximation' are to be interpreted for the purpose of the EU treaties, and especially what constitutes an approximating measure within

65 As already noted above, the EU treaties seem to use the terms 'approximation' and 'harmonization' interchangeably. Frequently they are followed by the same phrase, i.e. 'of the laws and regulations of the Member States': compare for example Arts. 81 & 149 TFEU. And sometimes they are even used in the same Treaty article: for instance, Art. 114 TFEU uses the phrase 'approximation of the provisions laid down by law, regulation or administrative action in Member States' in its first paragraph, but subsequently employs the term 'harmonization measure' in an apparently synonymous manner, particularly in its fourth and fifth paragraphs. Admittedly, it is not entirely clear whether these terms are to be interpreted synonymously, as this is not expressly stated at any point in the EU treaties. Nonetheless, this does appear to be the case. Also, it should be noted that the treaties sometimes speak of 'coordination' of Member State laws/regulations etc., rather than approximation or harmonization. For example, in a number of the company law directives that the EU legislator describes in the SE Regulation as 'approximation', the preambles actually refer to 'the coordination of national provisions', and this reflects the wording of the legal base for these directives contained in what is now Art. 50 (and particularly 50(2)(g)) TFEU (see further Chapter 3, EEIG description).

66 Other examples can be found in Arts. 19, 79, 84, 153, 165, 166, 167, 168, 173, 189, 195, 196, and 197 TFEU.

67 Art. 114(1) TFEU. Other examples of this include Arts. 81, 82 and 113 TFEU.

the meaning of the 'residual' internal market legal base contained in Article 114 TFEU.

(a) Do EU OIs Constitute Approximation for the Purpose of Article 114 TFEU?

Now, as in the case of the conceptual interpretation of approximation/ harmonization, it is clear that EU legislation approximating national laws in the narrow sense is covered by these terms as they are used in the EU treaties - and hence that similarization measures can be based on Article 114 TFEU. As Low puts it, '[t]he term "approximate" suggests some manner of harmonization or replacement of Member State laws, and there are countless examples of Union measures that bear out this suggestion'.[68] However, the question is whether 'approximation' can (or should) also be interpreted in a wider sense, and particularly whether EU legislation creating optional instruments can constitute approximation for the purpose of the Article 114 legal base. Admittedly, as we will see, all of the EU Optional Instruments under examination in this study that have been adopted to date have actually been based on the so-called 'flexibility clause' contained in Article 352 TFEU (ex. Art. 308 of the Treaty establishing the European Community (TEC), or Art. 235 of the Treaty establishing the European Economic Community (EEC)), with the exception of those in the area of procedural law, which for their part have been founded on a specific legal base for measures in the field of judicial cooperation in civil matters, and also the Unitary Patent Regulation, which was founded on the specific legal base for the creation of European intellectual property rights that was introduced following the Lisbon Treaty.[69] But still, this is not a purely theoretical question: In fact, it has already arisen.

First of all, the European Court of Justice (ECJ) was called upon to answer just such a question in relation to the Regulation establishing the SCE[70] in the *European Cooperative Society* case.[71] As just indicated, like most EU OIs, the SCE was based on what is now Article 352 TFEU, which allows the European legislator to simply adopt 'appropriate measures' (i.e. in principle any type of legislative measure)[72] in the event that 'action by the Union should prove necessary ... and the Treaties have not provided the necessary powers' (i.e. not even residually).[73] However, the original Commission proposal for a Regulation on the statute for a European cooperative society of 1992 had actually been based on ex Article 100a EEC (i.e.

68 Low 2012a, p. 136.
69 See further Chapter 3.
70 Council Regulation 1435/2003 of 22 July 2003 on the Statute for a European Cooperative Society (SCE).
71 Case C-436/03, *European Parliament* v *Council* ('European Cooperative Society') [2006] ECR I-3733.
72 Cf. Hesselink, Rutgers & De Booys 2008.
73 Art. 352(1) TFEU. Hence Art. 352 may only be used if Art. 114 (*inter alia*) could not serve as a legal base; see in more detail e.g. Wulf 2014, p. 30 *et seq*. (although, in spite of this mutual exclusivity, some have argued Art. 352 could potentially be used as a dual legal base along with Art. 114; see e.g. Van Schagen 2012, p. 89-90).

what is now, after amendment, Art. 114 TFEU).[74] This was only subsequently changed to (what was by then) Article 308 TEC (i.e. the current Art. 352 TFEU) as a result of '[d]iscussions which took place in the Council'.[75] And the European Parliament objected to this revised choice of legal base, to the extent that it brought an action for annulment before the ECJ, contending that the appropriate legal base was rather (what was by then) ex. Article 95 TEC (now Art. 114 TFEU).[76] The Parliament (which was also supported in its action by the Commission) was of the opinion that 'the approximation of the laws of the Member States may also be carried out by supplementing national law by creating European legal forms'.[77] The reason for this, according to the Parliament, was because 'the concept of "approximation" in Article 95 EC encompasses not only measures seeking to remove barriers resulting from the disparity of the different national legal orders but *also measures aimed at overcoming the territorial boundaries of the national legal orders* ...'.[78] By contrast, the Council, for its part, maintained that 'an approximation measure necessarily implies substitution, whether total or partial, for the national provisions'.[79] In other words, the Council argued that 'approximation' for the purpose of Article 95 TEC equated to similarization measures, and did not cover 'a new legal form, of a European dimension, additional to cooperative societies under national law'.[80]

In its ruling, delivered in 2006, the Court of Justice rejected the Parliament's arguments, *inter alia*, concerning Article 95 TEC, and dismissed the action. The Court began the key part of its judgment by stating that 'it is apparent from the content and the purpose of the contested regulation that it aims to introduce a new legal form in addition to the national forms of cooperative societies ... which has specific Community character'.[81] In particular, the Court found that it was clear from Article 9 of the contested Regulation, which requires all Member States to treat a European Cooperative Society as though it were a cooperative established under

74 Proposal for a Council Regulation on the statute for a European cooperative society, COM(91) 273 final.

75 Case C-436/03, *European Cooperative Society*, para. 12. It is worth noting that, as Advocate-General Stix-Hackl recognized in her opinion on this case, the Court of Justice has previously 'ruled that the Community may use Article 308 EC as the basis for creating new rights superimposed on national rights' (para. 66, referring to Opinion 1/94 [1994] delivered on 15 November 1994). See further Chapter 3, CTM description.

76 Case C-436/03, *European Cooperative Society*, para. 18. The Parliament's objection can be explained largely by the fact that whereas Art. 95 TEC required the use of what was formerly known as the 'codecision' procedure (now the 'ordinary legislative procedure' as stated in Art. 114 TFEU), under which the Parliament acts 'on an equal footing' with the Council, Art. 308 TEC provided for what was formerly known as the 'consultation' procedure (now the 'special legislative procedure' as stated in Art. 352 TFEU), pursuant to which the Parliament was only entitled to be consulted by the Council.

77 Case C-436/03, *European Cooperative Society*, para. 20.

78 *Ibid.*, para. 21 (italics added). On the aim of overcoming the territorial boundaries of the national legal orders see further Chapter 4, section A.1(a).

79 Case C-436/03, *European Cooperative Society*, para. 22.

80 *Ibid.*, para. 29.

81 *Ibid.*, para. 40.

the law of the State in which its seat is located, that 'the European cooperative society is a form which coexists with cooperative societies under national law'.[82] Then the Court went on to affirm that:

> 'In those circumstances, the contested regulation, which *leaves unchanged the different national laws already in existence,* cannot be regarded as aiming to approximate the laws of the Member States applicable to cooperative societies, but has as its purpose the creation of a new form of cooperative society in addition to the national forms.'[83]

So it appears from this judgment (at least prima facie) that the ECJ has already answered the question of whether EU legislation establishing OIs can amount to approximation within the meaning of Article 114 TFEU in the negative.

Yet, even after this ruling, the issue arose again only a few years later with the introduction of the Commission's proposal for a Common European Sales Law of 2011, a proposal for a Union OI in the area of contract law that has since been withdrawn.[84] As in the case of the original SCE proposal, the legal base selected by the Commission for the CESL proposal was (what was by then) Article 114 TFEU.[85] Of course, given the ECJ's judgment in *European Cooperative Society,* one could be forgiven for thinking that this was a rather odd choice of legal base, since the proposed CESL Regulation similarly had as its purpose, as the Commission expressly stated in its proposal, the creation of 'an optional regime in addition to pre-existing contract law rules without replacing them'.[86] However, in contrast to all of the previous Regulations establishing OIs, including the SCE Regulation, the Commission presented its proposal for a Regulation establishing an optional instrument as a so-called '*2nd national regime*' of contract law within the domestic law of each of the Member States.[87] Previously, the Commission had characterized the concept of introducing optional instruments in various fields as the '28th regime' method.[88] In fact, as the English Law Society has pointed out, the notion of an optional instrument in the area of contract law was initially also referred to by the

82 *Ibid.*, para. 43.

83 *Ibid.*, para. 44 (italics added).

84 Proposal for a Regulation of the European Parliament and of the Council on a Common European Sales Law, COM(2011) 635 final. See further description of CESL in Chapter 3.

85 The desire of the Commission to use Art. 114 TFEU and not Art. 352 TFEU can largely be explained by the fact that whereas the former allows for qualified majority voting in the Council under the ordinary legislative procedure, the latter requires the Council to act unanimously. See further description of CESL in Chapter 3.

86 COM(2011) 635 final, p. 10.

87 *Ibid.*, p. 4 *et seq.*

88 See Opinion of the European Economic and Social Committee on 'The 28th regime – an alternative allowing less lawmaking at Community level' (own-initiative opinion) CESE 758/2010, available at: <www.eesc.europa.eu/?i=portal.en.int-opinions.10007>, para. 2.5. In other words, as Low explains, '[t]here is a peculiar distinction between the CESL and all other optional instruments that have come before it. The CESL [was] not intended as a 28th legal system alongside national regimes, but [was] to be incorporated as a second set of rules within the national legal system': Low 2012a, p. 136.

Commission as a 28th regime,[89] meaning it would be available as an alternative contract law regime alongside pre-existing national regimes.[90] For example, in a press release as recent as 2010, the then European Commissioner for Justice, Viviane Reding, declared that '[a] possible solution is to have a *28th regime* for contracts. Such a European Contract Law would exist in parallel to the national contract laws and provide standard terms and conditions'.[91] But this approach was subsequently changed, with the result that the CESL was later described as a second set of rules incorporated within each of the Member State legal systems.[92] Hence, by the time the Commission published its Green Paper on a European Contract Law later that same year, it stated that the option of adopting a Regulation setting up an optional instrument 'would be conceived as a "2nd Regime" in each Member State, thus providing parties with an option between two regimes of domestic contract law'.[93]

And, on the basis of this distinction, the Commission maintained in its proposal for a Common European Sales Law that:

> '*The Proposal … harmonises the national contract laws of the Member States* not by requiring amendments to the pre-existing national contract law, but by creating within each Member State's national law a second contract law regime for contracts covered by its scope that is identical throughout the European Union and will exist alongside the pre-existing rules of national contract law.'[94]

In other words, the Commission took the position that, as a 2nd national regime, the proposed CESL was a *different type of EU optional instrument*, which would approximate national laws (also apparently within the meaning of Art. 114 TFEU), even if the previous EU OIs, as 28th regimes, did not.[95]

89 It should be noted that the expression '28th regime', which denotes an additional regime on top of those already existing in each of the Member States, is something of a misnomer. This was arguably already the case when the term was first used, as Scots law constitutes a distinct jurisdiction within the UK, meaning the additional regime of European origin would better have been called a '29th regime'. But also, since the accession of Croatia to the European Union in 2013, there are now 28 Member States, which means the expression 29th regime (if not '30th regime') would definitely be more appropriate. Notwithstanding this inaccuracy, however, the present study will also employ the term '28th regime' in order to avoid confusion, as this is the term that has consistently been used by others, including the EU institutions.

90 See the Law Society 2012, p. 2.

91 Press release, 'Making the Most of the Internal Market: Concrete EU Solutions to Cut Red Tape and to Boost the Economy', SPEECH/10/42 (24 February 2010), available at: <http://europa.eu/rapid/press-release_speech-10-42_en.htm> (italics added).

92 See The Law Society, 'Preliminary comments on the relationship between the proposal for a Common European Sales Law and the law applicable to contractual obligations (Rome I)' (2012), p. 2.

93 Green Paper from the Commission on policy options for progress towards a European Contract Law for consumers and businesses, COM(2010) 348 final, p. 9.

94 COM(2011) 635 final, p. 8 (italics added).

95 It should be added that the characterization of the CESL as a 2nd national regime was also significant for another reason, related to the applicability of Art. 6(2) of the Rome I Regulation: See further Chapter 3, CESL description.

(b) 28th Regime or 2nd National Regime?

So what exactly is this (alleged) difference between a 28th regime and a 2nd national regime, and how can the latter be said to approximate national laws while the former does not? In essence, the reasoning seems to be as follows.[96] The concept of a 28th regime, in general terms, denotes an optional legal regime that is independent (or at least largely independent) of existing domestic regimes, in the sense that it 'stands autonomously' within the EU next to the legal regimes available in the Member States.[97] More precisely, a Union OI is said to be a 28th regime if the Regulation establishing it 'relies on' pre-existing national law[98] to such a limited extent that it is identifiable as a distinct legal regime. It is not that the '28th regime' is entirely separate from existing national regimes, but rather that the references to pre-existing national law are so confined that it can be considered to all intents and purposes as a self-sufficient, 'supra-national' system. On the other hand, the 2nd national regime corresponds to the idea of an optional legal regime whose reliance on national law is 'so fundamental as to be inextricably intertwined in the national legal order'.[99] That is, a Union OI constitutes a 2nd national regime if the references to the laws of the Member States in the legislation establishing it are so extensive and/or significant that it should rather be seen as adding a 'hybrid' regime within each of the national legal systems.[100] Therefore, the argument is that, unlike the previous EU OIs, the CESL proposal of 2011 would (have) approximate(d) the laws of the Member States because, although it did not alter the pre-existing national contract laws per se, it would serve to change the 'reach' of (a number of) these laws, by making them applicable also to contracts selected to be governed by the CESL, 'coupled with the fact that all the hybridized portions of national regimes are the same'.[101]

The question, then, is whether this is an acceptable distinction. Or, put differently, should it be recognized that there are these fundamentally different types of EU OIs, one of which amounts to approximation within the meaning of the EU treaties, while the other does not? Certainly, a number of commentators have rejected this. According to Hesselink, for example,

> 'The ECJ has held explicitly that 'measures the for (sic) approximation' within the meaning of Article 95 EC do not include new Community instruments that co-exist with national rules ... This is highly relevant since the introduction of an optional instrument will not, as such, affect the national legal systems, but will rather co-exist

96 As Rühl notes (and as her article also demonstrates), the expressions '28th regime' and '2nd national regime' are also interpreted in different ways by different commentators. It should therefore be stressed that the explanation of these terms and the reasoning behind them given in what follows once again corresponds to the most common understanding in our context. See Rühl 2012. See also Fornasier 2012, p. 405.

97 See for example Fornasier 2012.

98 On the notion of a Union OI's 'reliance' on national law, see further Chapter 5, section A.2(b).

99 Low 2012a, p. 146.

100 Some have referred to this as a 'referential model'. See, for example, Fleischer 2012.

101 Low 2012a, p. 145-146. See also Wulf 2014, p. 34.

> with it (sic). Therefore, the conclusion seems to be that an optional instrument is not a measure of approximation within the meaning of Article 95 EC.'[102]

However, there are also those (along with the Commission) who have contended that such a distinction can be justified, and that the '2nd national regime' could be held to constitute approximation for the purpose of Article 114 TFEU (ex. Art. 95 TEC). It is possible to make this argument because in actual fact, as Hesselink also acknowledges, the question of how 'approximation' in Article 114 should be interpreted has not been elucidated completely by the case law of the European Court of Justice.[103] In particular, there are two other rulings of the Court of Justice that demonstrate that it is possible for EU measures to be based on Article 114 TFEU even if at first sight they do not harmonize Member State laws.[104] These are, firstly, the case of *Smoke Flavouring*,[105] in which the ECJ held that a Regulation creating a European agency to oversee a centralized procedure for the authorization of smoke flavourings for food products was 'designed in such a way that it leads to a harmonisation within the meaning of Article 95 EC',[106] in spite of the fact that the contested measure itself did not approximate the laws of the Member States in the narrow sense. And, secondly, the case of *ENISA*,[107] where the Court found that a Regulation setting up a European Network and Information Security Agency empowered to issue non-binding advice as a way of aiding the implementation of some other EU approximating legislation (in the narrow sense) also constituted approximation within the meaning of ex. Article 95 EC, because the tasks conferred on the agency in question were nevertheless 'closely linked to the subject-matter of the acts approximating the laws, regulations and administrative provisions of the Member States'.[108] The Court deemed this to be the case as 'the Community body thus established provides services to national authorities and/or operators which affect the homogenous implementation of harmonizing instruments and which are likely to facilitate their application.[109]

Thus, what has become clear from the ECJ's case law is that (contrary to the Council's position in *European Cooperative Society*) the term 'approximation' in Article 114 TFEU covers more than just approximation in the strict and narrow sense.[110] In other words, EU legislation does not necessarily need to modify the laws of the Member States 'upfront' in order to constitute approximation: Provided it is shown that the measure would lead to approximation in time, Article 114 could still

102 Hesselink, Rutgers & De Booys 2008, p. 26. See also e.g. Kuipers 2011; Wulf 2014, p. 25 *et seq.*; and, discussing the European Cooperative Society, Dashwood 1996.

103 See Hesselink, Rutgers & De Booys 2008, p. 25.

104 See Low 2012a, p. 138.

105 Case C-66/04, *United Kingdom* v *Parliament and Council* ('Smoke Flavouring') [2005] ECR I-10553.

106 *Ibid.*, para. 49.

107 Case C-217/04, *United Kingdom* v *Parliament and Council* ('ENISA') [2006] ECR I-3771.

108 *Ibid.*, para. 45.

109 *Ibid.*, para. 46.

110 For this reason it must also be acknowledged that the concept of approximation in the narrow sense may not necessarily be as straightforward as the outline of this concept in the previous section might suggest.

be a suitable legal base.[111] What has not been clarified, however, is how far this formula of an 'approximating effect' would extend to other kinds of EU measures than those at issue in the cases of *Smoke Flavouring* and *ENISA*. And this, in combination with the fact that more generally the Court of Justice has recognized that the European legislator has discretion in determining which measures to adopt on the basis of Article 114 TFEU, has led Low for one to argue that, as a 2nd national regime 'the CESL may be characterized as an intermediate step towards approximation',[112] in a similar way to the measures upheld in *Smoke Flavouring* and *ENISA*.[113] It is for this reason that Low arrives at the conclusion that 'the hybridization of national law can be equated with approximation'.[114]

Now while it is no doubt true that, taken together, the case law of the ECJ stands for the principle that the interpretation of approximation for the purpose of Article 114 TFEU depends on the 'approximating' (or converging) effect the EU legislation could have on national laws,[115] one can also not overlook the fact that in the cases of *Smoke Flavouring* and *ENISA* the measures at issue were not optional instruments - it was only in *European Cooperative Society* that the Court was posed the question specifically in connection with a Union optional instrument. For one thing, this means that the cases may be distinguishable on the facts,[116] in the sense that while the former two cases concerned measures that could be seen as a step towards approximation of national laws, even if an indirect one, the prospect of the SCE Regulation, *as an optional instrument*, contributing to the approximation of national laws was considered to be too distant.[117] But also, regardless of this, it is therefore undeniable that a measure *directly* comparable to the SCE Regulation (i.e. the so-called 28th regime) will not be considered by the ECJ to be an approximating measure, even if other measures that do not replace or amend national laws per se

111 See Low 2012a, p. 140.

112 Low 2012a, p. 141. It is important to clarify that, as Low observes, the characterization of the CESL as a 2nd national regime is not the only argument that could be made in support of it being an 'intermediate step towards approximation'. For example, another argument is that the CESL might (have) stimulate(d) regulatory competition, which could (have) lead to '*de facto* harmonisation' of Member State contract laws. However, apart from the fact that there are noteworthy doubts surrounding the possibility of regulatory competition leading to convergence in practice or even whether the CESL would (have) serve(d) to instigate regulatory competition (as Low acknowledges), it could also be argued that other EU OIs, including the SCE, may engender convergence between national laws in this way. On the possibility of OIs stimulating regulatory competition, and of this leading to convergence in practice, see further Chapter 4, sections A.2(b)(i) and (c), respectively. As for the doubts surrounding this, see further Chapter 4, sections A.3(b)(i) and A.3(c), respectively.

113 See also e.g. Van Schagen 2012.

114 Low 2012a, p. 147. In my opinion Low's thorough examination of this issue deserves acknowledgement as a particularly valuable contribution to informing the debate, not to mention for shaping and explaining my own views on the matter.

115 Cf. Low 2012a, p. 139.

116 Indeed, Hesselink appears to distinguish between these rulings in his analysis of the ECJ's case law: See Hesselink, Rutgers & De Booys 2008.

117 Cf. Low 2012, p. 140. Low describes this as the question of 'remoteness'.

could be.[118] Thus, the more fundamental question has to be whether the CESL is actually distinguishable from the SCE, inasmuch as the CESL, unlike the SCE, constitutes a 2nd national regime.

According to Low, the premise for classifying the CESL as 'a new breed of Article 114-based Euro-national optional instruments'[119] (i.e. the 2nd national regime) is that 'the CESL is not a completely self-contained system. It remains reliant on national law, for instance, to determine the proprietary effects of transactions'.[120] Indeed this is in line with the conceptual distinction between the 2nd national regime and the 28th regime outlined above which, as was indicated, rests on the extent to which a Union OI relies on pre-existing national rules. However, it is far from obvious that the SCE does differ from the CESL in this respect: In fact, the very same statement could be made about the SCE. As we shall see, the SCE Regulation (like the other EU OIs adopted in the area of company law, for that matter) makes numerous, non-peripheral references to national law, both on specific points, and for entire areas, such as taxation.[121] Furthermore, just as the proposed CESL Regulation of 2011 also contains a general stipulation deferring to 'pre-existing rules of the national law' for related matters that are not addressed in the Regulation,[122] so the SCE Regulation has a general provision stating that 'in the case of matters not regulated by this Regulation or, where matters are partly regulated by it, of those aspects not covered by it', an SCE is to be governed (*inter alia*) by 'the laws of Member States which would apply to a cooperative formed in accordance with the law of the Member State in which the SCE has its registered office'.[123] Indeed, the SCE relies on pre-existing national law to such an extent that it can be (and has been) maintained that there are actually as many forms of SCE in the EU as there are national jurisdictions.[124]

And yet, in the *European Cooperative Society* case, the European Court of Justice expressly rejected the argument – which was submitted by both the Commission and the Parliament – that the SCE constituted approximation because it

118 To quote Advocate-General Stix-Hackl, '[t]he fact is that certain aims, such as the creation of new Community legal forms, for instance, can only be achieved by recourse to Article 308 EC'; Opinion of Advocate-General Stix-Hackl delivered on 12 July 2005 on Case C-436/03, *European Cooperative Society*, para 96.

119 Low 2012a, p. 145.

120 Low 2012a, p. 146.

121 Indeed, Advocate-General Stix-Hackl recognizes as much in her opinion in *European Cooperative Society* (para. 84). Equally, the Commission itself has acknowledged this: see Report from the Commission to the European Parliament, the Council, the European Economic and Social Committee and the Committee of the Regions on the application of Council Regulation 1435/2003 of 22 July 2003 on the Statute for a European Cooperative Society (SCE), p. 9.

122 See Proposal for a Regulation of the European Parliament and of the Council on a Common European Sales Law, COM(2011) 635 final, considerations 27 and 28.

123 Art. 8.

124 See further Chapter 3, SCE description.

'systematically referred' to the laws of the Member States.[125] The Court stated that its finding that the SCE could not be regarded as approximating the different national laws applicable to cooperative societies was 'not affected by the fact that the contested Regulation does not lay down exhaustively all of the rules applicable to [SCEs] and that, for certain matters, it refers to the law of the Member State in the territory of which the [SCE] has its registered office, since ... that referral is of a subsidiary nature'.[126] So – assuming this is understood correctly as meaning that the SCE Regulation does not approximate national laws because, notwithstanding its reliance on national law, it is first and foremost the Regulation that is to apply in lieu of national law, and it is only where the Regulation 'runs out' that national law is to be applied – it is hard to see how the argument that the CESL is 'inextricably intertwined' with national law could (have) succeed(ed) where a very similar argument in relation to the SCE failed,[127] as the several references to pre-existing national law that the proposed CESL Regulation also makes are also for '[a]ll the matters ... that are not addressed in the Common European Sales Law.'[128]

Therefore, in my view, even if the case law of the ECJ should be interpreted as a connected line that points in the direction of a general test of 'harmonizing effects' for the purpose of determining what constitutes approximation under Article 114 TFEU, the Court has, at the same time, *effectively* excluded EU legislation creating optional instruments from the ambit of this legal base. Admittedly, the Court did not state as much in *European Cooperative Society*, choosing instead to pronounce itself only on the Union OI at issue (and arguably for good reasons).[129] But this does not prevent the conclusion that EU OIs have been 'all but' excluded from the ambit of Article 114. Moreover, leaving aside the issue of whether the Court of Justice would or would not recognize a difference in the case of a Union OI that is labelled as a second regime in national law,[130] it is my contention that this assertion of a

125 See Case C-436/03, *European Cooperative Society*, paras. 46 & 27. See also the discussion of this argument in the opinion of Advocate-General Stix-Hackl (who also rejected it) delivered on 12 July 2005 on Case C-436/03, *European Cooperative Society*, paras. 82-90.

126 Case C-436/03, *European Cooperative Society*, para. 45.

127 Of course, the argument made in relation to the SCE was not exactly the same because, as already stated, the CESL proposal was the first EU OI to be presented as a 2nd national regime.

128 Proposal for a Regulation of the European Parliament and of the Council on a Common European Sales Law, COM(2011) 635 final, consideration 27.

129 Apart from the fact that this was not necessary in order to arrive at a decision in the case at hand, it would have presumably required the Court to define Union optional instruments as a category of legislation. Furthermore, this can also be explained by the fact that, as noted above (and as Low emphasizes), the Court 'accords discretion to the Union legislator as regards its choice of instrumentality, for fear of otherwise dampening the quest for optimal governance structures'; Low2012, p. 144-145.

130 Of course, since the CESL proposal of 2011 has now been withdrawn, there is no longer a chance of the ECJ being called upon to answer this question in relation to this OI. However, it is certainly possible a challenge could have been brought (see on this e.g. paper of the Law Society entitled 'Common European Sales Law' of April 2013, available at: <http://international.lawsociety.org.uk/files/law%20society%20and%20bar%20council_cesl%20briefing%20for%20meps%20april%202013.pdf>, para. 51), and, in any case, as the experience with the →

dichotomy between 28th regimes and 2nd national regimes *should not* be recognized. Put simply, one might say that the extent to which a Union OI relies on national law must be understood as a question of variety, not type. That is to say, all EU OIs ultimately 'rely' on pre-existing national law;[131] it is just that some EU OIs do so more than others.[132] In this sense, as Fauvarque-Cosson & Behar-Touchais have (rightly) remarked, '[w]e have sometimes spoken of a "28th system", but in reality, to make it clear that this system integrates into national legal systems, it is more appropriate to use the term "second system" or "2nd system" ...'.[133] In other words, all EU OIs are probably best seen as hybridized legal regimes,[134] which, as explained previously,[135] are linked together (unlike the equivalent '1st' national regimes). Although, having said that, precisely because the additional legal regimes that result in each Member State legal system from EU legislation creating OIs are connected, the term '2nd national regime' is not ideal either, as it fails to capture the fact that the 2nd regime differs from the 1st regime in this important respect.[136] For this reason, one might argue that the label 28th (or 29th/30th) regime is actually more appropriate.

In any event, whether one calls a Union OI a '28th regime', or a '2nd national regime', or something else still, the point is that it would be incorrect to divide EU OIs into two different categories on the basis of their degree of reliance on national law. It may be that these terms serve as useful shorthand for Union OIs that rely to a large extent on national law versus those that place only limited reliance on pre-existing domestic rules, respectively, but this cannot alter the fact that they are all fundamentally the same kind of EU legislation, characterized by the same defining elements that were laid out before in this chapter.[137] In particular, apart from being optional, EU legislation creating OIs introduces alternative regimes in the legal systems of the Member States, meaning existing national law is thereby *supposed* to be left 'unaffected'.[138] Besides, at the technical level, the distinction between the 28th regime and the 2nd national regime is an unworkable one. For at what point does a Union OI become so reliant on national that it stops being a 28th regime and instead becomes a 2nd national regime? Perhaps one could distinguish relatively easily

CESL proposal shows, this question could potentially arise again in relation to another proposal for a Union OI (be it in the area of contract law and/or another) in future.

131 Note though that this 'national law' may also include (sets of) rules established by EU approximating legislation. Obvious examples would be the EU OIs in the area of procedural law (see further Chapter 3), as well as those in the area of company law (see further Chapter 4, section A.3(a)(i)).

132 See further Chapter 4, section A.3(a)(i) and Chapter 5, sections A.2(b) and C.

133 Fauvarque-Cosson & Behar-Touchais 2012, p. 29.

134 Once again, the term 'hybrid' in this context refers to the notion of an optional European legal regime interacting with the laws of each of the national legal systems in which it is introduced to a significant extent. It should not be confused with other notions of 'hybridity' in European law (see e.g. Micklitz & Svetiev 2012, and also Trubek & Trubek 2006; Kilpatrick 2006).

135 *Supra*, section B.2.

136 Cf. Dannemann 2013. Of course, this is not the only difference that can be identified.

137 *Supra*, section B.1.

138 See further Chapter 4, section A.1(b).

between a Union OI that makes only a few references to national law (such as the CTM Regulation)[139] and one that makes many such references (like the SE Regulation, for instance).[140] But what about a Union OI that falls somewhere in between (as is arguably the case with the European Small Claims Procedure (ESCP), for example)?[141] As we will see, it is actually very difficult to accurately compare EU OIs on this basis.[142] And given that at stake is the clarity of the term 'approximation' within the meaning of the EU treaties (notably Art. 114 TFEU), this would be particularly unsatisfactory.[143]

In short, then, just as we concluded in the previous section that there are good reasons not to blur the conceptual distinction between EU legislation establishing optional regimes and EU legislation approximating national laws, so it is argued here that the technical meaning of the term approximation should not be stretched to cover EU OIs (as they are defined in this study), which are another kind of EU legislation, regardless of (*inter alia*) the extent to which a given EU OI is reliant on national law. That is, to respond to the question posed at the start of this section, EU legislation creating optional instruments cannot - and at any rate should not - constitute 'approximation' for the purpose of Article 114 TFEU.

Conclusion

It follows from the above that the various EU measures mentioned at the beginning of the first chapter can be characterized collectively as 'EU Optional Instruments' on the ground that they all conform to an elementary definition, at least for the most part. Indeed, it was on the basis of a definition of this kind that the *Fauvarque-Cosson* study on European optional instruments (also mentioned in the previous chapter) was produced.[144] This alone serves to demonstrate that there is a case for viewing this range of EU initiatives in different fields of EU law as a distinct category of 'optional instruments', and hence for studying these initiatives as a separate 'family' of EU legislation.[145] Of course, this does not mean to say that EU OIs are a homogenous group of legislative instruments. On the contrary, we shall see that

139 See further description of CTM in Chapter 3, Chapter 4, section A.3(a)(i) and Chapter 5, section C.1.

140 See further description of SE in Chapter 3, Chapter 4, section A.3(a)(i) and Chapter 5, section C.2.

141 See further description of ESCP in Chapter 3 and Chapter 5, section C.2.

142 See Chapter 5.

143 Apart from overly stretching the meaning of approximation in Art. 114, there are also a number of other reasons why this would be unsatisfactory, including the point that this could undermine the choices of legal base made for previous optional European legal regimes: See further Wulf 2014, p. 29-30.

144 Although it should be noted that, in contrast to the present study, Fauvarque-Cosson & Behar-Touchais 2012 include instruments 'arising from ... an international convention signed solely by Member States of the European Union' within their definition of 'European optional instrument'.

145 Although to what extent these initiatives are actually perceived as optional instruments in practice is a separate matter: On this see Fauvarque-Cosson & Behar-Touchais 2012, p. 53 *et seq*.

there are a number of significant differences between them. But they can still be considered as a group, because they all share certain fundamental characteristics, including notably the elements of selection and choice – and these are characteristics that other kinds of EU legislation do not possess. In particular, these elements are what distinguish EU OIs from measures approximating national laws (in the narrow sense). In fact, I have argued that the difference between EU OIs and approximation goes further than this, insofar as the former affiliates national legal systems, whereas the latter similarizes them. But even if one does not accept this distinction, the point remains that EU approximating measures do not share the element of selection or the element of choice.

At the same time, I have also disputed the distinction some (including the Commission) have sought to draw between different types of EU OIs, and particularly between 'the 28th regime' and 'the 2nd national regime'. Again, notwithstanding that the specific features of EU OIs may differ, I maintain that EU OIs are all fundamentally the same kind of legislative instrument.[146] Hence, while one EU OI may rely on national law more than another, for example, this does not alter the essential nature of these instruments. Still, having said that, it is must be acknowledged that this is a difficult question, and the answer to it remains uncertain. Equally, the same can be said about the related question of whether a Union optional instrument can constitute approximation in the technical sense, within the meaning of the Treaties. In my opinion this is not (and should not be) the case, but the issue is debatable. And it is a debate that is likely to continue, at least until the Court of Justice of the EU pronounces itself directly on the matter (if not also beyond).

146 That is, I contend that the fundamental nature of all EU OIs is the same. At the same time, however, I certainly recognize that there exist important differences in the structure and design of EU OIs. Such differences are discussed further in the next chapter, and examined more closely in Chapters 4 & 5.

Chapter 3

OVERVIEW OF EU OPTIONAL INSTRUMENTS

INTRODUCTION

Having defined the fundamental nature of Optional Instruments of the European Union, it now becomes necessary to describe the various EU OIs under examination in this study in detail. Before commencing this overview of EU OIs, however, it should be reiterated that the present study does not cover (nor does it seek to cover) every single EU OI that has been adopted or proposed by the European legislator to date. Instead, our focus will rather be on three areas of European law in which a series of EU OIs have been adopted/proposed - namely European company law, European intellectual property law and European procedural law -, as well as on a proposal for an optional instrument in the area of European contract law that has since been withdrawn. As we shall see, all of these EU OIs have been around (in one form or another) for some years already, and many of them possess particularly interesting characteristics.

Thus, with this being said, in what follows an overview of each of these EU OIs (twelve in total) will be provided, charting their development since the European legislator enacted the very first optional instrument of the Community in the field of company law in 1985. This overview will systematically address a range of points, including the nature of, background to and legal base for the optional instrument; the aims and objectives behind the optional instrument; the legal and institutional framework, substantive content and scope of the optional instrument; and the advantages of the optional instrument, as well as (where appropriate) relevant statistics on its application. The chapter will then conclude with a brief comparison of these EU OIs, making reference to different aspects highlighted in the overview.

A. EU OIs in the Area of European Company Law

1. *The European Economic Interest Grouping (EEIG)*

As was already mentioned, the very first Optional Instrument (OI) to be formally adopted at EU-level was the European Economic Interest Grouping (EEIG), enacted by means of a Regulation on 25 July 1985.[1] Pertaining to the field of European Company law, this legislation created a new Community-wide form of corporate legal entity, to be added to the list of existing national company forms available to private actors in each of the Member States. As a result, private actors would now have an additional possibility of forming and operating an EEIG, 'upon the terms, in the manner and with the effects laid down' in the Regulation.[2] Moreover, the EEIG was eventually followed by two further Regulations establishing new European company forms to be made available to private individuals by the Member States in accordance with their terms. First, the Regulation on the Statute for a European Company, which was passed in 2001[3] (that is, some 16 years after the adoption of the EEIG) and, second, the Regulation on the Statute for a European Cooperative Society, of 2003.[4] Furthermore, in 2014 the Commission also submitted a formal proposal for a Directive on single-member private limited liability companies,[5] which would introduce yet another pan-European form of company (the Societas Unius Personae, SUP). Thus European Company law constitutes both a pioneering and prolific area of law as far as OIs are concerned, and as such an area of significant interest for our purposes.

While this analysis will focus especially on the European Company (or Societas Europaea, SE) - for reasons which will become apparent - it is useful to begin by considering the EEIG, not only because this was the first truly European business form to be created, but also because it marked the genesis of the Commission's new legislative strategy towards company law after the so-called 'first and second generation' directives adopted between the late sixties and early eighties.[6] This Community action preceding the EEIG sought to *harmonize* certain aspects of Member State company law regimes, including national mandatory rules

1 Council Regulation 2137/85 of 25 July 1985 on the European Economic Interest Grouping (EEIG). On this instrument see in general Santa Maria 2009, including the list of relevant literature on p. 173 (footnote 158); Van Gerven & Aalders 1990; Anderson 1990; De Bruycker 1991, p. 191; European Commission 1989; European Commission 1999.

2 EEIG Regulation, Art. 1.

3 Council Regulation 2157/2001 of 8 October 2001 on the Statute for a European company (SE).

4 Council Regulation 1435/2003 of 22 July 2003 on the Statute for a European Cooperative Society (SCE).

5 Proposal for a Directive of the European Parliament and of the Council on single-member private limited liability companies, COM(2014) 212 final.

6 The first generation directives comprise First Council Directive 68/151/EEC of 9 March 1968 and Second Council Directive 77/91/EEC of 13 December 1976, while the second generation comprises Third Council Directive 78/855/EEC of 9 October 1978, Fourth Council Directive 78/660/EEC of 25 July 1978, Sixth Council Directive 82/891/EEC of 17 December 1982, Seventh Council Directive 83/349/EEC of 13 June 1983 and Eighth Council Directive 84/253/EEC of 10 April 1984.

on disclosure of corporate data and minimum capital requirements, with the specific aim of removing restrictions on the freedom of establishment for companies. Hence the legal basis for these directives was Article 54(3)(g) of the Treaty establishing the European Economic Community (subsequently Art. 44(2)(g) of the Treaty establishing the European Community, now Art. 50(2)(g) of the Treaty on the Functioning of the European Union), which provided for the Community's power to *coordinate* 'the guarantees demanded in Member States from companies ... for the purpose of protecting the interests both of the members of such companies and of third parties'. These directives did not harmonize the core aspects of Member State company law (such as board structure, employee involvement, etc.), however, and indeed it soon became clear that, due to major disagreements between the Member States on such issues, 'the European Commission would be unable to remove the most intractable barriers to economic integration'.[7] Therefore while the Community's harmonization efforts did persist with later generations of directives, the Commission sought at the same time to develop an alternative approach aiming not at the harmonization of national (mandatory) rules, but rather the establishment of independent and uniform *European legal structures*.[8] And this was precisely the envisaged result of the EEIG Regulation: The creation of a European business form that would contribute to the 'smooth functioning of a common market offering conditions analogous to those of a national market'.[9] Accordingly, the EEIG Regulation was based on Article 235 of the EEC Treaty (subsequently Art. 308 TEC, now Art. 352 TFEU - the already mentioned 'flexibility clause'), which allowed the Community to simply 'enact the appropriate provisions' if it considered this necessary to achieve one of its aims 'in the functioning of the Common Market' and no other part of the EEC Treaty provided for the necessary powers of action.

The proposal for a Regulation introducing such a business form was submitted by the Commission to the Council in 1973[10] and, after some period of negotiation,[11] the EEIG Regulation was adopted. The Community aim which the EEIG was designed to achieve was that of 'harmonious development of economic activities', by allowing natural and legal persons to cooperate effectively across borders within the Common Market. Of course, as the Commission acknowledges in its EEIG handbook, such economic cooperation between enterprises in different Member States could take the form of a national company, or - at the other extreme - a temporary grouping of enterprises based on national law.[12] However, the EEIG possessed certain characteristics of both temporary groupings and company

7 McCahery & Vermeulen 2005, p. 794.

8 See McCahery & Vermeulen 2005, p. 794. See also Commission Memorandum to Parliament, Council and the two sides of industry on the Statute for the European Company of 8 June 1988, COM(88) 320 final, p. 11-12, and, in more detail, Cerioni 2007.

9 EEIG Regulation, consideration 1.

10 Proposal for a regulation of the Council on the European cooperation grouping (ECG), COM(73) 2046 (submitted to the Council by the Commission on 21 December 1973).

11 There seems to be some disagreement as to the duration and difficulty of the negotiations on the EEIG. According to some this period was relatively short, but others have described the deliberations as 'protracted and difficult': See Fleischer 2010, p. 1672 (footnote 8).

12 See European Commission 1999, p. 8-9.

structures, making it *sui generis* in nature. And prior to the entry into force of the EEIG Regulation, most of the Member States at the time, with the notable exception of France,[13] did not have a domestic business form directly corresponding to the EEIG at all. Thus, on the one hand, an EEIG was more akin to partnerships, business associations, joint ventures, consortia etc., since any profit or loss generated by an EEIG is attributed to its members and, moreover, the purpose of its activity must be 'to facilitate or develop the economic activities of its members and to improve or increase the results of those activities; its purpose is not to make profits for itself'.[14] In other words, the EEIG is a vehicle that is ancillary to its members. This is in contrast to the purpose of a company, which operates autonomously from its members, and seeks to make profits 'only part of which would be distributed, the rest being retained for its own purposes in the form of reserves, provision for depreciation etc.'.[15] On the other hand, though, the EEIG had other features which are shared by more permanent forms of cooperation. Most importantly, an EEIG has full and autonomous legal capacity, meaning it has 'the capacity, in its own name, to have rights and obligations of all kinds, to make contracts or accomplish other legal acts, and to sue and be sued',[16] in accordance with the provisions that are generally applicable to company structures.[17] It is for this reason that the EEIG was the first truly supranational corporate form to be created by European Community law.[18]

So the EEIG Regulation introduced an instrument of cooperation that allows private individuals to undertake joint commercial activities across borders for a limited or unlimited period within a legal framework that was previously unavailable to them. The list of activities that could be undertaken within this framework is long, ranging from common research and development programmes and the joint provision of goods or services to the creation of consortia for participation in public tenders (to name but a few);[19] and these could be in a wide array of sectors, including agriculture, finance, transport, the liberal professions,

13 In fact the EEIG was modelled on the French *groupement d'intérêt économique* (GIE), introduced in 1967. See for example De Bruycker 1991, p. 197; Santa Maria 2009. For details on the similarities between the French GIE and the EEIG, see Lefebvre 1992.

14 EEIG Regulation, Art. 3(1).

15 Proposal for a regulation of the Council on the European cooperation grouping (ECG), COM(73) 2046 (submitted to the Council by the Commission on 21 December 1973), p. 19-20.

16 EEIG Regulation, Art. 1(2).

17 Unlike in the case of the company law OIs that came after it, however, the EEIG Regulation does not accord legal personality to the EEIG, leaving this instead to the Member States to determine (see below). As the Commission explains in the Explanatory Memorandum accompanying its proposal for a regulation on a European cooperation grouping, this is due to differences in the meaning and consequences of the concept of legal personality between the laws of the Member States, and particularly differences in the fiscal consequences of granting such personality. See Proposal for a regulation of the Council on the European cooperation grouping (ECG), COM(73) 2046 (submitted to the Council by the Commission on 21 December 1973), p. 19 *et seq*. See also European Commission 1999, p. 20.

18 See Basedow 2015, p. 288; De Bruycker 1991, p. 197 & 199.

19 See Santa Maria 2009, p. 175.

etc.[20] For example, EEIGs have been set up by enterprises operating in the field of bio-fuels to develop common activities of research and development; by savings banks to provide clients with uniform cross-border services; and by transportation companies to coordinate international transport and removals.[21] As for the personal scope of the EEIG Regulation, the private individuals in question could be natural and/or legal persons, provided that they are 'attached' to a Member State. In the case of natural persons this means that they must perform an economic activity or service within the Community,[22] and as far legal persons are concerned, these can be companies, firms and other legal entities of any size governed by public or private law, but they must have been formed in accordance with the law of a Member State.[23] A European Economic Interest Grouping must comprise at least two natural and/or legal persons so defined, and the Regulation also requires a 'cross-border element', insofar as at least two of these persons must be attached to *two different Member States*. More precisely, there must be at least two legal persons 'which have their central administrations in different Member States', or two natural persons 'who carry on their principal activities in different Member States', or a combination of these.[24]

As noted above, binding rules governing the formation of a grouping are provided in the EEIG Regulation. In order to form an EEIG, the persons or bodies in question must draft a written contract of formation between themselves and subsequently register and file this contract at the designated registry of the Member State in which the grouping has its official address. This registration must then be published in both the appropriate official national gazette as well as the Official Journal of the European Communities, although the national registry remains the competent source of relevant information on the grouping, such as its official address, duration and details of its members. In addition, the Regulation also prescribes mandatory rules on the operation of EEIGs; for instance the principles of their internal organization and the protection of third parties and members.[25] This is only a 'rough legal framework',[26] however, and the Regulation left a number of choices to the discretion of national legislators in the process of implementation. These included not only whether to accord EEIGs legal personality as well as legal capacity,[27] but also whether to impose a limit on the number of members of an EEIG,[28] or whether to prohibit or restrict participation in groupings by certain classes of natural and/or legal persons.[29] Furthermore, subject to its basic

20 See De Bruycker 1991, p. 197, and also (referring to) European Commission 1989.
21 See European Commission 1999, p. 11 *et seq.* (also for numerous other examples of EEIGs).
22 EEIG Regulation, Art. 4(1)(b).
23 EEIG Regulation, Art. 4(1)(a).
24 EEIG Regulation, Art. 4(2).
25 See Santa Maria 2009, p. 173. For further details see European Commission 1989, p. 7-8.
26 Fleischer 2010, p. 1673.
27 Art. 1(3). Due to the tax consequences of having legal personality in their respective legal systems, Germany and Italy decided not to attribute legal personality to EEIGs. See European Commission 1999, p. 20.
28 EEIG Regulation, Art. 4(3).
29 EEIG Regulation, Art. 4(4).

provisions, the EEIG Regulation makes reference to the relevant national law of the State in which the EEIG's official address is located as the law applicable to the grouping's contract of formation and internal organization.[30] It also refers to national law on more specific points, such as for the consequences of the unlimited joint and several liability of the grouping's members,[31] or the liquidation resulting from the winding up of a grouping,[32] as well as deferring entirely to national law for matters such as social and labour laws.[33] Therefore, notwithstanding the Community legislator's goal of establishing a *uniform and independent* European legal framework, EEIGs are certainly not governed solely by the Regulation. Rather, the EEIG is governed *primarily* by the provisions of the Regulation, but these are supplemented by national laws (not to mention of course the grouping's formation contract itself)[34] in several respects.[35]

As regards the main advantage of the EEIG, on top of its sui generis nature, the EEIG Regulation also contained an additional element which could not be found even in the equivalent French business form, namely the possibility for the grouping to transfer its official address from one Member State to another without the need for it to be dissolved. In other words, as the Commission emphasized, '[t]he European nature of the grouping gives the EEIG's mobility a unique characteristic: the EEIG is the first body in Europe that can transfer its address from one State to another without having to be wound up and re-established, enabling economic operators to make substantial savings and to avoid complex procedures.'[36]

According to the Libertas European EEIG Information Centre, a total of 551 EEIGs were formed in the first five years of operation of the EEIG Regulation since it became applicable on 1 July 1989, of which 41 had subsequently been dissolved; and as of the end of 2014, a total of 2333 EEIGs have been formed, of which 391 have

30 EEIG Regulation, Art. 2(1). What the relevant national law is depends on the Member State in question. Since the promulgation of the EEIG Regulation a number of other Member States apart from France, including Germany, Belgium and Spain, now provide for a domestic body comparable to the EEIG, and in the case of these States the relevant law is therefore the law applicable to such bodies. Meanwhile in the case of other States which have not introduced a structure with legal similarities to the EEIG in their national systems, it is the law generally applicable to all legal persons. See European Commission 1999, p. 20.

31 EEIG Regulation, Art. 24(1).

32 EEIG Regulation, Art. 35(2).

33 EEIG Regulation, consideration 15.

34 See Santa Maria 2009, p. 173.

35 In fact the Commission has stated that the Regulation offers a 'very uniform legal framework for EEIGs' (see European Commission 1999, p. 19). However, it is not hard to find contrasting viewpoints in the literature. Fleischer, for example, states that the exact structure of the EEIG 'may vary considerably from Member State to Member State' (Fleischer 2010, p. 1673), while De Bruycker affirms that the EEIG Regulation 'leaves essential aspects of the EEIG's legal status and operation to the legislation of the Member States' (De Bruycker 1991, p. 197 (footnote 39)). And McCahery and Vermeulen also highlight the EEIG's references to national law (see McCahery & Vermeulen 2005, p. 794).

36 European Commission 1999, p. 59.

been dissolved.[37] A large proportion of these have been formed solely or largely by Small and Medium Sized Enterprises (SMEs),[38] although as the Commission notes, EEIGs have also been formed by large firms, public and semi-public bodies (e.g. chambers of commerce), professional groupings (e.g. lawyers, architects, consultants or engineers), etc.[39] And most of them have been formed in Belgium, France, Germany and the Netherlands.[40] This total of a little over 2000 formations in the whole of the EU over a period of 25 years is not a large number, and for this reason many have described the EEIG as an 'unpopular' business form in practice.[41]

2. *The European Company (SE)*

While the EEIG constituted the first (and for some years the only) OI to be introduced at Community level, the first OI to be formally proposed by the European Commission was actually the *Societas Europaea* (SE),[42] in 1970.[43] For some important reasons, however, the Regulation establishing a Statute for a European Company was finally adopted over 30 years after the Commission's initial proposal, and over 35 years after work on such a Statute first began.[44]

The SE was originally conceived of as a new form of public limited company (largely based on the German *Aktiengesellschaft*)[45] that could be utilized in the entire Community and would be governed by a fully autonomous body of European rules. Accordingly, the draft Statute for a European Company 'was a daunting and ambitious instrument comprising 284 articles' that was intended to regulate the European Company comprehensively, dealing with such matters as 'constitution, capital, organs, employee representation, accounts and audit, groups of companies, amendment of statutes, dissolution and liquidation, transformation into a national company, fusion, and tax'.[46] It is true that even this first draft, ambitious as it was, left certain matters of potential relevance to this proposed new company form to national law, such as the bankruptcy regime and criminal sanctions, but the fact remains that it was a comprehensive proposal, designed to establish a genuinely

37 See LIBERTAS - European Institute GmbH, EEIG Statistics from the European EEIG Information Centre, available at: <www.libertas-institut.com>.

38 Indeed, as Fleischer observes, 'the EEIG's legislative orientation is primarily geared towards small and medium-sized businesses, without being expressly limited to these' (Fleischer 2010, p. 1674).

39 See European Commission 1999.

40 See LIBERTAS, *supra* note 37. One of the most well-known EEIGs is ARTE, the Franco-German television channel: <www.arte.tv/fr>.

41 See e.g. Fleischer 2010, p. 1674; McCahery & Vermeulen 2005, p. 794.

42 Council Regulation 2157/2001 of 8 October 2001 on the Statute for a European company (SE). On this instrument see in general Rickford 2002; Cerioni 2007; Edwards 2003; Lenoir 2008.

43 Proposal for a Council Regulation Embodying a Statute for the European Company, COM(70) 600 final.

44 See Edwards 2003.

45 See McCahery & Vermeulen 2005, p. 797. Although De Bruycker identifies the French *Société Anonyme* as the company form that served as the model for the SE: De Bruycker 1991), p. 203 (footnote 77).

46 Edwards 2003, p. 444-445.

European form of commercial company. Indeed the very audacity of the Commission's original plan for the SE turned out to be a major factor in its protracted passage through the legislative process, as it soon became clear that the Member States were averse to the idea of a truly self-standing '28th regime' of company law co-existing with and largely independent of their own legal systems. In other words, '[t]he strong resistance of Member States to adopt the legislation, until recently, reflected their continued preference to retain legislative autonomy and control over core areas of company law.'[47] Moreover, in order to reach a compromise, the most far-reaching aspects of the first draft Statute were progressively watered down. In particular, the provisions on taxation, the requirement that the SE have a two-tier board structure, and the rules governing the involvement of employees in the SE proved to be insurmountable obstacles to reaching a consensus.[48] Thus, when the proposal was eventually relaunched in 1989,[49] many of these original provisions were abandoned. The proposed tax framework governing the SE's operations was reduced to one single fiscal provision, the mandatory two-tier board system was replaced with a choice for SEs between this and a one-tier system, and the issue of employee representation would now be addressed in a separate Directive supplementing the SE Regulation.[50] In addition, whereas the original SE proposal envisaged the creation of a centralized European company registry for the registration of SEs,[51] the revised proposal left it to the Member States to designate national registries for this purpose.[52] So the legislative text that was eventually adopted bore little resemblance to the autonomous statute governed by a uniform legal framework that had initially been foreseen.[53] As Edwards observes, '[t]hese changes ... and the increasing use of references to national law to govern certain issues, resulted in a shorter document: 137 articles, together with a further 13 in the complementary worker participation directive.'[54]

Like the EEIG Regulation, the Regulation on the Statute for a European Company which was eventually adopted in 2001, as well as its supplementing Directive, was based on the flexibility clause contained in what was by then Article 308 TEC. According to the European legislator, for the purpose of completing the internal market it was 'essential that companies the business of which is not limited to satisfying purely local needs should be able to plan and carry out the reorganisation of their business on a Community scale'.[55] However, companies from different Member States wishing to engage in restructuring operations faced 'legal

47 McCahery & Vermeulen 2005, p. 795.

48 See Edwards 2003, p. 445. See Rickford 2002, p. 18-19.

49 Proposal for a Council Regulation on the Statute for a European company, COM(89) 268.

50 See Edwards 2003, p. 446-447.

51 Proposal for a Council Regulation Embodying a Statute for the European Company, COM(70) 600 final, Art. 8.

52 Proposal for a Council Regulation on the Statute for a European company, COM(89) 268, Art. 8(1). On the registration of SEs see further below.

53 See also, for example, Cerioni 2007, p. 91; Burrows 2013, p. 158.

54 Edwards 2003, p. 447.

55 SE Regulation, consideration 1.

and psychological difficulties and tax problems' due to the fact that such operations would need to be governed by a particular national law.[56] And although, as we have seen, legislation harmonizing certain Member State company laws had already been passed, the core aspects of these laws remained unharmonized. For these reasons, the legislator considered that the existing legal framework posed a significant obstacle to the creation and management of groups of enterprises from different Member States as single economic units (as opposed to in the interests of their individual component companies).[57] Therefore the aim of the SE Regulation was to enable, by means of reorganization and restructuring on a Community scale, the creation of companies under a legal framework established by a Community Regulation directly applicable in all of the Member States, which would exist 'side by side with companies governed by a particular national law'.[58]

So with the entry into force of the SE Regulation in October 2004, firms (i.e. legal persons only) carrying on business in two or more Member States had the possibility to set up a European public limited-liability company 'on the conditions and in the manner laid down in this Regulation'.[59] Specifically, the Regulation stipulates four ways in which a European company may be formed.[60] First, SEs can be formed by merger of public limited-liability companies established under the law of a Member State and having their registered office within the EU, 'provided that at least two of them are governed by the law of different Member States'.[61] Second, public or private limited-liability companies founded under the law of a Member State and having their registered office within the EU can form a joint 'holding SE', as long as at least two of them are governed by the law of different Member States, or have had a subsidiary company governed by the law of another Member State or a branch located in another Member State for at least two years.[62] Third, public or private companies or other legal bodies governed by public or private law that were formed under the law of a Member State and have their registered office in the EU can set up a jointly held 'subsidiary SE', subject to the same cross-border requirement that applies to a holding SE.[63] Fourth, an existing public limited-liability company established under the law of a Member State that has its registered office in the EU can convert into a European company, provided that it has had a subsidiary company governed by the law of another Member State for at least two years.[64] Thus, the personal scope of the SE Regulation does not extend to

56 SE Regulation, consideration 3.

57 See SE Regulation, consideration 3 and Commission Memorandum to Parliament, Council and the two sides of industry on the Statute for the European Company of 8 June 1988, COM(88) 320 final, p. 11.

58 SE Regulation, consideration 6.

59 SE Regulation, Art. 1.

60 SE Regulation, Art. 2. For a detailed explanation of each of these modes of formation see Edwards 2003, p. 451 *et seq*.

61 SE Regulation, Art. 2(1) and Title II, Section 2.

62 SE Regulation, Art. 2(2) and Title II, Section 3.

63 SE Regulation, Art. 2(3) and Title II, Section 4.

64 SE Regulation, Art. 2(4) and Title II, Section 5. Unlike other EU company law OIs, however, formation of a European Company *ex nihilo* is not possible.

natural persons (unlike the EEIG Regulation), but rather only covers corporate bodies, which could be public- or private-limited liability companies or, in the case of joint subsidiary SEs, even other legal entities governed by public or private law, as long as they have been formed under the law of a Member State. SMEs are not excluded from this scope,[65] although as Drury notes, the SE 'is primarily designed for larger businesses, and its structure and attendant employee participation rules render it unsuitable for smaller firms wishing to collaborate in a joint project'.[66] As for the SE Regulation's territorial scope, like the EEIG Regulation it too provides for a cross-border element pursuant to which founding members (or in the case of subsidiary SEs, parent and subsidiary companies) must be connected with at least two different Member States - in the sense that they must be formed under (or governed by) the law of those States. Hence the SE is available 'neither for purely domestic operations nor as subsidiaries of companies governed by the law of third States ...'.[67]

Once an SE has been formed in one of these ways, it must be 'registered in the Member State in which it has its registered office in a register designated by the law of that Member State ...',[68] after which notice of this registration shall be published in the EU Official Journal.[69] When duly registered, the newly-formed company acquires legal personality[70] (and not merely legal capacity, as in the case of the EEIG), meaning the SE is necessarily recognized as having legal personality by the Member States. This entails that '[t]he existence of such a company cannot therefore be challenged by national courts or other national authorities,'[71] and, in particular, that the SE's members 'enjoy limited liability to the same degree as in respect of an ordinary registered company'.[72] As far as regards the SE's operation (as well as formation), the Regulation provides rules on, *inter alia*, minimum capital requirements, registered and head offices (including transfer thereof), board structure and shareholder rights, which are supplemented by the provisions on employee participation in the accompanying Directive.[73] Given the obstacles encountered in the process of adoption of these legislative instruments, however, there is a 'relative absence of mandatory rules' in the SE Regulation.[74] Therefore the Regulation makes frequent references to the national laws of the Member State

65 In fact according to the Commission the SE Statute was intended 'to provide a European form for already existing cross-border businesses of a reasonable size without making it difficult for small and medium sized enterprises to form SEs': Report from the Commission to the European Parliament and the Council on the application of Council Regulation 2157/2001 of 8 October 2001 on the Statute for a European Company (SE), COM(2010) 676 final, p. 6. See also SE Regulation, consideration 13.

66 Drury 2008, p. 126. See also Fleischer 2010, p. 1676.

67 Basedow 2015, p. 289-290.

68 SE Regulation, Art. 12(1).

69 SE Regulation, Art. 14(1).

70 SE Regulation, Art. 1(3).

71 Hirte & Teichmann 2012, p. 74.

72 Burrows 2013, p. 158.

73 Council Directive 2001/86/EC of 8 October 2001 supplementing the Statute for a European company with regard to the involvement of employees: See SE Regulation, Art. 1(4).

74 See McCahery & Vermeulen 2005, p. 798.

where the SE has its registered office (including both national laws implementing the SE and laws that are applicable to domestic public limited-liability companies). Apart from two general provisions that refer to Member State laws as the laws governing the SE subject to the Regulation itself (Arts. 9 and 10), there are also many particular references to national law, both in relation to specific matters like the organization and conduct of general meetings and voting procedures,[75] as well as for entire areas that are not regulated by the Regulation at all (i.e. not even partially), such as tax, liquidation and insolvency.[76] So while the SE is governed in the first place by the Regulation, the legal framework applicable to SEs is far from the autonomous body of European rules that was originally foreseen.[77] In fact, the legal framework governing SEs defers to national law to such an extent that it has led many to conclude 'there are as many versions of the SE as there are member states'.[78] Yet, in spite of this, the European Company has certain advantages that render it a helpful tool in facilitating the management of groups of companies that operate throughout the EU.[79] Most notably, the SE is able to transfer its registered office to another Member State without having to wind up the company or create a new legal person.[80]

Pursuant to the SE Regulation,[81] the European Commission published a report on the application of the European Company Statute towards the end of 2010.[82] This report found that in the period from the SE Regulation's entry into force in October 2004 until 25 June 2010 (i.e. its first five to six years of operation), a total of 595 SE's were registered throughout the entire EU (not to mention the European Economic Area (EEA)). Similarly, data compiled by the European Trade Union Insitute reveal that 656 SEs had been registered in the EU and EEA Member States by 2010, and that as of March 2014 the total reached 2,125.[83] The 595 SEs formed by June 2010

75 See SE Regulation, Art. 53. The Regulation itself provides that the SE must have a general meeting of shareholders (Art. 38), and also contains some provisions on the responsibilities of this general meeting (cf. Art. 52).

76 See SE Regulation, consideration 20.

77 Santa Maria 2009, p. 171. In fact, as much has even been acknowledged by the Commission: See Chapter 5, section C.2.

78 Burrows 2013, p. 158. Similarly, Siems states that '[s]ince the company laws of the Member States determine many features of the SE, there is no single but rather 25 [now 28] different types of SE ...': Siems 2005, p. 431. And, in the words of Rickford, 'the SE has become not a uniform European animal, but a chameleon, drawing its legal character largely from the law of its registration': Rickford 2002, p. 20. On the lack of uniformity of the SE see further Chapter 4, section A.3(a)(i).

79 See Lenoir 2008, p. 14.

80 See SE Regulation, Art. 8. Although, as Burrows notes, developments in the case law of the Court of Justice of the EU concerning European corporate mobility since the adoption of the SE Regulation have made this particular advantage 'less unique': Burrows 2013, p. 158.

81 Art. 69.

82 Report from the Commission to the European Parliament and the Council on the application of Council Regulation 2157/2001 of 8 October 2001 on the Statute for a European Company (SE), COM(2010) 676 final.

83 European Trade Union Institute European Company Database statistics, available at: <www.worker-participation.eu/europa-ag-se/facts-figures/total-number-of-registered-european-companies-ses>.

were registered in 21 of the 30 EU/EEA Member States that existed at the time, 'with the vast majority (around 70%) in the Czech Republic or Germany'.[84] A high number of the SEs registered in these Member States were so-called 'shelf SEs', though, which are essentially ready-made companies created by professional providers and available for sale.[85] Overall, of the 595 SEs noted in its report, the Commission found that 77 were shelf SEs.[86] And of course, as in the case of the EEIG, a few SEs have since been dissolved.[87] Notable and frequently cited examples of SEs include Porsche SE, and also Allianz SE (in fact around a quarter of all SEs pertain to the finance and insurance sector).[88] The Commission report does not provide indications as to the proportion of SEs set up by SMEs, although it does remark that SMEs in particular 'consider the current formation conditions very burdensome'.[89]

It is fair to say that there are mixed opinions on the popularity of the SE. Certainly there are plenty of commentators who agree that these figures serve to demonstrate the relative unpopularity of the European Company Statute with private actors. According to Rutgers, for example, the figures produced by the Commission (not to mention other surveys) show that '... there is a strong preference for national corporate entities rather than for the SE. The number of SEs is not that great if it is compared to the number of other corporate entities.'[90] Likewise, Fauvarque-Cosson & Behar-Touchais note that, although there has been an exponential increase in the number of SE registrations since 2004, 'these figures remain very low'.[91] Others, however, have interpreted these figures in more positive terms. For Eidenmüller *et al.*, for example, the growing number of SEs is rather an indication that '[f]ollowing a slow start, the European Company ... has become a

84 Report from the Commission to the European Parliament and the Council on the application of Council Regulation 2157/2001 of 8 October 2001 on the Statute for a European Company (SE), COM(2010) 676 final, p. 3. In fact, it has been observed that 40% of European Companies are of German origin: See for example Lenoir 2008, p. 15.

85 See Report from the Commission to the European Parliament and the Council on the application of Council Regulation 2157/2001 of 8 October 2001 on the Statute for a European Company (SE), COM(2010) 676 final, p. 6.

86 See Accompanying document to the Report from the Commission to the European Parliament and the Council on the application of Council Regulation 2157/2001 of 8 October 2001 on the Statute for a European Company (SE), SEC(2010) 1391 final.

87 Cf. LIBERTAS - European Institute GmbH, SE statistics, available at: <www.libertas-institut.com/de/se/se_statistics.pdf>.

88 See further, and for other examples, Lenoir 2008, p. 14-15. See also Fauvarque-Cosson & Behar-Touchais 2012, p. 164.

89 Report from the Commission to the European Parliament and the Council on the application of Council Regulation 2157/2001 of 8 October 2001 on the Statute for a European Company (SE), COM(2010) 676 final, p. 6.

90 Rutgers 2011, p. 356.

91 Fauvarque-Cosson & Behar-Touchais 2012, p. 159.

popular legal form amongst European firms.'[92] While according to Fleischer, '[in] legal practice, the SE is gradually gaining ground in some Member States.'[93]

3. *The European Cooperative Society (SCE)*

The adoption of the protracted proposal for a Statute for a European Company gave renewed impetus to other proposals for additional European company forms, including the European Cooperative Society (or *Societas Cooperativa Europaea*, SCE),[94] the European Private Company (*Societas Privata Europaea*, SPE)[95] and the European Foundation (*Fondatio Europaea*, FE)[96].[97] Admittedly (as was already noted in the previous chapter) two of these proposals - namely the Draft Statute for a European Foundation and that for a European Private Company - have since been withdrawn, due to a lack of progress in the legislative process.[98] Nevertheless, the SCE has already become a legal reality with the enactment of the Regulation on the Statute for a European Cooperative Society in 2003;[99] and the SPE proposal has been replaced by a proposal for a Directive on a single-member private limited liability company (SUP),[100] which is currently (at the time of writing) making its way through the ordinary legislative procedure.[101] We will now turn our attention to the last of the European company forms already in existence, the SCE, before proceeding to examine the SUP proposal.

Like the proposal for a Statute on a European Company, the proposal for a Statute on a European Cooperative Society, which was first submitted by the Commission in 1992, encountered considerable resistance in the course of the decision-making process, particularly with respect to proposed rules on employee involvement.[102] Shortly after the adoption of the SE legislation, though, the SCE was enacted 'without any fanfare',[103] and entered into force in August 2006. The basic

92 Eidenmüller, Hornuf & Reps 2013, p. 155. Whereas Lenoir even saw the start as a good one: See Lenoir 2008, p. 13.

93 Fleischer 2010, p. 1676.

94 Proposal for a Council Regulation on the statute for a European cooperative society, COM(91) 273 final.

95 Proposal for a Council Regulation on the Statute for a European private company, COM(2008) 396/3.

96 Proposal for a Council Regulation on the Statute for a European Foundation (FE), COM(2012) 35 final.

97 See Schmidt 2006, p. 99.

98 See Annex to the Communication from the Commission to the European Parliament, the Council, the European Economic and Social Committee and the Committee of the Regions 'Commission Work Programme 2015: A New Start', COM(2014) 910 final, Annex 2, item 61 (p. 12).

99 Council Regulation 1435/2003 of 22 July 2003 on the Statute for a European Cooperative Society (SCE). On this instrument see in general Cerioni 2007; Cerioni 2004, p. 296; Schmidt 2006.

100 Proposal for a Directive of the European Parliament and of the Council on single-member private limited liability companies, COM(2014) 212 final.

101 See <http://eur-lex.europa.eu/procedure/en/2014_120>.

102 See Fleischer 2010, p. 1677.

103 See Fleischer 2010, p. 1677.

legal framework of the SCE was constituted by a Regulation on its Statute (as just noted) supplemented by a Directive on employee participation,[104] both of which were - as in the case of the SE - based on the Article 308 TEC (now Art. 352 TFEU) flexibility clause.[105] This reflects the fact that the SCE represented a continuation of the EU legislator's attempts to provide for the organization of businesses on a Community scale with the aim of 'facilitating the development of their cross-border activities'.[106] Hence the aim of the SCE legislation was to facilitate the transnational operations of cooperative enterprises, by providing for a new European legal person in the form of a cooperative society, consisting of individuals that come together on a voluntary basis in order to meet the economic, social and cultural needs and aspirations they share in common, by means of a company that is owned collectively and wherein power is exercised democratically. The existing company law OIs at the time were considered to be inappropriate for the specific needs of cooperatives in the Member States because, as the preamble to the SCE Regulation explains, the SE, which was established 'according to the general principles of the public limited-liability company ... is not an instrument which is suited to the specific features of cooperatives'; while the EEIG, which 'allows undertakings to promote certain of their activities in common, while nevertheless preserving their independence ... does not meet the specific requirements of cooperative enterprise'.[107] And although cooperatives did already exist in all of the Member States, the territorially-limited rules governing them - like the rules governing public companies - also differed greatly from country to country. So the SCE was intended to 'fill the gap' by introducing an autonomous European form of cooperative with legal personality founded on uniform principles that would 'enable them to operate outside their own national borders in all or part of the territory of the Community'.[108]

Accordingly, a European Cooperative Society can be formed by private actors attached to different Member States on the conditions and in the manner laid down in the Regulation. More precisely, the SCE Regulation specifies five modes of formation of an SCE.[109] Firstly, by five or more natural persons resident in at least two Member States. Secondly, by five or more natural persons or companies or other legal bodies governed by public or private law that are resident in, formed under the law of, or governed by the law of at least two Member States. Thirdly, by companies or other legal bodies governed by public or private law formed under the law of a Member State which are governed by the law of at least two different Member States. Fourthly, by a merger between cooperatives formed under the law of a Member State with registered offices within the EU, provided at least two of them are governed by the law of different Member States. And finally, by

104 Council Directive 2003/72/EC of 22 July 2003 supplementing the Statute for a European Cooperative Society with regard to the involvement of employees.

105 Although, as was explained in the previous chapter, the original Commission proposal for a European cooperative society was founded on Art. 100a EEC (now Art. 114 TFEU).

106 SCE Regulation, consideration 6.

107 SCE Regulation, considerations 4 and 5, respectively.

108 SCE Regulation, consideration 12.

109 SCE Regulation, Art. 2.

conversion of a cooperative formed under the law of a Member State and having its registered office within the EU, provided it has had an establishment or subsidiary governed by the law of another Member State for at least two years. Thus, like the SE Regulation, the SCE Regulation requires in all cases a cross-border element within the EU, which means it is not available as an alternative form for cooperatives operating solely or even predominantly in a single Member State. By contrast to the SE, however, the SCE company form can be created by natural as well as legal persons, and *ex nihilo* too.[110]

Howsoever formed, the SCE must then be registered in the Member State in which its registered office is located, in a register designated by the law of that State.[111] And, again in a comparable fashion to the SE Regulation, the SCE Regulation contains various provisions on matters such as minimum capital requirements, board structure and transfer of registered office. Indeed, with respect to most of its key aspects, the regulatory model used for the SE was followed in the SCE legislation.[112] For this same reason, however, the SCE Regulation also makes numerous references to the laws of the Member State in which the SCE has its registered office (including both Member State laws implementing the SCE as well as domestic laws that are applicable to cooperatives).[113] This includes two general provisions referring to national law subject to the Regulation (Arts. 8 and 9), as well as a number of specific references to such law, some of which are partial (e.g. regarding the organization of the general meetings required by the Regulation),[114] and others total (e.g. with regard to taxation, which is not regulated at all in the Statute, thereby leaving this matter entirely to national law).[115] Therefore it can be said that the SCE legislation has also resulted in a different form of SCE in each of the Member States, rather than one single and uniform European company form as originally envisaged.[116]. In addition, like the SE, the SCE Regulation enables the

110 That is, in the case of the SCE, unlike the SE, there exists 'the possibility of *direct* creation by natural persons ... as an alternative to the choice of one of the cooperative forms governed by national laws' (italics added): Cerioni 2004, p. 300.

111 SCE Regulation, Art. 11(1).

112 Cf. Cerioni 2007, p. 125; Fleischer 2010, p. 1678; and also Report from the Commission to the European Parliament, the Council, the European Economic and Social Committee and the Committee of the Regions on the application of Council Regulation 1435/2003 of 22 July 2003 on the Statute for a European Cooperative Society (SCE), COM(2012) 72 final, p. 9.

113 Or in some cases public limited companies: See further Cerioni 2004, p. 298.

114 See SE Regulation, Art. 54(2).

115 See SCE Regulation, consideration 16.

116 According to Cerioni, for example, '[a]s a result of the extensive reliance on national laws, the outcomes of the SE Regulation and of the SCE Regulation are two vehicles which, on the whole - while keeping the basic identity - have in several important respects different working rules from one Member State to another': Cerioni 2004, p. 299. Similarly, Schmidt describes the SCE as 'a kind of "patchwork" of European and national fabrics', resulting in the 'emergence of 28 different types of SCE': Schmidt 2006, p. 106. See also Fleischer 2010, 1678. Although, having said that, it has been observed that the 'the SCE appears to be slightly more supranational from the company law viewpoint' (Cerioni 2007, p. 126. See also Cerioni 2004, p. 300 *et seq.*) This is because the European legislator sought to address some of the unclarities in the provisions of the SE Regulation and, as a result, the SCE provisions 'are →

European Cooperative Society to transfer its registered office to another Member State without resulting in the winding up of the SCE or in the creation of a new legal entity.[117]

Also in the case of the SE, the Commission produced a report on the application of the European Cooperative Society Statute[118] (a little over) five years after the SCE Regulation's entry into force in August 2006, as foreseen by the Regulation itself.[119] According to this report, by November 2011 a total of 24 SCEs had been registered in a total of 10 of the 30 EU/EEA Member States at the time, with exactly half of them being in Slovakia (seven) and Italy (five). This is also in line with unofficial data published by Libertas, according to which 27 SCEs have been formed as of the end of 2014.[120] The first of these to be formed was ESCOOP (on 6 July 2006), a cooperative between associations and bodies from six different Member States with the main goal of 'pursu[ing] the general interest of the community ... through the management of socio-health, education and training services for the benefit of underprivileged people ...'.[121] Clearly this total is a low number. Taking into account that the cooperative sector in Europe consisted of circa 300,000 businesses in 2007, as Fauvarque-Cosson & Behar-Touchais remark, 'it seems that the European Cooperative Society is struggling to get off the ground'.[122]

4. *The European Single-Member Private Limited Liability Company (SUP)*

As indicated above, apart from the three existing European business forms described in the preceding sections, a proposal for a fourth European-wide company form has recently been submitted by the Commission and is currently making its way through the EU decision-making process, namely the proposal for a

often a lot more precise and much more detailed than the equivalent provisions concerning the SE' (Schmidt 2006, p. 106. See also Cerioni 2007, p. 126.)

117 See SCE Regulation, Art. 7.

118 Report from the Commission to the European Parliament, the Council, the European Economic and Social Committee and the Committee of the Regions on the application of Council Regulation 1435/2003 of 22 July 2003 on the Statute for a European Cooperative Society (SCE), COM(2012) 72 final. See also previously the study conducted under the responsibility of A. Fici, EURICSE and the University of Molise for the European Commission on the implementation of the Regulation 1435/2003 on the Statute for European Cooperative Society (SCE), Executive Summary and Part I: Synthesis and comparative report of 5 October 2010, available at: <http://ec.europa.eu/enterprise/policies/sme/files/sce_final_study_part_i.pdf>, and Fauvarque-Cosson & Behar-Touchais 2012, p. 179 *et seq*.

119 SCE Regulation, Art. 79.

120 Cf. LIBERTAS - European Institute GmbH, List of European Cooperatives (SCE), available at: <www.libertas-institut.com/de/ewiv/list_sce.pdf>.

121 See <www.escoop.eu>.

122 Fauvarque-Cosson & Behar-Touchais 2012, p. 179. See also Fleischer 2010, p. 1677. In fact, even the Commission acknowledged the 'relative lack of success of the SCE statute' in its report: see Report from the Commission to the European Parliament, the Council, the European Economic and Social Committee and the Committee of the Regions on the application of Council Regulation 1435/2003 of 22 July 2003 on the Statute for a European Cooperative Society (SCE), COM(2012) 72 final, p. 7.

European single-member limited liability company (or *Societas Unius Personae*, SUP) of 2014.[123] In fact, as was already noted in the introductory chapter, the SUP proposal was actually put forward in place of a previous proposal for a European Private Company (or *Societas Privata Europaea*, SPE),[124] which was withdrawn earlier in the same year.[125] It is therefore useful to begin by briefly sketching the proposal for the SPE, before describing the alternate approach the Commission has taken with the SUP.

The background to the SPE proposal was comparable to that of the SCE, in the sense that just as the SCE was introduced to meet the specific needs of cooperatives operating or intending to operate on a Community scale, so the SPE was specifically designed for small and medium-sized enterprises (SMEs) with a view to facilitating their transnational activities in the EU. This is because the existing SE company form is also considered to be inappropriate for SMEs, as '[t]he minimum capital requirement for a SE and the restrictions on its formation make that form of company unsuitable for many businesses, in particular of a smaller size.'[126] For this reason, the Commission considered it necessary to create a European form of private company that would have a much lower minimum capital requirement, and would be subject simply to the applicable rules on worker participation of the host Member State. To that end, the Commission submitted the proposal for a Regulation on a European Private Company in 2008, which envisaged a minimum capital requirement of just €1,[127] as well as the general provision that '[t]he SPE shall be subject to the rules on employee participation, if any, applicable in the Member State in which it has its registered office ...'.[128] In addition, and again in contrast with the SE (not to mention also the SCE), the SPE proposal did not contain a cross-border condition, meaning a European Private Company could have been formed also in a purely domestic context.[129]

However, the proposed SPE Regulation, which like the previous company law OIs was based on the flexibility clause contained in what is now Article 352 TFEU,[130] encountered strong resistance from Member States, particularly on each of the aforementioned points. That is, notable controversies arose among the Member States in relation to precisely such issues as the minimum capital requirement, the (lack of) cross-border component, and the rules on worker involvement. As a result, revised texts of the proposal that were issued in the course of the negotiations began

123 Proposal for a Directive of the European Parliament and of the Council on single-member private limited liability companies, COM(2014) 212 final. On this instrument see in general Lutter & Kock 2015; Jung 2015; Wuisman 2015; Teichmann & Fröhlich 2014, p. 536.

124 Proposal for a Council Regulation on the Statute for a European private company, COM(2008) 396/3. On this proposal see for example Hirte & Teichmann 2012.

125 See Official Journal C 153, Volume 57 of 21 May 2014.

126 Proposal for a Council Regulation on the Statute for a European private company, COM(2008) 396/3, consideration 2.

127 *Ibid.*, Art. 19(4).

128 *Ibid.*, Art. 34(1).

129 *Ibid.*, Art. 3.

130 With the overall aim again being to further internal market integration by facilitating the cross-border activities of undertakings.

to look quite different to the text as originally proposed. For example, in the revised version issued by the Hungarian Presidency on 23 May 2011,[131] an option was inserted for Member States to set a higher minimum capital requirement up to €8,000 for SPEs registered in their territory if they wished;[132] a cross-border element was foreseen as a condition for incorporation of an SPE;[133] and while the general rule on worker involvement was still that the domestic legislation of the host State would apply, the formation of an SPE could in certain circumstances have been been subject to negotiations on arrangements for the participation of employees in a similar fashion to the SE.[134] And yet, notwithstanding significant revisions such as these, successive Council Presidencies failed to garner sufficient support on the proposal for an SPE Regulation, and ultimately it failed to secure the unanimity required for its adoption.

Accordingly, with a compromise on the SPE proposal proving too difficult to reach, the Commission decided to withdraw the proposal. At around the same time, though, the Commission also announced its intention 'to come up with the proposal of an alternative measure designed to address at least some of the problems addressed by the SPE',[135] and this is what eventually led to the submission of the proposal on the Societas Unius Personae. However, this proposal differs from the SPE proposal in a number of important respects. For one thing, as the name of the proposal suggests, the proposed SUP is intended as a single-member company form, which means 'a company whose shares are held by a single person'.[136] This is a more specific kind of private company than that envisioned in the SPE proposal, which could also have been formed by a plurality of distinct founding shareholders.[137] Therefore the material scope of the SPE proposal was considerably broader. But it is also the form of the SUP proposal that is different to the SPE, since the SUP is proposed in the form of a directive, which would need to be transposed into national law by each of the Member States. Moreover, the SUP is actually a cross between an optional instrument and an approximating measure, in the sense that it leaves Member States the choice to either apply the main provisions of the Directive to *existing* single-member private limited liability companies provided for in national law, 'so that all such companies would operate and be known as SUPs',

131 Interinstitutional File 2008/0130, Document No. 10611/11.

132 *Ibid.*, Art. 19.

133 *Ibid.*, Art. 3(3).

134 *Ibid.*, Arts. 35 and 35a-35d. On this issue see further Hommelhoff & Teichmann 2012, p. 23 *et seq*.

135 Proposal for a Directive of the European Parliament and of the Council on single-member private limited liability companies, COM(2014) 212 final, p. 2.

136 *Ibid.*, Art. 2(1). Art. 15(3) further provides that '[w]here in accordance with the applicable national law, a single share of an SUP is owned by more than one person, those persons shall be regarded as one member in relation to the SUP'.

137 See proposal for a Council Regulation on the Statute for a European private company, COM(2008) 396/3, Art. 3(1)(e). Hence, as the Commission acknowledges in the SUP proposal, it has been argued that the SUP 'should not be considered as a fully-fledged alternative to the SPE and that the efforts towards the SPE should continue'; Proposal for a Directive of the European Parliament and of the Council on single-member private limited liability companies, COM(2014) 212 final, p. 4.

or to provide for a *new* separate company law form 'which would exist in parallel with other forms of single-member private limited liability company provided for in national law'.[138] Hence it is only in those Member States that would eventually choose to introduce the SUP as a new company form that the SUP would constitute an additional, optional company form for private actors.[139]

This would also apparently explain why, unlike the SUP (and indeed all of the other European company law OIs), the legal base for the proposed SUP Directive is Article 50 TFEU (rather than the Art. 352 TFEU flexibility clause), which empowers the European legislator to enact directives in order to promote the right of establishment with respect to a particular activity, in accordance with the ordinary legislative procedure.[140] For, according to the Commission, the SUP proposal 'does not establish a new supra-national legal form for the single member company but rather contributes to the progressive abolition of restrictions on freedom of establishment as regards the conditions for setting up subsidiaries in the territories of Member States'.[141] Hence, the stated aim of the proposed Directive on single-member private limited liability companies is to facilitate the cross-border activities of SMEs by contributing to 'the progressive abolition of restrictions on freedom of establishment as regards the conditions for setting up subsidiaries in the territories of Member States ...'.[142] If adopted (and once transposed), the Directive would allow natural or legal persons to found an SUP in any Member State, either by establishing an SUP *ex nihilo*,[143] or by converting an existing company into an SUP.[144] Like the original SPE proposal, the proposed SUP Directive does not specify a cross-border requirement for this purpose, and requires a minimum share capital of only €1 (or one unit of the national currency in Member States which do not have the euro).[145] In addition, it does not contain any requirements regarding employee participation.[146] An SUP would need to be registered in the national company registry of the Member State in which it is to have its registered office,[147] although the Member States would have to ensure that the registration procedure for newly incorporated SUPs could be completed entirely online 'without it being necessary

138 Proposal for a Directive of the European Parliament and of the Council on single-member private limited liability companies, COM(2014) 212 final, consideration 10.

139 Cf. Malberti 2015, p. 245.

140 Hence, similarly to the CESL proposal, the motivation for the Commission to employ this legal base instead of Article 352 TFEU may be attributed in large part to the fact that Article 50 TFEU does not require the Council to reach unanimous agreement.

141 Proposal for a Directive of the European Parliament and of the Council on single-member private limited liability companies, COM(2014) 212 final, p. 5.

142 *Ibid.*, consideration 8.

143 *Ibid.*, Art. 8.

144 *Ibid.*, Art. 9.

145 *Ibid.*, Art. 16(1).

146 Teichmann & Fröhlich 2014, p. 544.

147 Proposal for a Directive of the European Parliament and of the Council on single-member private limited liability companies, COM(2014) 212 final, Art. 14(1) and (2).

for the founding member to appear before any authority in the Member State of registration'.[148]

B. EU OIs in the Area of European Intellectual Property Law

1. *The Community Trade Mark (CTM)*

In addition to the field of company law, another area of European law which has experienced a proliferation of legislation establishing Optional Instruments in recent years is that of European Intellectual Property (IP) law. Since the adoption of the first Regulation on the Community Trade Mark (CTM) in 1993,[149] two further IP OIs have been created in the form of the Community Plant Variety Right (CPVR) in 1994 and the Community Design (CD) in 2001, and long-awaited plans to institute an equivalent OI (among other things) for patents are finally coming to fruition. On the other hand, as we will see, these OIs exhibit a number of peculiar features that distinguish them from the company law OIs considered thus far. Accordingly, European IP law is equally a field of particular relevance for this study. It will be seen that the general approach taken for the CTM has been followed with both the CD and the CPVR, and it is therefore for reasons of both chronology and practicality that we turn our attention first to the Community Trade Mark.

As in the case of European company law, the Commission's initial action in the area of IP law addressed disparities in the respective national laws of the Member States 'which may impede the free movement of goods and freedom to provide services and may distort competition within the common market ...'.[150] In other words, the Commission sought to harmonize certain aspects of Member State IP laws, with a view to improving the functioning of the internal market. After a first directive on the legal protection of topographies of semiconductor products adopted in 1986,[151] the Community legislator passed another directive approximating the laws of the Member States relating to trade marks (hereinafter referred to as the 'Trade Mark Directive') in 1988,[152] which was to be transposed within four years thereof. Unlike in the case of the legislator's harmonization efforts in the area of company law, however, this directive provided a framework of fundamental substantive provisions harmonizing those areas of national trade mark

148 *Ibid.*, Art. 14(3). On the possibility of online registration see further Teichmann & Fröhlich 2014, p. 542-543.

149 Council Regulation 40/94 of 20 December 1993 on the Community trade mark (now, as amended, Council Regulation 207/2009 of 26 February 2009 on the Community trade mark - although in this study reference is made to the original Regulation, unless otherwise indicated). On this instrument see in general Jehoram, Van Nispen & Huydecoper 2010; MacQueen *et al.* 2010; Seville 2007.

150 First Council Directive 89/104/EEC of 21 December 1988 to approximate the laws of the Member States relating to trade marks, consideration 1.

151 Council Directive 87/54/EEC of 16 December 1986 on the legal protection of topographies of semiconductor products.

152 First Council Directive 89/104/EEC of 21 December 1988 to approximate the laws of the Member States relating to trade marks.

law which most directly affect the functioning of the internal market,[153] including such matters as the definition of a trade mark, the registrability of a trade mark, and the rights conferred by a trade mark.[154] Still, while this did serve to bring a large degree of consistency in the key provisions of Member State laws relating to trade marks, the Commission was desirous to achieve more than a mere removal of potential barriers to trade; that is, it also wished to create legal conditions 'which enable undertakings to adapt their activities to the scale of the Community ...'.[155] And, as far as Intellectual Property Rights (IPRs) are concerned, such conditions correspond to the availability of EU-*wide IP instruments* governed by a uniform Community law, which thereby transcend the inherent territorial limitation of (harmonized) national IPRs.[156]

In fact, as the Commission explained in a Memorandum[157] over ten years prior to the adoption of the Trade Mark Directive, the need to approximate the national trade mark laws of Member States actually *resulted* from the decision to implement such a Community instrument relating to trade marks (i.e. the CTM Regulation, which was first formally proposed by the Commission in 1980),[158] since it was considered that the former would complement the latter.[159] This is because the existing national trade mark rights would not be replaced by the CTM, as they would continue to be necessary for undertakings that do not wish to obtain EU-wide protection for their trade marks.[160] Instead, the CTM would 'feature amongst the legal instruments which undertakings have at their disposal'[161] and, therefore, potential obstacles and confusion could arise if CTMs and national trade marks were subject to (substantially) different legal requirements. Indeed, the original intention was for the Trade Mark Directive and CTM Regulation to be implemented at the same time, but due to 'political difficulties over the CTM, especially the location of the CTM office, the Commission pushed ahead first with its harmonisation program'.[162] So the Community Trade Mark Regulation was eventually adopted a few years after the Trade Mark Directive, and a good thirteen years after the Regulation was first proposed.

153 See First Council Directive 89/104/EEC of 21 December 1988 to approximate the laws of the Member States relating to trade marks, considerations 1 and 10.

154 A trade mark is defined as 'any sign capable of being represented graphically, particularly words, including personal names, designs, letters, numerals, the shape of goods or of their packaging, provided that such signs are capable of distinguishing the goods or services of one undertaking from those of other undertakings' (First Council Directive 89/104/EEC of 21 December 1988 to approximate the laws of the Member States relating to trade marks, Art. 2; see also CTM Regulation, Art. 4). Examples include word marks (e.g. 'Nike'), logos (e.g. the Nike 'swoosh') and even shapes (e.g. the Coca-Cola bottle), etc.

155 CTM Regulation, consideration 1.

156 Basedow 2015, p. 292.

157 Commission Memorandum on the creation of a community trade mark, SEC(76) 2462.

158 Proposal for a Council Regulation on Community trade marks, COM(1980) 635.

159 See also Tritton *et al.* 2007, p. 261.

160 Cf. Seville 2009, p. 221.

161 CTM Regulation, consideration 1.

162 Tritton *et al.* 2007, p. 262.

Once again, the CTM Regulation was based on the flexibility clause contained in ex. Article 235 EEC (later Art. 308 TEC, now Art. 352 TFEU). Unlike the Trade Mark Directive, the CTM Regulation could not be based on Article 100a EEC (later Art. 95 TEC, now Art. 114 TFEU) because, as the Court of Justice confirmed in an opinion of 1994, this accorded the Community the competence to harmonize national laws in the field of intellectual property, but not 'the basis for creating new rights superimposed on national rights', which was rather provided by Article 235 EEC.[163] And the Community aim the CTM Regulation was designed to achieve was precisely that of 'completing an internal market which functions properly and offers conditions which are similar to those obtaining in a national market', by making 'arrangements for trade marks whereby undertakings can by means of one procedural system obtain Community trade marks to which uniform protection is given and which produce their effects throughout the entire area of the Community ...'.[164] In other words, the purpose of the CTM Regulation was to create a unified European trade mark registration system, under which one single registration provides the trade mark proprietor with a uniform right which is automatically applicable and enforceable in the whole of the EU as a single territory.[165] To this end, the Regulation established an Office for Harmonisation in the Internal Market (OHIM, located in Alicante, Spain), which was charged with the task of administering the system. So trade mark applicants wishing to obtain protection on a Community-scale could now submit a single application to OHIM to register a CTM (possibly via a national IP Office or WIPO, the World Intellectual Property Organization), rather than seeking protection in each of the Member States individually. This application may be filed in any of the Community's official languages, although if the language selected is not one of OHIM's official languages (English, French, German, Italian or Spanish), '[t]he applicant must indicate a second language which shall be a language of the Office the use of which he accepts as a possible language of proceedings for opposition, revocation or invalidity proceedings'.[166] For its part, OHIM has the competence to assess and decide on the application (as well as any revocation or invalidity proceedings) according to the uniform conditions for registrability laid down in the Regulation *as regards each and every Member State*, and provided it meets these conditions, the applicant will be granted a CTM. Exclusive jurisdiction over any eventual infringement actions or counterclaims for revocation or invalidity is, however, accorded to national courts,

163 Opinion 1/94 [1994], delivered on 15 November 1994, para. 59. See also Opinion of Advocate-General Stix-Hackl delivered on 12 July 2005 on Case C-436/03 *European Cooperative Society*, para. 66, and Basedow 2015, p. 294.

164 CTM Regulation, considerations 1 and 2, respectively.

165 It is important to note that a centralized system for the international registration of trade marks had already been provided for by many countries, in the form of the so-called 'Madrid system' (i.e. the Madrid Agreement Concerning the International Registration of Marks of 1981, as well as the related Protocol Relating to the Madrid Agreement of 1989, administered by the WIPO). However, this is purely a procedural system, which results not in the registration of a uniform right applicable in different countries, but rather a collection of national trade mark rights.

166 CTM Regulation, Art. 115(3).

albeit national courts designated by the respective Member States as 'Community trade mark courts'.[167] And (just like with the Trade Mark Directive) such courts have the right or in some cases even the obligation to submit preliminary references to the Court of Justice of the European Union (CJEU) concerning questions of interpretation of the Regulation, pursuant to the current Article 267 TFEU.

With regard to the personal scope of the CTM Regulation, this extends to any natural and legal person, including authorities established under public law, who may be 'based' in or outside the EU.[168] Also, the CTM Regulation does not require any cross-border element, which entails that Community trade mark protection is available as an alternative to corresponding Member State systems in purely domestic cases as well. In fact, it is even possible to obtain cumulative protection for the same sign in relation to the same goods and services by both a Community trade mark and a national trade mark (or several).[169] Although, as was already explained, the CTM is tailored to the needs of cross-border operators,[170] so in practice (taking into account relative costs etc.) it is a viable option for applicants seeking trade mark protection in multiple Member States.

In terms of its specific content, for the reasons noted above '[t]he substantive provisions of the Trade Mark Directive are virtually identical to those of the CTM Regulation'.[171] In other words, the provisions of the CTM Regulation concerning, *inter alia*, definition,[172] registrability[173] and rights conferred[174] are essentially reproductions of the corresponding provisions in the Trade Mark Directive. This concordance between the two pieces of legislation is significant in a number of respects. Firstly, it entails that CTM applicants find themselves in a familiar environment to that with which they are confronted at national level in the EU, only on a larger scale. Secondly, the national courts having the competence to adjudicate actions relating to CTMs are also faced with substantive rules to which they have already become accustomed in the domestic setting. And, thirdly, CJEU interpretations of provisions of the Trade Mark Directive apply equally to corresponding provisions in the CTM Regulation and *vice-versa*, the consequence being that 'national decisions of Member States have receded in importance and there is now considerable uniformity in Member States to the interpretation of the Directive and the Regulation'.[175] The Regulation also contains references to

167 CTM Regulation, Arts. 91 and 92.

168 In fact the original CTM Regulation Article 5 provided a few conditions in this respect, so that nationals of countries that were not Community Member States or parties to the Paris Convention for the Protection of Industrial Property (adopted in 1883 and amended in 1979) did not necessarily fall within the scope of the Regulation. In the amended CTM Regulation, however, Article 5 simply states: 'Any natural or legal person, including authorities established under public law, may be the proprietor of a Community trade mark.'

169 Cf. CTM Regulation, Art. 105.

170 On this see also further Chapter 4.

171 Tritton *et al.* 2007, p. 262.

172 CTM Regulation, Art. 4.

173 CTM Regulation, Arts. 7 & 8.

174 CTM Regulation, Arts. 9-13.

175 Tritton *et al.* 2007, p. 262.

applicable national law (as determined by rules of private international law)[176] on certain specific matters, including both entire references for actions relating to civil liability and unfair competition,[177] as well as partial references with respect to, for instance, the CTM as an object of property[178] and the effects of CTMs.[179] As regards the latter, these include, for example, certain effects vis-à-vis third parties[180] and also certain sanctions for infringement (or threatened infringement).[181] Apart from such matters, however, '[t]he effects of Community trade marks shall be governed solely by the provisions of [the] Regulation'.[182]

The latest OHIM statistics concerning the CTM[183] reveal that in the first five years of operation of the Community Trade Mark system since its inception in 1996 a total of 93,920 CTMs were registered, and that, as of 2015, the total number of registrations has reached 1,144,554 CTMs. As for the number of annual CTM registrations, this has risen steadily from 24,266 in 1998 to a peak of 103,763 in 2014. In a similar vein, the annual number of CTM applications filed has progressively increased, from 43,708 in the first year of operation to a peak of 117,475 in 2014, amounting to 1,436,835 applications in total. Applications have been received from all over the world, with the highest number coming from private actors in Germany (198,874), followed by the US (187,923) and the UK (116,094). The OHIM statistics do not indicate which private actors have applied for CTMs, but it is apparent that SMEs are important users of the system as well as large enterprises.[184] Given this sizable number of, and increase in, CTM registrations and applications, it has been observed that 'the Community trademark is perhaps the most successful optional instrument'.[185]

2. *The Community Design (CD)*

In many respects, the background to and concept of the Community Design (CD) mirrors that of the CTM. Already in 1991 the Commission published a Green Paper on the Legal Protection of Industrial Design,[186] in which it expressed the view that '[t]he single Community market will become a reality for European design industries only insofar as the territorial effects and limitations of national

176 See CTM Regulation, Title X.
177 CTM Regulation, Art. 14(2).
178 CTM Regulation, Art. 16(1).
179 CTM Regulation, Art. 14(1).
180 CTM Regulation, Art. 23.
181 CTM Regulation, Art. 98.
182 CTM Regulation, Art. 14(1).
183 OHIM Statistics of Community Trade Marks 2015 (SSC009), last updated on 7 July 2015, available at <https://oami.europa.eu/ohimportal/en/the-office>.
184 See for example the 'Allensbach survey': Institut für Demoskopie Allensbach, 'Survey of Market Participants Who Use the CTM System: The Findings of a Survey Among CTM Applicants/Owners and their Professional Representatives in All EU Member States' (2010), available at: <www.ip.mpg.de/fileadmin/user_upload/ctm-systema.h.jan.2011. pdf>.
185 Fauvarque-Cosson & Behar-Touchais 2012, p. 116.
186 Commission Green Paper on the Legal Protection of Industrial Design, III/F/5131/91, of June 1991.

intellectual property law are set aside and replaced by Community wide legislation'.[187] However, since a unitary Community-wide Design right could not simply supersede national design protection (or at least not immediately), the main aspects of Member State design protection laws also needed 'to be harmonised by way of a Directive in accordance with the provisions for a possible future Community design'.[188] So in this Green Paper the Commission envisaged the institution of a Community Design Regulation accompanied by a directive harmonizing the registered design laws of the Member States, and it submitted formal proposals for both of these instruments two years later. Yet, while the Design Directive was founded on Article 100a EEC, for the reasons already explained in relation to the CTM this legal base could not be used for the Community Design Regulation, and therefore the Regulation had to be based on Article 308 TEC (ex. Art. 235 EEC).[189] Coupled with the fact that the proposed Design Regulation was of course more far-reaching, this resulted in the Design Directive being adopted first, in October 1998, with a three-year period prescribed for its implementation by the Member States.[190] It was only after the end of this period, in December 2001, that the corresponding Community Design Regulation finally received Council assent.[191]

Equally, the Commission's concern with overcoming the limitations of national IPRs *vis-à-vis* the wider internal market was again reflected in the Community objective behind the CD Regulation. As the preamble makes explicit, it is the multiplicity and diversity of Member State systems of design protection that leads to a situation where, '*[i]n comparison with domestic trade in,* and competition between, products incorporating a design, trade and competition within the Community are prevented and distorted ...'.[192] For this principal reason it was necessary to introduce a uniform Registered Community Design (RCD) right with equal effect across the entire EU,[193] which could be acquired by private individuals on the strength of a single application to OHIM in any of the Community's official languages, according to common registration criteria specified in the Regulation. On the other hand, the CD Regulation went one step further by also providing for an Unregistered Community Design (UCD) right. This is because, as the preamble to the CD Regulation acknowledges, many industrial designs in certain sectors (such as fashion, children's toys, etc.), are intended to be sold on the market only for a relatively short time, and for this reason it was considered necessary to offer the

187 *Ibid.*, p. 4.

188 *Ibid.*, p. 6.

189 Cf. Tritton *et al.* 2007, p. 559; Levin & Richman 2003, p. 114.

190 Directive 98/71/EC of the European Parliament and of the Council of 13 October 1998 on the legal protection of designs.

191 Council Regulation 6/2002 of 12 December 2001 on Community designs. On this instrument see in general MacQueen *et al.* 2010; Seville 2009; Tritton *et al.* 2007; Levin & Richman 2003.

192 CD Regulation, consideration 3 (italics added). Cf. Seville 2009, p. 183.

193 Similarly to the CTM, an international registration system for industrial designs did already exist, known as the 'Hague System' (i.e. the Hague Agreement Concerning the International Registration of Industrial Designs, first adopted in 1925, which is also administered by WIPO). Again, though, this international procedure does not result in a uniform design right that is enforceable in multiple states.

possibility of obtaining short-term design protection without the need to undergo a procedure of registration.[194] The UCD is therefore a significantly less extensive right than the RCD, in the sense that the term of protection it confers is limited to 3 years from the date on which the design is first disclosed in the EU (as opposed to 25 years from the date of registration in the case of the RCD), and the scope of this protection is limited to the prevention of copying (meaning it does not cover designs resulting from the independent work of creation of another designer, unlike the RCD). And, on this point, it is also interesting to note that the Design Directive expressly did not harmonize Member State laws governing unregistered designs, so there remain notable differences between certain national unregistered design rights and the UCD. In any event, the point remains that as far as the RCD is concerned,[195] this is 'administered by OHIM in a broadly similar manner to the CTM'.[196] Furthermore, exclusive jurisdiction over invalidity and infringement actions in relation to both RCDs and UCDs is again accorded to national courts, designated by their respective Member States as 'Community design courts'.[197]

Like the Community trade mark, the Community design is available to natural and legal persons based in or outside the EU, and the CD Regulation does not contain an actual cross-border requirement (although it is targeted at cross-border operators), nor does it exclude the possibility of simultaneous protection by Community and national design rights.[198] In addition, as in the case of trade marks, '[t]he substantive law under the Directive and the Regulation is virtually the same',[199] thereby ensuring that the definition of designs,[200] conditions for registrability[201] and scope and effects of the rights conferred[202] that are specified in the CD Regulation are consistent with those applied at national level, and that a CJEU interpretation given in response to a preliminary reference concerning one of these legislative instruments is applicable equally to the other. However, this alignment is not quite so straightforward as it is with the trade mark legislation, since many Member States have other intellectual property laws applicable to designs (including not only unregistered design rights but also patents, utility models, etc.), and the Design Directive was not intended to have any effect on these alternative mechanisms of protection in national law. Hence the CD Regulation

194 See Tritton *et al.* 2007, p. 561.

195 For the purposes of simplicity, the term 'Community Design' will henceforth be used to refer only to Registered Community Designs, unless specified otherwise.

196 Tritton *et al.* 2007, p. 561.

197 CD Regulation, Arts. 80 and 81.

198 Cf. CD Regulation, Art. 95.

199 Tritton *et al.* 2007, p. 559. See also Levin & Richman 2003, p. 114-115.

200 A design is defined as 'the appearance of the whole or part of a product resulting from the features of, in particular, the lines, contours, colours, shape, texture and/or materials of the product itself and/or its ornamentation' (Directive 98/71/EC of the European Parliament and of the Council of 13 October 1998 on the legal protection of designs, Art. 1; CD Regulation, Art. 3). Examples of Registered Community Designs range from the design of chairs and vacuum cleaners through wristwatches and handbags to garden sheds and even automobiles, etc.

201 CD Regulation, Arts. 4-9.

202 CD Regulation, Arts. 10 and 19-23.

does not preclude the application of Member State industrial property laws relating to such alternative protection mechanisms to (Registered and Unregistered) Community Designs.[203] On top of this, the CD Regulation, like the CTM Regulation, also defers to other relevant laws of the Member States concerning civil liability and unfair competition,[204] as well as making more restricted references to national law with regard to, for example, Community Designs as objects of property,[205] effects of CDs vis-à-vis third parties[206] and sanctions in actions of infringement.[207] Still, these matters aside, the references to national law in the CD Regulation are limited.

According to the most recent OHIM figures,[208] in the first five years of operation of the Community Design system since the Office began to accept RCD filings in 2003, 303,278 Community Designs were registered, and the total number of registrations as of 2015 stands at 902,737. Also like the CTM the number of annual CD registrations has grown over time, from 40,422 in the system's first year of operation to a peak of 86,995 in 2014. Similarly, the number of designs applied for each year has risen steadily from 40,500 in 2003 to a height of 87,532 in 2014, making a total of 907,694. And again as in the case of the CTM, these applications have been submitted by private actors across the globe, with the largest number coming from Germany (213,326). The second highest number has been received from Italy (119,389), and the third from the US (76,250). So the Community design has also been described as a 'successful' optional instrument.[209] According to Tritton, for example, '[i]f quantity of filings are a measure, the scheme has been an instant success ...'.[210]

3. *The Community Plant Variety Right (CPVR)*

It was already mentioned in the introduction to the present account of EU intellectual property law OIs that, broadly speaking, they all follow a similar approach. So we will see that the Regulation on Community plant variety rights[211] adopted a year after the CTM Regulation (and some years before the CD Regulation) is based on many of the same fundamental concepts. Viewed from another perspective, however, the case of the Community Plant Variety Right (CPVR) has a number of idiosyncrasies - not least due to the very nature of this intellectual property right - that renders it a slightly more distant relative in the family of existing IP law OIs. Plant variety rights (PVR), also known as Plant

203 Cf. CD Regulation, consideration 31.
204 *Ibid.*
205 CD Regulation, Art. 27.
206 CD Regulation, Art. 33.
207 CD Regulation, Art. 89.
208 OHIM Statistics of Community Designs 2015 (SSC007), last updated on 6 July 2015, available at: <https://oami.europa.eu/ohimportal/en/the-office>.
209 See Fauvarque-Cosson & Behar-Touchais 2012, p. 134.
210 Tritton *et al.* 2007, p. 561. See also in more detail Izquierdo Peris 2006.
211 Council Regulation 2100/94 of 27 July 1994 on Community plant variety rights. On this instrument see in general Würtenberger *et al.* 2006; Llewelyn & Adcock 2006; Seville 2009; Kiewiet 2005, p. 321; Millett 1999; Van der Kooij 1997.

breeders' rights (PBR), are perhaps best understood as a special title of protection of intellectual property positioned in the vicinity, and available in lieu of, a general patent regime. The intellectual property in question consists of new and distinct varieties of plants that are capable of cultivation,[212] created by breeders in the agricultural or horticultural market. These innovative varieties will usually offer benefits such as greater yields or stronger resistance to pests and disease or ornamental qualities.[213] Breeders therefore acquire plant variety rights in order to ensure a return on their investment in developing a novel plant grouping, as PVR allow them to prevent others from freely propagating it.[214] In precise terms, then, PVR are exclusive rights over the commercial sale or marketing of a new variety[215] of a botanical genus or species, for a certain period of time.

Since new plant varieties have a certain similarity to inventions, the notion that they could be protected by a regular patent regime is certainly not unfathomable. In fact, the international framework laid down by the Convention for the Protection of New Varieties of Plants (hereinafter 'the UPOV Convention'), originally agreed in 1961 by Germany, the Netherlands and the UK,[216] expressly allowed member countries to recognize the rights of breeders 'by the grant either of a special title of protection or of a patent' (Art. 2(1)).[217] However, in contrast to the more conventional objects of patent protection, living creations (particularly plants) do not fit comfortably within the architecture of patent law. As Millett explains:

> 'Unlike a machine, an electronic circuit or an industrial process, plants are not susceptible of being manufactured wholly by man, and hence the definition of a new variety poses certain specific problems. Furthermore as plants reproduce, they have a natural propensity to spontaneous genetic variation, and so the stability of the object of these rights poses a problem generally unknown to patents.'[218]

So, for reasons such as these, many countries have eschewed the possible application of patent law in favour of a *sui generis* form of IP protection for plant breeders' rights. As far as European states are concerned, the majority opted to introduce specialized PVR regimes so that, by the time the European Community itself acceded to the UPOV Convention in June 2005, tailor made protection systems for plant varieties based on the Convention were already available in most of its

212 As follows from the legal definition of the term 'variety' provided in the International Convention for the Protection of New Varieties of Plants ('UPOV Convention') 1961 (Art. 2(2)).

213 See Millett 1999, p. 231.

214 See Millett 1999, p. 231.

215 Cf. UPOV Convention, Art. 5(1).

216 The UPOV Convention has since been revised on three occasions, in 1972, 1978 and 1991, and its list of signatory states now totals 70 worldwide.

217 This was in compliance with the Agreement on Trade-Related Aspects of Intellectual Property Rights ('TRIPS') agreement, which simply obliges signatories to 'provide for the protection of plant varieties either by patents or by an effective *sui generis* system or by any combination thereof (Art. 27(3)).

218 Millett 1999, p. 231.

Member States.[219] Similarly, before the adoption of the CPVR Regulation at the beginning of the 1990s, nine of the then twelve Member States had a specific law for the protection of plant varieties, while Greece, Luxembourg and Portugal did not.[220]

Yet, this convergence towards *sui generis* protection does not mean to say that the plant variety laws enacted by Member States were uniform, and especially not on the question of patentability of plant varieties. On the basis of the foregoing this may at first sight appear nonsensical for, by deciding to establish special systems of protection for plant varieties, it would seem to follow that the Member States had by implication also chosen to exclude the possibility of protecting such inventions through their respective patent systems. And to an extent as much does follow, but only as far as *certain* inventions of this kind are concerned. To clarify this rather cryptic statement, it is necessary to delve a little further and more broadly into the international intellectual property regime relating to living (plant) matter, starting with the aforementioned UPOV Convention. The original UPOV Convention, as well as both the first (1972) and second (1978) revised versions thereof, were founded on the assumption that plant varieties would be developed (at least mainly) by means of traditional breeding techniques, like crossing or selection (sometimes referred to as 'early' biotechnological processes). The reason for this is a simple one: 'Techniques of genetic engineering now used to manipulate DNA and fabricate genes were scarcely conceivable in 1961; and although such techniques were being developed in the mid-1970s, they were little discussed when the UPOV Convention was revised in 1978.'[221] In other words, the UPOV Convention (prior to its latest revision in 1991) was not designed with 'modern' biotechnology (or 'microbiological processes') such as genetically modified varieties in mind,[222] and consequently a number of States, including in Europe, retained the possibility for plant breeders to obtain patents over plant material where the PVR system was deemed to be insufficient. Among several perceived shortcomings, the UPOV Convention was considered to suffer from the deficiency that the exclusive scope of protection it offered was more limited than that provided by a patent, since it covered 'only the production and commercialization of the reproductive or propagative material, as such, of the protected variety, but not the whole plants or parts of plants, such as cut flowers as end products'.[223] Furthermore, a PVR holder had no entitlement to profit in any way in the event that another breeder made use

219 To be precise, prior to the accession of the EC to the UPOV Convention in June 2005, 21 of the then 25 EU Member States had established *sui generis* plant variety protection systems (Cyprus, Greece, Luxembourg and Malta being the ones that had not). See Kiewiet 2005.

220 See Opinion of Advocate General Ruiz Jarabo-Colomer delivered 21 March 2002 in case C-305/00, *Schulin* v *Saatgut-Treuhandverwaltungs*, para. 14. Portugal has since introduced a national system of plant variety protection.

221 Millett 1999, p. 232.

222 Although, in principle, the intellectual property rights contained in the UPOV Convention can be granted for genetically modified crops as well as traditionally bred varieties.

223 Commission Proposal for a Council Directive on the Legal Protection of Biotechnological Inventions, COM(88) 496 final, p. 27 (para. 48).

of the protected plant variety as a basis for the propagation and marketing of a new variety.[224]

The European Patent Convention (EPC) of 1973, to which six Member States were originally party, with others joining in the years that followed, sought to entrench the dichotomy between early and modern biotechnology in European patent practice, with a view to avoiding future clashes between PVR and patent systems.[225] Article 53(b) EPC provides that European patents (that is, 'bundles' of national Member State patent rights)[226] shall not be granted in respect of 'plant or animal varieties or essentially biological processes for the production of plants or animals; this provision shall not apply to microbiological processes or the products thereof'.[227] That is, the EPC closed the door for its Members to provide patent protection for plant varieties 'as such', leaving open only the possibility of patenting all other kinds of plant innovation and, as a result, 'all European countries exclude plant varieties from patent protection; none excludes plants from patent protection'.[228] Nevertheless, in spite of this attempt to 'settle' the matter, there remained divergences between the legal systems of the Member States even after the advent of the EPC, for various reasons. First and foremost, being an international agreement that is not self-executing, the EPC relies on its Contracting States to give effect to its provisions through the enactment of domestic legislation. It is true that, by referring to the EPC framework, the patent laws of the EU Member States share a considerable degree of consistency in their content,[229] but the point is that the implementation of the EPC is still ultimately a matter for the States themselves. In addition, just as the provisions of the EPC hold merely persuasive authority in respect of national patent laws, so the decisions of the European Patent Office (EPO) - the body responsible for the grant of European patents - are not binding on national intellectual property offices.[230] And given that the patentability of living matter poses specific ethical difficulties as well as legal ones (relating particularly to the application of conventional patent law requirements such as novelty or industrial applicability), it was therefore almost inevitable that these issues would continue to be 'handled in some respects in a different manner in different [EEC] Member States ...'.[231]

224 *Ibid.*

225 Cf. Opinion of Advocate General Ruiz Jarabo-Colomer delivered 21 March 2002 in case C-305/00, *Schulin* v *Saatgut-Treuhandverwaltungs*, para. 11.

226 See further the next section on the European Patent with unitary effect.

227 This borderline between PVR and patents was also subsequently affirmed by the Board of Appeal of the European Patent Office (EPO) in the *Novartis* case (G0001/98, O.J. EPO 3/2000, 20 December 1999). See further Kiewiet 2003.

228 Llewelyn & Adcock 2006, p. 4.

229 See further the section on the European Patent with unitary effect.

230 See Llewelyn & Adcock 2006, p. 5 *et seq*. This is significant in this context as the EPO has endeavoured to clarify the demarcations laid down in Art. 53(b) EPC on several occasions, both in its 'Guidelines for Examination' and in its case law.

231 Commission Proposal for a Council Directive on the Legal Protection of Biotechnological Inventions, COM(88) 496 final, p. 7 (para. 14). For further explanation of why plants do not easily fit within patent principles, see Funder 1999.

Thus, when the European Commission formally announced its intention to 'propose to the Council measures concerning patent protection of biotechnological inventions' in the White Paper 'Completing the Internal Market' of 1985,[232] it was clear that these measures would include some harmonization of Member State laws in the field, as in the areas of trade marks and designs. However, unlike in the case of these other constituents of European IP law, the Commission did not attempt to approximate all of the main aspects of national laws protecting plant varieties because, '[n]otwithstanding extensive criticism of certain UPOV principles by major users of plant variety protection based on the UPOV system, an approach directing the Member States to revise the obligations into which they entered under international conventions outside of the Community legal framework appears inappropriate...'.[233] Instead, the Commission decided to concentrate its harmonization efforts on *modern* plant biotechnology, leading to a proposal for a directive on the legal protection of biotechnological inventions in October 1988.[234] The principal purpose of this proposed directive was to 'establish harmonised, clear and improved standards for protecting biotechnological inventions ... with the aim of securing the application of patent laws in this important area as effective [sic] as possible'.[235] More precisely, this directive was intended, in the first place, to actualize the distinction between plant variety and patent protection (as foreseen by the EPC) in the Community Member States, by prescribing simply that plant varieties and essentially biological processes for the production of plants 'shall not be patentable'.[236] Then, in turn, the proposed directive sought to establish conditions under which other types of inventions relating to plant varieties (i.e. microbiological processes and processes which are not 'essentially biological' for the production of plant varieties, as well as specific uses of plant varieties)[237] could be protected as biotechnological inventions under Member State patent laws, as well as the scope such protection entailed.[238]

In the intervening period between the initial presentation of the proposal for a directive on biotechnological inventions in 1988 and its eventual adoption ten years later, the Regulation on Community plant variety rights was both proposed (in 1990) and adopted (in 1994). This legislation was also intended to contribute to the implementation of the EPC's ban on patenting plant varieties as such, by providing for a *sui generis* system of plant variety protection 'as the sole and exclusive form of

232 White Paper from the Commission to the European Council, COM(85) 310 final, p. 37 (para. 149).

233 Commission Proposal for a Council Directive on the Legal Protection of Biotechnological Inventions, COM(88) 496 final, p. 26 (para. 47).

234 Commission Proposal for a Council Directive on the Legal Protection of Biotechnological Inventions, COM(88) 496 final.

235 *Ibid.*, p. 6 (para. 8).

236 Directive 98/44/EC of the European Parliament and of the Council of 6 July 1998 on the legal protection of biotechnological inventions, Art. 4(1).

237 See Commission Proposal for a Council Directive on the Legal Protection of Biotechnological Inventions, COM(88) 496 final, p. 37.

238 Directive 98/44/EC of the European Parliament and of the Council of 6 July 1998 on the legal protection of biotechnological inventions, Arts. 3-4 and 8-9, respectively.

Community industrial property rights for plant varieties'.[239] In addition, the proposed Regulation offered a definition of the concept of plant variety rights,[240] reference to which would be made in the subsequently promulgated 'Biotech' Directive.[241] So in this sense, the CPVR Regulation was intrinsically related to the Biotech Directive, just as the CTM Regulation was to the Trade Mark Directive, and the CD Regulation would be to the Design Directive. However, the parallelism between the background to the CPVR Regulation and that of these other IP law ends here for, as indicated above, the proposed CPVR Regulation was not preceded by any legislation harmonizing corresponding plant variety (as such) protection systems at national level, meaning the requirements (or even the very existence) of such systems would continue to diverge *as between the Member States*. Hence in the particular case of plant variety rights, it should be noted that the Commission was (and remained) desirous to ensure 'the establishment, at Community level, of a special form of industrial property rights for the development of new plant varieties'[242] *in the absence of* any accompanying European legislation addressing the multifarious plant variety protection laws existing in the Member States.

Still, this anomaly aside, there is a great deal of correspondence between the overarching aim and underlying foundations of the CPVR Regulation and those of the CTM and CD regulations. The purpose of creating a Community-level plant variety title was to enable breeders 'to acquire, upon a single application and through a single decision, direct and uniform protection throughout the Community for varieties of all botanical taxa and hybrids of taxa'.[243] In doing so, the CPVR Regulation would serve to 'adapt the current situation determined by various national plant variety protection laws to the circumstances of the single market',[244] thereby strengthening the protection available to plant breeders in the European Community. The Regulation was therefore also founded on the Article 235 EEC legal basis 'of last resort', as an action considered necessary to achieve a Community objective in the functioning of the common market. In fact, the CPVR proposal was originally to be based on the then Article 43 EEC, relating to the implementation of the Community's common agricultural policy, but it 'was later considered that no specific provision of the Treaty authorised the Community to legislate on that matter [of plant varieties] and, consequently, it used the provisions contained in Article 235 ... concerning implied powers, in order to adopt the regulation'.[245]

So with the creation of the Community plant variety right, a breeder would be liberated from the need to obtain plant variety protection in individual Member States on the basis of separate applications, as he would now have the option to

239 CPVR Regulation, Art. 1. Cf. Millett 1999, p. 235 *et seq.*

240 CPVR Regulation, Art. 5. See further below.

241 Directive 98/44/EC of the European Parliament and of the Council of 6 July 1998 on the legal protection of biotechnological inventions, Art. 2.

242 Proposal for a Regulation on Community plant variety rights, COM(90) 347 final, p. 2.

243 *Ibid.*, p. 3.

244 *Ibid.*, p. 2.

245 Opinion of Advocate General Ruiz Jarabo-Colomer delivered 21 March 2002 in case C-305/00, *Schulin* v *Saatgut-Treuhandverwaltungs*, para. 16. The most important criteria are those of distinctness, uniformity and stability (known as the 'DUS requirements').

seek protection on a Community scale through an intellectual property right equally valid and operative in the territory of all of the Member States.[246] The personal scope of the CPVR Regulation originally covered natural persons who were nationals of (or domiciled in) one of the EU Member States or member countries of the UPOV Convention, and legal persons that had their seat or an establishment in one of these states.[247] In addition, natural and legal persons 'located' in other countries could also have been entitled to obtain CPVRs, but - unlike the CTM and CD - this was subject to the Commission so deciding, which may in turn have been dependent on reciprocity with the given state.[248] This was fundamentally changed by an amending Regulation of 2007, however, so that now, as in the case of the CTM and CD, any natural or legal person whatever their nationality is entitled to apply for a CPVR.[249] As for the Regulation's territorial scope, like the CTM and CD there is no formal cross-border requirement for obtaining a CPVR, although if the breeder 'sees a market for a new variety in more than two Member States the Community option is the logical choice'.[250] By contrast to the CTM and CD, however, the CPVR Regulation expressly excludes the possibility of protection of a variety by means of a Community plant variety right simultaneously with other national plant variety rights (or indeed patents).[251]

For the purpose of administration of the CPVR system, the Regulation introduced a new Community agency, the Community Plant Variety Office (CPVO, based in Angers, France),[252] to perform a similar role to that carried out by OHIM in respect of the Community Trade Mark (and later also the Community Design). Breeders can submit an application for plant variety protection, in any of the official languages of the European Union,[253] either directly to the CPVO or via a national agency of a Member State.[254] The CPVO is accorded the exclusive competence to examine CPVR applications and ultimately to grant Community plant variety rights.[255] This examination is again conducted on the basis of uniform criteria laid down in the Regulation itself[256] (which 'to a large extent ... follows the framework established by the UPOV Convention in the Act of 1991').[257] On the other hand, unlike the CTM and CD regulations, the CPVR Regulation does not provide for a system of designated national courts in the Member States with jurisdiction over infringement and other civil law actions relating to CPVRs. Instead, the CPVR

246 See CPVR Regulation, Art. 2.

247 CPVR Regulation, Art. 12(1)(a).

248 CPVR Regulation, Art. 12(1)(b).

249 Council Regulation 15/2008 of 20 December 2007 amending Regulation 2100/94 as regards the entitlement to file an application for a Community plant variety right.

250 Kiewiet 2005, p. 321.

251 CPVR Regulation, Art. 92; see also Seville 2009, p. 174.

252 CPVR Regulation, Art. 4.

253 Cf. CPVR Regulation, Art. 34.

254 CPVR Regulation, Art. 49.

255 See for further details Kiewiet 2005, p. 319-320 and also Millett 1999, p. 244 *et seq.*

256 As elaborated in test guidelines adopted by the Administrative Council of the CPVO.

257 Opinion of Advocate General Ruiz Jarabo-Colomer delivered 21 March 2002 in case C-305/00, *Schulin* v *Saatgut-Treuhandverwaltungs*, para. 17.

Regulation simply refers to 'competent' national courts to adjudicate upon such actions.[258]

Similarly to the CTM and CD Regulations, the CPVR Regulation provides not only the conditions governing the grant of Community plant variety rights,[259] but also rules concerning the effects of these rights.[260] Furthermore, the references to applicable national law in the CPVR Regulation are limited to a few partial references on specific matters, such as supplementary rules governing CPVRs as objects of property[261] and restitution rules in cases of infringement.[262] In all other respects, though, the effects of CPVRs are to be determined solely in accordance with the Regulation.[263]

According to the most recent figures published by the CPVO at the end of 2014,[264] a total of 38,950 CPVRs have been granted since the Community plant variety protection system started operating in 1995, and a total of 51,681 applications have been received during this period. As for the annual number of applications for CPVRs, this has evolved from a total of 1,394 in 1996 to a peak of 3,626 in 2014.[265] The largest number of applications in 2014 (by far) were filed in the Netherlands (1,324 applications), followed by France (463), the United States (462) and Germany (376) - though CPVRs have also been filed in other EU Member States and third countries.[266] On the basis of these figures, the CPVO asserts that the CPVR system 'has been a success story from the start'[267] - and certainly many would agree. In the opinion of Llewelyn and Adcock, for example, the figures produced by the CPVO 'indicate the success of the system'.[268] Of course, as these authors point out, when appraising these figures 'it is important to bear in mind the size of the industry concerned and the fact that it relates to a single type of subject matter',[269] so the fact that the numbers are considerably lower than in the case of the CTM and CD is to be expected.

258 Cf. CPVR Regulation, Art. 101. See further Millett 1999, p. 254.

259 CPVR Regulation, Arts. 5-10.

260 CPVR Regulation, Arts. 13-18.

261 CPVR Regulation Art. 22.

262 CPVR Regulation Art. 97(1) & (2).

263 CPVR Regulation Art. 97(3).

264 Community Plant Variety Office statistics of 31 December 2014, available at: <www.cpvo.europa.eu/main/en/home/about-the-cpvo/statistics>.

265 See Community Plant Variety Office Annual Report 2014, available at: <www.cpvo.europa.eu/main/en/home/documents-and-publications/annual-reports>.

266 *Ibid.*

267 *Ibid.*, p. 8. See also Kiewiet 2005, p. 324. Kiewiet points out that the number of applications received by the CPVO by 2004 (over 20,000) was 'higher than the sum of the national applications received by the national PVR authorities within the European Community over the same time period ...'.

268 Llewelyn & Adcock 2006, p. 241.

269 Llewelyn & Adcock 2006, p. 242.

4. *The European Patent with Unitary Effect (UP)*

The last EU OI to be discussed in the area of European IP law is the European patent with unitary effect (or 'Unitary Patent', UP).[270] As we shall see, similarly to the Regulation on Community plant variety rights, the Regulation of 2012 creating unitary patent protection again adheres to the overall approach underpinning the IP law OIs that came before it. At the same time, however, the Unitary Patent Regulation also has a number of peculiarities, which are not shared by any of these previous IP law OIs, and which make it a particularly interesting OI to look at.

As was alluded to in the introduction of our account of the European IP law OIs, the plan to make available within Europe an optional instrument for patents has a long history. In fact, the first such initiative can be traced as far back as 1959, shortly after the creation of the European Economic Community (EEC) itself, when the EEC began working towards an agreement on a system of patents with unitary character[271] - making the unitary patent arguably the first optional instrument to actually be conceived of by the Community. These efforts eventually resulted in the Community Patent Convention of 1975 (CPC),[272] an international agreement between the (by then) nine Member States of the EEC to provide for a patent that would 'have equal effect throughout the territories to which this Convention applies ...',[273] and which would 'be without prejudice to the right of the Contracting States to grant national patents'.[274] This particular agreement never entered into force, however, as it was not ratified by all of the Member States, and this proved to be the sign of things to come until 2012 (but also beyond). That is, the failure of the CPC marked the beginning of a period of decades of discord among the Community Member States on the matter of unitary patent protection, which ultimately reached a conclusion (though not an end) in the next century with the adoption (by most but not all of the Member States) of the Unitary Patent Regulation. The CPC was followed by an amended Agreement relating to Community patents (known as the Luxembourg Agreement) of 1989,[275] but this was again ratified by not all the Member States. Then, another dozen years later, the European Commission attempted to revive the idea of a Community patent with a move away from the intergovernmental approach, by submitting a proposal for a Regulation on a

270 Regulation 1257/2012 of the European Parliament and of the Council of 17 December 2012 implementing enhanced cooperation in the area of the creation of unitary patent protection. On this instrument see in general Pila & Wadlow 2015; Ilardi 2015; Luginbuehl 2011; Pila 2013; Mahne 2012; Ullrich 2012.

271 See Pila 2013. In fact, as Pila points out, initiatives to create a common patent protection system in Europe even pre-date the EEC, to the extent that, by 1959, 'the creation of such a system was already considered "an old and vexing problem"'; referring to Spencer 1959. See also Pila 2015.

272 Convention for the European Patent for the Common Market (Community Patent Convention), 76/76/EEC (Luxembourg, 15 December 1975).

273 *Ibid.*, Art. 2(2).

274 *Ibid.*, Art. 6.

275 Agreement relating to Community patents, 89/695/EEC (Luxembourg, 15 December 1989).

Community Patent in 2000 on the basis of ex Article 308 TEC.[276] However, while the Council did initially reach consensus on the proposal at the political level in early 2003, arriving at a unanimous agreement on the details of the Regulation once again proved too difficult, and in the spring of the following year this proposal was also abandoned. Then, finally, after continued discussions in the course of the subsequent years and a revised proposal for a Community Patent Regulation presented by the Slovenian Presidency in 2008[277] failed to make a breakthrough, the Council authorized the use of the enhanced cooperation procedure (for only the second time in the procedure's history) by a Decision of March 2011.[278] This led to a Commission proposal for a Regulation implementing enhanced cooperation in the area of unitary patent protection being published shortly thereafter,[279] and it was this proposal that was ultimately adopted by the participating Member States as the Unitary Patent Regulation at the end of 2012.

As in the case of the CPVR, there has been no attempt by the European legislator to approximate the main laws of the Member States governing patent protection. Apart from a Community measure dealing with certain specific aspects of patent law, i.e. the previously mentioned directive on the legal protection of biotechnological inventions,[280] the only European-level legal instrument that existed in this area prior to the adoption of the UP Regulation was the (again already mentioned in the previous section) European Patent Convention, which was signed in Munich in 1973, two years before the CPC. Still, the EPC is an important instrument in the context of patent law (and certainly of more direct relevance to this area of law than it is to that of plant variety protection), for a number of reasons. First and foremost, the EPC, which is an international treaty to which EU Member States as well as a number of other European countries are party, established a centralized registration system, administered by an international body created for this purpose, namely the European Patent Office (EPO),[281] which enables private actors to obtain, through a single procedure and subject to common registration criteria, a 'bundle' of individual national patent rights, one for each of the countries they designate in their application (the so-called 'European patent' system). That is, since the entry into force of the EPC in 1977, there already exists the possibility for private actors to obtain protection for their patentable inventions covering multiple European countries via a single registration procedure, in accordance with a single set of criteria. Prior to this, it was necessary to apply for a

276 Proposal for a Council Regulation on the Community Patent, COM(2000) 412 final.

277 Council document 9465/08 (Brussels, 23 May 2008).

278 Council Decision 2011/167/EU of 10 March 2011 authorizing enhanced cooperation in the area of the creation of unitary patent protection.

279 Proposal for a Regulation of the European Parliament and of the Council implementing enhanced cooperation in the area of the creation of unitary patent protection, COM(2011) 215/3.

280 Directive 98/44/EC of the European Parliament and of the Council of 6 July 1998 on the legal protection of biotechnological inventions. Cf. Arnold 2013, p. 29.

281 In fact, the EPO is just one organ of the international organization whose task it is to grant European patents (i.e. the European Patent Organisation); the other organ being the Administrative Council. See European Patent Convention, Art. 4.

patent in each desired country separately, following the application procedures of each national system. Secondly, the fact that the EPC laid down substantive patent rules – and notably the common registration criteria – was significant, as it stood the EPC apart from comparable international registration systems in the fields of trade mark law and design law (i.e. the Madrid system and the Hague system, respectively). As a result, the EPC has had some degree of converging effect on core national patent laws in the signatory States, even though, as an international agreement, it is not directly effective. And, last but not least, the EPC constitutes the basis for the Unitary Patent, insofar as the main aim of the UP Regulation is to accord European patents granted by the EPO unitary effect vis-à-vis EU Member States. Since the European patent is not a unitary right, the rights granted under a European patent must still be maintained and enforced in each of the jurisdictions individually, in the same way as national patents granted pursuant to national registration procedures.[282] In other words, a European patent has the same effects as a national patent, meaning patentees must still maintain the validity of the patent (including paying renewal fees) in each jurisdiction, and 'the national designations of European patents must be separately enforced through the national court systems'.[283] For this reason, as is explained in the preamble to the Unitary Patent Regulation, the EU legislator considered it necessary to add to the European patent system by introducing the possibility of obtaining a European patent *with unitary effect*, the main feature of which 'should be its unitary character, i.e. providing uniform protection and having equal effect in all the participating Member States'.[284] This way, as in the case of the other European IP law OIs, private actors would only need to obtain, maintain and enforce a *single* right in order to protect their intellectual property in the European Union (or, when it comes to the Unitary Patent, 'the participating EU Member States'), rather than a portfolio of national patent rights.

The UP therefore differs from the CTM and CD because it was not preceded by EU legislation approximating the core areas of Member State patent law, and it differs from all other IP law OIs adopted to date because it seeks to build on an already established European registration system, rather than creating a new one. Furthermore, whereas the Regulations creating the CTM and CD provided for a system of designated national courts as 'Community courts' with the exclusive jurisdiction to decide on issues of enforcement of rights, and the CPVR Regulation did not provide for any particular court system, in the Unitary Patent Regulation the European legislator maintains that the establishment of 'a Unified Patent Court to hear cases concerning the European patent with unitary effect is essential in order to ensure the proper functioning of the patent, consistency of case-law and hence legal certainty ...'.[285] That is to say, in the case of the Unitary Patent, it is also envisaged that a newly-established European-level court will have exclusive jurisdiction over actions relating to the validity and infringement of UPs (as well as

282 Cf. Ullrich 2012, p. 14.
283 Arnold 2013, p. 27.
284 UP Regulation, consideration 7.
285 UP Regulation, consideration 25.

European patents without unitary effect within the EU), in place of existing national court systems. In fact, the proposal for a Community Patent Regulation of 2000 had actually '*included provision for* a centralized Community Patent Court with an appeal to a specialist chamber of the General Court and the possibility of a further appeal to the CJEU',[286] which would have had exclusive jurisdiction over invalidity and infringement proceedings.[287] However, the UP Regulation itself does not contain any provisions directly addressing the Unified Patent Court to which it refers. Instead, this is provided for in a separate intergovernmental agreement on a Unified Patent Court (UPC),[288] outside of the framework of the EU, which was signed at the beginning of 2013 and is currently in the process of being ratified by the signatory EU Member States.[289]

This parallel initiative to create a pan-European specialized patent court is significant for many reasons; not least because it explains why the UP Regulation has (at the time of writing) yet to become applicable, even though it was adopted by enhanced cooperation already some time ago. Bearing in mind the importance of the Unified Patent Court for the 'proper functioning' of the Unitary Patent, the Regulation declares that the UP 'shall apply from 1 January 2014 or the date of entry into force of the Agreement on a Unified Patent Court ... whichever is the later'.[290] Thus, the Unitary Patent will only start operating once the UPC agreement has come into effect. In fact, the plan to confer jurisdiction on a European-level court in parallel has been one of the major stumbling blocks in the effort to introduce a European patent with unitary effects[291] ever since the CPC of 1975, which sought to accord supreme jurisdiction to the European Court of Justice (while at the same time maintaining the jurisdiction of national courts).[292] The idea of 'setting up a Community patent appeal court common to the Contracting States (Common Appeal Court) to hear on appeal referrals on questions of infringement and validity ...'[293] was also a divisive issue in the discussions surrounding the Luxembourg

[286] Arnold 2013, p. 28 (italics added).

[287] See Proposal for a Council Regulation on the Community Patent, COM(2000) 412 final, Art. 30.

[288] Agreement on a Unified Patent Court, 16351/12 (Brussels, 11 January 2013).

[289] At the time of writing 9 signatory Member States have ratified the Agreement on a Unified Patent Court. In order for the agreement to enter into force a total of at least 13 states must accede to it, and these must include France, Germany and the United Kingdom. Of these Member States currently only France has completed its ratification of the agreement (in March 2014).

[290] UP Regulation, Art. 18(2).

[291] There have been several stumbling blocks in this effort. As Pila observes, '[p]ost-War European patent initiatives were vexed by a wide range of issues: substantive, procedural, institutional, political, and constitutional in nature'. Pila 2013, p. 921.

[292] Cf. Convention for the European Patent for the Common Market (Community Patent Convention), 76/76/EEC (Luxembourg, 15 December 1975), notably recital 7 and Art. 5. For a detailed account of the background to the UPC see e.g. Wadlow 2015.

[293] Agreement relating to Community patents, 89/695/EEC (Luxembourg, 15 December 1989), recital 9.

Agreement of 1989,[294] as was that of establishing a Community Patent Court with exclusive jurisdiction to adjudicate on infringement and invalidity claims in the discussions relating to the Community Patent. Indeed, the level of discord among the Member States was such that a subsequent draft agreement on a European and Community Patents Court (as it was called by then) presented by the Council Presidency in 2009[295] was considered by several Member States to be incompatible with the EU Treaties, and the Council requested an opinion from the European Court of Justice in this respect.[296] And even the agreement that was eventually reached on a Unified Patent Court, which is still awaiting ratification, was not signed by all of the-then EU Member States, as Spain and Poland decided not to participate (at least for the time being).

In addition to this, another recurring issue of particular importance in the strive to create a unitary patent has been that of the applicable language arrangements. Applications for existing European patents can be filed with the EPO in any one of the EPO's three official languages, namely, English, French and German,[297] and the same will be true of European patents with unitary effect. Yet, as Pila explains, unlike the European Patent Convention, the Unitary Patent 'package' will also 'reliev[e] patentees of any obligation to furnish additional translations of patents other than at the request of a defendant in patent infringement proceedings'.[298] By contrast, under the EPC, European patent proprietors can be required by Contracting States that do not have as an official language English, French or German to supply a translation of their European patents as granted in one of the official languages of those States, in order for the patent to be valid in said States.[299] This EPC system was essentially also the arrangement foreseen by the CPC, which allowed the Contracting States to reserve the right to prescribe that 'if the specification of a Community patent has been published in a language which is not one of the official languages of that State, the proprietor of the patent may ...

294 To be precise, the detailed provisions on this 'Common Court of Patent Appeals' were contained in a Protocol on Litigation added to the Luxembourg Agreement: Protocol on the Settlement of Litigation Concerning the Infringement and Validity of Community Patents (Luxembourg, 15 December 1989).

295 Council document 5072/09 (Brussels, 8 January 2009).

296 Opinion 1/09, delivered on 8 March 2011. In this opinion, the Court of Justice expressed the view that the draft agreement would indeed be incompatible with the EU treaties, as it purported to confer exclusive jurisdiction over matters of EU law on an international court outside the framework of the EU, and involving also non-EU Member States. For this reason, the agreement that was eventually reached on the UPC is open to EU Member States only, and characterizes the UPC as 'a court common to the Contracting Member States and thus subject to the same obligations under Union law as any national court of the Contracting Member States': Agreement on a Unified Patent Court, 16351/12 (Brussels, 11 January 2013), Art. 1 (see further below).

297 Cf. European Patent Convention, Art. 14.

298 Pila 2013, p. 937, referring in particular to Arts. 3(1) and 4 of the Regulation on translation arrangements accompanying the UP Regulation (i.e. Council Regulation 1260/2012 of 17 December 2012 implementing enhanced cooperation in the area of the creation of unitary patent protection with regard to the applicable translation arrangements; see further below).

299 Cf. European Patent Convention, Art. 65.

avail himself, in that State, of the rights conferred by that patent, only under the condition that he files ... a translation of the specification ...'.[300] However, with the introduction of the proposal for a Regulation on a Community patent in 2000, the European Commission sought to change this approach, affirming in the preamble of this proposal that '[t]he objective of an affordable Community patent militates in favour of a patent that is valid throughout the Community in the language in which it was granted under the Munich Convention'.[301] Hence, the linguistic system provided for the Unitary Patent was envisaged already in the proposed Community Patent Regulation - and this was met with strong objections from certain Member States. Most notably, Italy and Spain objected to the proposed translation arrangements, as each wanted to see their official language included in the list of those in which Community patents could be granted. Such was the extent of disagreement on this issue that it eventually led to the enhanced cooperation procedure being used for the unitary patent package, without the involvement of Spain or Italy.[302]

The legal base used for the Unitary Patent Regulation that was finally adopted by enhanced cooperation (as authorized by Council Decision 2011/167/EU) is Article 118 TFEU, a provision that was inserted after the Lisbon Treaty, which provides a specific competence for Union measures in the area of IP law.[303] More precisely, Article 118 TFEU affirms that '[i]n the context of the establishment and functioning of the internal market', the Parliament and the Council, following the ordinary legislative procedure, 'shall establish measures for the creation of European intellectual property rights to provide uniform protection of intellectual property rights throughout the Union ...'. Prior to the entry into force of the Lisbon Treaty at the end of 2009 there was no such competence - hence the fact that, by contrast, all of the previous EU OIs adopted in this field were based on the flexibility clause in what is now Article 352 TFEU. In addition, concurrently with the UP Regulation (and again unlike the other IP law OIs), the European legislator enacted by the same enhanced cooperation a separate Regulation on the translation arrangements applicable to the Unitary Patent.[304] This was also based on Article 118 TFEU, but more specifically on the second paragraph thereof, which provides that the Council, acting unanimously and after consulting the Parliament (i.e. in accordance with a special legislative procedure), 'shall by means of regulations

300 Convention for the European Patent for the Common Market (Community Patent Convention), 76/76/EEC (Luxembourg, 15 December 1975), Art. 88.

301 Proposal for a Council Regulation on the Community Patent, COM(2000) 412 final, consideration 5.

302 Spain and Italy did actually challenge the Council's Decision to authorize the use of enhanced cooperation for the unitary patent package, but this action was dismissed by the CJEU (see judgment in Joined Cases C-274/11 and C-295/11 *Spain and Italy* v *Council* [2013] ECR I-0000, not yet reported).

303 Recourse to the flexibility clause for EU legislation establishing unitary intellectual property rights is therefore no longer necessary: Cf. Basedow 2015, p. 294.

304 Council Regulation 1260/2012 of 17 December 2012 implementing enhanced cooperation in the area of the creation of unitary patent protection with regard to the applicable translation arrangements.

establish language arrangements for the European intellectual property rights.' Indeed, it is because of this second paragraph that the translation arrangements for the unitary patent system had to be established by a separate regulation.[305]

Once it becomes operational, the UP Regulation will provide natural and legal persons with the possibility to obtain a European patent that benefits from unitary protection in the participating Member States (i.e. all of the EU Member States except Spain,[306] as well as Poland,[307] and Croatia),[308] 'provided that its unitary effect has been registered in the Register for unitary patent protection'.[309] Just like European patents without unitary effect, European patents with unitary effect will be available for any inventions, in all fields of technology, provided that they satisfy the criteria for patentability required for European patents under the European Patent Convention (and particularly the requirements of novelty, inventive step and industrial application).[310] Accordingly, unlike the other Regulations creating IP law OIs, the UP Regulation does not contain detailed provisions laying out the conditions for registrability of Unitary Patents, but instead defers to the rules laid down in the European Patent Convention,[311] adding (along with the requirement of registration in the Register) only the condition that the European patent must be 'granted with the same set of claims in respect of all the participating Member States'.[312] Furthermore, although the proposal for a UP Regulation implementing enhanced cooperation had contained provisions on the scope of the protection conferred on proprietors of European patents with unitary effect,[313] these were transferred to the UPC agreement at the eleventh hour in the negotiations over the unitary patent package,[314] so the UP Regulation (again unlike the IP law OIs) also does not specify the effects of Unitary Patents. Instead, for the acts against which the Unitary Patent provides protection and the applicable limitations, the

305 See proposal for a Regulation of the European Parliament and of the Council implementing enhanced cooperation in the area of the creation of unitary patent protection, COM(2011) 215/3, p. 2 and 3.

306 Italy, on the other hand, has now joined the UP package, pursuant to a request it submitted to the Commission under Article 331 TFEU. Italy's participation in enhanced cooperation in the area of the creation of unitary patent protection was confirmed at the end of September 2015, by Commission Decision (EU) 2015/1753.

307 This is because the UP cannot take effect in Poland as long as Poland does not participate in the UPC agreement, even though Poland did participate in the enhanced cooperation that led to the adoption of the UP Regulation.

308 This is because Croatia was not a European Union Member State at the time of the enhanced cooperation on the UP Regulation, and (at the time of writing) it has not (yet) submitted a request to join the UP package, nor signed the UPC agreement.

309 UP Regulation, Art. 3(1).

310 See European Patent Convention, Arts. 52 *et seq*.

311 UP Regulation, Art. 2(b).

312 UP Regulation, Art. 3(1).

313 Proposal for a Regulation of the European Parliament and of the Council implementing enhanced cooperation in the area of the creation of unitary patent protection, COM(2011) 215/3, Arts. 6-8.

314 This was due in particular to the concern felt by some Member States (especially the UK) over possible delays that could result from the need to refer preliminary questions on the interpretation of these articles to the CJEU.

Regulation refers to 'the law applied to European patents with unitary effect in the participating Member State whose national law is applicable ...',[315] which in turn would lead to the applicability of the relevant articles that were transferred to the UPC agreement (i.e. articles 25-27 thereof).[316] Then, on top of this, the Regulation states that it 'shall be without prejudice to the application of competition law and the law relating to unfair competition'.[317]

As already indicated, the system of European patents with unitary effect is to be administered by the EPO,[318] a non-EU body, just as European patents without unitary effect. This is obviously in stark contrast to the existing IP law OIs, which are administered by EU bodies established for that purpose. In addition, the system of adjudication envisaged for the UP is peculiar, in that European patents with unitary effect (not to mention European patents without unitary effect, as regards the Member States that participate in the UPC agreement) are to be adjudicated upon by the newly-created Unified Patent Court, a European-level court common to the participating Member States. The UPC is to be composed of a Court of First Instance, consisting of a central division - having its seat in Paris but with regional sections (dealing with particular classifications of patents) in Munich and London - as well as local and regional divisions in participating Member States (at their request),[319] and also a Court of Appeal located in Luxembourg.[320] And, just as any national court in the Member States, the UPC is to collaborate with the Court of Justice of the European Union via the preliminary ruling procedure.[321]

It is likely that, like the IP law OIs that came before it, the Unitary Patent, which also offers an IP right with uniform protection across the EU (albeit in most rather than all Member States), will prove a popular instrument with private actors when it finally comes into being. This is not to say that there are no points of concern surrounding the unitary patent package, but the general idea of creating

315 UP Regulation, Art. 5(3). More precisely, this article specifies that the applicable law in these respects is that of the participating Member State 'whose national law is applicable to the European patent with unitary effect as an object of property in accordance with Article 7'. In turn, Article 7 provides that this Member State will be the State in which the applicant had his residence or principal place of business (or, if this does not apply, *a* place of business) on the date of filing of their application; or, failing that, the State where the European Patent Organisation has its headquarters (i.e. Germany).

316 Cf. UP Regulation, consideration 9.

317 UP Regulation, Art. 15.

318 On the functions of the EPO relating to the UP see further Luginbuehl 2015.

319 Agreement on a Unified Patent Court, 16351/12 (Brussels, 11 January 2013), Art. 7.

320 Agreement on a Unified Patent Court, 16351/12 (Brussels, 11 January 2013), Art. 9. The partitioning of the central division between France, Germany and the United Kingdom is the result of another compromise, proposed in order to resolve a dispute between these States over the seat of the central division, which was one of the last major obstacles to reaching agreement in the negotiations, this time on the UPC. See e.g. Mahne 2012, p. 187; Ilardi 2015, Chapter 5 (III).

321 See Agreement on a Unified Patent Court, 16351/12 (Brussels, 11 January 2013), Art. 21. On the role of the CJEU in relation to the UP see further Dimopoulos 2015.

unitary IP rights certainly seems to be a sound one, which is strongly supported by interested individuals.[322]

C. EU OIs in the Area of European Procedural Law

1. *The European Enforcement Order for Uncontested Claims (EEO)*

The third area of European law in which a series of optional regimes have already been established is that of civil procedure or, more precisely, 'judicial cooperation in civil matters having cross-border implications, based on the principle of mutual recognition of judgments ...'.[323] The development of Optional Instruments in this field began with the adoption of a Regulation creating a European Enforcement Order for uncontested claims in 2004, and continued with two further Regulations adopted shortly thereafter; one creating a European Order for Payment Procedure, and the other establishing a European Small Claims Procedure. Being of a procedural nature, these OIs are quite a different variety to those described thus far in the areas of European company and intellectual property law. For these reasons, Judicial Cooperation in Civil Matters (JCCM) is the third field of importance for the present study.

Like the vast majority of the European legislator's initiatives, including those discussed up to this point, the strive to facilitate the 'free movement of judgments' in the EU is linked to the better functioning of the internal market. As the Commission points out on its website, '[t]he increasing use of the rights of free movement of persons, goods and services results inevitably in an increase in the potential number of cross-border disputes'.[324] Therefore, it is considered necessary to ensure that cross-border litigation is not impeded or hindered by obstacles to the recognition and enforcement of judicial decisions in different Member States of the EU. This was explicitly affirmed in the well-known Tampere European Council Presidency Conclusions of October 1999, which noted that '[i]n a genuine European Area of Justice individuals and businesses should not be prevented or discouraged from exercising their rights by the incompatibility or complexity of legal and administrative systems in the Member States'.[325] And it was in these Conclusions that the European Council also invited the Council to adopt 'special common procedural rules for simplified and accelerated cross-border litigation on small consumer and commercial claims ... and on uncontested claims'.[326] So it makes sense to take the Tampere European Council as a starting point for our account of procedural law OIs. However, that is not to say that the movement towards the simplification and acceleration of cross-border civil justice was initiated in 1999. In fact, the first step in this process actually came three decades earlier in the form of an inter-governmental measure: the Brussels Convention on jurisdiction,

322 See further Chapter 6, section 2(b).
323 Treaty on the Functioning of the European Union, Art. 81.
324 See Commission, 'Civil Justice': <http://ec.europa.eu/justice/civil/index_en.htm>.
325 Tampere European Council, 15 and 16 October 1999, Presidency conclusions, No. 28.
326 *Ibid.*, No. 30.

recognition and enforcement of judgments in civil and commercial matters of 1968 ('the Brussels Convention').[327] Subsequent actions taken in the JCCM area, including the above-mentioned OIs, *build on* this initial endeavour to improve the conditions of enforceability of foreign judgments. Accordingly, it is after a brief prologue elucidating this wider context that our discussion of procedural OIs must begin.

At this point, it should be recalled that the EU's competence in the JCCM field was only 'communitarized' following the amending Treaty of Amsterdam of 1997, which transferred this competence from the third to the first of the EU's (now defunct) pillars. Among other things, this entails that before 1997 any European measure in this area took the form of one of the particular intergovernmental legislative instruments available, rather than a *Community* instrument. The Brussels Convention was one such measure, agreed at the time of the European Economic Community (EEC). Its central objective was 'to secure the simplification of formalities governing the reciprocal recognition and enforcement of judgments of courts or tribunals'[328] in disputes of a civil or commercial nature. To this end, the Convention prescribed common EEC private international law rules assigning jurisdiction and determining entitlement of foreign judgments to recognition and enforcement, subject to certain exceptions.[329] In so doing, the Convention reduced the possibilities for national courts to refuse to recognize foreign judgments under a so-called *exequatur* procedure (that is, the national procedure through which courts in a given member state determine whether foreign judgments can be declared enforceable).[330] Subsequently, after the renegotiation of JCCM as a Community competence at the end of the 1990s, the EU used its newly-acquired supranational legislative powers in the field to convert the Brussels Convention into a Council Regulation ('the Brussels I Regulation'),[331] thereby making its rules directly applicable in all the Member States. This Regulation reduced the reach of Member State *exequatur* procedures still further by limiting the scope for refusal of recognition to an exhaustive list of four (narrower) exceptions.[332] As a result, the Brussels Convention of 1968 and Brussels Regulation of 2000 went quite some way

327 Brussels Convention on jurisdiction, recognition and enforcement of judgments in civil and commercial matters, Convention adopted on 27 September 1968 (1972) OJ L 299. On this point see Cuniberti 2008, p. 372.

328 Brussels Convention on jurisdiction, recognition and enforcement of judgments in civil and commercial matters, (2001) OJ L 12, Recital 1.

329 See Crifò 2005, p. 201. The exceptions were contained particularly in Article 27 of the Brussels Convention.

330 See Cuniberti 2008.

331 Council Regulation 44/2001 of 22 December 2000 on jurisdiction and the recognition and enforcement of judgments in civil and commercial matters. This has since been replaced by a recast Brussels I Regulation (Regulation 1215/2012 of the European Parliament and of the Council of 12 December 2012 on jurisdiction and the recognition and enforcement of judgments in civil and commercial matters), which entered into force on 10 January 2015. However for the purposes of this thesis (and unless specified otherwise) reference will be made to the original Brussels I Regulation.

332 Council Regulation 44/2001 of 22 December 2000 on jurisdiction and the recognition and enforcement of judgments in civil and commercial matters, Art. 34. See also Crifò 2005, p. 201-202.

towards facilitating the cross-border recognition and enforcement of judgments delivered by Member State courts in civil and commercial cases.[333]

In spite of these achievements, however, the limitations of this 'Brussels regime' are equally well-documented. First and foremost, the fact that the regime continued to retain an *exequatur* procedure at all[334] (even if it is 'a mere control of formal regularity')[335] 'was perceived as not only unnecessary with regard to judgments on claims uncontested by their debtor but very much as a [sic] incentive for recalcitrant or fraudulent debtors to (further) delay in making payment'.[336] In other words, the Brussels regime was considered to be intrinsically constrained by its maintenance of an intermediary procedure, particularly in cases of uncontested claims for payments of sums of money that have fallen due. Furthermore, it failed to address the obstacles to cross-border enforcement of debts posed by disparities in the procedural laws of the Member States governing pecuniary claims and their execution.[337] The primary aim of the Brussels regime was to *coordinate* national procedures; it was never concerned with the procedures themselves.[338]

It is with these limitations in mind that we can now return to the Tampere European Council, for it was here that the desire to move from the coordination provided by the Brussels regime to the 'approximation' of national procedural laws was declared.[339] Concretely, the European Council requested the Council and the Commission to bring forth a programme of measures to implement the principle of mutual recognition (which the Heads of State and Government endorsed as the 'cornerstone of judicial cooperation in both civil and criminal matters within the Union')[340] by the end of the year 2000. The programme of measures that duly followed envisaged, as a priority, the abolition of *exequatur* in cases of uncontested claims, which were seen as the inevitable point of departure for a wider suppression of national intermediary procedures. According to the programme drafters, '[t]he fact that an *exequatur* procedure can delay the enforcement of judgments concerning uncontested claims is a contradiction in terms. It fully justifies this area being the first in which *exequatur* is abolished'.[341] More precisely, the abolition of intermediary procedures in this area was to take the form of a 'European enforcement order', a

333 See Fiorini 2008, p. 449.

334 It should be noted that this has changed with the entry into force of the recast Brussels I Regulation (Regulation 1215/2012 of the European Parliament and of the Council of 12 December 2012 on jurisdiction and the recognition and enforcement of judgments in civil and commercial matters), Art. 39 of which provides for the abolition of *exequatur* proceedings.

335 See Crifò 2005, p. 201. Others, though, would not espouse this view of the *exequatur* procedure. See, for instance, Cuniberti 2008.

336 Fiorini 2008, p. 450.

337 On such disparities see further Crifò 2009, p. 2 *et seq*.

338 See further Crifò 2009, p. 11 *et seq*.

339 See Fiorini 2008, p. 450. Note that the term 'approximation' must be understood in a wide sense here, comprising also EU legislation establishing optional instruments. Indeed, as we shall see, rather than adopting similarizing measures, the European legislator subsequently concentrated on the enactment of EU OIs.

340 Tampere European Council, 15 and 16 October 1999, Presidency conclusions, No. 37.

341 Draft programme of measures for implementation of the principle of mutual recognition of decisions in civil and commercial matters, 2001 OJ (C 12) 01.

concept which the Commission had begun contemplating as far back as 1995[342] and to which the European Council had specifically referred in its Tampere Conclusions. This led to the adoption of the Regulation creating a European Enforcement Order for uncontested claims ('the EEO Regulation') on 21 April 2004 (which entered into force in 2005).[343] Thus, the enactment of the EEO Regulation followed *directly* from the assault on *exequatur* initiated by the Brussels *acquis*; 'its position therefore is within the conflict of laws discipline, specifically dealing with the recognition of foreign judgments'.[344]

As in the case of the Brussels I Regulation adopted four years earlier, the EEO Regulation was founded on the legal basis provided by the new Title IV of the Treaty establishing the European Community. This was contained in Article 61(c) TEC, which - with reference to Article 65 TEC - allowed the legislator to take measures in the field of judicial cooperation in civil matters 'having cross-border implications ... insofar as necessary for the proper functioning of the internal market'. Whereas the Brussels I Regulation was passed through the consultation procedure specified for a transitional period in Article 67(1) TEC, however, the EEO Regulation of the Council and Parliament was adopted via the general Article 251 TEC co-decision procedure, as prescribed by Article 67(5) TEC. In line with its fundamental aim of abolishing *exequatur vis-à-vis* uncontested claims, the European Enforcement Order was grounded on the principle of mutual recognition, so that '[a] judgment that has been certified as a European Enforcement Order by the court of origin should, for enforcement purposes, be treated as if it had been delivered in the Member State in which enforcement is sought'.[345] This would of course entail a considerable advantage over the existing procedure provided by the Brussels regime, as the judicial enforcement of the foreign decision would not be subject to any additional declaration of enforceability.[346] Nevertheless, the EEO would not supplant the Brussels regime in the area of uncontested claims, since the application for EEO certification of such a claim would be '... optional for the creditor, who may instead choose the system of recognition and enforcement under Regulation (EC) No. 44/2001 ...'.[347] In other words, a creditor could still pursue enforcement on the

342 See Commission Communication to the Council and the European Parliament 'Towards greater efficiency in obtaining and enforcing judgments in the European Union', COM(97) 609 final, p. 7. On this Communication see further Crifò 2009, p. 15 *et seq.*

343 Regulation 805/2004 of the European Parliament and of the Council of 21 April 2004 creating a European Enforcement Order for uncontested claims. On this instrument see in general Crifò 2009, including the list of relevant literature on p. 61-62 (footnote 2); De la Oliva Santos & Calderón Cuadrado 2011; Crifò 2005; Zilinsky 2006; Demeyere 2008.

344 Crifò 2005, p. 203. See also Crifò 2009, p. 17-18.

345 EEO Regulation, consideration 8.

346 Obviously with the recast Brussels I Regulation abolishing the *exequatur* procedure (as was noted above), this advantage has now ceased to exist: Cf. Deloitte 2013, p. 31. However, as this report also points out, certain advantages nevertheless remain in this respect, since all of the grounds for refusal of recognition of a foreign judgment provided by Article 34 of the original Brussels I Regulation (which are more extensive than those contained in the EEO Regulation, as is explained below) have been maintained in Article 45 of the recast Brussels I Regulation.

347 EEO Regulation, consideration 20.

basis of the Brussels I Regulation, even if they met the conditions for requesting an EEO.

Certification of enforcement titles as EEOs is available for 'judgments, court settlements and authentic instruments on uncontested claims'[348] in all Member States except Denmark, to whom the EEO Regulation does not apply.[349] The Regulation is applicable 'whatever the nature of the court or tribunal',[350] and applicants may be natural or legal persons. In cases where the debtor is a consumer, however, the judgment for which EEO certification is sought must have been given in the Member State of the debtor's domicile.[351] By its very nature the EEO is available for cross-border cases, although (save where the debtor is a consumer) the debtor does not necessarily need to be resident in a Member State of the EU.[352] Rather, it is sufficient that the enforcement of a judgment delivered in one Member State is sought in another Member State. An 'uncontested claim' is defined in Article 3 of the Regulation as covering four scenarios, the first and last of which concern situations where the debt due has been expressly accepted by the debtor.[353] Of greater note are the second and third scenarios, which deal with those cases where a claim is 'uncontested' (only) insofar as the debtor has failed to maintain a formal objection thereto (sometimes referred to as 'procedural default'). To use the wording of Article 3(1), a claim shall (also) be regarded as uncontested if:

> '[...]
> (b) the debtor has never objected to it, in compliance with the relevant procedural requirements under the law of the Member State of origin, in the course of the court proceedings; or
>
> (c) the debtor has not appeared or been represented at a court hearing regarding that claim after having initially objected to the claim in the course of the court proceedings, provided that such conduct amounts to a tacit admission of the claim or of the facts alleged by the creditor under the law of the Member State of origin
> [...]'

348 Certain categories of claims are excluded from the scope of the Regulation, including rights in property arising from a matrimonial relationship, will or succession, bankruptcy and social security (Art. 2(2)).

349 EEO Regulation, Art. 2(3). Denmark did not take part in the adoption of the EEO Regulation (or the EOP and ESCP Regulations for that matter) in accordance with its 'opt out' from measures in the area of judicial cooperation contained in the Protocol on the position of Denmark annexed to the Treaties (now Protocol 22 of the TFEU).

350 EEO Regulation, Art. 2(1).

351 EEO Regulation, Art. 6(1)(d).

352 See Zilinsky 2006, p. 478.

353 Art. 3(1)(a) covers situations in which the debtor has expressly agreed to the claim by admission or by a court settlement, while Article 3(1)(d) refers to debtor admissions by way of authentic instruments.

Given that such cases involve some absence of participation of the debtor in the proceedings,[354] the EEO Regulation provides certain procedural requirements if a claim is uncontested in one of these two senses. These 'minimum standards for uncontested claims procedures', set out in Chapter III of the Regulation, prescribe safeguards in relation to three main aspects of proceedings: the service of documents, the provision to the debtor of due information about the claim, and the possibilities for review.[355] The rationale behind these provisions is clear. Since the EEO Regulation would have the effect of removing the need for an *exequatur* procedure in the Member State of enforcement, which is precisely the means by which national courts can verify whether a party's rights of defence have been observed (that is, considerations of 'procedural public policy'), it was necessary that the Regulation compensate for this by providing 'a sufficient guarantee of observance of the rights of the defence' in cases of debtor absence.[356] At any rate, this still represented an improvement on the Brussels I Regulation as regards the conditions of enforceability of foreign judgments, partly because it limited the grounds for disputing a foreign judgment still further[357] and, in addition, because any substantive review of a certified EEO is to be carried out by the court of origin rather than that of enforcement.[358] The Regulation does actually allow courts of Member States of enforcement to limit or even refuse the enforcement of an EEO in certain exceptional circumstances,[359] but the point remains that the instances in which certification of uncontested claims as EEOs can be challenged on the basis of the law of the State of enforcement are more restricted as compared to the Brussels regime.

Having said this, the EEO Regulation does make a number of references to national law. Firstly, the assessment of whether the requirements for EEO certification are met that is performed by the court of origin is done on the basis of that court's domestic law which, depending on the Member State in question, may

354 Art. 3(1)(b) applies where a debtor fails to appear at a court hearing or fails to respond to a court invitation to give a written notice of their intention to defend the case – see EEO Regulation, consideration 6.

355 Cf. Arts. 13-15, 16-17, and 19, respectively. On this point see Mourre & Lahlou 2004, p. 541.

356 EEO Regulation, consideration 10. See also Cuniberti 2008, p. 373, where the Regulation's procedure for review of minimum procedural standards is described as 'the alibi of European authorities for suppressing exequatur'. It should also be clarified that these are 'minimum' standards in the sense that (atypically for a Regulation) Member States are entitled to require higher standards than those provided in the Regulation. On this point see Crifò 2011, p. 286 *et seq*.

357 Whereas Article 34 of the Brussels I Regulation allows national courts to refuse to recognize a foreign judgment, *inter alia*, 'if such recognition is manifestly contrary to public policy in the Member State in which recognition is sought', Article 21(2) of the EEO Regulation expressly excludes the possibility for Member States of enforcement to review the substance of a European Enforcement Order.

358 See Mourre & Lahlou 2004, p. 551.

359 Mourre & Lahlou 2004, p. 552. In particular the court of enforcement may, upon application by the debtor, limit or stay the proceedings in the event that the debtor has applied for substantive review of the EEO before the court of origin (Art. 23), or may even refuse to enforce an EEO in specific cases of irreconcilability with an earlier judgment in another Member State or third country (Art. 21).

go further than the test laid down in the EEO Regulation.[360] Secondly, even the requirements specified in the Regulation itself cannot be described as uniform. For example, the minimum standards concerning the service of documents actually list the various methods of service existing in all of the Member States, thereby permitting them all.[361] As Crifò puts it, the EEO Regulation '"sits on the fence" with regard to any normative object of service: systems of rules of service are deeply entrenched in differing legal cultures, and an extensive, wide-ranging and in-depth comparative analysis of those systems would be required in order to reach a scientifically acceptable "uniform" rule ...'.[362] Last but certainly not least, the procedures for *execution*[363] of an EEO are governed virtually entirely by the law of the Member State of enforcement[364] (and, as we will see, the same goes for the other EU procedural optional instruments). This is considered by many to be regrettable, since national rules governing execution procedures differ significantly as between the Member States.[365] In fact, the Commission is also of the view that the fragmentation of national rules on enforcement within the EU 'severely hampers cross-border debt-collection',[366] and therefore that action also needs to be taken in order to ameliorate the conditions of execution (as well as enforceability) of foreign judgments.

So in summary, under the EEO Regulation claimants desirous to have their claim enforced in another Member State can elect to apply to the court judging the claim for certification of its judgment as an EEO, for the purpose of enforcement in another Member State. This application can be made at any time, be it during the actual proceedings on the claim or after the delivery of the judgment.[367] It is then the task of the national court of origin to ascertain whether all the requirements for EEO certification in their Member State (which may or may not correspond entirely to those provided in the Regulation) are met,[368] and the task of courts in States of enforcement simply to execute the EEO (albeit subject to some limited exceptions). Thus in the case of the European Enforcement Order optional instrument (and indeed the other EU optional instruments in the area of procedural law, as we shall see), its application is dependent on the request of a single private individual being granted by a *national court*, which constitutes the entity responsible for the administration of the instrument (in cooperation with other Member State courts),

360 This results notably from Article 19(2) EEO Regulation, which allows Member States 'to grant access to a review of the judgment under more generous conditions than those mentioned ...'.

361 Mourre & Lahlou 2004, p. 544.

362 Crifò 2011, p. 287.

363 As Crifò explains, the term 'execution' in this context refers to 'the provision of effective further procedures whereby satisfaction of a judicially declared debt can be obtained' (Crifò 2009, p. 34).

364 EEO Regulation, Art. 20(1).

365 See Fiorini 2008, p. 452. See also Crifò 2009, p. 95.

366 Commission Green Paper on improving the efficiency of the enforcement of judgments in the European Union: the attachment of bank accounts, COM(2006) 618 final, p. 2.

367 See Van der Grinten 2006, p. 78.

368 And, if so, to issue a European Enforcement Order certificate using a standard form annexed to the Regulation (see Art. 9(1)).

as well as its adjudication (in collaboration with the Court of Justice of the EU under the preliminary ruling procedure). The advantage of the EEO lay (until the entry into force of the recast Brussels I regulation) in particular in the nullification of the *exequatur* procedure, as this would otherwise be required under the system of coordination of Member State laws provided by the Brussels I Regulation (before it was recast). On the other hand, like the Brussels I Regulation that preceded it, the EEO Regulation also relies on the procedural laws of the Member States for the assessment of claims that form the object of EEO certification, as well as for their subsequent execution.

There is at present a paucity of data regarding the operation of EEOs to date since their entry into force in 2005. In fact a study of 2012 commissioned by the European Parliament's Committee on Legal Affairs found that there are virtually no official statistics at all.[369] Luxembourg was identified as the only Member State with official statistics on the European Enforcement Order, with a few other Member States, notably Slovakia, Hungary and the UK, including some unofficial figures in their reports. To take the UK's unofficial statistics, for example, these indicate that, in 2010/11, the courts of England and Wales sent a total of 121 EEOs to other Member States for enforcement, and received from the courts of other Member States 2,761 EEO's. In any case, it seems to be generally accepted that the level of use of the European Enforcement Order has been relatively low.[370]

2. *The European Order for Payment Procedure (EOP)*

Returning by way of recollection to the EU Council's programme of measures for the implementation of the principle of mutual recognition of decisions in civil and commercial matters,[371] it was already mentioned that one of the main focal points of the programme was the suppression of national intermediary procedures in general, starting with uncontested claims. But it should also be recalled that in its 1999 Tampere Conclusions, the European Council had foreseen the establishment of *common rules* of procedure in order to facilitate cross-border civil litigation. For it is with these associated yet separate goals in mind that one may better understand the progression from the European Enforcement Order (EEO) to the European Order for Payment Procedure (EOP), and on to the European Small Claims Procedure (ESCP).

Certainly from one perspective, the European Order for Payment Regulation[372] that followed two years after the European Enforcement Order can be viewed as a further step in the EU legislator's suppression of *exequatur*, at least insofar as it, like

369 Fauvarque-Cosson & Behar-Touchais 2012, p. 90.

370 See Fauvarque-Cosson & Behar-Touchais 2012, p. 92-93. And with the revision of the Brussels I Regulation, one wonders whether the EEO might not be used even less.

371 Draft programme of measures for implementation of the principle of mutual recognition of decisions in civil and commercial matters, 2001 OJ (C 12) 01.

372 Regulation 1896/2006 of the European Parliament and of the Council of 12 December 2006 creating a European order for payment procedure. On this instrument see in general Crifò 2009; De la Oliva Santos & Calderón Cuadrado 2011; Kramer 2010; Fiorini 2008; Demeyere 2008.

the EEO Regulation, does not permit any national intermediary procedure prior to enforcement of the Order in a State other than that in which the procedure was conducted.[373] But to suggest, as some have done,[374] that all of the EU procedural OIs under consideration are merely concerned with the elimination of the *exequatur* procedure in respect of different types of judgments, is to somewhat misrepresent the nature of the OIs that followed the EEO. As the Commission itself explained in its 2002 Green Paper on a European order for payment procedure and on measures to simplify and speed up small claims litigation:

> '... the abolition of exequatur and the harmonization of procedural law are two distinct issues. The former presupposes the delivery of a decision and concerns the access to enforcement where a border has to be crossed for the purposes of enforcement whereas the latter relates to the efficient access to justice in order to obtain a decision regardless of whether or not this decision has to be enforced abroad. In spite of the interrelation between these matters...it is important to bear in mind their separate nature and the fact that both of them can be addressed independently and on their own merits.'[375]

From this perspective, the EOP and the ESCP are more extensive optional instruments than the EEO, as they are the first to address the procedures for the recovery of debts in the EU themselves. As noted previously, the use of the term 'harmonization' here is to be understood in a wide sense, however, since rather than harmonizing the procedures of varying efficiency existing within the Member States - not all of whom used a specific payment order or small claims procedure[376] - the Commission was seeking to create autonomous Union procedures for the recovery of debts within the EU.[377] Indeed this reflects more clearly the idea of affiliation, as the optional instrument is again seen as the way to establish a *European-level* regime, rather than achieving convergence between national legal regimes. The EEO can also be said to follow from this account in the sense that it offers a form of 'European *exequatur*', but the EOP constituted a so-called 'second-tier' in the EU's approach to procedural law, focusing on the facilitation of trans-frontier access to justice for creditors to recover apparently undisputed debts, rather than purely on

373 Cf. EOP Regulation, Art. 19.

374 See notably Cuniberti 2008, p. 373 *et seq*.

375 COM(2002) 746 final, p. 14-15. The Commission had also made this point previously in its Communication 'Towards greater efficiency in obtaining and enforcing judgments in the European Union', COM(97) 609 final.

376 A survey of 2000, sent by the Commission to the then 15 EU Member States in preparation for the 2002 Green Paper preceding the EOP and ESCP, revealed that any one (or more) of three principal kinds of procedures were available in those States for the streamlined administration of certain categories of claims: payment order procedures, small claims procedures or so-called 'ex parte mechanisms' (see further Fiorini 2008, p. 454; see also Crifò 2009, p. 18).

377 Cf. Kramer 2008, and Crifò 2005. This understanding is also supported by the preamble to the EOP Regulation, which states that 'this Regulation neither replaces nor harmonises existing mechanisms for the recovery of uncontested claims under national law' (consideration 10): See further Chapter 4, section A.1(b).

the cross-border enforcement of judgments on uncontested claims delivered on the basis of differing national procedures.[378]

Thus the purpose of the EOP Regulation adopted in December 2006 was to introduce a European order for payment procedure available in cross-border cases for the recovery of uncontested pecuniary claims,[379] as well as to ensure the free movement of European orders for payment in the EU through the use (again) of minimum standards, 'compliance with which renders unnecessary any intermediate proceedings in the Member State of enforcement prior to recognition and enforcement'.[380] With the establishment of this procedure, citizens and businesses would therefore have a simple and relatively inexpensive method for the enforcement of uncontested payments at their disposal in all of the Member States (again save Denmark).[381] In particular it was envisaged that SMEs would benefit from the introduction of such a procedure, as it would allow them for example to recover the payment of unpaid invoices for Internet sales or mail orders[382] from consumers domiciled in different Member States more easily.[383] Consumers would also stand to profit though, as they too would be able to make use of the procedure in order to recover an outstanding debt from a fellow individual or a trader based in a Member State other than their State of domicile.

The legal basis on (and decision-making procedure by) which the European Order for Payment Regulation was enacted was identical to those used for the European Enforcement Order. The matter of the legal base for the EOP was less straightforward than in the case of the EEO, however, as the Commission originally proposed that the new EU procedure should be available in purely domestic as well as cross-border cases.[384] This of course gave rise to the issue of whether the combination of Articles 61(c) and 65 TEC allowing for EU measures of civil procedure 'having cross-border implications' that are needed for the proper working of the internal market would suffice in the case of the proposed EOP, bearing in mind also the limitations of subsidiarity and proportionality contained in

378 On this point see Fiorini 2008, p. 454.

379 Like the EEO Regulation, the material scope of the EOP Regulation does not extend to certain rights in property, bankruptcy and social security. In fact the EOP Regulation is restricted still further by the exclusion of claims arising out of non-contractual obligations, unless such claims have been the subject of an agreement between the parties or there has been an admission of debt, or they are related to liquidated debts from joint ownership of property (Art. 2(2)).

380 EOP Regulation, consideration 9.

381 See EOP Regulation, Art. 2(3).

382 See EP Press Release 20061002IPR11283, 'Go-Ahead for the European Payment Order', 10 March 2006, available at: <www.europarl.europa.eu/sides/getdoc.do?language=mt&type=im-press&reference=20061002ipr11283>.

383 For another example illustrating also the difference between the EEO and the EOP, see Crifò 2011, p. 285.

384 COM(2004) 173 final. In the Explanatory Memorandum the Commission states that it would 'consider it not only inappropriate but counterproductive to constrain the scope of application of this procedure to cross-border cases only' (p. 7). A parallel can be drawn here with the Commission's original approach to the proposed optional instrument in the area of sales law. See further below.

Article 5 TEC.[385] The Commission maintained that the requirement of cross-border implications '... did not mean that the rules that can be adopted pursuant to this basis could only apply to cross-border *litigation*, i.e. to cases of a concrete cross-border nature',[386] for the principal reason that the availability of an efficient procedure for the payment of apparently undisputed debts in purely internal cases within each of the Member States would also play a role in eliminating distortions of competition and facilitating access to justice for the better functioning of the internal market.[387] This broader interpretation of Article 65 TEC was not espoused by the other decision-making institutions in co-decision though, and in an amended proposal adopted two years after the original the Commission accepted the restriction of the Regulation to cross-border cases, inserted in its provision on 'scope' (Art. 2).[388]

Hence the EOP Regulation applies to civil and commercial cases (whatever the nature of the court or tribunal)[389] involving natural and/or legal persons in which 'one of the parties is domiciled or habitually resident in a Member State other than the Member State of the court seized'.[390] The procedure is available 'for the collection of pecuniary claims for a specific amount that have fallen due at the time when the application for a European order for payment is submitted'[391] although, being optional in nature, claimants are not precluded from making use of other procedures available under the law of a Member State or under EU law.[392] In order to initiate an EOP procedure a claimant must apply to a competent court, the jurisdiction of which is determined by reference in particular to the Brussels I Regulation.[393] If the defendant is a consumer, the only competent courts will be those in the Member State in which the consumer is domiciled, within the meaning of Article 59 of the Brussels I Regulation.[394] The application must be made using the standard form annexed to the EOP Regulation, which requires the claimant to provide various details including, apart from the particulars of the parties and the sum claimed, the cause of action, a description of evidence in support of the claim and the cross-border nature of the case.[395] The court seized of the application must then determine, on the basis of the completed standard form, whether the criteria for the issuance of an EOP are satisfied, 'and whether the claim appears to be

385 See Kramer 2008, p. 357-358. The reason this issue did not arise in the case of the EEO is that, as we saw, the EEO is by its very nature a cross-border instrument.

386 COM(2004) 173 final, p. 7.

387 COM(2004) 173 final. The Commission also pointed to the difficulty of distinguishing internal from cross-border scenarios and the optional character of the proposed instruments, not to mention the 'undesirable political and economic results' that such a distinction would have.

388 COM(2006) 57 final. On this debate over the Commission's first proposal see further Crifò 2009, p. 104 *et seq.*

389 EOP Regulation, Art. 2(1).

390 EOP Regulation, Art. 3(1).

391 EOP Regulation, Art. 4.

392 EOP Regulation, Art. 1(2).

393 EOP Regulation, Art. 6(1). On the jurisdiction rules under the Brussels I Regulation see Crifò 2009, p. 24 *et seq.*

394 EOP Regulation, Art. 6(2).

395 EOP Regulation, Art. 7.

founded'.[396] If so the court cannot reject the application[397] but rather must grant the EOP, which will then be served on the defendant through one of the means prescribed by the Regulation.[398] Upon being served the defendant is left with a choice between paying the sum claimed in the EOP or, in the alternative, lodging an opposition to the payment order with the court of origin (again using a standard form attached to the Regulation) within 30 days of its service.[399] Should they opt for the latter, the proceedings will continue before that court in accordance with its ordinary domestic rules of civil procedure.[400] If on the other hand they neither oppose nor settle the debt within the time limit, the EOP will be declared enforceable by the court of origin.[401]

Upon such a declaration by the court, the claimant will be entitled to have the EOP enforced under similar conditions to an EEO. This means that if the claimant wishes the judgment to be executed in a Member State other than that in which the judgment was handed down, the rules '... are broadly similar to the rules set out in the EEO Regulation: the EOP will be automatically recognized and enforced in the other Member States, the enforcement procedures being governed by the law of the State of enforcement'.[402] This also entails that, as in the case of the EEO, the 'automatic' recognition of an EOP in another Member State is still in fact subject to the possibility for defendants to request an exceptional review of the EOP from the court of origin even after it has been declared enforceable,[403] or to raise an objection to its execution[404] before the court of enforcement.[405] Furthermore, the EOP Regulation relies on national law in the same areas; the law of the State of the court of origin for the purpose of conduct and review of the EOP (bearing in mind that this may go beyond the minimum standards laid down in the Regulation), and (as just indicated) the procedural law of the State of enforcement for the purpose of its execution.[406] It is therefore clear that the additional contribution of the EOP over the

396 EOP Regulation, Art. 8. Note that, as is also true of the EEO, the application for an EOP can be rectified or modified upon review by the court of origin (cf. EOP Regulation, Arts. 9 and 10).

397 EOP Regulation, Art. 12.

398 EOP Regulation, Arts. 13-15. These methods of service mirror those specified in the EEO Regulation (Arts. 13-15), and as previously mentioned are also based on the same 'minimum standards' approach.

399 EOP Regulation, Art. 16.

400 EOP Regulation, Art. 17. Unless the claimant has expressly requested that the action be terminated in that event (Art. 17(1)).

401 EOP Regulation, Art. 18.

402 Fiorini 2008, p. 456. These provisions are contained in Arts. 20-23 of the EOP Regulation. As was already remarked in relation to the EEO, the fact that a judgment delivered in the EOP in one Member State is automatically enforceable in another is in itself no longer an advantage since the entry into force of the recast Brussels I Regulation, for this now provides the same rule abolishing *exequatur*.

403 EOP Regulation, Art. 20.

404 EOP Regulation, Arts. 22 and 23.

405 For further details see Kramer 2010, p. 25 *et seq*.

406 EOP Regulation, Art. 21. In addition, the EOP Regulation also contains a general clause stating that '[a]ll procedural issues not specifically dealt with in this Regulation shall be governed by national law' (Art. 26).

EEO lies not in the provisions for its enforcement, but rather in the optional procedure outlined above, designed to engender 'a simplified, accelerated hybrid judicial/administrative order for payment, directly enforceable throughout the EU'.[407] As a result of this, creditors in cross-border cases would now have a number of different procedural routes available to them: any applicable national procedure for the recovery of debts via the Brussels I Regulation; the same but in conjunction with the EEO Regulation for the purpose of recognition and enforcement; or the European order for payment procedure, which regulates both of these phases.[408]

As in the case of the EEO, there is currently a scarcity of official and unofficial figures on the practical application of the EOP since the date on which it became applicable, i.e. 12 December 2008, with many Member States having no statistics on the use of the procedure whatsoever.[409] Unlike the EEO Regulation, the EOP Regulation did impose an obligation on the Commission to present a report reviewing the operation of the EOP procedure by 12 December 2013, but this report does not appear to have been made public.

3. *The European Small Claims Procedure (ESCP)*

The Regulation establishing a European Small Claims Procedure[410] is comparable to the EOP Regulation in many ways, not least inasmuch as it too was designed to create an optional Union procedure for the cross-border recovery of debts (in this case of a limited amount, viz. €2000)[411] that would be independent of existing national procedures.[412] As follows from the Tampere conclusions and the Commission's Green Paper on a European order for payment and small claims litigation, this action would be in line with the second tier of the Union's strategy towards procedural 'harmonization', as the second initiative in the JCCM field '… directly concerning the rules that govern the procedure to obtain an enforceable decision'.[413] So it should come as little surprise that, as we shall see, the content of the ESCP Regulation adopted in July 2007 (and which entered into force in 2009) to a noticeable extent coincides or even matches with the EOP Regulation promulgated less than a year earlier. Upon closer inspection, however, it will also be seen that the European Small Claims Procedure actually embodies yet another expansion of the EU procedural law *acquis* into previously unchartered territory.

The numerous affinities between the ESCP with the EOP begin already with their respective legislative backgrounds. The proposal for the ESCP Regulation[414]

407 Crifò 2011, p. 290.

408 Cf. Fiorini 2008, p. 464.

409 See Fauvarque-Cosson & Behar-Touchais 2012, p. 108.

410 Regulation 861/2007 of the European Parliament and of the Council of 11 July 2007 establishing a European Small Claims Procedure. On this instrument see in general De la Oliva Santos & Calderón Cuadrado 2011; Kramer 2008; Fiorini 2008.

411 ESCP Regulation, Art. 2.

412 Art. 1 of the Regulation refers to the availability of the ESCP as 'an alternative to the procedures existing under the laws of the Member States'.

413 COM(2002) 746 final, p. 6.

414 COM(2005) 87 final.

was founded on the same legal base as the two procedural OIs discussed thus far, and because it also anticipated in its original form a territorial scope covering domestic as well as cross-border cases, it faced the same opposition and ultimately modification in the course of the decision-making process. Consequently the scope of the ESCP is restricted to the latter category of case as well.[415] The definition of a cross-border case in the ESCP Regulation is also virtually identical,[416] meaning that, like the EOP, the ESCP may (in certain circumstances) even be used by a claimant (or against a defendant) domiciled or habitually resident in a State that is not a Member State of the EU, provided the other party is domiciled or habitually resident in a Member State, and this is not the Member State of the court seized.[417] Equally, the motivation behind the ESCP Regulation corresponds with that of the EOP: disparities in both the content and performance of procedures available in the Member States hinder access to efficient justice in intra-EU cases and distort competition to the detriment of the internal market, and therefore a European option offering common rules - governing both the procedure itself and the enforcement of resulting decisions - is required in order to achieve a level playing field.[418] More specifically, the ESCP was intended to address a particular problem related to small claims, namely that claimants may be especially dissuaded by costs, delays and complexities of proceedings when the debt is small, as '... the weight of these obstacles increases in small claims litigation'.[419] For this reason, the EU legislator considered the availability of a simple, speedy and cost-effective procedure to be of particular importance when it comes to claims of low value.[420] Thus the aim of the ESCP Regulation is 'to simplify and speed up litigation concerning small claims in cross-border cases, and to reduce costs'[421] throughout the EU and, as in the case of the other procedural law OIs, this is in order to facilitate access to justice for businesses (especially SMEs) and consumers alike.[422] To give an example this time of the latter as claimant, the ESCP would allow, say, a consumer domiciled in Finland who has purchased a tablet PC for €750 while on holiday in Ireland and uncovered a defect after returning home to initiate the common

415 ESCP Regulation, Art. 2(1), which states that '[t]his Regulation shall apply, in cross-border cases, to civil and commercial matters, whatever the nature of the court or tribunal ...'.

416 ESCP Regulation, Art. 3(1). The one difference in the ESCP definition is that it refers not only to courts but also tribunals. Still, as we have seen, the EOP Regulation does mention the latter too, notably in its Art. 2.

417 Cf. Commission Practice guide for the application of the European Small Claims Procedure (2014), available at: <http://ec.europa.eu/justice/civil/files/small_claims_practice_guide_en.pdf>, p. 22.

418 See Proposal for a Regulation establishing a European Small Claims Procedure, COM(2005) 87 final, p. 5.

419 Kramer 2008, p. 359.

420 As the Commission stated in its Proposal for a Regulation establishing a European Small Claims Procedure, '[t]he lack of such procedures which are proportional to the value of the litigation make judicial recourse economically questionable in many cases and often creditors abstain from taking legal action'; COM(2005) 87 final, p. 6.

421 ESCP Regulation, Art. 1.

422 Cf. Proposal for a Regulation establishing a European Small Claims Procedure, COM(2005) 87 final.

procedure against the vendor,[423] either in Finland or in Ireland (keeping in mind the definition of 'cross-border cases' noted previously). As for the basic fee for the procedure, this is not the same in each of the Member States, but should in any event be affordable. Sticking with our hypothetical example, it would range from €25 in Ireland to roughly €85 in Finland.[424]

In terms of its substance, the ESCP is predicated on a number of fundamental elements, many of which either replicate or borrow from those underlying the previous procedural law OIs. Firstly, the ESCP is initiated and progresses by means of standard forms, which are adjoined to the Regulation itself.[425] The form commencing the procedure is to be lodged with a competent court in one of the Member States,[426] which - presuming it does indeed have jurisdiction[427] - then becomes the authority to administer and adjudge the claim. Secondly, the ESCP Regulation also adopts a minimum standards approach to both the initial application (which must include a description of the supporting evidence along with the details of the claim)[428] and the review of judgments,[429] thereby again leaving the precise requirements and level of scrutiny to the Member States to determine. As regards the service of documents, however, the ESCP only invokes the minimum standards provided in the EEO Regulation in the event that service by post 'attested by acknowledgement of receipt' is not possible - this being the primary method of service for the ESCP.[430] Thirdly, the ESCP had the particular advantage at the time the procedure came into being that judgments given in the procedure in one Member State would be recognized in another Member State 'without the need for a declaration of enforceability and without any possibility of opposing its recognition' (albeit with a few exceptions).[431] Finally, in addition to

423 It is worth adding that such a claim could be founded on rights derived from EU consumer law, and most notably Directive 1999/44/EC of the European Parliament and of the Council of 25 May 1999 on certain aspects of the sale of consumer goods and associated guarantees (as amended). On the connection between the European Small Claims Procedure (and also the European Order for Payment Procedure) and EU consumer law, see further Loos 2011.

424 According to the European Consumer Centre Finland the fee in that Member State was €86 in 2014; see: <www.ecc.fi/en/about-us/court-proceedings-in-cross-border-trade-con sumer-dis putes/european-small-claims-procedure/>. While, for its part, the European Consumer Centre Ireland indicates a current court fee of €25 in Ireland; see: <www.eccireland. ie/popular-consumer-topics/european-small-claims-procedure/>.

425 Apart from the standard form to commence the procedure (Form A), there is also one for the claimant to complete and/or rectify the application (Form B), one for the defendant to respond to the claim (Form C), and one for the competent court or tribunal to certify judgments resulting from the procedure (Form D).

426 ESCP Regulation, Art. 4. Again, the term 'Member States' here excludes Denmark (see Art. 2(3)).

427 As in the case of the EOP, this is determined in accordance with the Brussels I Regulation: See Kramer 2008, p. 363. Although, as Kramer also points out, unlike in the case of the EEO and EOP, the ESCP Regulation does not provide a special jurisdiction rule for consumers.

428 Cf. ESCP Regulation, Art. 4(1).

429 ESCP Regulation, Art. 18.

430 ESCP Regulation, Art. 13.

431 ESCP Regulation, Art. 20(1). Once again, this rule is now provided by the recast Brussels I Regulation; see Deloitte 2013, p. 31.

relying on the law of the State in which the competent court is located to supplement the rules governing the conduct and the review of the procedure, the ESCP Regulation also defers to the procedural rules of the Member State of enforcement for the purpose of cross-border execution of judgments given in the ESCP.[432]

Yet the European Small Claims Procedure exhibits certain key features that are peculiar to it and that all stem from one salient difference: the ESCP is not limited to cases of procedural default, but rather is also (or even especially) applicable in cases involving claims that *are* contested.[433] In other words, the ESCP is 'a full, adversarial procedure ... in a way more essential than the primarily administrative European Order for Payment Procedure for uncontested claims'.[434] Upon receipt of an ESCP application, the competent court is not called upon simply to determine whether the claim meets the necessary formal requirements before rendering judgment.[435] Instead, since the procedure is in principle two-sided, the court shall also hear the response of the defendant.[436] This means that this EU procedure, while starting in a similar fashion, actually takes a different course to those described up to this point. After receiving the standard form commencing the ESCP, the given court must determine that the claim has been completed correctly and comprehensively, that it falls within the scope of the Regulation, and that it is not unfounded or inadmissible. In the event of a shortcoming with the application (i.e. a negative finding on the first question), the court will give the claimant the opportunity to complete or rectify the claim form (as in the case of the other EEO and EOP), unless it finds that the claim does not meet the third criterion, in which case it will be dismissed (again, similarly to the EOP). And if the claim falls outside the scope of the Regulation,[437] the claimant remains entitled to proceed on the basis of the relevant procedure available in the State of the court.

If, on the other hand, the claim is found to meet all of the applicable criteria, a copy of the claim form as well as any supporting documentation and the standard answer form C 'shall be served on the defendant in accordance with Article 13' within 14 days of the court's receipt of the application.[438] The defendant is then given a period of 30 days in which to submit his response (and where appropriate, supporting documents) to the court using the standard form 'or in any other

[432] See notably ESCP Regulation, Art. 21. And, again, the ESCP Regulation also contains a general provision stating that '[s]ubject to the provisions of this Regulation, the European Small Claims Procedure shall be governed by the procedural law of the Member State in which the procedure is conducted' (Art. 19).

[433] Cf. Kramer 2008, p. 363. See also Loos 2011, p. 503.

[434] Kramer 2008, p. 355-356.

[435] This and the following procedural steps are all contained in ESCP Regulation Art. 4.

[436] Cf. ESCP Regulation, Art. 5.

[437] On this point it should also be noted that, as in the case of the other procedural law OIs, a number of categories of claims are excluded from the scope of the ESCP Regulation (see Art. 2(2)).

[438] ESCP Regulation, Art. 5(2). Art. 13 provides for the primary and secondary methods of service of the documentation mentioned above.

appropriate way'.[439] If he fails to respond within this time limit, the court will then render judgment on the claim by default.[440] If on the contrary the defendant does respond in the time allotted, the response may comprise not only his answer to the claim but potentially also a counterclaim, which must be made using the same form as the claimant to commence the procedure (i.e. standard Form A).[441] The court then has a further 14 days from the time it receives the response to send it to (or, in the event of any counterclaim, serve it on) the claimant.[442] If the defendant does make a counterclaim, it is the claimant who in turn is accorded a period of 30 days in which to submit her own response[443] (and who faces the same consequence as the defendant if she fails to do so).

As transpires from the summary of the ESCP up to this point, the procedure is in principle a written one.[444] This is only in principle, however, because the possibility of oral hearings being held in the course of the proceedings is not precluded. Both of the parties may request the court to hold an oral hearing, either in the standard forms or at some other stage in the proceedings,[445] and such a request can only be refused by the court if it considers such a hearing to be obviously unnecessary for the proceedings' 'fair conduct'.[446] Furthermore, the court can hold an oral hearing of its own motion if it considers this necessary. And this latter possibility is specifically foreseen at the concluding stage of the ESCP.[447] In fact, within 30 days of receiving the defendant's response (or the claimant's in the event of a counterclaim), the court has a number of options available to it. Of course it may simply proceed directly to giving judgment on the claim(s) but, alternatively, it can request further information from the parties within a specified time no longer than 30 days; take written or if necessary (and taking costs into account) oral evidence in accordance with Article 9; or summon the parties to an oral hearing to be held within 30 days of the summons. If the court does take one of these alternative steps, it will then give its judgment 'either within 30 days of any oral hearing or after having received all information necessary for giving the judgment'.[448] So it is the judgment delivered either before or after these steps that marks the end of the procedure on the form and substance of the claim(s), albeit subject to the possibility of appeal depending on the Member State.[449] Finally, as far as regards the execution of European Small Claims judgments, it was already

439 ESCP Regulation, Art. 5(3).

440 Cf. ESCP Regulation, Art. 7(3). As noted below, this also applies to the claimant's response to any counterclaim of the defendant.

441 Cf. ESCP Regulation, Art. 5(6).

442 ESCP Regulation, Art. 5(4).

443 ESCP Regulation, Art. 5(6).

444 Cf. ESCP Regulation, Art. 5(1), which begins by stating: 'The European Small Claims Procedure shall be a written procedure.'

445 The standard claim and answer forms themselves include a statement to this effect.

446 ESCP Regulation, Art. 5(1).

447 Prescribed in ESCP Regulation Art. 7.

448 ESCP Regulation, Art. 7(2).

449 Cf. ESCP Regulation, Art. 17.

mentioned that the ESCP Regulation also relies on the laws of procedure of the Member States in this respect.

Statistics on the operation of the ESCP are again hard to come by,[450] for the reason that most Member States do not compile separate data on this European procedure.[451] However, like the EOP, the ESCP Regulation required the Commission to report on its practical application, before 1 January 2014, and – unlike in the case of the EOP – this report is freely accessible.[452] The Commission found that the use of the ESCP by private actors was 'still rather limited compared to the number of potential cases'.[453] This was also the conclusion of the external study produced for the Commission by Deloitte, which estimated that in 2012 a total of around 3,500 applications to initiate the European Small Claims Procedure were filed in the entire EU.[454]

Once again, then, the latest procedural EU OI goes a step further than those that came before; in this case, the step from a one-sided and predominantly administrative procedure, like both the EEO and EOP, to a bona fide contentious claims procedure, available as an alternative to the existing EU procedures as well as those provided by the laws of the Member States, that is the ESCP. This means that creditors in cross-border cases have been offered another route still by the ESCP, this time for claims that are typically contested, albeit limited to a certain value. So while it is indubitably correct to state that the EOP and ESCP had a broader 'reach' than the EEO, a more apt description of these OIs (as well as the legislation that preceded them) would be that in writing each subsequent measure, as Crifò puts it, 'the drafters sought time after time to rely on, but also extend, the *acquis* derived by a previous measure'.[455] Indeed it is also important to remember that while each of these measures do exhibit novel features, at their core lie the same principles and foundations.

450 See Deloitte 2013, p. 62. In fact according to the *Fauvarque-Cosson* study for the European Parliament Legal Affairs Committee, '[f]igures on small claims are even rarer than those on the EEO'; Fauvarque-Cosson & Behar-Touchais 2012, p. 101.

451 See European Consumer Centres Network ECC-Net, European Small Claims Procedure Report, September 2012, available at: <http://ec.europa.eu/consumers/ecc/docs/small_claims_210992012_en.pdf>, p. 6.

452 Report from the Commission to the European Parliament, the Council and the European Economic and Social Committee on the application of Regulation (EC) No. 861/2007 of the European Parliament and of the Council establishing a European Small Claims Procedure, COM(2013) 795.

453 *Ibid.*, p. 2.

454 See Deloitte 2013, p. 62 and 63.

455 Crifò 2011, p. 284.

D. EU OI in the Area of European Contract Law

1. *The Common European Sales Law (CESL)*

The last EU Optional Instrument of especial significance for this study is the 2011 proposal for a Regulation on a Common European Sales Law (CESL),[456] in the field of European contract law. Admittedly, this is the only Union OI to have been formally proposed in this field, and it is a proposal that has since been withdrawn (at the end of 2014).[457] But it is also one that has been discussed extensively, both before and after the publication of the Commission's proposal, due to its significance in the overall context of European private law. And, in turn, this discussion has fuelled the debate concerning optional instruments in the European Union more generally. So this proposal of 2011 is therefore still very much of interest.

The idea of creating an optional instrument in this field was first put forward by the Commission in 2001 in its Communication on European contract law.[458] In this Communication, the Commission laid out different possible approaches for future Community initiatives in the area of contract law, including that of '[a] purely optional model which has to be chosen by the parties', such as 'a Regulation which applied when the parties agree that their contract was to be governed by it'.[459] And in the ten years that followed, the idea of introducing this 'optional model' was taken up in each successive Commission policy paper in the field.[460] Notably, the 2001 Communication was followed by an Action Plan in 2003, in which the Commission announced its intention 'to examine further whether problems in the European contract law area may require ... solutions such as an optional instrument;[461] and a Green Paper in 2010, where the Commission presented a series

456 Proposal for a Regulation of the European Parliament and of the Council on a Common European Sales Law, COM(2011) 635 final. On this instrument see in general Schulze 2012; Dannemann & Vogenauer 2013; Alpa *et al.* 2013; Basedow 2015; Smits 2012b; Whittaker 2012; Eidenmüller *et al.* 2012; the collection of articles in 50 *Common Market Law Review* 1-2, 2013.

457 See Annex to the Communication from the Commission to the European Parliament, the Council, the European Economic and Social Committee and the Committee of the Regions 'Commission Work Programme 2015: A New Start', COM(2014) 910 final, Annex 2, item 60 (p. 12). In place of the CESL proposal, the Commission has since published (at the end of 2015) two legislative proposals to approximate certain Member State contract laws governing online sales and the supply of digital content: Proposal for a Directive of the European Parliament and of the Council on certain aspects concerning contracts for the supply of digital content, COM(2015) 634 final, and Proposal for a Directive of the European Parliament and of the Council on certain aspects concerning contracts for the online and other distance sales of goods, COM(2015) 635 final. For an early contribution (and critique) on these new proposals of the Commission see Smits 2016.

458 Communication from the Commission to the Council and the European Parliament on European Contract Law, COM(2001) 398 final.

459 *Ibid.*, para. 66.

460 Cf. Low 2012a, p. 134.

461 Communication from the Commission to the European Parliament and the Council, 'A more coherent European contract law: An action plan', COM(2003) 68 final, p. 2.

of seven 'policy options' for a future instrument of European contract law, the fourth of which was a 'Regulation setting up an optional instrument'.[462] Then, after the decision was taken to pursue precisely this fourth option, this finally culminated in the publication of a proposal for a Regulation establishing such an optional instrument (i.e. the CESL proposal) in October 2011.

The essential motivation behind this now defunct proposal was, in the words of the Commission, 'to improve the establishment and the functioning of the internal market by facilitating the expansion of cross-border trade for business and cross-border purchases for consumers'.[463] This was in line with previous similarization efforts in the field of contract law by the European legislator, who from 1985 onwards adopted a series of directives approximating certain aspects of the Member State laws governing specific types of contract, and especially different types of consumer contract (a body of EU legislation that is typically referred to as the 'consumer *acquis*'),[464] all of which were 'directly based on the rationale of furthering the European internal market: differences among national contract laws would hinder cross-border trade and would lead to distortions of competition'.[465] Likewise, the reason given by the Commission for the need for the CESL proposal was that '[d]ifferences in national contract laws...constitute barriers which prevent consumers and traders from reaping the benefits of the internal market'.[466] However, whereas the principal objective of the preceding directives in the area of European contract law was to approximate certain domestic contract laws of the Member States with a view to reducing or eliminating such disparities, the stated aim of the CESL was rather to enable these private actors to *bypass* differences in national contract laws 'by making available a self-standing uniform set of contract law rules including provisions to protect consumers, the Common European Sales Law'.[467] That is, the Commission envisaged that the enactment of an optional sales contract law regime that is common to each of the Member States would allow market actors (particularly traders) to select this regime as the law (primarily) governing their various transactions within the European Union, 'instead of having to adapt to different national contract laws, provided that the other party to the contract agrees'.[468]

As was discussed in the preceding chapter,[469] the legal base chosen by the Commission for the proposed CESL Regulation was Article 114 TFEU, which as a residual possibility permits the European legislator to 'adopt the measures for the

462 Green Paper from the Commission on policy options for progress towards a European Contract Law for consumers and businesses, COM(2010) 348 final. Interestingly, the first three policy options were soft law measures, whereas the last three options corresponded to traditional hard law measures.

463 COM(2011) 635 final, p. 4.

464 See further Smits 2010a, p. 6; and also Smits 2002a.

465 Smits & Bull 2013, p. 41.

466 COM(2011) 635 final, consideration 6. On this rationale see also further Chapter 4 section A.1(a).

467 COM(2011) 635 final, p. 4.

468 *Ibid.*

469 Chapter 2.

approximation of the provisions laid down by law, regulation or administrative action in Member States which have as their object the establishment and functioning of the internal market'.[470] Following directly on from the point just made, this choice certainly made sense to the extent that, like the approximating directives that came before it (many of which had also been based on (what is now) Article 114 TFEU), the CESL proposal also had as its stated goal the better functioning of the internal market. Equally, however, this was in stark contrast to other EU Optional Instruments that had been introduced until then in other fields, the majority of which were founded on the legal base 'of last resort' contained in Article 352 TFEU,[471] and it is questionable whether the proposed CESL Regulation could be held to constitute a measure 'for the approximation' of Member State laws within the meaning of Article 114 TFEU.[472] Indeed, the Commission's proposal expressly states that the CESL 'will be an optional regime in addition to pre-existing contract law rules without replacing them'.[473] At the same time, it is of course understandable why the Commission had a preference for Article 114, as it provides for the use of the ordinary legislative procedure specified in Article 294 TFEU – and therefore the possibility for the Council to adopt the measure by qualified majority, rather than by unanimity, as is the case under the special legislative procedure required for Article 352 TFEU.[474]

In any event, whether on the basis of Article 114 TFEU or eventually perhaps Article 352 TFEU, had it been adopted as proposed the Regulation would have made available the Common European Sales Law to contracting parties 'for cross-border transactions for the sale of goods, for the supply of digital content and for related services'.[475] In fact, as in the case of the EOP and ESCP Regulations, the Commission had originally foreseen the possibility of extending the territorial scope of the CESL, so that it would be applicable in both cross-border contracts involving at least one Member State and in domestic contracts.[476] But ultimately this approach was not followed (although peculiarly in the case of the CESL the Member States were to be given the option to make the CESL available also to 'purely domestic' transactions, should they wish to do so).[477] Hence the provision in Article 4(1) of the Regulation that '[t]he Common European Sales Law may be used for cross-border contracts', these being defined as contracts between parties 'in' different countries of

470 Art. 114(1) TFEU.

471 And those which were not, i.e. the OIs in the area of procedural law, were founded on a specific legal base for measures in the field of judicial cooperation in civil matters.

472 See Chapter 2, section B.3.

473 COM(2011) 635 final, p. 10.

474 In addition, of course, this would also have the consequence that the European Parliament would participate in the decision-making process on an equal footing with the Council, which is not the case in the special legislative procedure. See further Hesselink 2008.

475 COM(2011) 635 final, Art. 1(1).

476 See Green Paper from the Commission on policy options for progress towards a European Contract Law for consumers and businesses, COM(2010) 348 final, p. 9.

477 See COM(2011) 635 final, Art. 13(a).

which at least one is a Member State.[478] As for who the parties to such contracts could be, the personal scope of the proposed CESL Regulation covered both business-to-consumer ('B2C') and business-to-business ('B2B') transactions, but the latter was limited to contracts between large parties on the one hand and small or medium-sized enterprises on the other. That is, according to Article 7(1) of the Regulation, the CESL could 'be used only if the seller of goods or the supplier of digital content is a trader. Where all the parties to a contract are traders, the Common European Sales Law may be used if at least one of those parties is a small or medium-sized enterprise ('SME')' (though, again, Member States were accorded the option to extend the availability of the CESL to 'contracts where all the parties are traders but none of them is an SME within the meaning of Article 7(2)').[479]

Accordingly, the proposed Common European Sales Law contained provisions regulating a whole range of aspects of such transactions, from pre-contractual obligations and requirements for the conclusion of a contract, not to mention defects of consent, through rules on interpretation of contracts, to contractual remedies.[480] In addition, as was already alluded to, the CESL also prescribed (a vast array of) rules on consumer protection, which provided 'for a high standard of protection throughout the whole of the European Union',[481] and most of which would have been mandatory (including provisions involving 'remedies, withdrawal rights, risk of loss, warranties, notices and communications, disclosure rules, and more').[482] All of these rules were contained in a separate text (i.e. the Sales Law that parties would opt into), which was annexed to the proposed Regulation that would be directly applicable in the Member States.[483] The CESL proposal was therefore unprecedented in the area of European contract law, as it was the first Union instrument that sought to regulate the contracts to which it would have applied in a *comprehensive* manner. By contrast, the various directives approximating national contract laws that preceded the CESL proposal (the so-called consumer *acquis*) only regulated certain aspects of the contracts that fell within their scope, in what many would call a 'piecemeal' fashion. For this reason, notwithstanding these prior approximating measures, there remained many divergences between the Member State contract laws, even in the case of consumer contracts (and let alone as regards other types of contracts).

478 See COM(2011) 635 final, Art. 4(2) and 4(3). More precisely, the Regulation states that 'a contract between traders is a cross-border contract if the parties have their habitual residence in different countries of which at least one is a Member State', while 'a contract between a trader and a consumer is a cross-border contract if (a) either the address indicated by the consumer, the delivery address for goods or the billing address are located in a country other than the country of the trader's habitual residence; and (b) at least one of these countries is a Member State'. This also means that the CESL could eventually have been opted into by contracting parties based in third countries, although it would not have been available in situations where none of the contracting parties were based in a Member State.

479 COM(2011) 635 final, Art. 13(b).

480 See COM(2011) 635 final, Annex I.

481 COM(2011) 635 final, p. 4. In fact this is required under Art. 114 TFEU.

482 Gar-Gill & Ben-Shahar 2013, p. 109; see this contribution for a detailed account (and critique) of the numerous consumer protection rules provided by the CESL.

483 COM(2011) 635 final, Annex I. Cf. Fauvarque-Cosson & Behar-Touchais 2012, p. 22.

There did also already exist a number of general 'non-official' soft law instruments (or 'model rules') in the field of European contract law (and beyond) created by academics, such as the Principles of European Contract Law (PECL), produced by the *Lando* Commission in three parts between 1995 and 2003,[484] and later the Draft Common Frame of Reference (DCFR), published by the 'Study Group on a European Civil Code' and the 'Research Group on EC Private Law (Acquis Group)' in 2009.[485] These instruments, and particularly the latter in the view of the European Commission, could be used as a source of inspiration by the European legislator, national legislators, courts and practitioners,[486] or even 'serve as the basis for the development of a possible optional instrument'.[487] In fact, the Expert Group (consisting of legal practitioners, former judges and academics) that was charged by the Commission with the task of carrying out a so-called 'feasibility study'[488] on the development of a possible European contract law instrument (be it an optional instrument or something else) a few months before the publication of the Commission's 2010 Green Paper was asked 'to select those parts of the Draft Common Frame of Reference ... which were of direct relevance to contract law and to simplify, restructure, update and supplement the selected content'.[489] And it was this feasibility study that eventually formed the basis for the CESL proposal that was published shortly thereafter. However, being non-legislative instruments, these model rules have no legal force in themselves.[490]

Still, even if the proposed CESL was an unparalleled attempt by the European legislator to provide comprehensive and detailed legal rules governing certain types of contracts, the CESL Regulation was far from exhaustive. For one thing, the proposed Regulation deferred entirely to the existing rules of national law applicable under private international law on a number of particularly significant issues, including notably 'legal personality, the invalidity of a contract arising from lack of capacity, illegality or immorality ... matters of non-discrimination, representation ... change of parties including assignment, set-off and merger,

484 Lando & Beale 1995-2003.

485 Von Bar & Clive 2009.

486 See Möslein 2010, p. 184.

487 Communication from the Commission to the European Parliament and the Council, 'European Contract Law and the revision of the *acquis*: the way forward', COM(2004) 651 final, p. 5.

488 This study was published in 2011: 'A European contract law for consumers and businesses: Publication of the results of the feasibility study carried out by the Expert Group on European contract law for stakeholders' and legal practitioners' feedback (3 May 2011), available at: <http://ec.europa.eu/justice/contract/files/feasibility_study_final.pdf>.

489 'A European contract law for consumers and businesses: Publication of the results of the feasibility study carried out by the Expert Group on European contract law for stakeholders' and legal practitioners' feedback (3 May 2011), available at: <http://ec.europa.eu/justice/contract/files/feasibility_study_final.pdf>, p. 5.

490 Indeed it is for this reason that model rules such as the PECL and the DCFR are not considered as optional instruments for present purposes, as the focus of this study is on optional regimes created by binding instruments (or 'hard law').

property law including the transfer of ownership ... and the law of torts'.[491] Also, more generally, the Preamble to the Regulation stated that '[a]ll the matters of a contractual or non-contractual nature that are not addressed in the Common European Sales Law are governed by the pre-existing rules of the national law outside the Common European Sales Law'.[492]

In order to opt in to the CESL, as indicated previously contracting parties falling within its scope would have had to agree on it as the legal regime to govern their transaction. More precisely, such parties would have needed to include a statement in their contractual agreement to this effect,[493] which would then have made the CESL applicable to the contract from the moment the contract was concluded.[494] This means that, in contrast to other EU OIs (except the EEIG), it would not have been possible for an individual party to opt into the CESL unilaterally: Rather, agreement between two or more individuals would have been required. Furthermore, and again by contrast with the EU OIs described until now, this also entails that parties wishing to opt into the CESL would not have been required to apply to any particular institution in order to do so. In the event of an action being brought on the contract by one of the parties, the validity of their selection of the CESL as the applicable regime could potentially have been examined and eventually rejected by the court hearing the action (say, because the transaction did not fall within the scope of the CESL Regulation), but this determination (if required at all) would not have needed to be made at the time of the conclusion of the contract.[495] As for which courts would have had jurisdiction to hear actions founded on the CESL, the proposed Regulation did not provide for any particular rules in this respect. Hence, as with domestic contract law regimes, these would simply have been any competent national courts (again as determined under the rules of private international law); albeit that, as EU law, the CESL Regulation would have been interpreted by such courts in collaboration with the Court of Justice of the European Union, via the preliminary ruling procedure.[496] The only

[491] COM(2011) 635 final, consideration 27. For details on how the CESL interfaces with various areas of law from a conflict of laws viewpoint see further Dannemann 2013.

[492] COM(2011) 635 final, consideration 27.

[493] See in particular COM(2011) 635 final, Arts. 3 and 8(1). It should be added that in the case of B2C contracts, the proposed CESL Regulation further specified that in order for the agreement to use the CESL to be valid the consumer's consent would need to be given 'by an explicit statement which is separate from the statement indicating the agreement to conclude a contract' (Art. 8(2)). As regards online sales contracts in particular, the idea of a so-called 'blue button' that consumers would be able to click on in order to indicate their assent to the CESL has been mooted (see further e.g. Schulte-Nölke 2011, and also Beale 2010, p. 142-143).

[494] Cf. COM(2011) 635 final, Art. 11.

[495] Hence e.g. COM(2011) 635 final, Art. 4(6). In other words, as Basedow explains, '[r]egistration, a constitutive prerequisite for the optional institutions of intellectual property and company law ... cannot have the same significance in contract law. Contracts do not come into existence through registration; they are usually perfected through mere consent. ... The application of an optional European contract law, therefore, can only occur when resulting from an agreed upon choice-of-law clause, this clause perhaps requiring a specific form but not being subject to registration': Basedow 2015, p. 297.

[496] Cf. COM(2011) 635 final, consideration 34.

'special' provision of the CESL Regulation to be found in this regard is Article 14, which envisaged the setting up of a database of final judgments of Member State courts applying the CESL (as well as relevant rulings of the CJEU) that would be 'accessible to the public'.[497]

In terms of the potential advantages the CESL would have offered contracting parties, as mentioned at the outset of this account, the Commission foresaw that the availability of a uniform sales law regime throughout the EU would allow private actors (and especially businesses) to avoid the need to adapt to divergent national contract laws (while also offering a 'high level of protection' for consumers). More particularly, the CESL was intended to liberate cross-border traders from the burdens (especially financial) that arise 'in finding out about the provisions of an applicable foreign contract law, obtaining legal advice, negotiating the applicable law in business-to-business transactions and adapting contracts to the requirements of the consumer's law in business-to-consumer transactions'.[498] In fact, as was indicated in the previous chapter, it is already possible for parties contracting between different jurisdictions to select the contract law regime of another jurisdiction as the regime governing their transactions, through a 'choice-of-law' clause. In the European Union, this possibility is (now) enshrined in the so-called 'Rome I' Regulation,[499] Article 3(1) of which affirms that '[a] contract shall be governed by the law chosen by the parties. The choice shall be made expressly or clearly demonstrated by the terms of the contract or the circumstances of the case ...'. This entails that, in situations involving a conflict of laws,[500] contracting parties (whether business-to-business or business-to-consumer) are free to choose the law applicable to the contract, be it the law of a Member State or a third country.[501] However, as Article 6(2) of the same Regulation makes clear, when it comes to consumer contracts a choice of law made by the parties in accordance with Article 3 cannot 'have the result of depriving the consumer of the protection afforded to him by provisions that cannot be derogated by agreement by virtue of the law which, in the absence of choice, would have been applicable ...'. That is to say, the mandatory consumer protection rules of the law of the country where the consumer has his habitual residence[502] remain applicable to B2C contracts in which a choice for the law of another country has been made, to the extent that those rules offer greater

497 COM(2011) 635 final, Art. 14(2). See also p. 10.

498 COM(2011) 635 final, p. 2.

499 Regulation 593/2008 of the European Parliament and of the Council of 17 June 2008 on the law applicable to contractual obligations (Rome I).

500 Cf. Regulation 593/2008 of the European Parliament and of the Council of 17 June 2008 on the law applicable to contractual obligations (Rome I), Art. 1(1).

501 It is worth adding that the Rome I Regulation does not recognize soft law optional codes such as the PECL and the DCFR as valid choices of law for cross-border transactions in the EU (although some argue that it should; see e.g. Wulf 2014, p. 139). Of course it is still possible for contracting parties to make reference to such optional codes in their contracts, but this would amount to an extension of the parties' agreement, which would then still need to be governed by the 'law' of some jurisdiction within the meaning of the Rome I Regulation.

502 See Regulation 593/2008 of the European Parliament and of the Council of 17 June 2008 on the law applicable to contractual obligations (Rome I), Art. 6(1).

protection than the law of that other country. Hence the reason why the Commission refers to the continued need for cross-border traders to 'adapt' their contracts specifically in relation to B2C transactions, and only of the need for such parties to 'negotiate the applicable law' as regards B2B transactions. For it is only in the case of the former that, even with the possibility of choosing the applicable law, it can still be necessary for businesses to adapt to different (mandatory) national contract law rules. In the case of the B2B contracts, the businesses essentially just need to agree on which law should be applicable to the contract.[503]

Thus, as far as regards B2C contracts, it was envisaged that the creation of a European sales law providing also its own set of rules of consumer protection – which would be made available as a second contract law regime in each of the Member States[504] – would enable traders to make use of a common contract law regime to govern their dealings with consumers throughout Europe, while at the same time avoiding the residual application of national mandatory rules pursuant to Article 6(2) of the Rome I Regulation – since that Regulation only applies to choices of 'foreign' law, and not 'second national' regimes.[505] On the other hand, as far as B2B contracts are concerned, the CESL was intended more to provide a contract law regime that would be familiar to businesses from different jurisdictions, which these businesses could agree on as the applicable regime, rather than choosing a 'foreign' law as their 'common' regime instead. Whether or not the CESL would have proved a 'success' with businesses (not to mention consumers)[506] is a matter of some debate, and a question to which we shall return in the concluding chapter.[507] Although two Eurobarometer surveys of 2011 (one regarding business-to-business transactions and the other consumer transactions) did find that the proposal to introduce a single EU contract law for cross-border transactions 'was strongly favoured by the surveyed enterprises'.[508] What does at any rate seem

503 Although, as the Commission clarifies in the CESL proposal, one could further distinguish here between contracts between SMEs, where there is a need to *negotiate* the applicable law, and contracts between SMEs and large companies, where SMEs 'generally have to agree to apply the law of their business partner and bear the costs of finding out about the content of the foreign law applicable to the contract and of complying with it': COM(2011) 635 final, p. 3.

504 See COM(2011) 635 final, p. 8.

505 Indeed, apart from being of relevance to the issue of whether the CESL could be said to constitute approximation within the meaning of Article 114 TFEU (as was already explained in the previous chapter), the conception of the CESL as a second national regime was also significant for this reason: On this see further Low 2012a; Fornasier 2012.

506 The focus on businesses here can be explained by the fact that it would have essentially been up to businesses in the first place to determine whether or not to offer consumer contracts governed by the CESL; and only then would consumers have had the possibility to opt in; see further Chapter 4, section C.1(a).

507 See Chapter 6, section 2(b).

508 Commission, Flash Eurobarometer 320, European contract law in business-to-business transactions, Analytical Report (2011) and Commission, Flash Eurobarometer 321, European contract law in consumer transactions, Analytical Report (2011), p. 7. However, some have argued that the empirical data gathered in such Eurobarometer surveys do not actually provide support for the use of the CESL proposal; see e.g. Hubbard 2012.

clear is that, in order to really facilitate cross-border trade, the CESL would have needed to attract parties to opt in.[509]

CONCLUSION

It would appear from the preceding overview of EU Optional Instruments in various policy areas that there are a number of noteworthy similarities and differences between these EU OIs on a range of points. It is therefore useful to conclude with a brief comparison of the EU OIs that have been discussed in this chapter.

As far as the more foundational aspects are concerned, we have seen that, firstly, most EU OIs have not been preceded by EU legislation harmonizing the core Member State laws applicable to the corresponding national regimes in the given field, but also that this is not true of the CTM and CD, which were introduced shortly after a directive approximating the core national trade mark and design laws, respectively. Secondly, most EU OIs have been adopted on the basis of the same provision in the treaties, namely the flexibility clause contained in what is now Article 352 TFEU, but a number have not. Those in the area of procedural law were founded on a specific legal base for measures in the field of judicial cooperation in civil matters, and the Unitary Patent Regulation was founded on the specific legal base for Union measures in the area of IP law inserted into the TFEU following the Lisbon Treaty. Also, in the case of the proposal for a CESL Regulation of 2011, the legal base envisaged was by contrast the residual Article 114 TFEU legal basis for the internal market, and as for the SUP proposal, this is based on Article 50 TFEU, which is contained in the treaty chapter on the right of establishment. Thirdly, most EU OIs have been established solely by means of regulations, but the SE and the SCE have been created by regulations supplemented by accompanying directives. And when it comes to the SUP proposal, this is proposed in the form of a directive alone.

In addition, we have also seen commonalities and points of divergence as regards the respective scope of the various EU OIs. Firstly, as regards personal scope, the vast majority of EU OIs may be opted into by both natural and legal persons, but this is not the case with the SCE and the SE, which can only be selected by legal persons. Also the vast majority of EU OIs can be opted into by one individual person or legal entity unilaterally, but this is not true of the EEIG, and would not have been true of the CESL, each of which rest on there being agreement between a plurality of individuals. Secondly, regarding territorial scope, most EU OIs require a cross-border element to be present, but those in the area of IP law do not. The SUP proposal does not contain a cross-border requirement either, and although the 2011 CESL proposal did cover only cross-border cases, it left open the possibility for individual Member States to extend its territorial scope so as to cover purely domestic cases as well. Thirdly, as for geographical scope, most EU OIs are available only (or at least primarily) to private actors 'based' within the EU, but the

509 See further below, Chapter 4, section D.3(b).

European IP law OIs are again exceptional here, since these are available also to individuals located in third countries. Also, while most EU OIs are applicable in all EU Member States, the procedural law OIs do not apply in Denmark, and the Unitary Patent Regulation, which was adopted via the enhanced cooperation procedure, will not apply (at least initially) in three EU Member States.

Furthermore, the statistics on the number of 'opt ins' that have taken place for the various EU OIs already in existence also seem to reveal some notable similarities and differences in terms of the level of 'uptake' of these OIs, insofar as some of the existing OIs appear to have been selected by many individuals on a consistent basis, while others do not. For example, while there have been a large number of Community trade mark and Community design registrations since the entry into force of the CTM and CD Regulations, the number of European Company and European Cooperative Society registrations appears to have been more modest.

Of course, there are also a number of other important points of similarity and divergence between EU OIs that can be drawn from the overview of EU OIs provided in this chapter - and indeed these will be brought into focus in the next chapters - but this initial comparison will suffice for the time being.

PART 2

EU OPTIONAL INSTRUMENTS: A NORMATIVE AND EXPLANATORY FRAMEWORK

Chapter 4

NORMATIVE FRAMEWORK

INTRODUCTION

The possibility of grouping and comparing distinct pieces of EU legislation applicable in diverse fields of law under a single heading on the basis that they are all birds of a particular legislative feather is an appealing one, for it can lead to a whole host of intriguing observations and questions.

First and foremost, the aggregation of various existing and proposed Regulations in the areas of company law, intellectual property law, contract law and procedural law (not to mention others) according to an elemental definition of 'optional instrument'[1] supports the finding of a certain *trend* arising in European Union legislation.[2] That is, it may be observed that the EU legislator is increasingly looking to such 'optional instruments' as an alternative way of regulating various areas of (private) law that fall under its competence. In turn, this growing reliance of the EU legislator on OIs begs the question whether this tendency is to be welcomed; or, in more concrete terms, whether this alternative legislative approach is desirable, and for what reasons? Clearly this question can itself give rise to various others, depending on the considerations one might deem relevant in this regard, not to mention the perspective one takes. What are the motivations behind the shift towards OIs in the European Union, and is the reasoning of the European legislator well-founded? More generally, what are the arguments in favour of and against OIs as a method of EU lawmaking? Are OIs a better means of attaining the legislator's goals than other methods available to it and, in particular, is the OI-based approach preferable to that of similarization[3] in achieving the EU's objectives in the different fields of European law? Is the effectiveness of OIs in reaching their stated aims dependent on their being selected by a sufficient number of private individuals on a sufficiently consistent basis? Even though OIs apparently leave national laws unmodified, do/can they still have a converging effect in the relevant field of law at *national* level? That is, can EU legislation creating OIs still lead to legal convergence

1 See Chapter 2.
2 On the finding of such a trend see *supra* Chapter 1, section 1(a).
3 This term is explained in Chapter 2.

in some other way? And if so, to what extent is this (also) dependent on the instrument being chosen by natural and legal persons? What does the optional instrument method mean for the EU Member States and private actors? Are OIs less disruptive for national legal systems than traditional similarization measures, and if so does this render them more readily acceptable for the Member States? Or perhaps the fact that EU OIs may instigate a form of 'regulatory competition' between the national and supra-national levels actually provides a reason for greater resistance on their part? Does the introduction of additional, EU legal options empower individuals to derive greater benefit from the internal market (and if so, is this only limited to certain groups of individuals)? Or does an increased number of options simply lead to greater complexity for private actors in the European legal environment, by providing them with too many different possibilities from which to choose? All of these questions and more could form the basis for a general normative assessment of EU Optional Instruments.[4]

A second observation, which follows from the description of the various EU OIs in the previous chapter, is that they seem to differ in certain noteworthy respects. For example, while some OIs have been preceded by an equivalent approximating directive, others have been created in the absence of any parallel approximating measure. Or, whereas the application of some OIs is subject to the presence of a certain cross-border element, the application of others is not subject to any such condition. It is idiosyncrasies such as these that provide grounds for the impression that EU OIs are far from a homogeneous group of legislative instruments - and this impression also leads to a series of compelling questions. Does the fact that there exist notable differences between EU OIs entail that the conclusions emanating from any general assessment of this legislative method do not hold true *in concreto*? In particular, does the effectiveness of the OI-based approach (as compared to similarization) vary depending on the specific OI and EU policy area in question? Are OIs even feasible in all EU policy fields? If not, how can this be explained? Undoubtedly a comprehensive normative evaluation of EU OIs would also need to take into account both the extent and the significance of heterogeneity in the 'family'.[5]

Finally, our overview of EU OIs in distinct fields of EU law - and particularly the statistics relating to those OIs already in existence for a certain period of time - also signalled the possibility of a third observation, which is that some OIs appear to be more 'attractive' to private actors than others, in the sense that some OIs have apparently been opted into by a relatively large number of individuals on a relatively consistent basis since they entered into force, while others have not. Naturally this observation incites one to ask whether this is indeed the case, and if so, why - and this question again provokes a number of others in turn. Perhaps the lack of demand for certain OIs could be explained simply by the fact that there is no need for an OI at all in the areas of law in which these OIs have been introduced, at least not from the perspective of private actors. Alternatively, maybe it is something about the particular OIs in question that makes them unappealing to individuals,

4 See sections A-C.

5 See section D.

even if there may be a demand for an optional instrument in principle. If so, what are the features of these OIs that render them less attractive, and how could/should these be reformed so as to make them more attractive? Do these unalluring characteristics differ as per each of these OIs, or do unpopular OIs suffer from the same (or at any rate similar) perceived shortcomings? Last but by no means least, assuming the latter is true, could this lead to certain lessons for the European legislator when elaborating optional regimes in future? Given that, as Smits points out, '[a]lthough the popularity of these regimes differs considerably, the European legislator aims at creating optional regimes in other fields as well',[6] the potential significance of these questions cannot be overstated. At least to the extent that the effectiveness of EU optional regimes can be said to depend on their popularity, it would be important to offer an explanation of this aspect of EU OIs too.[7]

In summary, the rise of optional instruments within the European Union calls for both a normative and an explanatory framework to be developed. Yet, in spite of the growing prominence of EU OIs, the debate surrounding them still lacks such theoretical underpinnings. Work towards this goal has already begun,[8] but a great deal of progress still needs to be made. Accordingly, one of the central aims of the present study is to *expand* the theory behind EU OIs, addressing the array of issues outlined above along the way. Of course, as EU OIs are a large and rapidly evolving family of legislative instruments, it would be unrealistic to expect that a study of this magnitude could offer an all-encompassing analysis of the phenomenon. Inevitably, a number of these issues will not be discussed exhaustively, and many other pertinent issues may not be covered at all. So the ambition is a more modest one: to contribute to the development of a conceptual footing for EU OIs based on normative and explanatory structures framed around a number of central questions. This should lead not only to a more reasoned view of the matter of EU OIs, but also to the identification of potential lines of further research and eventually the stimulation of further debate in the process.

Each of the many issues raised above will therefore be addressed to one degree or another at different stages in the analysis. The contribution begins in this chapter, which seeks to evaluate EU OIs from different perspectives, taking into account also their heterogeneity (i.e. the first and second aspects mentioned). As was explained in the introductory chapter, the reason for looking at EU OIs from different perspectives is essentially because the assessment of EU OIs could differ depending on the perspective one takes.[9] Accordingly, this chapter commences with an examination of the EU legislator's rationale underlying the use of optional instruments, before undertaking a broader evaluation of EU OIs, considering not only the 'European' perspective (section A) but also the perspective of the Member States (section B) as well as private actors (section C). From each of these perspectives, it will be seen that the appraisal focuses in particular on the question of utility of the OI-based approach relative to the similarization method. Then, the

6 Smits 2010b, p. 348.
7 See Chapter 5.
8 See Chapter 1, section 1(b).
9 See Chapter 1, section 2(b). Also see further *infra* section D.3(a).

issue of divergences between EU OIs is also discussed, which ultimately leads to the question of whether it is possible to identify pertinent criteria on the basis of which the desirability of EU OIs *in general* may be assessed (section D). As for the usage of EU OIs (i.e. the third aspect), the attempt to explain this is left to the next chapter.

A. Evaluation of EU OIs and the Reasoning of the EU Legislator

1. *EU OIs as an Alternative Form of EU Lawmaking*

The most obvious place to begin searching for the EU's reasoning behind the increasing reliance on optional instruments is in the legislative texts themselves, as well as other relevant EU documentation. There may well be other more implicit justifications that can be identified, but it makes sense to start with the express motivations given by the European legislator for using EU OIs before moving to consider what other reasons there may be for doing so. It should also be stressed that at this juncture the objective is merely to describe the stated arguments of the EU legislator in favour of creating OIs, and not to comment on their validity or persuasiveness. The analysis of the legislator's rationale is left to a later stage too, as part of our broader assessment of arguments pro and contra EU OIs from the 'European perspective' (i.e. including the views of not only the European legislator but also academics).

(a) Creating EU Regimes for EU Activities

The first (and the primary) motivation for the shift towards OIs expressed by the EU legislator corresponds to the notion that the completion of the internal market and its attendant improvements necessitates the removal of barriers to (particularly cross-border) activities of private actors, not only through the similarization of Member State laws, which seeks to attain greater uniformity among the various domestic regimes governing such activities, but also via the establishment of European Union legal regimes adapted to the Union's dimension, which allows such actors to *transcend* the disparate rules and territorial boundaries of the national legal systems. In a nutshell, the desire to create 'EU regimes for EU activities'. Arguably the most lucid expression of this underlying logic is to be found in the *Monti* Report on the re-launch of the Single Market,[10] where the ex-Commissioner put it as follows:

> 'The advantage of the 28th regime is to expand options for business and citizens operating in the single market: if the single market is their main horizon, they can opt for a standard and single legal framework valid across Member States; if they move in a predominantly national setting, they will remain under the national regime.'[11]

10 Monti 2010.

11 Monti 2010, p. 93.

As this statement implies, it is considered that by introducing sets of uniform rules at the European level, which are not territorially limited because all of the Member States are affiliated to them, EU optional regimes can offer something that national legal systems, regardless of the extent to which they are similarized, are not able to, and this is of benefit to those private actors in the internal market whose main operations extend beyond the frontiers of individual Member States. Thus, offering additional EU-level legal options for such actors is a way of complementing measures aimed at approximating national laws in the strive to improve the functioning of the internal market.

Now while this may be taken as a starting point, a proper understanding of this line of reasoning can only be arrived at with reference to concrete examples of European Union optional instruments in which it is reflected. In this regard, it is useful to look first and foremost at the optional instruments in the field of European intellectual property law, since it is these instruments that provide the clearest illustration of the EU regimes for EU activities rationale.

EU OIs in the area of intellectual property law

To begin with EU trade mark law, it will be recalled that prior to the adoption of the first Community trade mark (CTM) Regulation in 1993,[12] the core substantive rules of Member State trade mark law were approximated through a directive adopted five years earlier.[13] The purpose of similarizing these rules was to ensure that the free movement of goods and services would not be impeded by disparities in national trade mark laws, so that, following the implementation of the directive, private actors seeking trade mark protection in another Member State would find themselves in a substantially similar legal environment. Yet, as the legislator expressly noted in the preamble to the Trade Mark directive, it was still 'important not to disregard the solutions and advantages which the Community trade mark system may afford to undertakings wishing to acquire trade marks',[14] because, even if companies active in a plurality of jurisdictions within the Community would no longer be confronted with major divergences between national trade mark laws, they would still be faced with the need to obtain a series of territorially-limited trade mark rights. Hence it was also considered necessary to establish an additional '28th' trade mark system at Community-level that would allow undertakings to obtain a unitary trade mark right, via a single procedural system, which would take effect throughout the whole of the Community's territory.[15] This way, a private actor wishing to acquire trade mark protection in a number of (if not all) EU Member States would have access to a trade mark system tailored to their needs as cross-border operators. That this did constitute the main *raison d'être* of the CTM Regulation subsequently enacted is borne out in its own preamble, in which the

12 Council Regulation 40/94 of 20 December 1993 on the Community trade mark (now, as amended, Council Regulation 207/2009 of 26 February 2009 on the Community trade mark).

13 First Council Directive 89/104/EEC of 21 December 1988 to approximate the laws of the Member States relating to trade marks.

14 Consideration 2.

15 See Regulation 207/2009 on the Community trade mark, consideration 3.

legislator explains that in order to achieve an internal market that 'offers conditions which are similar to those obtaining in a national market', it is necessary not only that 'barriers to free movement of goods and services be removed and arrangements be instituted which ensure that competition is not distorted, but, in addition, legal conditions must be created which enable undertakings to adapt their activities to the scale of the Community'.[16] Accordingly, a trade mark right that produces its effects in the entire area of the Community irrespective of internal borders 'should feature amongst the legal instruments which undertakings have at their disposal'.[17]

The field of European design law supplies an equally intelligible depiction of the idea of EU regimes for EU activities. As has also already been mentioned, like the CTM Regulation, the Regulation establishing the Community Design (CD) of 2002[18] was preceded by a directive approximating the most salient features of Member State design protection laws a few years prior.[19] This similarization measure was again designed to address distortions of competition within the internal market, this time caused by divergences in the design protection prescribed by the legislation of the Member States directly affecting goods embodying industrial designs. However, as the European legislator again observed in the preamble to the directive itself, it was also 'important to take into consideration the solutions and the advantages with which the Community design system [would] provide undertakings wishing to acquire design rights'.[20] In other words, in much the same vein as the legislative train of thought behind the CTM, there was seen to be an enduring need to introduce a unified system of registered design protection available under a uniform procedure according to common registration criteria and having uniform effect across the Community, in order to allow private actors to escape the territorial limitations of national IP rights. And once again, this reasoning was later made explicit in the preamble of the CD Regulation, where it is stated that 'a more accessible design-protection system adapted to the needs of the internal market is essential for Community industries',[21] for the reason that '[t]he effect of design protection being limited to the territory of the individual Member States whether or not their laws are approximated, leads to a possible division of the internal market ...'.[22]

As far as the area of European plant variety protection is concerned, we have seen that the picture is not exactly identical, as the Regulation establishing the Community Plant Variety Right (CPVR)[23] was not preceded by any measure approximating national plant variety protection systems (that is, in those Member States where such systems existed). As a result, the preamble to the CPVR Regulation contains a slightly different explication of the need for a CPVR, to the

16 *Ibid.*, consideration 2.
17 *Ibid.*
18 Regulation 6/2002 on Community designs.
19 Directive 98/71/EC of the European Parliament and of the Council of 13 October 1998 on the legal protection of designs.
20 Consideration 4.
21 Consideration 8.
22 Consideration 4.
23 Council Regulation 2100/94 of 27 July 1994 on Community plant variety rights.

effect that it was the lack of harmonization of core domestic rules in this field that called for the establishment of a corresponding Community-wide system. To quote the phraseology employed in the preamble, it is in circumstances where 'industrial property regimes for plant varieties have not been harmonised at Community level'[24] - and therefore where the content of such regimes is not uniform - that 'it is appropriate to create a Community regime which, although co-existing with national regimes, allows for the grant of industrial property rights valid throughout the Community'.[25] So it could be inferred from this that, in contrast to the CTM and the CD, the CPVR was intended to overcome the obstacles to the smooth functioning of the internal market caused by the divergences between plant variety protection laws in existence in the Member States, rather than the difficulties posed by the inherent territorial limitations of national plant variety rights. Yet to reach such a conclusion on the basis of the above statement alone would be misguided, for other preparatory documentation relating to the CPVR Regulation suggests that the fundamental legislative motivation for the instrument was in fact the very same. In particular, the proposal for the CPVR Regulation indicates that, by enabling breeders to obtain uniform plant variety protection throughout the Community on the strength of a single registration procedure, the Regulation would 'adapt the [then] situation determined by various national plant variety protection laws to the circumstances of the single market'.[26] Understood in this light, it is perfectly conceivable that the CPVR would have been introduced even if there had been some prior similarization of Member State laws in the field, as in any event such similarization would not have achieved the kind of *adaptation* foreseen by the legislator.

Lastly, as we have also seen, the case of European patent law has a somewhat peculiar background as well. In terms of EU legislation, as in the case of plant variety protection law, there has been no similarization of the *core* areas of patent law. On the other hand, a considerable degree of spontaneous convergence between Member State provisions in some of these areas (such as the criteria for patentability) has been achieved as a result of agreements at the international level, and particularly the European Patent Convention (EPC) 1973. Moreover, the EPC established a single procedure for the acquisition of patent rights in the EU Member States (as well as a number of third countries) administered by an international body (the European Patent Office (EPO)), meaning that a common European registration procedure for patent rights already exists. So, at first sight, this might lead one to think that in the field of patent law there would actually be no need for a Union optional instrument of the kind introduced in the other aforementioned areas of intellectual property law. However, the outcome of this international procedure is not a unitary right with uniform effect throughout the participating States, but rather a 'bundle' of national rights subject to national laws as regards most notably their validity and scope. For this reason, as the EU legislator makes clear in the preamble to the Regulation on the European patent with unitary effect (or 'Unitary

24 Consideration 2.

25 Consideration 3.

26 COM(90) 347 final, p. 2.

Patent', UP), '[u]nitary patent protection should be achieved by attributing unitary effect to European patents in the post-grant phase by virtue of this Regulation and in respect of all the participating Member States'.[27] In other words, there remains a need for a patent granted by means of the common registration procedure that also offers uniform protection and has equal effect in all of the EU Member States proceeding with enhanced cooperation, in much the same way as the CTM, CD and CPVR. It makes sense, therefore, that in the Unitary Patent Regulation the legislator refers once more to the establishment of 'legal conditions enabling undertakings to adapt their activities in manufacturing and distributing products across national borders' as the reason why '[u]niform patent protection within the internal market, or at least a significant part thereof, should feature amongst the legal instruments which undertakings have at their disposal'.[28]

EU OIs in the area of company law

It appears, then, that the intention on the part of the European legislator to create EU regimes for EU activities is expressly cited in the legislative texts of all of the European intellectual property law OIs under scrutiny. Now can the same explicit intention be identified in the EU OIs adopted in the area of European company law? The Regulation on the Statute for a European Company (or *Societas Europaea*, SE)[29] provides possibly the most palpable indication that this is indeed the case. Recalling our description of the European company law OIs, it was observed that the essential purpose of the SE Regulation was to make available a European public-limited liability company form accessible to companies from different Member States involved in restructuring operations (i.e. the creation of groups of companies) which, when carried out in the framework of national regimes, gives rise to legal difficulties due to divergences in as well as territorial limitations of Member State laws. And while, as is indicated in the prelude to the SE Regulation, a degree of Community action approximating domestic company laws was taken before the introduction of the EU OIs in the field[30] in order to surmount some of these difficulties, the Community legislator considered that '[s]uch approximation does not, however, release companies governed by different legal systems from the obligation to choose a form of company governed by a particular national law'.[31] It was therefore envisaged that the adoption of a Regulation allowing companies to form and carry on business under the law that it provides would 'permit the creation and management of companies with a European dimension, free from the obstacles arising from the disparity and the limited territorial application of national company law'.[32] This way, the structures of production could be 'adapted to the

27 Regulation 1257/2012 of the European Parliament and of the Council of 17 December 2012 implementing enhanced cooperation in the area of the creation of unitary patent protection, consideration 7.

28 Consideration 1.

29 Council Regulation 2157/2001 of 8 October 2001 on the Statute for a European company (SE).

30 Albeit not the most fundamental of these laws, as in the case of the CTM and the CD.

31 Consideration 3.

32 SE Regulation, consideration 7.

Community dimension'.[33] The recurrent reference to the term 'adaptation' is telling in itself as a sign that the common theme of EU regimes for EU activities underpinning the European IP law OIs also lies at the heart of the European company; an OI in a distinct area of EU law.

The express motivations given for the European Cooperative Society (SCE) Regulation adopted two years later are formulated in an equivalent manner to those put forward in justification of the SE Regulation. Bearing in mind the similarity in the background to the two measures, this is hardly surprising. As has been noted previously, like the public-limited liability form, the legal form of cooperatives was widely available within the national systems of the Member States prior to the introduction of the corresponding EU OI, but these domestic legal options were seen by the Community institutions as inadequate when it came to the transnational establishment and operation of cooperative societies, taking into account also the dissimilarities between the respective Member State rules. And since neither the existing SE form nor the European Economic Interest Grouping (EEIG) could match the specific features and requirements of cooperative enterprises,[34] an additional European legal form was considered necessary, as this could allow cooperatives to function 'outside their own national borders in all or part of the territory of the Community'.[35] So from the perspective of the Community legislator, the SCE Regulation was needed to extend the opportunity offered by the EEIG and the SE to cooperative societies because, for the purpose of adapting structures of production to the Community dimension, it was 'essential that companies of *all types* the business of which is not limited to satisfying purely local needs should be able to plan and carry out the reorganization of their business on a Community scale'.[36] Accordingly, the main aim of the SCE Regulation was to supply cooperatives also with 'adequate legal instruments capable of facilitating the development of their cross-border activities'.[37]

When it comes to the EEIG – the first of the European OIs to be introduced – the idea of creating a Community regime for operations with a European dimension is expressly referred to in the Regulation establishing this OI as well, although its reflection in the EEIG form is rather blurred by the fact that, before the adoption of the Regulation, only one of the then Member States offered a corresponding business form in its domestic legal system. As noted in our outline of the EEIG, possibilities for groupings between natural and legal persons did exist within the legal systems of the Member States, and these could be of a more temporary nature, such as a partnership, or a more permanent nature, like a national company. However, the kind of grouping made possible by the EEIG was *sui generis* insofar as it combined elements of both partnerships and more permanent forms of cooperation. For this reason, one does not find a reference to equivalent national

33 SCE Regulation, consideration 1.
34 See Council Regulation 1435/2003 of 22 July 2003 on the Statute for a European Cooperative Society (SCE), considerations 4 and 5 respectively.
35 SCE Regulation, consideration 12.
36 SCE Regulation, consideration 2 (italics added).
37 SCE Regulation, consideration 6.

structures being inadequate in the Community legislator's explanation behind the EEIG Regulation, as in the vast majority of Member States at the time no such structure was available.[38] Nevertheless, the absence of directly corresponding legal forms at national level does not mean that the EU regimes for EU activities rationale underlying the other European company law OIs cannot have been behind the EEIG too, for the existence or otherwise of direct national equivalents is not an essential competent of this rationale. Fundamentally, the idea is one of establishing European legal regimes for intra-Community activities, and for this to make sense it is not a prerequisite that there be parallel frameworks provided by the domestic laws of the Member States. That this is so is evidenced by the preamble to the EEIG Regulation, where it is stated that, in order to increase the unity of the single market, 'a legal framework which facilitates the adaptation of their activities to the economic conditions of the Community should be created for natural persons, companies, firms and other legal bodies [by allowing them] to cooperate effectively across frontiers'.[39] Thus, the legislator's conception of 'adaptation' of economic activities to the Community dimension can be traced all the way back to its very first optional regime.[40]

EU OIs in the area of procedural law

What, then, of the European OIs in the area of procedural law? Are these measures also expressly motivated by the rationale of EU regimes for EU activities? Given that this appears to be the case with the OIs in the areas of European IP law and company law, one might expect the answer to this question to be in the affirmative. Yet, this is by no means self-evident. In fact, what is certain is that the EU regimes for EU activities rationale is not immediately apparent from a perusal of the legislative considerations put forward in support of the EU procedural law OIs. In particular, the preambles of the Regulations establishing the European Enforcement Order (EEO),[41] European Order for Payment Procedure (EPO)[42] and European Small Claims Procedure (ESCP)[43] do not employ the kind of phraseology with which we have become familiar in discussing the motivations provided for the company and IP law OIs. One does not find any use of the language of 'adaptation' of private

38 Although one does find in the Commission's original proposal for a Regulation on a European cooperation grouping the affirmation that the various forms available under national laws under which cooperation of this nature *could* take place 'are not suitable for cooperation at Community level precisely because they are the creatures of national legal systems'; Proposal for a regulation of the Council on the European cooperation grouping (ECG), COM(73) 2046 (submitted to the Council by the Commission on 21 December 1973), consideration 2.

39 Consideration 1.

40 See also Basedow 2015, p. 288.

41 Regulation 805/2004 of the European Parliament and of the Council of 21 April 2004 creating a European Enforcement Order for uncontested claims.

42 Regulation 1896/2006 of the European Parliament and of the Council of 12 December 2006 creating a European order for payment procedure.

43 Regulation 861/2007 of the European Parliament and of the Council of 11 July 2007 establishing a European Small Claims Procedure.

activities to the scale of the Community, or of offering legal conditions similar to those obtaining in a national market, or of releasing individuals from the obligation to make use of territorially-limited national legal systems. Of course the use of such phrases is not decisive, but they do serve to render the rationale more explicit, and so the fact that they are not present in the considerations behind the procedural law OIs entails that the rationale will only be identifiable through close examination – if at all.

Now, before enquiring more deeply into the question of whether the logic of EU regimes for EU activities features among the EU legislator's justifications for the EEO, EPO and ESCP, it is worth briefly recalling its key elements. These are, first, the provision of a European-level legal regime to which Member States are affiliated that is, second, designed for private actors engaged primarily in cross-border operations within the internal market, inasmuch as it allows such actors to transcend the territorial constraints and legal idiosyncrasies of national regimes. This reminder is useful because, with this in mind, it could still be expected that the logic may be detectable in the explanatory texts pertaining to the EU procedural law OIs. For, as we saw from our depiction of these OIs, the European legislator's determination to adopt common procedural rules on small claims and uncontested claims stemmed from a desire to facilitate cross-border litigation and the free movement of judgments, given the rise in the potential number of cross-border disputes resulting from the growing use of the basic rights of free movement in the internal market. In other words, as the European Council put it in its Tampere Conclusions of 1999,[44] a 'genuine European Area of Justice' necessitates that natural and legal persons in this Area not be dissuaded from seeking to assert legal rights by the incongruity and complexness of the territorially-constrained Member State legal systems. So it would not come as too much of a surprise to find that the Community legislator does actually evince the EU regimes for EU activities logic in the explicative passages relating to these OIs.

Sure enough, this line of argumentation is expressed in the preambles to both the Regulation establishing the European Order for Payment Procedure and that establishing the European Small Claims Procedure. To begin with the former, it was noted that the main purpose of the EOP Regulation was to introduce a pan-European procedure for the recovery of undisputed debts in cross-border cases, and to expedite the cross-border enforcement of judgments delivered following this procedure.[45] And while the European legislator acknowledges in the preamble to the Regulation that '[a]ll Member States are trying to tackle the issue of mass recovery of uncontested claims', it nevertheless maintains that 'both the content of national legislation and the performance of domestic procedures vary substantially' and that 'the procedures currently in existence are frequently either inadmissible or

44 Tampere European Council, 15 and 16 October 1999, Presidency conclusions.

45 Hence, as the Community legislator explains in the preamble to the EOP Regulation, this was considered to be a measure 'in the field of judicial cooperation in civil matters having cross-border implications and needed for the proper functioning of the internal market', or, more specifically, for the gradual establishment of 'an area of freedom, security and justice in which the free movement of persons is ensured' (consideration 1).

impracticable in cross-border cases'.[46] In other words, according to the legislator, existing national procedures for the recovery of uncontested claims are hindered by the territorial limitations as well as the peculiarities of national legal systems, and this is why it was necessary to establish a European Order for Payment procedure in order to ensure efficient access to justice in cross-border cases.[47] This is therefore consistent with the idea that this EU optional instrument in the area of procedural law is also directed towards the promotion of Community-scale activities - the activity here consisting of freedom of movement and ensuing litigation - by enabling private actors to surmount the constraints of domestic procedures, which create particular difficulties in cross-border cases.

Equally, a similar concern is articulated as part of the motivation for the ESCP Regulation adopted some months later, which as we have seen was also intended to make available a EU-wide procedure (this time for the cross-border recovery of claims of a limited amount) accompanied by common rules for the recognition and enforcement of resulting judgments. In the preamble reference is again made to the drawbacks of national systems, and once more an emphasis is put on cross-border cases, in which the legislator considers that '[t]he obstacles to obtaining a fast and inexpensive judgment are exacerbated'.[48] And this accentuation of the obstacles faced by litigants involved especially in cross-border situations is even more evident in the proposal for the ESCP Regulation,[49] in which the Commission explains that, whereas 'the potential number of cross-border disputes is rising as a consequence of the increasing use of the ... rights of free movement of persons, goods and services', individuals and businesses 'may face difficulties when they want to pursue their claims in another Member State', particularly extra costs (of legal representation, translation, travel etc.).[50] Admittedly, the Commission does also give reasons for extending the availability of the ESCP to purely 'internal' cases because, as was noted previously, it had originally envisaged that the scope of the procedure would cover such cases too.[51] Nonetheless, its focus in the ESCP proposal remains unequivocally on the needs of litigants active in more than one Member State, and especially on the question of 'accessibility', which in the Commission's view is 'particularly relevant for those operating in several Member States and being spared the need to make themselves familiar with the procedural law of every one of them by the availability of a uniform European Small Claims Procedure'.[52] Here too, then, the legislator's argumentation is consonant with the notion of a European regime

46 Consideration 7.

47 See EOP Regulation, consideration 8.

48 Consideration 7.

49 Proposal for a Regulation establishing a European Small Claims Procedure, COM(2005) 87 final.

50 *Ibid.*, p. 3.

51 Indeed this is also the case with the Commission's original proposal for the EOP Regulation (COM(2004) 173 final), which also emphasizes the needs of cross-border litigants while at the same time putting the case for including wholly domestic disputes within the scope of the procedure (cf. p. 6 *et seq.*).

52 Proposal for a Regulation establishing a European Small Claims Procedure, COM(2005) 87 final, p. 7.

that is designed to enable private actors engaged in intra-EU activities to transcend domestic legal systems; although in the case of the ESCP, the legislator's explanation appears to concentrate more on the differences between national procedural laws and less on the territorial limitations on their applicability.

So while it may not be instantaneously recognizable, the rationale of EU regimes for EU activities is at any rate discernible in the legislator's explanation behind the EOP Regulation, as well as (at least to a certain extent) the ESCP Regulation, even if it is not made explicit. When it comes to the first EU procedural law OI to be adopted, however, the rationale is all but imperceptible. The single noteworthy indication in the preamble to the EEO Regulation is contained in the first recital where, as in the Regulations that followed it, the legislator affirms the need for the Community to adopt measures in the area of judicial cooperation in civil matters for the proper functioning of the internal market, in order to ensure 'the free movement of persons' in an area of freedom, security and justice.[53] Even in this one familiar passage, however, there is no mention of 'cross-border implications', in spite of the fact that, as has been observed, the EEO Regulation was founded on a legal base authorizing measures having such implications, like the EOP and ESCP Regulations. Nor is there any discussion of cross border cases in the subsequent passages. To be sure, it is still arguable that the EEO, as an optional instrument intended to accelerate and simplify 'access to enforcement in a Member State other than that in which' a judgment on an uncontested claim has been given[54] (and thereby a measure meeting a legal requirement of 'cross-border implications') *is* in fact inspired by the same ideology of EU regimes for EU activities recited by the Community legislator in the EOP and ESCP Regulations. But the point here remains that, if this is so, it is certainly not mentioned by the legislator in the background to the EEO Regulation.

EU OI in the area of contract law

The remaining EU OI to be considered is the 2011 proposal for a Common European Sales Law.[55] Speaking always about *express intentions*, the picture in the case of this EU OI is clearer than it is with regard to the EEO. Indeed it is largely comparable to the example of the ESCP, in the sense that while the Commission does not utilize the tell-tale terminology of 'adaptation', the conception of EU regimes for EU activities is still visible to a degree in the proposal's Explanatory Memorandum, which again focuses on the needs of cross-border operators in the internal market. In fact the Commission highlights this concern from the very beginning of its explanation, proclaiming in the first paragraph that:

> 'Differences in contract law between Member States hinder traders and consumers who want to engage in cross-border trade within the internal market. The obstacles which stem from these differences dissuade traders ... from entering cross border trade

53 EEO Regulation, consideration 1.
54 EEO Regulation, consideration 8.
55 Proposal for a Regulation on a Common European Sales Law, COM(2011) 635 final.

> or expanding to new Member States' markets. Consumers are hindered from accessing products offered by traders in other Member States.'[56]

It then goes on to explain that the reason why different national contract laws render cross-border trade more complicated and expensive vis-à-vis domestic trade is that traders in cross-border transactions must discover and adhere to potentially applicable provisions in the legal systems of the various Member States. More precisely, traders need to negotiate the applicable contract law in transactions with other businesses, and adapt their contracts with consumers to the requirements of the law of the consumer's 'home' State.[57] Therefore, as already mentioned in our presentation of the CESL, the main aim of the proposal was to expand intra-EU business trade and consumer purchases by giving market actors the possibility to opt into a uniform contract law regime common to all of the EU Member States. This way, according to the Commission, traders would be able to apply the CESL 'in all their cross-border dealings within the European Union instead of having to adapt to different national contract laws, provided that the other party to the contract agrees'; and, as a result, 'take better advantage of the internal market by expanding their trade across borders'.[58] So, in other words, the CESL was foreseen as a single set of common rules at European level permitting private actors involved in trans-frontier dealings to overcome the divergent (though not territorially limited)[59] contract laws of the Member States.[60]

To sum up, then, the expression of the conception of EU regimes for EU activities can be identified, at least in one form or another, in virtually all of the existing and proposed optional instruments within the EU legal order.

(b) Avoiding Undue Disruption of National Legal Systems

The second (and secondary) justification for the shift towards OIs expressed by the EU legislator is the desire to avoid undue disruption of national legal systems, which is premised on the idea that EU OIs leave national legal orders 'untouched' because – as ex-Commissioner Monti also notes in his independent study of 2010 – the 28th regime is 'a EU framework alternative to but not replacing national rules'.[61] In other words, unlike EU similarization measures, Union optional instruments do not in principle require any modification or amendment of *existing* provisions in the Member States[62] and, as such, they constitute a way for the Union to attain its objectives while at the same time ensuring that disturbance of domestic legal orders

56 *Ibid.*, p. 2.
57 *Ibid.*
58 *Ibid.*, p. 4.
59 Since it is already possible for cross-border operators to choose the law of a national jurisdiction as a 'common regime' to govern their transactions. See *supra* Chapter 3, CESL Description.
60 See also Proposal for a Regulation on a Common European Sales Law, COM(2011) 635 final, consideration 8.
61 Monti 2010, p. 93.
62 On this point see Chapter 2, section B.

is kept to a *minimum*. In order to demonstrate this contributory rationale, it is of course necessary to refer again to the various specific examples of EU OIs. It is helpful to discuss them in a different order to the preceding section, however, since (as we will see) the rationale of leaving national legal orders untouched is also (and even more so) cited to varying degrees, and in some cases not at all. The most unequivocal indication is furnished this time by the European procedural law OIs, and so it is with these OIs that we shall begin.

EU OIs in the area of procedural law

The desire to avoid undue disruption of the domestic legal orders of the Member States patently features as an element in the legislative reasoning put forward for both the EOP and the ESCP. Starting with the former, the original proposal for a Regulation creating a European Order for Payment Procedure[63] contains an intriguingly elaborate explanation of this aspect of the optional instrument method, which is worth quoting at length. In explaining why the proposed EOP Regulation met the requirement of proportionality, the Commission stated:

> 'It is particularly essential to underscore the effects of the combination of the legal instrument chosen (Regulation) with the optional nature of the European order for payment procedure in relation to comparable mechanisms under the national procedural law of the Member States. Whilst ensuring the uniformity and direct applicability of the procedure, the Regulation proposed here would only oblige Member States to make the European recovery mechanism available as an additional tool. It would force them neither to abandon their pre-existing legislation on orders for payment or any other procedure for the collection of undisputed debts nor to modify such legislation to bring it into line with Community law. Hence this proposal for a Regulation which leaves untouched the Member States' right to continue the application of the domestic rules alongside the European order for payment encroaches much less on their procedural systems than a Directive that would require an adaptation of national legislation to the standards set in that instrument. This legislative technique, in fact, assures a minimum level in the efficiency of the recovery of uncontested claims but it permits Member States that have developed an even better-functioning domestic system to retain it.'[64]

The value of this passage for our purposes lies not only in the fact that it expounds the avoidance of undue disruption argument in unambiguous terms, but also that it clearly relates this argument to the distinct 'legislative technique' that is the EU optional instrument. As stated, the premise for the argument is the fact that the optional instrument is available as an alternative to existing legal equivalents (direct or otherwise) at national level, thereby recalling one of the defining characteristics of EU OIs. This is said to entail that the application of the equivalent regimes of the Member States continues 'untouched', in the specific sense that the OI requires them neither to be abandoned nor modified. However, the Commission does not mean to say that the OI leaves national systems entirely unaffected. Bearing in mind that OIs are established by means of Regulations, they are still directly applicable in the

63 COM(2004) 173 final.

64 *Ibid.*, p. 8.

Member State legal orders. Hence the conclusion is that the OI is *less* intrusive of national systems than EU legislation necessitating approximation of domestic rules (i.e. similarization). And this contrast between the nature of the OI and the similarization method is also emphasized in the preamble to the EOP Regulation that was subsequently adopted, where it is stated that the EOP 'should serve as an additional and optional means for the claimant, who remains free to resort to a procedure provided by national law. Accordingly, this Regulation neither replaces nor harmonises the existing mechanisms for the recovery of uncontested claims under national law'.[65]

The rationale of avoiding excessive interference in national systems is expressed in a similarly overt way in the legislative background to the ESCP Regulation as well. Indeed the proposal for the ESCP contains an identical passage to that just described in the original EOP proposal, meaning the above account of this rationale is reproduced in full. Furthermore, the Commission adds that since, beyond the provisions of the Regulation itself, the ESCP is to be governed by the domestic procedural law of the Member State in which it is pursued, 'the introduction of a European Small Claims Procedure does not entail the need for further approximation of national procedural legislation and thus keeps interference with domestic law to an absolute minimum'.[66] In other words, the Commission observes that not only does this OI technique not require any approximation of national laws per se, but it also does not require any such approximation for the purpose of its application when it is selected because, in those areas or on those points not regulated by its establishing Regulation, an optional instrument relies on the residual applicability of pre-existing national laws,[67] without necessitating the approximation of such laws. Thus, according to the Commission, as an alternative to national regimes EU OIs do not entail approximation of national laws, whether they are applicable or not. And equally, like the EOP Regulation, the preamble to the ESCP Regulation also stresses the alternative nature of optional instruments, noting that the ESCP 'should simplify and speed up litigation concerning small claims in cross-border cases, whilst reducing costs, by offering an optional tool in addition to the possibilities existing under the laws of the Member States, which will remain unaffected'.[68] Again, the use of the term 'unaffected' here is intended to mean that the OI does not necessitate the abandonment or modification of regimes already existing in the Member States, in the same manner as the word 'untouched' is used in the European legislator's explanation behind the EOP Regulation. It should not be understood in the wider sense of leaving domestic regimes completely uninfluenced, as the legislator does not claim that the OI does not encroach at all upon national procedural systems.

On the other hand, there is no comparable statement in the preamble to the EEO Regulation. This may be understandable because, as we have seen, the European Enforcement Order (unlike the EOP and ESCP) was envisaged as a direct

65 Consideration 10.
66 COM(2005) 87 final, p. 7.
67 On this see further Chapter 5, section A.2(b).
68 Consideration 8.

extension of the legislator's efforts to bypass the *exequatur* procedure that commenced with the Brussels *acquis*, and notably the Brussels I Regulation of 2000, which similarized Member State procedural rules regulating the circumstances in which recognition of a foreign judgment could be refused. In this sense, the EEO was proposed as an alternative to an already similarized legal framework, albeit for the specific case of uncontested claims, inasmuch as creditors meeting the relevant conditions would have the option of pursuing enforcement either on the basis of the EEO or the Brussels I Regulation. Therefore, it would not be entirely correct to describe the EEO purely as an alternative to existing 'national' regimes, nor for that matter to speak of leaving such regimes untouched, at least as long as the EEO is viewed as following directly on from a broader legislative move against intermediate recognition procedures that also includes measures of similarization. At any rate, the fact is that the desire to avoid undue disruption of domestic legal orders is not mentioned among the legislator's express justifications for the EEO. It is true that the preamble does point out that the EEO Regulation 'does not imply an obligation for the Member States to adapt their national legislation to the minimum procedural standards set out [in the Regulation]. It provides an incentive to that end by making available a more efficient and rapid enforceability of judgments in other Member States only if those minimum standards are met'.[69] But the preamble does not characterize the EEO as a whole as an optional tool introduced with the aim (*inter alia*) of leaving national regimes provided under the laws of the Member States unaffected, in contrast to the procedural law OIs that were subsequently adopted.

EU OI in the area of contract law

Like the EOP and ESCP, the justification of avoiding undue encroachment upon domestic legal orders is also clearly declared in the 2011 proposal for a Regulation on a Common European Sales Law.[70] The explanation is not identical in the case of the CESL, however. Owing to its conception not as a 28th regime but as a 'second contract law regime' existing within the legal orders of all of the Member States,[71] the European legislator discusses it as an alternative *form of* (rather than an alternative *to*) harmonization. Hence, according to the European Commission, the CESL 'harmonises the national contract laws of the Member States not by requiring amendments to the pre-existing national contract law, but by creating within each Member State's national law a second contract law regime ... that is identical throughout the European Union and will exist alongside the pre-existing rules of national contract law'.[72] Still, as this statement makes clear, this 'other form of harmonization' consists of providing an alternative to existing national regimes and therefore, notwithstanding the difference in the way it is described, it is plainly the same premise as that noted in relation to the procedural law OIs (and connected to

69 Consideration 19.
70 COM(2011) 635 final.
71 See Chapter 2, section B.3.
72 COM(2011) 635 final, p. 8.

the very nature of OIs). Indeed it is on the basis of this premise that the Commission goes on to make the point (again in sustaining the proportionality of the proposed optional instrument) that '[t]he fact that the Common European Sales Law represents an optional set of rules applying only in cross-border cases means...it can lower barriers to cross-border trade without interfering with deeply embedded national legal systems and traditions'; the reason being that the CESL would be 'an optional regime in addition to pre-existing contract law rules without replacing them'.[73] So even if the OI proposed in the area of contract law was labelled as a second domestic regime common to the Member States - and, as such, was not contrasted with the similarization method - like other EU OIs it too was explicitly intended to leave the application of existing national contract law regimes unaffected insofar as they were to be neither repealed nor reformed. At the same time, the Commission did not seek to claim that the CESL, as a second contract law regime available within each of the Member States, would not affect national legal systems at all, but concluded instead that it would only go 'as far as necessary'.

EU OIs in the area of intellectual property law

As far as regards the EU OIs in the area of intellectual property law, one also finds allusions to the notion of averting excessive disturbance of the legal systems of the Member States in the legislative explanations behind some of these instruments, although it is not laid out in quite so categorical terms. The preamble to the Community Trade Mark Regulation, for example, affirms that the 'Community law relating to trade marks nevertheless does not replace the laws of the Member States on trade marks',[74] thereby alluding once more to the premise of leaving domestic legal orders untouched (in the specific sense noted above). Yet the legislator does not use this premise as a basis for arguing that the CTM Regulation is intended to avoid unnecessary intrusion into the pre-existing Member State regimes, as it does in the case of the EOP, the ESCP and the CESL proposal. Instead, it cites a more specific train of thought, according to which '[i]t would not in fact appear to be justified to require undertakings to apply for registration of their trade marks as Community trademarks. National trade marks continue to be necessary for those undertakings which do not want protection of their trade marks at Community level'.[75] In other words, rather than explaining the desire to limit EU legislative intervention through the CTM from the perspective of the Member States, the legislator does so with reference to the position of private individuals making use of pre-existing national regimes. In a comparable way to the EEO Regulation (but even more so), this may be explicable for the simple reason that, as previously indicated, the main rules of Member State law in the field were similarized by means of an approximating measure (i.e. the Trade Mark Directive) prior to the introduction of the CTM Regulation, which was considered to be a corollary to the CTM Regulation itself. Of course, it still makes sense to speak of the CTM providing an alternative to

73 *Ibid.*, p. 10.
74 Consideration 6.
75 *Ibid.*

national trade mark regimes, even if these have been similarized. However, the adoption of a parallel directive modifying and/or replacing national laws does mean that it would make considerably less sense for the legislator to point to a desire to leave national legal systems unaffected (or again at least as long as the CTM is regarded as part of broader legislative action in the field including also measures of approximation).

Equally, a comparable explanation can be found in the preamble to the Regulation implementing enhanced cooperation in the area of the creation of unitary patent protection, where the legislator maintains that the Unitary Patent Regulation 'should be without prejudice to the right of the participating Member States to grant national patents and should not replace the participating Member States' laws on patents. Patent applicants should remain free to obtain ... a national patent'.[76] Although, as this statement indicates, the decision not to replace national patent rights with the UP actually stems from an express desire to protect the existing powers of *both* Member States (i.e. the power to grant national patent rights) and private actors (i.e. the ability to obtain national patent rights). In fact, it would be reasonable for the legislator to argue that the UP is intended to avoid unnecessary disruption of national legal systems on the ground that it leaves national patent laws unaffected (that is, not replaced or modified), for unlike the CTM and CD Regulations, the UP has not been preceded by any accompanying EU measure similarizing the main rules on patent protection in the Member States. However, this argument is not made explicit in the UP Regulation.

On the other hand, there is no reference whatsoever to the rationale of avoiding excessive interference in domestic legal orders in the proposal for or preamble to the Community Design Regulation (perhaps because the core rules of Member State design law would also be similarized by a related directive on the legal protection of designs), and only a small hint to this effect in the preamble to the Community Plant Variety Right Regulation (where it is stated that 'it is appropriate to create a Community regime which, *although co-existing with national regimes,* allows for the grant of industrial property rights valid throughout the Community').[77]

EU OIs in the area of company law

Finally, it must be acknowledged that the logic of avoiding undue disruption of the legal systems of the Member States does not feature in the legislative background to any of the OIs in the area of European company law. One does come across traces of this reasoning along the lines of that just mentioned in relation to the CPVR Regulation. For instance, the preamble to the Regulation on the Statute for a European Company asserts that 'provision should be made for the creation, side by *side with companies governed by a particular national law,* of companies formed and carrying on business under the law created by a Community Regulation directly

[76] Consideration 26.

[77] Consideration 3 (italics added).

applicable in all Member States',[78] which implies that the legislator wishes existing domestic company regimes to remain unaffected by the SE.[79] However, a more elaborate and explicit indication of the rationale is not present in any of the company law OIs under scrutiny.

So the rationale of leaving national legal orders unaffected is also identifiable to some degree or another in many EU OIs, although there are at the same time a number of EU optional instruments where an apparent reference to this reasoning cannot be found.

2. *The Case for EU OIs*

It was acknowledged at the outset of the preceding account of the EU legislator's express motivations that these are unlikely to constitute the only reasons driving the legislator's increasing use of the OI method in order to attain its goals, and in any event they certainly do not encompass all of the arguments that can and have been made in favour of legislating by means of OIs. Nonetheless, our description of the explicit justifications for OIs is helpful, not only because it serves as a natural point of departure for a deeper exploration into the arguments supporting EU OIs, but also because the double-edged rationale we identified revealed a common theme that, as we shall see, pervades both the broader political debate within the EU and the academic discourse to date. For, in our discussion of the justification of EU regimes for EU activities and that of leaving national legal orders unaffected, it became clear that both are presented as advantages EU OIs offer over the similarization method which, due to its very essence, cannot provide the same benefits. And it is this line of reasoning, based on a comparison of these two methods of EU lawmaking, that recurs time and again in the case for EU OIs. The arguments put forth may be, *inter alia*, of a political, practical, and/or economic nature, but in every case reference is made to a comparative advantage of the OI method over measures similarizing national laws.

Now it becomes necessary to examine these other reasons that have been adduced for legislating by means of EU OIs, in order to gain a more complete understanding of the general case for the OI method. Only once these arguments have been elaborated will our attention shift to the case against EU OIs, with a view to eventually arriving at an overall evaluation of this legislative method. For the purposes of clarity, the arguments are discussed in the following under separate headings, but this is not intended to imply that there are no inter-connections between them. On the contrary, it will also be seen that many of the reasons are inextricably intertwined.

78 Consideration 6 (italics added).

79 See also Commission Memorandum to Parliament, Council and the two sides of industry on the Statute for the European Company of 8 June 1988, COM(88) 320 final, p. 7, where the Commission affirms that '[a]s an optional instrument, the European Statute will coexist with the other national company forms, which will remain in being'.

(a) Political Impracticability of Similarization in Certain Areas

The first additional argument sustaining the OI method that should be noted is a relatively simple one. This is the view that, in certain fields of EU competence, legislation approximating the laws of the Member States is impracticable, if not impossible, whereas legislation establishing an optional instrument in such fields is not. This is very much a political argument, according to which the *form* of EU OIs, being, so as it is claimed, binding instruments that are less disruptive of national legal orders, renders them - and therefore also their legal *content* - more readily acceptable to and easily receivable by the Member States than binding measures approximating national laws. As such, the EU OI is believed to be a legislative method that can overcome the political impasse preventing EU proposals for measures similarizing domestic provisions from being adopted in certain more 'sensitive' areas of law (and particularly of private law). By framing the substance of proposals in the form of an optional instrument instead, political agreement on the given legislative proposal as a whole and its proffered legal content in particular is said to become a more feasible prospect. Clearly then, this argument is closely linked to the motivation of avoiding excessive interference in national legal systems discussed in the previous section, and also more broadly a continuation of the comparative advantage line of argumentation underlying both stems of the EU legislator's express rationale behind EU OIs. In fact, the consideration that optional instruments are a form of legislation capable of being adopted in cases where the necessary political consensus on similarization measures is unattainable could be characterized as an implicit motivation of the European legislator for making use of OIs.

That political expediency is another element in the rationale of the legislator can actually be gleaned from official texts and studies at European level pertaining to EU OIs. In particular, the European Commission itself has asserted this viewpoint by way of follow-up to an own-initiative opinion of the European Economic and Social Committee (EESC) published at the end of May 2010. It is, however, best classified as an implied and not an express motivation behind the legislator's employment of the OI method, for two reasons. Firstly, it is not mentioned in any of the EU Regulations or Commission proposals for EU Regulations establishing any of the optional instruments that have been proposed and/or adopted to date. Furthermore, as we shall see, even in those instances in which mention of this argument has been recorded in some form of EU documentation, it has been set out in rather vague terms.

In its own-initiative opinion of May 2010, entitled 'The 28th regime - less lawmaking',[80] which was adopted almost unanimously,[81] the EESC offered insights into the perceived advantages of EU OIs over harmonizing measures at the political level. It began with the observation that '[i]n recent times, on many occasions and

80 Opinion of the European Economic and Social Committee on 'The 28th regime - an alternative allowing less lawmaking at Community level' (own-initiative opinion) CESE 758/2010, available at: <www.eesc.europa.eu/?i=portal.en.int-opinions.10007>.

81 To be precise, the opinion was adopted by 124 votes to 8 with 20 abstentions.

during numerous events, several voices from civil society have raised the question as to whether an optional regime could be adopted as an alternative to the traditional way of harmonising legislation in specific areas',[82] thereby immediately emphasizing the significance of comparison between EU OIs and the similarization method in the case for using the 28th regime. Next, it added that, 'also, references to the possible use of a so called 28th regime began to appear in various Commission and EP documents, mainly relating to important subjects where the desired full harmonisation was expected to be neither easy nor achievable'.[83] In other words, according to the EESC, the main reason for these EU decision-making institutions to pursue the OI method was as an alternative to similarization in cases where the latter was unrealistic from a legislative perspective. Hence the EESC considered this as a motivation for EU OIs being used in such circumstances. The EESC's opinion then went on to identify a number of concrete examples of occasions in which this approach has been followed (not to mention of other areas in which this approach could need to be taken). Specifically, it indicated, *inter alia*, company law, intellectual property law, contract law and succession law as areas in which this reasoning has prompted the EU legislator to move to legislating by means of OIs, suggesting that most if not all of the fields of European law under scrutiny in the present study constitute examples of situations where the legislator is having recourse to the OI method because the desired full harmonization is 'neither easy nor achievable'. The EESC regarded this to be the case especially in the area of contract law, on which it focuses the attention of its opinion; and this is hardly surprising. Certainly, given the well-documented resistance of Member States to similarization proposals in the (consumer) contract law field to date, one might expect that the EU legislator could be resorting to the OI method in this area due to the political impracticability of similarizing measures.

And sure enough, in its response to the EESC opinion[84] (as expounded by Commissioner Reding), the Commission confirmed that the perception of the EESC is correct. After noting that '[t]he idea for optional instruments has been embraced by independent studies, such as the Monti Report … and by political authorities, such as the European Parliament',[85] the follow-up goes on to affirm that 'the Commission is considering a complementary optional instrument among other solutions for areas *where full harmonisation is not possible* (e.g. general contract law)'.[86] So the Commission plainly recognizes that the unfeasibility of traditional approximating measures does form part of the rationale behind the reliance of the EU legislator on the OI method in certain areas of competence, including notably the field of contract law. In addition, as regards why this legislative method could be especially pertinent for European contract law, the Commission's response

82 Opinion of the European Economic and Social Committee on 'The 28th regime – an alternative allowing less lawmaking at Community level' (own-initiative opinion) CESE 758/2010, 1.1.
83 *Ibid.*, 1.2.
84 Follow-up of the European Commission on the EESC opinion on 'The 28th regime – an alternative allowing less lawmaking at Community level', available at: <www.eesc.europa.eu/resources/docs/int-499_table_follow-up-by-the-commission_13012011_int-499.pdf>.
85 *Ibid.*, p. 1.
86 *Ibid.*, p. 2 (italics added).

points out that '[i]t would be a "neutral" additional and voluntary regime that would co-exist in parallel to the national contract laws. It would not interfere with national law …'.[87] So it is also apparent that the reason why the Commission believes that similarization measures constitute a legislative impossibility in such areas and why, on the other hand, legislation enacting optional instruments would be realizable, lies in the extent to which the former, by contrast to the latter, intrudes into national legal systems.

Having said this, neither the Commission nor the EESC provides a precise explanation of the connection between the (averred) less interfering nature of the OI method and the instrument's legislative feasibility. The argument is not articulated in a comprehensive manner and, as a result, is not directly intelligible. An additional hint is contained in the *Monti* Report cited by Commissioner Reding, where it is stated that:

> 'Harmonisation through regulations can be most appropriate when regulating new sectors from scratch and easier when the areas concerned allow for limited interaction between EU rules and national systems. In other instances, *where upfront harmonisation is not the solution*, it is worthwhile exploring the idea of a 28th regime, a EU framework alternative to but not replacing national rules.'[88]

This implies that it is in more traditional sectors necessitating more than limited interaction between EU rules and national systems that the '28th regime', as an alternative legal framework, is a legislative 'solution'; or at least an easier one than similarization, which would impinge to a significantly greater extent upon domestic systems. However, this still does not expressly clarify why exactly the OI method, by leaving national rules unaffected in such areas, is more appropriate or easier than similarization in such areas of law. It is therefore necessary to 'read between the lines' in order to arrive at a complete understanding of this line of argumentation. Of course one could well imagine what the connecting factor might be, but the point is that this is not stated explicitly.

At any rate, it is submitted that the connection is in all likelihood the one indicated at the outset, namely that the OI method is considered to be more politically palatable to the Member States. In other words, since European rules embodied in OIs do not require any modification of existing rules at national level, the argument is that Member States are more inclined to accept them, and this is what makes OIs a more suitable solution in certain fields of EU competence. Thus, the difficulty or even impossibility of attaining the necessary political agreement on legislation similarizing national rules in certain areas is indubitably another important argument made in favour of, and by the European legislator to support, legislating by means of OIs. This is not to say, however, that this argument necessarily holds true. Rather, just as the veracity of the claim that the EU OIs avoid disruption of national legal orders itself is yet to be scrutinized, the question

87 *Ibid.*, p. 1.
88 Monti 2010, p. 93 (italics added).

whether the OI method does actually provide a legislative solution in areas of law where similarization is impracticable is also addressed at a later stage.[89]

(b) Regulatory Competition and the Law Market

The next prominent argument advanced in support of the case for EU OIs that should be considered is of a more theoretical, if not ideological, nature than the relatively pragmatic point regarding the political impracticability of similarization. Also, unlike the latter, it is an argument that has been made predominantly by legal commentators in academic circles, and not so much in the context of the democratic process at EU-level (although the European Commission has alluded to it in two of its proposals establishing an optional instrument). For both of these reasons, it is a rather more complex rationale, comprising a number of constituent elements. Still, in essence, it can be boiled down to the following fundamental contention: that EU OIs are preferable to the similarization method because they allow for the possibility of what is commonly referred to as *regulatory competition*, whereas similarization does not. Generally speaking, the term 'regulatory competition' denotes a phenomenon whereby different legislative authorities compete with each other in the legal rules that they provide to govern a given area of activity, with the aim of alluring private actors to make use of their respective laws and legal regimes. In other words:

> '[T]here are producers of individual legal rules and entire legal regimes (contract laws, company laws, laws of procedure, etc.), as well as customers who shop for these products. The customers will make choices and 'buy' or 'opt into' those rules or sets of rules that best meet their preferences. Thus, there is 'regulatory competition' between the producers to the extent that they will only be able to 'attract business' if they offer an attractive regulatory framework ...'[90]

Accordingly, regulatory competition can only arise (if at all) in situations where there is a plurality of distinct legal regimes that 'not infrequently attach different legal consequences to identical fact patterns',[91] and private parties have at least some degree of freedom to choose – in one way or another – between such regimes. In the absence of either one of these basic conditions, there can be no competition in the regulatory sense.[92]

In itself, regulatory competition is not a new phenomenon. In fact, regulatory competition has been an important topic of discussion among lawyers and economists for many years.[93] The concept first surfaced at the turn of the 20th

89 See section B.
90 Vogenauer 2013, p. 228.
91 Vogenauer 2013, p. 230.
92 In fact, many would add a third basic condition, namely the availability of information on solutions offered by different regimes, so that private parties have not only the freedom but also the *means* to choose between them (see notably Kieninger 2002). For the purposes of the present study, however, the issue of information is discussed as an additional (rather than a fundamental) requirement for regulatory competition; see *infra*, section A.3(b)(i).
93 See Rühl 2013a, p. 63.

century in the context of US company law, and specifically the now-infamous 'charter competition' that emerged between different US states seeking to entice companies to incorporate in their jurisdiction. This competition began in 1888, when the US state of New Jersey enacted a modernized, liberalized incorporation statute.[94] Attracted by the financial benefit New Jersey derived from this reform in the course of the subsequent decade - with a number of 'industry-dominant' companies all having incorporated in that state during that period - 'other states sought to both emulate and compete with New Jersey by offering even more "liberal" state corporation laws or by charging lower incorporation fees and franchise taxes'.[95] In particular, Delaware adopted a similarly reformed corporate charter in 1889, which eventually led to it becoming the preeminent state of incorporation in the US from the 1920s onwards.[96] This series of events was made possible because the federal US legal system has traditionally treated company law as a matter for the states' governments,[97] and because private actors, in this case, businesses, 'found that they could choose their place of incorporation and could also cheaply reincorporate in any state they preferred'.[98] That is, both essential conditions for regulatory competition to be possible were satisfied: the existence of multiple regimes providing different rules, and the ability of private actors to choose between them.

These developments sparked a great deal of discussion in the next decades, with the debate initially focusing on the particular case of US charter competition, especially after the publication of a seminal work on American corporations by Berle and Means in 1932, who pleaded against the onset of such competition.[99] In later years, attention started to shift to the idea of competitive governance in general, inspired by Charles Tiebout's economic theory of public finance published in 1956,[100] which was the first to consider the abstract notion of law as 'a product that is supplied by states and asked for by businesses and consumers'.[101] Then, following the creation of the European Economic Community and the development of the principle of mutual recognition in the internal market by the European Court of Justice, the possibility of regulatory competition in European company law began to be discussed. This signalled an expansion of the relevance of the concept beyond conflict of laws at the internal, interstate level (i.e. within a national, federal jurisdiction) to conflict of laws at the international level (i.e. between nation-states). Also, more recently, the concept has pervaded academic discourse in other areas of law (as well as other legal contexts). Most notably, it has been observed by a number of authors in the area of contract law (and again at both the interstate and international level), based on the possibility for parties to various types of contracts,

94 See McCahery & Vermeulen 2005, 789, and also Yablon 2007, p. 323 *et seq.*
95 Yablon, p. 325.
96 See McCahery & Vermeulen 2005, p. 789.
97 See McCahery & Vermeulen 2005, p. 789.
98 O'Hara & Ribstein 2009, p. 10.
99 Berle & Means 1932. The reason for the opposition of these authors to regulatory competition is discussed *infra*, section A.3(b)(i).
100 Tiebout 1956.
101 Rühl 2013a, p. 64.

commercial and consumer, to include a clause in the contract specifying the state law that is to govern their agreement.

In short, the concept of regulatory competition has long been debated in relation to situations where there is some choice of law between different national (or sub-national) jurisdictions; that is, a *horizontal choice of law*. What is novel, however, is the notion of regulatory competition arising in a supra-national context, in which private actors have a *vertical choice of law* between a regime at national- and one at supra-national level, as in the case of optional instruments in the European Union.[102] It is therefore useful to examine the principal arguments in the regulatory competition debate, with a view to seeing how these have been or can be applied to the peculiar context of EU OIs. We shall commence with the main reasons that have been advanced to explain why enabling regulatory competition (particularly between the EU decision-making bodies and the Member States) should be seen as desirable, before turning our attention to contradictory standpoints in our account of the case against EU OIs.

(i) Allowing for Legal Experimentation at EU- and National-Level

In his oft-cited article of 1956, Tiebout formulated a so-called 'exit' model of political economy. This model was predicated on the consideration that individuals are able to determine the government-provided services (or 'public goods') – including the laws – available to them, not only by voting in political elections, but also by exiting their jurisdiction and moving to another one. That is to say, governments determine the services they want to make available to individuals residing within their jurisdictions, and 'people gravitate to those places that provide the services that they desire'.[103] From this perspective, Tiebout saw the law of a given jurisdiction as part of a package of public goods available for individuals to choose by deciding where to reside. In such circumstances, he argued, a process of selection driven by the satisfaction of individual preferences occurs, ultimately resulting in a 'general equilibrium solution',[104] whereby residents are optimally distributed among different jurisdictions. This way, Tiebout sought to propose a 'market-type' basis for the satisfaction of individual preferences at the local level.

The importance of this model has endured to the present day, not least because it 'laid the foundations for this view of people not voting through parliaments, but voting with their feet',[105] a view that has since been taken up by several legal academics. One recent example[106] is a work of 2009 by O'Hara and Ribstein,[107] who build upon Tiebout's idea of law as a product to construct a conception of lawmaking competition per se. These authors agree with Tiebout that the type of consumer market in governments he describes can 'embrace laws, which

102 On this distinction see, for example, Eidenmüller 2013b.
103 O'Hara & Ribstein 2009, p. 27.
104 Tiebout, p. 424.
105 Smits 2010c, p. 72.
106 For an earlier example see in particular the seminal contribution by Romano 1985.
107 O'Hara & Ribstein 2009.

after all, are an important type of government-provided goods'.[108] However, they identify two fundamental limitations with his conception of the market for packages of public goods. The first is that the choice on which it is based is a rather crude one, in the sense that, by literally voting with their feet, individuals can only select the 'whole package' offered by a given jurisdiction. In other words, 'consumers of governments must "buy" the entire bundle of public goods associated with a particular place'.[109] This is a problem because it entails that such consumers 'may not be able to find just the right bundle of laws and other public goods. Businesses, for example, might like the regulatory environment in Nevada and South Dakota, but not the labour market or the weather'.[110] Therefore voting by physical exit is a somewhat imperfect means of satisfying individual preferences. For this reason, O'Hara and Ribstein propose a more refined form of selection, which enables people to 'choose the law separately from both other government-supplied public goods and other attributes of geographic location'.[111] This form of selection involves voting not by exit, but through (horizontal) choice of law; like, for instance, in the aforementioned areas of company law and contract law. Admittedly, as Rühl notes, the choice of law is actually often distinguished as direct in the case of, for example, contract law, where parties are able to determine the applicable law through a choice of law clause, and indirect if parties can affect facts that determine the governing law, as in the case of company law, where 'parties may - indirectly - choose the applicable corporate law by choosing the state of incorporation'.[112] But the point remains that, in either case, the individual is able to choose the law applicable to them without the need to physically move between jurisdictions. As a result, according to O'Hara and Ribstein, 'a separate market for each type of relationship can form, enabling people and firms to choose the law that suits each aspect of their economic and social lives - that is, Delaware for corporations, New York for commercial contracts, Massachusetts for mutual funds ...'.[113] This is what these authors call 'the law market'.

As well as offering a more expansive account of the market for laws, O'Hara and Ribstein also consider the implications of such a market to be wider than Tiebout's theory on public goods suggests. Specifically, this second important limitation they individuate is that Tiebout concentrates on the influence the laws and other public goods in a given jurisdiction have on an individual's decision as to where to reside, rather than contemplating the reverse. In other words, 'Tiebout never explored the fact that people's choices also may affect government-provided services, including laws. Thus, the exit option may not only give people and firms a way to avoid undesirable laws, but also provide a mechanism for pressuring governments to change those laws.'[114] This pressure is said to stem from the desire

108 O'Hara & Ribstein 2009, p. 14.
109 O'Hara & Ribstein 2009, p. 14.
110 O'Hara & Ribstein 2009, p. 14.
111 O'Hara & Ribstein 2009, p. 14.
112 Rühl 2013a, p. 65.
113 O'Hara & Ribstein 2009, p. 14.
114 O'Hara & Ribstein 2009, p. 28.

of legislators to attract individuals based in other jurisdictions to make use of their legal systems, in order to secure pecuniary and other benefits of the kind obtained by Delaware, which now derives a significant portion of its tax revenues from the initial incorporation fee and continuing franchise taxes.[115] Hence the law market O'Hara and Ribstein envision is one 'created by the mobility of at least some people, firms, and assets *and* the incentives of at least some states to compete for people, firms, and their assets by creating desired laws';[116] as it is this second element that gives rise to actual competition between legislators. For both of these reasons, then, it is utile to take these authors' depiction of law as a product as the starting point for a deeper inquiry into the concept of regulatory competition.

According to O'Hara and Ribstein, one of the central policy arguments supporting the law market they describe is that the regulatory competition that is promoted by choice-of-law clauses incentivises states and parties to experiment with novel legal rules.[117] In other words, by enabling regulatory competition through the rules of private international law, whereby private actors choose between the laws of different states, not only are the states incentivised to *introduce* legislative reforms in order to attract such individuals, but they are also induced to *test* these reforms - and eventually revise them again - according to how attractive they prove to be to private actors, as determined by their own process of experimentation. In this sense, party choice also 'provides feedback to the states regarding the appeal of the new laws'.[118] The advantage of legal experimentation of this kind, so the argument goes, is therefore that it 'can help legal systems to generate better legal rules'.[119] That is, the process of experimentation can lead states to promulgate laws that are more attractive to market actors. As one illustration of this, O'Hara and Ribstein point to another aspect of US company law, namely the occurrence of limited liability companies (LLCs). In this case, the state of Wyoming adopted the first LLC statute in 1976, allowing companies to be formed with limited liability for the owners, but 'without forcing them to incur the extra burden of the corporate tax'.[120] As firms started increasingly to form LLCs, so other states began to respond with legislation of their own; and eventually this induced *all states* in the US to adopt LLC statutes. Thus, these authors argue, regulatory competition in this instance led to improvements in the laws of various jurisdictions, at least from a market perspective.

And O'Hara and Ribstein are far from alone in making this point. Indeed prominent commentators in the European context have also adduced the advantage of legal experimentation as an argument for fostering regulatory competition between states in Europe. One of the leading proponents is Smits, who shares the view of a law market based on choice of law rather than physical exit. Smits also maintains that one of the principal advantages of competition between regulators in

115 Cf. Grundmann 2002, p. 563.
116 O'Hara & Ribstein 2009, p. 65 (italics added).
117 See O'Hara & Ribstein 2009, p. 32.
118 O'Hara & Ribstein 2009, p. 32.
119 O'Hara & Ribstein 2009, p. 32.
120 O'Hara & Ribstein 2009, p. 32.

such a market is that 'it allows experiment: looking at other countries' solutions to legal problems shows whether or not these solutions function in any way. In this respect States can indeed be seen as "experimenting laboratories"'.[121] In fact this has been a key tenet underpinning many of Smits' claims concerning law and legal systems, initially - and perhaps most markedly - against the promulgation of EU measures approximating the domestic (private) laws of the Member States. Already in an early piece on legal transplants, he defends the position that the ideal means of achieving legal uniformity in Europe is through jurisdictional competition not least because 'the insight into the way in which a (private) legal system evolves and has evolved in the past, may raise awareness as to what is the most successful road towards a future European private law'.[122] He also reaffirms this view in subsequent articles discussing European law from the perspective of evolutionary theory ('In transplanting legal rules from one country to another...the best legal rule for Europe may survive')[123] and of mixed jurisdictions ('It is likely that these types of experiment will lead to innovation: countries that see how certain legal rules and solutions are successful abroad will be tempted to adopt these for their own citizens').[124] Hence the preservation of legal experimentation is one important reason for Smits to oppose EU legislation approximating national law; as such legislation has the effect of eliminating (or at least limiting) the possibility of 'organic' legal development through international (and particularly European) regulatory competition, by imposing legal uniformity on the Member States in a centralist fashion.[125]

Similarly, other European scholars have also expressed their belief in the need to allow for legislative experimentation through regulatory competition.[126] As mentioned above, the possibility of regulatory competition itself first surfaced in European academic discourse in the specific field of company law, mirroring developments across the Atlantic. And although in Europe too the idea of jurisdictional competition was initially viewed as unsound from a legislative perspective,[127] more recently views in favour of regulatory competition and its attendant advantages have been expressed by European company law experts. To name but one, Grundmann has voiced the opinion that 'one answer cannot be doubted: competition with little or without market failure should be strived for and is then also desirable'.[128] The reason for this, according to Grundmann, is that 'it is rare that a system without competition produces a better outcome than one with intense competition', albeit provided this is 'within a framework designed to reduce market failure even if the framework never eliminates market failure completely'.[129]

121 Smits 2008, p. 3.
122 Smits 1998, p. 335.
123 Smits 2002b, p. 80.
124 Smits 2008, p. 3.
125 See Smits 2002b; notably also Smits 2006.
126 For a more complete list of these scholars, see Vogenauer 2013, footnote 3.
127 Grundmann 2002), p. 565. This position was adopted by Schmitthoff, for example, already back in the 1970s; cf. Schmitthoff 1973.
128 Grundmann 2002, p. 568.
129 Grundmann 2002, p. 567-568.

Then, as also indicated before, similar discussions emerged over the potentiality of regulatory competition in the field of contract law, and here again legal commentators in Europe (not to mention elsewhere) have pointed to its advantages, including that of permitting legal experimentation. Rühl, for instance, maintains that regulatory competition in contract law should, in general, be promoted, because it 'will generally induce a race to the top'.[130] In other words, regulatory competition in the area of contract law will (typically) foster the development of legal rules through states seeking to satisfy the preferences of businesses and consumers[131] and, as a result, 'the evolution of new and arguably better rules'.[132] The line of thought espoused by these European legal scholars in distinct fields of law had also previously been advanced by a number of economists in Europe, who emphasized the utility of regulatory competition as a system allowing for the testing and amelioration of national laws governing private actors. Siebert, for example, argued that under conditions of regulatory competition, 'Firms will migrate ... to the most favourable location ... The arbitrage of consumers and firms will show which national regulatory system is best in the eyes of the consumer or the producer: national regulation has to pass a litmus test of private agents voting with their purses and their feet.'[133]

Most recently, following the use of this line of argumentation in relation to European (private) law in general - and particularly to plead against the promulgation of EU similarizing law - it has also been employed in a supra-national context, to support the idea of EU optional law as an alternative. On this view, EU OIs are said to be preferable to measures of similarization, firstly, because they preserve the possibility of horizontal regulatory competition between the laws (as well as the jurisdictions) of the Member States, but also, secondly, because they create the possibility of vertical regulatory competition between Member State law and EU law.[134] Or, to put it the other way around, it is argued that approximating measures constitute a less desirable method not only because they impede international regulatory competition (between legal regimes provided by Member States), but also because they do not allow for competition at the supra-national level (between Member State and EU legal regimes). Again Smits has been a leading exponent of this perspective, and again for the reason, *inter alia,* that competitive pressure on legislatures (in this case both national and EU) can occasion a long-term learning process in the adaptation of laws. In fact he goes a step further, arguing that (depending on the design of the given EU OI) vertical competition has the potential to avoid some of the problems of traditional jurisdictional competition,

130 Rühl 2013a, p. 89. The origins of the term 'race to the top' again lie in the US company law debate. As early as 1977 Winter foresaw such a race (or 'rush', or 'rise') to the top between state company laws: Winter 1977.

131 The reference to consumers as well as businesses here reflects the fact that contract law covers both B2B- and B2C-transactions, in contrast to company law, which deals exclusively with legal persons.

132 Rühl 2013a, p. 79.

133 Siebert 1990b, p. 56.

134 On the possibility of vertical regulatory competition triggered by optional instruments in European private law see for example Fleischer 2012; Leible 2012.

particularly as regards the availability of information on possible options to users of law (i.e. private actors).[135] And Rühl has also pointed to the possibility of a race to the top in the context of vertical regulatory competition as well. Once more subject to certain conditions being met (especially in terms of design of the OI), Rühl claims 'optional instruments may be driving forces on the market for law',[136] meaning this kind of competition on the law market in Europe could well lead to legislative improvements of its own.

In fact, even the European Commission has alluded to the notion of (vertical) regulatory competition in its explanations behind proposals for two EU OIs in the area of procedural law, which in itself provides an indication of the significance of this viewpoint. Specifically, in both the original proposal for a European Order for Payment Procedure and its proposal for a European Small Claims Procedure, the Commission states that the result of legislating by means of OIs in this area is that '[u]ltimately, it will be left to the creditors to judge which procedure [national or European] they consider as being either superior in performance or more convenient in terms of accessibility, the latter being particularly relevant for those operating in several Member States ...'.[137] Admittedly the Commission does not explicitly refer to the concepts of legal experimentation or a race to the top in this regard, but it nevertheless seems reasonable to presume that this may be at least part of the reason why the Commission considers competition between EU and national regimes to be a good thing. At the same time - or, if not, alternatively - it may be that the Commission has in mind another arguable benefit of EU OIs, seen from the perspective not of improved lawmaking, but rather of enhanced choice for private actors. Whether or not this is the case is difficult to say for certain, but in any event it is to this other asserted advantage that our attention must now turn.

(ii) Providing Additional Options for Private Actors

It will be remembered that the learning process for legislators induced by regulatory competition as just described is informed by party choice, which is also one of the fundamental prerequisites for the very existence of such competition. This is not the only benefit that can be attributed to party choice, however. More obviously, as we have already seen that Tiebout observed, the possibility of party jurisdictional choice can give natural and legal persons a way to avoid undesirable laws or, as O'Hara and Ribstein put it, 'to avoid the results of failed experiments ...'[138] (as determined by their respective preferences). In other words, the provision of additional legal options to private actors can enable them, through their own process of experimentation, to better satisfy their needs. The increased availability of legal options for parties is therefore in itself another important reason that has

[135] Smits 2013. This point is discussed further below.
[136] Rühl 2013a, p. 84.
[137] Original proposal for the EOP Regulation (COM(2004) 173 final), p. 8; Proposal for a Regulation establishing a European Small Claims Procedure, COM(2005) 87 final, p. 7.
[138] O'Hara & Ribstein 2009, p. 32.

been advanced to sustain a systemic approach founded on regulatory competition, as seen from the perspective of private actors themselves.

Indeed this advantage of the regulatory competition model for private actors is another central argument made by O'Hara and Ribstein in support of their vision of a law market based on horizontal (and particularly direct) choice of law, as this 'dramatically expands parties' jurisdictional choice'.[139] In other words, choice of law clauses offer parties considerably more options than those available both at the political level and through physical exit, and this is another ground for these authors' position that they should be enforced, because of the benefit this can confer on individuals and firms. By way of example, O'Hara and Ribstein note that, 'a small business in Delaware, whose corporate law is designed for large corporations, may never be able to persuade the Delaware legislature to enact a law that reflects its needs. But the firm can contract to be governed by the corporate law of North Carolina, which might better reflect the needs of closely held firms'.[140] Hence these authors argue that expansion in choice for private parties 'potentially produces legal improvements even for those people who lack both voice and physical exit options in any single state'.[141] Equally, the opportunities that enhanced jurisdictional choice can create for private actors is also another key tenet supporting Smits' plea against the adoption of harmonizing measures in the EU (particularly in the area of European private law). According to Smits, 'citizens' interests are often much better represented by leaving it to them to decide which jurisdiction they like best rather than adopting a binding European Code with only weak parliamentary input',[142] and this is therefore a further reason for him to oppose top-down harmonization, as such harmonization also has the effect of reducing the legal options available to citizens. In fact, Smits describes this as the main reason why in his opinion the regulatory competition model should be fostered. This can be explained by the significance he attaches to the availability of diverse legal options for the empowerment of citizens as an alternative theory of democracy and justice, which he has consistently advocated. Since 'the question of what is fair and just necessarily receives different answers from different people, also if these people live in the same country', Smits maintains that, particularly following developments in the direction of globalization, it is 'less and less convincing to force all citizens to accept the solution of 'their' own national parliament'.[143] For this reason, he argues that an international system of 'legal pluralism' in which citizens can choose between sets of norms existing in distinct jurisdictions should be supported, as this 'provides them with an enormous potential to shape their lives in the way they want. They would be able to invoke the rules they prefer, regardless of whether these are produced by their 'own' State, by other States, by local communities, or by international human rights treaties'.[144]

139 O'Hara & Ribstein, 2009, p. 28.
140 O'Hara & Ribstein, 2009, p. 28.
141 O'Hara & Ribstein, 2009, p. 28.
142 Smits 2010c, p. 70.
143 Smits 2013, p. 54.
144 Smits 2012c, p. 169.

Now most recently (and again similarly to the argument regarding legal experimentation), the advantage of enhanced party choice for individuals has also been put forward to support the case for EU optional instruments. And here too the point has been made that EU OIs have a dual edge over the similarization method, inasmuch as they not only conserve the existing degree of availability of horizontal choice of law between different Member State jurisdictions, but also furnish private actors with additional options at the supra-national level that are capable of being selected without the need to physically move between jurisdictions. Once more Smits has been pre-eminent in expressing this point of view, in the belief that optional regimes can offer 'high quality alternatives that differ considerably from existing options and thus reflect alternative views of justice'.[145] Along with the preceding argument concerning the advantage of the increased party choice brought about by EU OIs for national and EU lawmaking, as well as the argument expressly referred to by the Commission according to which EU OIs are less disruptive of national legal orders, this is the third principal argument that Smits says speaks in favour of the increased use of EU optional law.[146] This is not to say that he does not see any other arguments in favour of EU OIs,[147] but rather that it is a fundamental posit for his support (at least in principle) of the optional instrument method that '[t]he hypothetical consent of the social contract for (nearly) everything the state does is then replaced by the *real* consent of the governed for those sectors of life they opt into',[148] as this allows citizens to choose for the solution that they prefer, and it is also from this consent that an optional instrument derives its democratic legitimacy.[149] Furthermore, as in the case of legal experimentation, Smits even contends that vertical choice of law has the potential to function more effectively still than horizontal choice of law, and that consequently this argument regarding the satisfaction of divergent preferences of private actors holds even more weight when it comes to EU OIs.[150]

So, in summary, the alleged advantages of the regulatory competition model constitute other, more theoretical reasons that have been adduced to sustain the case for EU OIs. Still, like the previous, more practical arguments considered thus far, this view relies on drawing a contrast between optional instruments and the similarization method, and particularly on the nature of EU OIs as alternative legal regimes to existing frameworks at Member State-level. In this sense, the regulatory competition argument is nevertheless clearly linked to the other arguments examined up to this point. In turn, it will be seen that the next line of reasoning to be considered is itself closely connected with the notion of regulatory competition.

145 Smits 2013, p. 54.
146 See Smits 2010b.
147 These other arguments are discussed further below.
148 See Smits 2010b, p. 352.
149 See, for example, Smits 2009.
150 Smits 2013.

(c) The Converging Effect of EU OIs

Already in the discussion of the first point in our exposition of the case for EU OIs, not to mention in that of all the other points examined subsequently, it became abundantly clear that, in principle, EU optional regimes do not, and certainly are not intended to, reform or repeal existing regimes in the legal orders of the Member States. It should not be forgotten, however, that the overall aim of EU similarizing measures, which do necessarily require Member States to amend and/or abolish domestic provisions, is (again in general terms) to achieve *greater uniformity in national laws*, on the ground that the divergences that exist between national regimes in different areas of law in themselves (that is, independently of the actual content of their provisions) create obstacles to the activities of private actors within the internal market. Obviously, the degree of uniformity a given EU similarizing measure is aimed at achieving varies (not least depending on whether the measure takes the form of a minimum harmonization directive, a maximum harmonization directive, or a 'unifying' regulation, for example), but the fact is that, by definition, such measures are intended to effectuate convergence between the laws of the Member States; hence the copious examples one can find of EU similarizing legislation in the preamble of which the legislator identifies the lack of uniformity among domestic laws as the issue that the similarizing measure is designed to address.[151] Now it is true that, as we have also seen in our account of the 'EU regimes for EU activities' rationale, Union legislation introducing optional instruments is in most cases (with the noteworthy exception of the CTM and the CD) spurred by the same express motivation of overcoming the (alleged) obstructions to the functioning of the internal market caused by disparities between national laws, *as well as* (i.e. and not only) by their territorial limitations. It is essentially just the solution offered by these EU OIs to this perceived problem that differs, since, rather than pursuing uniformity among the regimes existing within the legal orders of the Member States, the European legislator, by adopting these instruments, is seeking to create *uniform regimes available at the supra-national level.*[152] But still, the point remains that the legal divergence that exists at national level is not addressed by legislation establishing EU OIs, or at least not directly. In fact, we have already seen that this is precisely what many, including the EU legislator,

151 An early example one could mention is the commonly-termed 'doorstep selling directive' of 1985 (Council Directive 85/577/EEC of 20 December 1985 to protect the consumer in respect of contracts negotiated away from business premises), the motivation for which read: 'Whereas it is a common form of commercial practice in the Member States for the conclusion of a contract or a unilateral engagement between a trader and consumer to be made away from the business premises of the trader, and whereas such contracts and engagements are the subject of legislation which differs from one Member State to another; Whereas any disparity between such legislation may directly affect the functioning of the common market; Whereas it is therefore necessary to approximate laws in this field...' (Recital 3).

152 I.e. what some have described as 'identity' rather than 'uniformity' (see e.g. Fauvarque-Cosson & Behar-Touchais 2012). Of course, the extent to which such uniformity at the supra-national level is achieved by the creation of EU OIs is another matter. On this point see the discussion *infra* in section A.3(a).

perceive to be the beauty of the OI method, as it is aimed at neutralizing the obstructive effects of national legal diversity, without eliminating legal diversity itself.

(i) Why the Need for National Legal Convergence may be felt even if a Union Optional Regime is Available for Selection

Yet, it could be argued that the need for greater convergence between national regimes in various fields of law may be felt even if an alternative EU regime is available in such areas, for two main reasons.

Firstly, it is inevitable that a certain group of the natural and/or legal persons who could/would conceivably make use of any given EU OI will not be eligible to do so, because they do not satisfy one or other or more of the criteria for eligibility specified in the corresponding Regulation; that is, because they do not fall within the scope of application of the optional instrument. Even if their intended legal act falls within the material scope of the instrument, such persons may not be covered by the OI's territorial scope of application, meaning that their situation is a 'purely domestic' one, whereas the OI in question requires some cross-border element to be present in order for them to be entitled to select it. Indeed we saw from our description of EU OIs that most of those in existence, with the exception of the ones in the area of intellectual property law, contain a cross-border requirement of some kind. So, for example, a group of public limited-liability companies formed under the law of a Member State wishing to form a European Company by means of a merger will not be able to do so if each of the companies in the group is governed by the law of the same Member State, just as a claimant desirous to initiate a European Small Claims Procedure will not be able to do so if none of the parties to the case are domiciled or habitually resident in a Member State other than the court or tribunal seized. In addition, as we also saw, even those OIs the applicability of which is not made subject to any cross-border requirement, like the IP law OIs, are still at any rate explicitly designed with cross-border operators in mind. But it could also be (alternatively if not in addition) that such persons do not fall within the personal scope of the particular optional instrument. For instance, a public and a private limited-liability company formed under the law of a Member State that want to form an SE by means of a merger will not be eligible to do so because this possibility is only available to a plurality of public limited-liability companies, unless of course such companies are formed under the law of a country that is not a Member State of the EU, in which case they will not be eligible either. Or it may be that these private actors do not fall under the geographical scope of the OI, because they are operating from a Member State in which the Regulation establishing the OI does not apply. An example of this would be a claimant that seeks certification as a European Enforcement Order of a judgment on an uncontested claim delivered in Denmark, which they would not be entitled to do since this Member State is not subject to the application of the EEO Regulation.[153]

[153] Cf. EEO Regulation, Art. 2(3).

Secondly, and moreover, it is also inevitable that even among those natural and/or legal persons who are eligible to select a certain EU OI (i.e. that do fall within its scope of application), there will be a number who choose not to do so, as they do not consider the optional regime necessary or find it attractive. There could of course be any number of potential reasons for eligible persons to arrive at such a conclusion, which is a point that is explored further in the next chapter. But whether it is for one reason or another (or a combination thereof), a proportion of eligible private actors will not (and do not) opt in to EU OIs.

Therefore, the point could be made that even where an OI is available for selection, more convergence between corresponding regimes at national level would still be desirable from the internal market perspective because, in the absence of such convergence, a significant proportion of private actors would continue to be faced with obstacles to their activities caused by disparities in the domestic laws by which they are governed. Clearly, this point would hold true more in those areas where a Union optional instrument has 'complemented' similarization merely in the sense that it has provided an alternative way forward for the EU legislator, after having only attained a limited degree of convergence in national provisions through similarization efforts (such as the fields of European company law and European procedural law), or even having adopted no approximating law whatsoever (as in the case of plant variety protection). By contrast, in areas such as trade mark law and design law, where EU OIs may be said to have complemented similarization measures in the specific sense of 'accompanying' such measures (meaning the legislator has adopted the EU OI in parallel with approximating legislation of similar scope that is aimed at achieving a comparable degree of uniformity among national regimes), this point would surely be less compelling.

(ii) Why EU OIs could also have Some Converging Effect at National Level

In any event, the point just mentioned is an interesting one, for it begs the question whether, particularly in those areas where it is not accompanied by corresponding similarization measures, the OI method itself has anything to offer in respect of the attainment of greater uniformity at the national level (as well as at the supra-national level). In other words, even though in principle EU OIs are not directly intended to bring about convergence in the legal orders of the Member States, can they nevertheless in practice have some kind of indirect *converging effect*?

Naturally the instinctive answer to this question would most probably be that the fact that EU OIs are not targeted at national laws means that they are unlikely to have any impact upon such laws whatsoever. However, it is possible to identify two arguments that suggest this is not necessarily the case, both of which are very much related to the notions of regulatory competition and particularly legal experimentation.

The first argument is that if one does subscribe to the view that EU OIs can stimulate a race to the top between national and EU legislatures, this view implies not only that domestic and Union legal systems 'improve', but also that they converge around a certain point (i.e. the proverbial 'top'). That is to say, as a result of the competitive process fostered by EU OIs, private actors within the internal market would be confronted with legal regimes that are both more attractive *and* less diverse. Siems, for example, states that '[t]he American experience demonstrates that competition among legal rules leads to convergence rather than divergence in formal law ...'.[154] In fact, even if one takes the conflicting view that, by encouraging regulatory competition, EU OIs may actually give rise to a 'race to the bottom',[155] this would still logically entail that legal systems converge, albeit at a different meeting point. Having said that, as we shall see,[156] there are also those who argue that for any race to emerge at all (i.e. be it to the top or to the bottom), certain additional conditions need to be satisfied, including not least the condition that a significant number of private actors must actually choose between different legal regimes (be they domestic or European). This view therefore suggests that EU OIs may not have a converging effect through regulatory competition if only a few individuals opt into the legal regimes that are made available to them.[157] And even if a given EU optional regime is selected by relatively many private actors, then logically speaking there would be less of a need to reach greater uniformity at national level in the first place, as the relevance of the second main reason for such a need noted above would be diminished. In other words, it is precisely in cases where EU OIs that are unaccompanied by similarization measures are *not* selected by a considerable segment of eligible private actors that the assertion of a continued need for national legal convergence could hold most weight and, accordingly, the question of the whether EU OIs can also satisfy this need could be most important. So, assuming it is considered that the stimulation of regulatory competition by EU OIs is dependent on their being chosen by a significant number of private actors, it could be contended that any converging effect they might have at national level would likely be either limited or, at best, inessential.

This brings us to the second argument as to why the OI method may also indirectly impact upon the laws of the Member States, and concretely to the area of European company law, for it is in this area that the exact situation of an OI not accompanied by approximating legislation being selected by relatively few private actors in the years since its entry into force has (at least arguably) already arisen. This second argument sustaining a 'converging effect' of EU OIs is that EU OIs can have such an effect even in the event that they do prove unpopular with eligible natural and/or legal persons. In other words, on this view, convergence between the legal orders of the Member States can be fostered by the creation of EU optional regimes even if the latter are not selected by a significant number of private actors. This view has been expressed specifically in the context of the debate over the European Company (SE), as an OI whose 'popularity' to date is questionable to say the least. Certainly, as we have seen, there are many who would agree with the proposition that the SE has proven relatively unpopular with eligible private actors

154 Siems 2005, p. 439. On this see also Smits 2006, and Wagner 2009.

155 On the concept of the 'race to the bottom' see *infra*, section A.3(b)(i).

156 *Infra*, section A.3(b)(i).

157 Being a qualification to this first argument in favour of the notion that EU OIs can have a converging effect, this point is discussed further in the section on the lack of converging effect of EU OIs, *infra*, section A.3(c).

since its entry into force in 2004.[158] Rutgers, for example, arrived at the conclusion in 2011 that private actors strongly prefer national corporate forms to the SE, and that the number of SEs relative to the number of corporate entities is 'not that great'.[159] As much had also been predicted by Siems in an article published shortly after the entry into force of the SE Regulation, who felt that 'its success could be doubted'.[160] Yet, even though Siems also recognized the unpopularity of the SE (at least in the beginning),[161] he took the position that its existence alone could still lead to convergence in national company laws, regardless of the extent to which it is selected. Siems identified a number of grounds for holding this belief, two of which merit particular attention because they could equally apply in the case of EU OIs in other fields of European private law.

One noteworthy ground mentioned by Siems is the idea that 'the SE law can serve as a model' for domestic regimes,[162] in the sense that the rules it contains provide a source of inspiration and a frame of reference for national legislators to reform their respective legal systems.[163] As an example of this, Siems pointed to the rules on board structure, which in the national legal orders of many Member States provide for either a one-tier or a two-tier system whereas, as stated previously, those in the SE Regulation offer a choice between both. In this situation, he argues, 'conferring companies a choice between a one tier and a two tier system can inspire national legislators ...'.[164] Viewed in this way, then, the SE OI in any event acts as a body of 'model principles', almost as if it were a form of soft law of the kind that has been created in other fields of private law, such as the Principles of European Contract Law (PECL) or the Principles of European Tort Law (PETL). For this reason it is one of the more significant grounds identified by Siems for present purposes, as the notion of an EU OI serving the supplementary function of a model law is also applicable to OIs in areas beyond the domain of European company law. In the field of European contract law, for instance, it would entail that the proposed Common European Sales Law OI (Option 4 of the Commission's 2010 Green Paper)[165] could simultaneously have performed the role of a soft law instrument allowing the Member States to gradually incorporate the instrument into their national laws on a voluntary basis (i.e. like the Commission Recommendation suggested in Option 3 of the Green Paper). In fact, some have already asserted that

158 On the other hand, as we have also seen, there are those who interpret the experience of the SE in more positive terms. These opposing viewpoints are also indicated in Chapter 5.

159 Rutgers 2011, p. 356.

160 Siems 2005, p. 431.

161 In fact, Siems believes the SE could yet prove to be an attractive instrument for private actors. See *infra*, section A.3(b)(i).

162 Siems 2005, p. 433. In fact Siems goes even further, arguing that the SE could also serve as a model for the EU legislator in the promulgation of future approximating legislation in the area of company law (particularly the directives on cross-border mergers and transfer of seat).

163 On this see also Fleischer 2010, 1696, who speaks of a *circolazione di modelli* (i.e. an exchange of models).

164 Siems 2005, p. 433.

165 'Green Paper from the Commission on policy options for progress towards a European Contract Law for consumers and businesses', COM(2010) 348 final.

this constitutes an added use of EU OIs in general. Former Commissioner Monti, for example, states in his report on the Single Market cited above that '[a]n additional benefit of [the 28th regime] model is that it provides a reference point and an incentive for the convergence of national regimes'.[166]

The other ground put forward by Siems of particular interest for present purposes is that, apart from communicating *to* national legislators a *European* legal model that they can use as guidance for domestic legal reforms, the SE optional regime can also promote communication *between* the Member States and induce national lawmakers to draw inspiration from the regimes of their *counterparts*, thereby fostering convergence in a more practical manner (or, as Siems terms it, 'a European legal culture').[167] His basis for this argument is the fact that, as we have seen, the Regulation establishing the SE leaves a range of issues to be settled in accordance with the laws of the Member States. In other words, '[a]s the regulation aims only at establishing a framework, national company laws are a crucial complement to the SE law'.[168] According to Siems, this has the result (among other things) that cross-border communication regarding national company laws is increased, not only through the process of implementation of the SE Regulation into the Member State legal orders, but also through its operation, since 'the establishment of an SE demands that for some questions the laws of different Member States have to be applied'.[169] As an example of this he points to the case of formation of an SE by merger, in which, pursuant to Article 24(1) of the SE Regulation, 'The law of the Member State governing each merging company shall apply as in the case of a merger of public limited-liability companies …'. In other words, regardless of where a European Company is incorporated, the national rules on mergers continue to govern respectively each of the companies involved in the cross-border merger forming the SE. For this reason Siems maintains that 'it is not only necessary that it is communicated how the SE laws have been implemented in the Member States, but also communication and translation of general national company laws … will increase'.[170] Again, this is a significant ground for our purposes, because it could also conceivably be applied to other EU OIs (or at least other EU OIs that leave many matters to be decided by national law).

So both of these grounds hold that an EU OI may prompt national legislators to adopt converging reforms - even if the OI proves unpopular with private actors and therefore fails to stimulate (vertical) regulatory competition - through what Siems categorizes as 'communication'. In summary, then, there are reasons for thinking that EU OIs can have an indirect 'converging effect' in one way or another, and this even goes for OIs that are considered by many to be unpopular, like the SE.

166 Monti 2010, p. 93. See also Hesselink 2010, who notes that an optional instrument 'could become a source of inspiration for the CJEU and for national courts when interpreting and further developing European and national private law, even in cases where the instrument is not the applicable law. Such optional-instrument-friendly interpretation would have a harmonising and integrating effect' (p. 15).

167 Siems 2005, p. 432.

168 Siems 2005, p. 432.

169 Siems 2005, p. 433.

170 Siems 2005, p. 433.

(d) The Economic Case for EU OIs

The final point in our delineation of the case for EU OIs concerns the economics behind the OI method. Of course, as is the case with other legislation made by the EU (not to mention other legislators), there are various economic arguments underpinning the debate over EU OIs. These arguments are made in relation to both EU OIs as an overall legislative method as well as to specific optional instruments pertaining to particular areas of EU law. Therefore any discussion of the case for and against EU OIs must take into account this economic perspective. Having said that, it is beyond the scope of the present study (not to mention the expertise of its author) to undertake a detailed economic evaluation of EU OIs. So the aim here is limited to providing an overview of the main arguments that have been made in the economic debate underlying EU OIs, in order to construct a more complete normative framework. In what follows we will consider the alleged economic advantages of EU OIs, with a view to returning to opposing views in our presentation of the case against Union optional regimes.[171] In both instances the focus will be on economic claims that have been made about the OI method in general, although a few examples of claims made about particular EU OIs will also be mentioned. It will be seen that, in line with the other normative arguments in favour of EU OIs noted up to this point, the economic discourse is also grounded on comparison between the OI and the similarization method, and especially on the 'alternative' nature of EU OIs.

As with EU similarization measures, the starting point for the economic assessment of EU OIs is the cost of disparities in Member State laws, particularly in terms of the obstacles these pose for the functioning of the internal market. It makes sense to depart from this point because, as was noted in the preceding section, EU optional law - like EU harmonizing law - is generally inspired, *inter alia*, by the desire to address such obstacles. Hence '[d]emands for a more comprehensive harmonization of law between legal areas are generally based on the assumption that legal diversity causes transaction costs and lowers economic trade and welfare, in particular by creating legal uncertainty',[172] and the same is true of demands for optional regimes. Specifically, the European legislator considers that national legal diversity discourages suppliers of goods and services from operating in other Member States, and equally natural persons from engaging in cross-border transactions. As regards the former, '[a]ccording to the Commission, companies lose out on at least EUR 26 billion of sales every year because of obstacles linked to differences in national legislation'.[173] Meanwhile, the latter are said to be 'deprived of a greater and more competitive choice of products, not only because businesses refuse to sell in their countries, but also because consumers lack knowledge about their rights when making purchases abroad'.[174]

171 See section A.3(d).
172 Wagner 2009, p. 1.
173 Fauvarque-Cosson & Behar-Touchais 2012, p. 32.
174 Fauvarque-Cosson & Behar-Touchais 2012, p. 33.

More precisely, at the level of theory, various kinds of financial costs stemming from national legal diversity have been distinguished in the literature. Helmut Wagner, for example, identifies two main types, namely 'the costs of information (about the law, about administrative procedures, about competent legal advice) and ... the costs of enforcement (by way of litigation or alternative forms of dispute resolution) ...'.[175] In other words, divergences between domestic rules lead to two principal forms of 'transaction cost', which arise from the need to obtain information on the applicable law in other Member States, as well as from the need to determine how to bring a claim against parties in other jurisdictions. And, in addition to these transaction costs, Ribstein and Kobayashi also pinpoint a number of other kinds of cost attached to legal diversity, such as inconsistency costs and externalities.[176] 'Inconsistency costs' are essentially costs directly connected to divergences between national rules: 'Inconsistent state laws can impose costs by, for example, exposing a manufacturer that sells its products nationally to many different product liability design standards or a business association to varying governance rules.'[177] Whereas 'externalities' are costs related to the introspective nature of national law. That is, domestic legislation 'typically takes into account the national interests: the national legislator in inclined to help its constituents and not groups outside the state, such as foreign manufacturers', which leads to the externalization of costs, thereby reducing the efficiency of the single market.[178]

So, in summary, many argue that national legal diversity entails higher costs, particularly for private actors, as a result of which prices increase and national income decreases;[179] and EU legislation is typically aimed at reducing such costs. Now, for reasons that will become plain, it is useful to examine the main economic arguments surrounding the use of similarizing legislation to constrain these costs, before discussing the asserted economic gains offered by legislation establishing EU OIs.

(i) *The Benefits and Costs of Similarization*

Through the adoption of approximating legislation, the EU legislator seeks of course to diminish the transaction costs relating to disparities in the laws of the Member States by attaining greater uniformity in these laws. The logic supporting this approach is self-evident: Given that national legal diversity gives rise to transaction costs for private individuals within the EU, less diversity should lead to a decrease in these costs. For this reason, as Wagner observes, 'full harmonization may (at first sight) seem to be an adequate instrument for reducing the costs of cross-border legal uncertainty'.[180] Indeed this cost-reducing effect of harmonization is acknowledged by Wagner and again also by Ribstein and Kobayashi, who affirm

175 Wagner 2009, p. 1.
176 See Ribstein & Kobayashi 1996.
177 Ribstein & Kobayashi 1996, p. 138.
178 See Smits 2005b, p. 168. See also Chirico 2010, p. 26 *et seq.*
179 Cf. Smits 2005b, p. 171.
180 Wagner 2009, p. 2.

that more uniform law serves to curtail each of the types of cost they describe (including transaction (i.e. information and litigation) costs, but also inconsistency costs and externalities). Firstly, information costs decrease as a result of harmonizing legislation, because '[u]niform laws make it easier for firms or individuals that travel or transact business in several states to determine what law applies in each state'.[181] Equally, greater unity among domestic provisions can also facilitate private actors' ascertainment of available means of enforcement, so '[u]niform law will therefore make litigation less expensive'[182] too. Furthermore, inconsistency costs are obviously reduced by legislation establishing greater uniformity in national standards, as such costs are a direct result of divergence between such standards. And finally, externalities may also be diminished by EU harmonizing law, since '[u]niform lawmakers presumably must take into account interstate social welfare rather than only the narrow constituent interests that would matter to state legislators'.[183] This is not to say that similarization measures completely eliminate all of these costs, since such measures (regardless of whether they aim at minimum or maximum harmonization) inevitably leave divergences at national level. But these authors do recognize that the similarization method has the effect of *lowering* the costs of legal diversity.

Yet, both Wagner and Ribstein and Kobayashi maintain that, by removing disparities between national legal systems, harmonization implies costs of its own; and it is therefore not as economically advantageous as it might seem. Starting with the former again, Wagner states that '[t]here is a good deal of evidence that complete harmonization would lead to substantial costs. These include not only direct costs for developing new bureaucracies or demolishing old structures, but also costs arising from renouncement of *advantages of system competition* ...'.[184] In other words, Wagner considers that harmonizing law itself gives rise to costs not least due to the fact that it represses (horizontal) regulatory competition. Concretely, he identifies a number of economic benefits of regulatory competition that are reduced by similarization measures. Two of these are especially noteworthy for present purposes, since they mirror the normative arguments in favour of regulatory competition expounded above.[185] Thus, one is the advantage emanating from the efficiency gains jurisdictional competition offers to national legislators, as 'a process for discovering the regulations that fulfil the desired purpose with the lowest costs. Diversity in laws enables states to experiment in their search for efficient and workable rules of law'.[186] While the other is the benefit accruing from the efficiency gains that regulatory competition provides to private actors, by allowing legal systems to adapt to the variety of preferences. 'In other words: If

181 Ribstein & Kobayashi 1996, p. 138.
182 Smits 2005b, p. 168.
183 Ribstein & Kobayashi 1996, p. 139.
184 Wagner 2009, p. 9. Of course, the costs of producing the harmonizing law and of developing new bureaucracies to administer it would also arise in the case of other legislation, including legislation introducing an optional instrument; see further below.
185 Section A.2(b).
186 Wagner 2009, p. 10.

states compete with their legal systems, more preferences may be satisfied.'[187] For these reasons, Wagner argues that '[w]hen economic policy conclusions are drawn, attention should be paid to more than just the costs of legal uncertainty. The (transaction) costs of eliminating legal uncertainty ... also have to be taken into account, if a balanced cost-benefit analysis is to be carried out'.[188] And, similarly, Ribstein and Kobayashi also argue that harmonization brings about new losses of growth or efficiency by restricting regulatory competition, because 'uniform state laws tend to decrease exit opportunities', and 'innovation and experimentation through a decentralized lawmaking process may produce at least some laws that are better than what a single uniform lawmaker could write'.[189]

Evidently, the plea for a balanced cost-benefit analysis does not lead inexorably to the conclusion that similarization never brings about economic gains, as it is perfectly possible that in certain cases similarization measures would still be cost-effective and should therefore be taken. In other words, as Smits puts it, '[a]ll this does not mean that diversity is always to be preferred above unification. It could well be that the costs of diversity...are larger than the costs of unification. Uniform law should thus still be adopted if the benefits of uniformity outweigh the costs'.[190] What it does entail, however, is that the removal of legal diversity is not necessarily an appropriate means of tackling the financial costs to which such diversity gives rise. For this reason, from the arguments he raises, Wagner reaches the conclusion that they speak 'in favour of - at most - only partial harmonization of law due to possible advantages resulting from system competition ...'.[191]

Hence the economic viability of similarizing law varies according to the circumstances; and the question of *when* the benefits of establishing greater uniformity outbalance the costs cannot be answered in the abstract. Instead, this can only be addressed on a case-by-case basis, pursuant to an individual cost-benefit analysis. Moreover, as Smits also points out, even in concrete areas, such as contract law, 'it seems impossible to calculate either the cost of legal diversity or the cost of uniform law'.[192] This is mainly due to the complexity of the analysis and the variables involved. Indeed, even if one frames the issue in terms of comparison, Smits maintains that there cannot be a definitive answer to the question whether the reduction in transaction costs achieved by the elimination of legal diversity is higher than 'the losses caused by the termination of competition of legal systems'.[193] This is not to say that arguments (and estimates) concerning the economic impact of similarization have no role to play;[194] but it is contended that these arguments must be appreciated with this important limitation. So, in short, not only are the

187 Wagner 2009, p. 9.
188 Wagner 2009, p. 8.
189 Ribstein & Kobayashi 1996, p. 140-141. See also Chirico 2010, p. 26 *et seq*.
190 Smits 2005b, p. 178.
191 Wagner 2009, p. 10.
192 Smits 2005b, p. 178.
193 Smits 2005b, p. 179. See also Sefton-Green 2011, p. 138 et *seq*.
194 On this point, suffice to say that we have already seen examples of the European Commission providing financial estimates to make the economic case for legislative intervention (most recently *supra*, section A.2(d)).

advantages and costs of EU approximating law unsusceptible to generalization, but they are also uncertain.

(ii) The Economic Advantages of EU OIs

Having briefly considered the alleged financial benefits and costs of similarization, we can now return to the economic arguments that have been made in support of the OI method.

The first argument to be noted in this respect is that EU OIs can bring most (if not all) of the economic benefits that approximating legislation is said to bring, insofar as the aim of EU optional law is (in part) also to reduce the very same transaction costs arising from divergence between national laws by securing greater uniformity.[195] The only difference in this regard is that the uniformity is sought not in the domestic laws of the Member States, but rather in the availability of a common EU regime that is uniform across the Member States. Thus, EU legislation establishing OIs can also lead to a reduction in information costs, as firms and natural persons that select a Union OI are facilitated in determining the law that applies in each Member State in which they operate, since (generally speaking) optional regimes apply in all EU Member States. In fact, it could be argued that EU OIs would serve to reduce information costs even further, as such individuals would (for the most part)[196] need to familiarize themselves with just a single, common regime, as opposed to various - similarized - national regimes. And, by the same token, inconsistency costs would also decrease, as private individuals are also able to avert disparities in national standards by opting into a common EU-wide body of rules.[197] A prime example of a Union OI that has been supported by this argument would be the proposed Common European Sales Law[198] in the area of European contract law - in which it will be recalled that there have been no *comprehensive* EU similarization measures. As indicated before, as part of its motivation for the CESL proposal, the Commission affirmed that this EU OI was needed to allow private actors to escape the extra contract law-related costs that they usually face in cross-border as compared to domestic situations *due to differences in national laws*. These costs are said to 'include the difficulty in finding out about the provisions of an applicable foreign contract law, obtaining legal advice, negotiating the applicable law in business-to-business transactions and

[195] See section A.1(a).

[196] This caveat is needed because, just like similarization measures, EU OIs cannot and do not eliminate the possibility of divergences at the Member State-level altogether; see further *infra*, section A.3(a)(i).

[197] Furthermore, since the lawmaker behind the legislation is the same, the possibility of a reduction in externalities is present in the case of EU OIs too.

[198] Proposal for a Regulation of the European Parliament and of the Council on a Common European Sales Law, COM(2011) 635 final.

adapting contracts to the requirements of the consumer's law in business-to-consumer transactions' (i.e. both transaction and inconsistency costs).[199]

Indeed, the argument that EU OIs can have the same economic advantages as EU approximating law is one reason why the digression into the economic theory behind similarization was useful, as the case made in support of the latter can and has been applied *mutatis mutandis* to the former. But there is another important reason for this, which has to do not with the economic advantages of similarization measures, but rather the alleged financial costs of such measures. For it is in the comparison (or perhaps better, the contrast) drawn between EU approximating law and EU optional law on the question of the costs of the EU legislation itself that one of the main economic arguments sustaining EU OIs lies.

This is the argument that, unlike similarization measures, EU OIs do not also import the same costs - particularly the costs of constraining jurisdictional competition, but also the 'direct costs' of adaptation. As regards the former, first and foremost, the assertion is more precisely that, by allowing for regulatory competition, the OI method does not give rise to costs attached to the limitation of exit opportunities for private individuals and of possibilities for lawmakers to engage in legislative experimentation as the similarization method does. In fact, EU OIs actually *promote* regulatory competition and therefore, conversely, they can serve to increase the economic benefits derived from such competition, while at the same time procuring the financial advantages associated with overcoming national legal diversity. This point is well-summarized by Kerber and Grundmann's statement that 'The introduction of an Optional EU Code can be recommended, because it can combine important advantages of centralization (e.g. economies of scale-effects and saving of information and transaction costs) and decentralization (e.g. heterogeneity, innovation, and adaptability).'[200] Patently this is a reflection of the theoretical arguments in favour of EU OIs according to which optional regimes are to be supported because, by virtue of their alternative nature, they allow national and EU legislators the opportunity to engage in legal experimentation at national- and EU-level, as well as preserve and provide additional legal options for private actors. Furthermore, regarding the latter, it has also been contended that the OI method does not entail the same level of 'direct costs' as approximating legislation (although it does give rise to such costs as well), since it does not require pre-existing national legal frameworks to be reformed or abolished, and private actors do not need to adapt to the optional regime unless they opt into it. Hesselink, for example, asserts that 'the economic costs of introducing an OI (in terms, especially, of adaptation by economic and legal operators to the new rules) seem to be rather modest, certainly much lower than the costs of e.g. full harmonization ...'.[201] And this point is also linked to one of the claims noted in our account of the

199 *Ibid.*, p. 2. On the other hand, there are also those who dispute the significance of the problems caused by national legal diversity in the area of contract law; see further Chapter 5, section A.3(a).

200 Kerber & Grundmann 2006, p. 215. See also Wagner 2002.

201 Hesselink 2010, p. 8.

theoretical case for EU OIs, namely the claim that optional instruments leave pre-existing national legal frameworks unaffected.

Last but not least, the third (and perhaps the central) economic argument sustaining EU OIs is that - unlike similarization measures - the aim of optional instruments (at least generally speaking) is not merely to reduce the costs of national legal diversity; it is also (if not primarily) to tackle the costs of national territorial limitations.[202] Or, phrased in a more positive fashion, EU OIs are also intended to provide efficiency gains by making available to private actors legal regimes the applicability of which extends throughout the entire territory of the European Union, rather than being confined within the borders of a given Member State.

It will be remembered that the notion of EU regimes for EU activities was exemplified most clearly by the OIs in the area of intellectual property law, and particularly by the way in which '[t]hese optional instruments are used to go beyond the territoriality of the rights granted by national legislation'.[203] And here again it is the IP law OIs that provide arguably the most perspicuous illustration of the potential efficiency savings private actors engaged in cross-border activities can achieve by opting into a Union optional regime *due to the territorial limitations of national regimes*. An unequivocal indication to this effect is contained in the Community Trade Mark Regulation itself, the fourth recital of which states:

> 'The barrier of territoriality of the rights conferred on proprietors of trade marks by the laws of the Member States cannot be removed by approximation of laws. In order to open up unrestricted economic activity in the whole of the internal market for the benefit of undertakings, trade marks should be created which are governed by a uniform Community law directly applicable in all Member States.'[204]

And a detailed elaboration of this argument can be found in the proposal for the Community Design, which identifies a number of different costs incurred by private actors resulting from this barrier of territoriality of national IP rights (and that therefore can be eliminated by the availability of an IP right with uniform effect throughout the territory of the EU). In particular, the 'exclusively territorial application' of Member State IP protection systems is said to impose on users 'the burden of multiple registrations, of the payment of different fees in different Member States and monitoring of rights in different Member States ...'.[205] In other words, because the protection of national IP rights ends at the borders of the Member State in which that protection has been acquired, private actors that are economically active in a plurality of Member States - and therefore desirous to acquire protection extending beyond the frontiers of a single Member State - must

202 This, along with the first argument noted above, again reflects a point already identified in the theoretical case for EU OIs, namely the notion that Union OIs offer 'EU regimes for EU activities'. See section A.1(a).

203 Fauvarque-Cosson & Behar-Touchais 2012, p. 382.

204 CTM Regulation, consideration 4.

205 Proposal for a European Parliament and Council Regulation on the Community Design, COM(93) 342 final, p. 2.

obtain (and maintain) multiple IP rights, typically through separate registration (and renewal) procedures, with different criteria and their own distinct fees. Without such trans-frontier protection, 'the risk that conflicting rights could exist in other Member States would still be real'.[206] But perhaps the most concrete expression of this economic argument is to be found in the legislative background to the Unitary Patent. In the very first paragraph of its explanatory memorandum to the proposal for a Regulation implementing enhanced cooperation in the area of unitary patent protection, the Commission estimated that the 'overall cost of validation of an average European patent reaches 12.500 EUR if validated only in 13 Member States and over 32.000 EUR if validated in the whole EU'.[207] While, in a related press release of 2011, the Commission predicted that '[i]n the long run, in the territories of the 25 participating Member States unitary patent protection will cost €680 ...'.[208]

The various asserted costs of the barrier of territoriality – as well as those resulting from national legal divergence – can be illustrated using EU OIs in other areas too, though. Take, for instance, the field of European procedural law. As noted previously, the Commission maintains that the expense of obtaining a judgment is 'clearly intensified in a cross-border context. It will often be necessary to hire two lawyers, there are additional translation and interpretation costs and miscellaneous other factors such as extra travel costs of litigants, witnesses, lawyers etc.'.[209] These costs are said to arise from a combination of both the territorial limitations of and the differences between national procedures. It is for this reason that the availability of a uniform Union procedural regime in each of the EU Member States that is admissible and applicable in cross-border cases (like, say, the European Order for Payment Procedure) is seen to be necessary, as a means of allowing private actors to obviate the additional costs caused by the barrier of territoriality along with national legal divergence.

To sum up, then, the economic arguments in favour of EU OIs are essentially three-fold, and may be boiled down to the fundamental contention that, at least in certain cases, legislation creating EU OIs can be more cost-effective than similarization measures, especially (but not only) for private actors operating in a cross-border context. There are two final points, however, that should be noted with regards to the economic case for EU OIs.

The first is that it is important to bear in mind that the arguments just outlined are by no means exhaustive of the economic case for EU OIs. On the contrary, other economic arguments have also been made in support of EU OIs, although these tend to be of a more indirect kind, in the sense that they centre on the wider

206 *Ibid.*, p. 1.

207 Proposal for a Regulation of the European Parliament and of the Council implementing enhanced cooperation in the area of the creation of unitary patent protection, COM(2011) 215 final, p. 1.

208 Press release, 'Commission proposes unitary patent protection in 25 Member States – Frequently Asked Questions', Memo/11/240 (13 April 2011), available at: <http://europa.eu/rapid/press-release_memo-11-240_en.htm?locale=en>.

209 Proposal for a Regulation of the European Parliament and of the Council establishing a European Small Claims Procedure, COM(2005) 87 final, p. 3.

economic implications of optional instruments for the EU internal market. In the Community Design proposal, for example, the Commission draws a connection between the need for a unitary system of design protection and the free movement of goods within the EU: 'To allow goods embodying designs to flow freely within an internal market a protection system at the level of the Community is necessary.'[210] While, in the EOP proposal, the Commission points to a link between the lack of common EU procedures for the recovery of uncontested debts and the collapse of economic enterprises (particularly of small- and medium-size) in the EU, where it states that '[l]ate payments are a major reason for insolvency threatening the survival of businesses ...The need to engage in lengthy, cumbersome and costly court proceedings even for the collection of uncontested debts inevitably exacerbates those detrimental economic effects'.[211]

On the other hand, the second point is that, just as in the case of similarization, one cannot reasonably generalize about the financial effects of EU optional law, and at any rate the cost reductions offered by EU OIs are not certain, even in particular cases. We have already observed the difficulty of ascertaining savings in transaction costs in the area of European contract law, for instance, and this naturally also extends to the proposed CESL. But even in the case of an OI like the Regulation establishing the European patent with unitary effect, for example (in support of which, as was just indicated, the Commission published specific estimates as to the eventual savings that the Unitary Patent could provide for private actors), the extent of potential cost savings envisaged by the Commission is questionable. This is mainly because the Commission based its comparison on the cost of validating a current European patent in all EU Member States, in spite of the fact that, according to its own Impact Assessment accompanying the unitary patent proposals (of 2011), 'only around 1 000 out of approx. 50,000 annually validated patents (2%) are validated in all 27 Member States'.[212] If one were to compare the cost of validating a European patent in, say, 5 Member States (which, according to the same Commission statistics, account for around 40 per cent of the 50,000 annually validated patents), however, the cost savings that can be expected would no doubt be considerably lower. For reasons such as these, the economic effects of the UP Regulation, should it be adopted, are far from settled. Once again, the point here is not that discussion of the economic impact of EU OIs is futile, but simply that it must be appreciated taking such limitations into account.

210 Proposal for a European Parliament and Council Regulation on the Community Design, COM(93) 342 final, p. 2. This is also declared in the preamble of the Community Design Regulation itself (see consideration 4).

211 Proposal for a Regulation of the European Parliament and of the Council creating a European order for payment procedure, COM(2004) 173 final, p. 5.

212 European Commission Impact Assessment, Accompanying document to the Proposal for a Regulation of the European Parliament and the Council implementing enhanced cooperation in the area of the creation of unitary patent protection and Proposal for a Council Regulation implementing enhanced cooperation in the area of the creation of unitary patent protection with regard to the applicable translation arrangements, SEC(2011) 482 final, p. 17.

This being said, it is necessary to conclude our discussion of the economic case for EU OIs - and indeed our account of the case for EU OIs in general - at this juncture, and turn our attention to the case against EU optional instruments.

3. *The Case against EU OIs*

Having presented the key tenets of the case for EU OIs, coupled with those of the European legislator in creating OIs, we must now consider the essential elements of the case against this legislative method, in order to come to a balanced overall assessment of Union optional instruments. Again, it is useful for presentational purposes to divide the key points into different categories, notwithstanding the fact that many of them are unquestionably related. Moreover, it will be seen that a number of the claims discussed in what follows constitute counter-arguments to those explored in the preceding part, in the sense that they deny, or at least qualify, the arguments that have been made in favour of EU OIs.

(a) The Limitations of EU OIs

The first point that should be noted in our account of the case against EU OIs is that the OI method suffers from two fundamental limitations, each of which lessens the usefulness of legislation establishing optional instruments. One of these limitations is that EU OIs are not as uniform as has been suggested up to now - and, as we shall see, this lack of uniformity can defeat part of the aim behind EU optional regimes. While the other is that, for various reasons, EU OIs could never eliminate the need for legislation approximating national laws; as a matter of fact, it may be contended that, at least for the most part, EU OIs do not constitute a genuine alternative to similarization at all. We shall now examine each of these claims in turn.

(i) The Lack of Uniformity of EU OIs

It will be remembered that the premise for the primary motivation given by the EU legislator for using the OI method (i.e. that of creating EU regimes for EU activities) is not merely that EU optional regimes are recognized *in unison* by all of the Member States. It is also that these regimes equate to *uniform* legal institutions across the domestic legal orders, in the sense that they are subject to the same rules - namely those provided in the very regulations that establish them. Indeed this explains why all OIs in the different EU policy areas, both existing and proposed, are embodied (primarily if not solely)[213] in regulations,[214] as this is the only type of

213 In fact, as we have seen (in Chapter 3), the only EU OIs that have not been created exclusively by means of Regulations are the European Company and European Cooperative Society, as in the case of each of these OIs the rules governing employee participation were ultimately adopted in the form of a Directive. Even in these anomalous cases, however, it is indisputable that the primary provisions are contained in the SE Regulation and SCE Regulation, respectively.

secondary legislation that is 'binding in its entirety and directly applicable in all Member States'.[215] It is not that it is inconceivable to set up an optional regime that Member States subscribe to in common by means of, say, a directive.[216] But the problem with this is that, since directives leave to the Member States 'the choice of form and methods', there would be a risk of significant divergence between the implementing legislation adopted within the various domestic legal orders.[217] And this would of course run counter to the EU legislator's vision of the optional instrument as a common legal construct that is also uniform in each of the Member States.

Clearly, the reason the EU legislator considers that the optional regimes it creates should be standard as well as shared between all of the Member States is that this is essential for the dual aim it is (at least in most cases) expressly seeking to achieve by promulgating OIs, which is to enable private actors to surmount the barrier of national legal diversity *as well as* the barrier of territoriality. For, while the simple fact that a Union optional regime is recognized by the Member States in unison may of itself allow private individuals to 'transcend the territorial limitations of national law', it is the uniformity of the optional regime made available for selection in each of the Member State legal systems by EU legislation establishing OIs that enables such individuals to overcome obstacles caused by disparities between domestic rules. Once again, the field of European intellectual property rights is probably the most convenient to use by way of illustration here. Take, for example, the Community Plant Variety Right. The fact alone that the CPVR has effect in all Member State legal systems as a single IP right entails that private actors do not need to obtain multiple domestic rights in order to secure protection for their new plant varieties throughout the territory of the EU (which in practical terms allows them not least to avoid paying multiple registration fees). However, if the CPVR Regulation did not also prescribe, say, standard criteria for determining the infringement of a Community plant variety right, and instead left this to be governed by applicable domestic rules (which, as we have seen, have not been similarized), the scope of the protection accorded to this unitary right could potentially differ to a significant degree from one Member State legal system to another. So even if holders of CPVRs would be able to surpass the barrier posed by the restricted territorial effect of domestic plant variety protection systems, they would still be faced with the hurdle of particular rules *within* these unsimilarized national systems governing their non-territorially limited plant variety rights.

214 See Chapter 2, section B.1(a).

215 Art. 288 TFEU.

216 See *supra*, Chapter 2, section B.1(a).

217 Cf. Opinion of Advocate-General Stix-Hackl delivered on 12 July 2005 on Case C-436/03 *European Cooperative Society*, para. 54. This does not necessarily mean to say that the content of the rules would differ because, if it were a maximum harmonization directive, it could in principle ensure that the rules applicable to the optional regime are standardized across the national legal systems. However, there would remain the possibility (or, rather, the probability) that the type of national legislation used to give effect to the aims of the Directive would diverge, and this could potentially lead to noteworthy disparities in the legal standing or the interpretation of the rules within the context of the domestic legal orders.

Hence the utility of the CPVR as a unitary right for persons engaged in cross-border activities could be severely diminished if the rules applicable to it varied considerably between the Member States.

Now, it was already acknowledged when discussing EU approximating legislation[218] that the idea that such measures (even in the form of regulations) can attain complete uniformity among national legal orders is an unrealistic one, since there inevitably remain divergent laws at national level, no matter how much the domestic rules are similarized.[219] In addition, even those rules that are similarized may be applied differently at national level, since this depends on factors that lie beyond the black-letter law. As Wagner puts it, 'uniformity of law cannot be created by just imposing rules through public policy. Compliance with the law requires more than just rules; it must match the (legal) culture of a country'.[220] And, obviously, the same caveat applies in the case of regulations establishing EU OIs. In other words, even if the legislator adopts the most comprehensive and uniform set of rules it possibly can to govern a Union optional regime, it cannot hope to achieve absolute uniformity. This hardly serves to negate the legislator's premise that EU OIs amount to uniform regimes, though, principally because this is not what the legislator intends by the adjective 'uniform' anyway. Rather, the legislator simply presupposes that the main rules governing EU optional regimes are the same in all Member States, albeit accepting that the enactment of absolute legal uniformity is unachievable. Yet, even this understanding of EU optional regimes can be questioned, on the ground that EU OIs are not actually uniform (in a black-letter sense) across the Member States. On the contrary, all EU optional regimes lack uniformity, even in this narrower sense of the word. In fact, some of the EU OIs in existence would be more veraciously described as positively *disuniform*.

The most conspicuous example of an OI that lacks uniformity to such a large extent would be the SE. As was explained in our presentation of the European Company,[221] the SE Regulation that was eventually adopted in 2001 makes numerous references to pre-existing Member State rules applicable to domestic company forms. More precisely, many of the requirements of the SE Regulation are made subject to rules of national law governing public companies of the State in which the SE's registered office is located, and there are also two general stipulations making SEs subject to this national law (i.e. Arts. 9(1)(c) & 10).[222] Some of these references may be described as minor or subsidiary, inasmuch as the Regulation lays down a basic norm (or norms), while leaving certain ancillary matters to national law so defined. For instance, Article 38 provides that the SE shall comprise, *inter alia*, a general meeting of shareholders, and the Regulation also

218 See section 2(d)(i).

219 In this respect it is important to bear in mind that the EU has limited competences to enact legislation, and particularly when it comes to the field of private law; Cf. Micklitz 2012. In fact this is a relevant point for EU intervention in general, including also EU legislation creating OIs (see further Ch. 5, section A.2(b)). Although, being a more general question of EU law, the issue of competence is not addressed directly in the present study.

220 Wagner 2009, p. 11.

221 See description of SE in Chapter 3.

222 See Edwards 2003, p. 451.

contains some provisions concerning the functions of this general meeting,[223] but then Article 53 states that 'the organisation and conduct of general meetings together with voting procedures' is to be governed by national law. However, others are undeniably more fundamental in nature, insofar as the SE is made subject to national rules as regards entire 'sub-fields' of company law, such as corporate taxation.[224] Admittedly some aspects of the pre-existing national law to which the Regulation defers have previously been similarized by European company law directives, but equally a number of others (including the sub-field of taxation) have not. Thus, as Edwards explains, the SE Regulation can be criticized on the basis that:

> 'The legislation provides *too many options and references to national law* – in such important areas of company law as minority protection, directors' liability, audit and accounts, capital changes and insolvency – *to promote genuine uniformity* and too many sources of rules – Statute, statutes, national law both harmonized and un-harmonized.'[225]

In particular, the fact that the Regulation fails to establish uniformity in the area of tax is seen as potentially crucial, because tax considerations are often the most important factor for cross-border corporate structures.[226] As a result, according to Edwards, 'the availability of a pan-European instrument which leaves the existing mosaic of fiscal regulation untouched may prove to be irrelevant'.[227] In other words, even though this company form is recognized by all Member States in unison, its usefulness could be seriously tempered by the fact that the laws applicable to it in each Member State are far from uniform.

On the other hand, other EU OIs appear to lack uniformity to a much lesser extent. The Community Trade Mark Regulation, for example, contains a relatively complete set of rules governing various aspects of Community Trade Marks, from procedural rules regulating the process of application for a CTM, to substantive provisions determining the effects of CTMs. Nevertheless, as we observed in our summary of this OI, the CTM Regulation does also defer to pre-existing national rules in certain 'sub-fields' of trade mark law. For instance, it does not establish any rules in the areas of civil liability or unfair competition; instead, Article 14(2) simply states that the Regulation 'shall not prevent actions concerning a Community trade mark being brought under the law of Member States relating in particular to civil liability and unfair competition'. In addition, while the CTM Regulation does prescribe some rules governing the CTM as an object of property (e.g. concerning transfer, licensing, insolvency proceedings, etc.).[228] Article 16 affirms that, subject to these rules, 'a Community trade mark as an object of property shall be dealt with … as a national trade mark registered in the Member State in which … (a) the proprietor has his seat or his domicile …; (b) where point (a) does not apply, the

223 Cf. SE Regulation, Art. 52.
224 SE Regulation, consideration 20.
225 Edwards 2003, p. 463 (italics added).
226 See Edwards 2003, p. 463.
227 Edwards 2003, p. 463.
228 See Regulation 207/2009 on the Community trade mark Arts. 17-24.

proprietor has an establishment ...'. So even the more comprehensive OIs such as the CTM are not exactly uniform, as the regulations that establish them still redirect users to pre-existing national laws on certain points, rather than providing 'their own' rules. Therefore it may be concluded that the degree of uniformity of EU OIs is at best variable, ranging from not entirely uniform, to barely uniform at all.

To sum up, then, the first notable limitation of EU OIs also constitutes the first counter-argument in our account of the case against EU OIs, since it calls into question the very rationale behind EU legislation establishing optional instruments. The EU legislator conceives of its optional instruments as uniform regimes available in the legislation of all the Member States, but an inspection of the OI regulations that it has adopted so far reveals that this understanding does not quite correspond with the reality. This is significant because the lack of uniformity of an optional instrument may affect the ability of private actors to overcome the barrier of national legal diversity by opting into it. The question of how uniform an optional regime needs to be in order to achieve this goal is impossible to answer, particularly in the abstract. But what one may venture to say is that the less uniform a given optional regime is, the less likely it will be to enable private actors to avoid obstacles to their cross-border activities caused by divergences in the laws of the Member States.

(ii) The Limits of the Conception of EU OIs as an Alternative to Similarization

The second important limitation of EU OIs is that, for a number of different reasons, they do not actually always constitute an alternative to EU approximating law. All of these reasons can actually be educed from our discussion up to this point, but it is useful at this stage to state them in more explicit terms.

The first (and primary) reason why EU OIs are not always an alternative to similarization is that, while similarization measures may not be practicable in certain areas of EU law, there are many other fields where the European legislator cannot achieve its objectives by adopting an optional instrument, and must instead proceed by means of similarizing legislation.[229] The Czech response in the 2012 study on optional instruments conducted for the Legal Affairs Committee of the European Parliament provides some examples of such fields, where it states that:

> 'These instruments are undoubtedly useful for the internal market in their own context. However, there are other field (sic) in which the discretionary systems do not allow [the objective of facilitating the creation of the single market] to be achieved and in which unified or harmonised solutions are necessary (for example a customs union, the basic system of the four fundamental freedoms, etc.).'[230]

Indeed, this goes a long way towards explaining why - as was implicit in the exchange between the European Economic and Social Committee and the

229 There are also other fields where optional instruments may be of only limited use; see *infra*, section D.2.

230 Fauvarque-Cosson & Behar-Touchais 2012, p. 330.

Commission noted above[231] – the similarization method continues to be viewed as the prime method for the EU legislator to achieve its goals, whereas optional instruments are attributed a mere 'supporting' role, in the sense that they are considered mainly for areas where similarization is expected to be 'neither easy nor achievable' (such as general contract law, or company law, etc.). Admittedly this is not the case with all EU OIs (we shall return to this point in a moment), but it is at any rate consistent with the majority of EU optional regimes, existing and proposed. Thus, the characterization of EU OIs as an 'alternative' to similarization should not be taken to mean that these legislative methods are in some way 'on a level par', since the OI method only offers a plausible alternative to the EU legislator in a limited number of areas of European law.

In the case of certain EU OIs, particularly the Community Trade Mark and the Community Design, this depiction of the OI method as an alternative to similarization measures *when such measures are impracticable* does not fit because, as we have seen, the core provisions of the Member States in these areas were *also* approximated, shortly before the introduction of the Union optional regimes. Instead, these OIs are perhaps better described as 'complementary' to similarization measures,[232] in the specific sense that they build on the latter. This is clearly reflected, for example, in the preamble to the trade mark directive, where the legislator, apart from explaining the motivation behind the approximating directive, also declares that it is 'important not to disregard the solutions and advantages which the Community trade mark system may afford to undertakings wishing to acquire trade marks'.[233] On the other hand, the 'flip side' of this is of course that the legislator also considered it 'necessary, in view of the establishment and functioning of the internal market, to approximate the laws of the Member States',[234] so that the various national trade mark rights available within the EU's borders would be subject to the same basic rules (i.e. a 'level playing field', if you will). Hence this is also a second reason why the description of EU OIs as an 'alternative' to similarization does not tell the whole story, as in some cases the legislator has seen the need to utilize both of these legislative methods simultaneously. In fact, one could even go as far as to argue that in the case of the CTM and the CD, the legislation establishing the OI was partially *dependent* on the approximating legislation, in the sense that the preceding directives 'laid the groundwork' for the Member States' reception of the subsequent regulations (the main substantive provisions of which are largely similar if not identical).

Last but not least, the third qualification to the conception of EU OIs as an alternative to similarization that should be mentioned is that, as was just remarked in the preceding section, none of the EU optional regimes that have been introduced to date are completely uniform, since they all make references to pre-existing

231 See section A.2(a).

232 Cf. Fauvarque-Cosson & Behar-Touchais 2012, p. 384 (section entitled 'Are optional instruments only used in the absence of maximum harmonization standards?').

233 Council Directive 89/104/EEC of 21 December 1988 to approximate the laws of the Member States relating to trade marks, consideration 2.

234 *Ibid.*, consideration 1.

national laws. And, given that at least some of these domestic laws to which the regulations establishing OIs refer have not been similarized, private actors who opt into a Union optional regime could therefore still be faced with obstacles to their economic activities caused by national legal diversity. Consequently, even for those individuals who are able to and indeed do avail themselves of a Union regime in a certain field of law - let alone those who are or do not - there may be a lingering need for (further) EU measures similarizing national laws in that field, due to the fact that the Union regime that has been made available lacks uniformity to one degree or another. An SE, for example, is still governed by disparate national corporate taxation laws, and so even for those legal persons that form an SE (and, in the case of this OI, contrary to what was originally envisaged), the availability of a European Company has not eliminated the necessity for these domestic company laws to be approximated.[235] In other words, for such persons the SE has served as an alternative to similarization only up to a point.

For all of these reasons (and particularly the first), the extent to which EU OIs constitute a genuine alternative to similarization measures is dubitable to say the least. Not only is the OI method 'not always' an alternative to similarization, but one could go a step further and argue that it is not an alternative in many (or even most) cases. If anything, what becomes apparent from the above is rather the enduring relevance of similarization, even in those areas where optional regimes have been created. Bearing in mind that the juxtaposition of EU optional law and EU approximating law is a recurring theme in the case for EU OIs, this point is a significant one too. For while it may be true that the OI method can have numerous advantages over the similarization method, the limitation we have just noted suggests that this line of argumentation holds weight in but a few areas of European law.

(b) An Alternative View of Regulatory Competition and the Law Market

The second contention in the case against EU OIs is also the second counter-argument, as it offers a conflicting view of regulatory competition and the idea of a law market. Put succinctly, this corresponds to the view that, even though EU OIs provide additional options to private actors, and even if EU OIs do in fact serve to stimulate (both horizontal and vertical) regulatory competition - a claim that is disputed in and of itself - these are anything but desirable effects. On the contrary, such a law market-based approach should be discouraged, for two main reasons: First, because, if anything, regulatory competition engenders a 'race to the bottom' rather than a 'race to the top'; and, second, because, while the law market model may provide more freedom of choice for some individuals, it leads to more social injustice for many others. It is again conducive to discuss each of these points in turn.

235 This is without prejudice to the discussion as to whether OIs like the SE could still have some effect on the domestic laws of the Member States in the sections on the converging effect of EU OIs and on the lack thereof, *supra* section A.2(c) and *infra* section A.3(c).

(i) The 'Race to the Bottom', if a Race at All

As became clear from our account of the case for EU OIs, one of the main theoretical arguments advanced by legal commentators in support of EU optional instruments is that, unlike similarization measures, they preserve the possibility for jurisdictional competition between Member State regimes, while at the same time creating the possibility for regulatory competition between Member State and Union regimes. This was said to be beneficial because it allows both the Member State and the EU legislators to engage in legal experimentation, which can instigate the development of novel and arguably 'better' laws. This argument has been challenged, however, with one line of attack targeting its premise, and another countering its conclusion.

Starting with the former, the very idea of a law market driven by regulatory competition has been questioned by various experts in the European context, dealing with different areas of law. In particular, doubt has been cast upon this idea by a number of commentators in the field of contract law. Vogenauer, for example, has recently disputed the notion of lawmakers within the EU competing for private actors to choose their respective regimes of contract law on both conceptual and empirical grounds. On the conceptual level, Vogenauer argues that there is no reason to expect such competition to emerge between contract law regimes, because '[n]either the contracting parties as customers of contract law and dispute resolution regimes nor lawmakers as producers of such regimes have sufficient incentive to engage in true market behaviour'.[236] In other words, although Vogenauer accepts that the area of contract law does meet the basic conditions for regulatory competition outlined at the outset of our discussion of this phenomenon,[237] he maintains that there are insufficient incentives on both the demand side and the supply side for meaningful competition between contract law (and dispute resolution)[238] regimes in Europe to arise.

As far as the demand side is concerned, Vogenauer says this is so partly because parties to a contract regularly differ as to their preferred contract law regime (and dispute resolution system, albeit to a lesser extent), which means that 'there are no preferences of 'business' as such; they can only be determined for a given party entering into a given transaction'.[239] But it is also because contracting parties typically cannot be sure what their preferences are at the time they conclude the contract and, moreover, are not in a position to obtain all of the information that would be needed to determine which contract law (and dispute resolution) regime comes closest to satisfying their preferences. This is essentially because the costs of

236 Vogenauer 2013, p. 274.

237 *Supra*, section A.2(b). In particular, Vogenauer observes that there is a multitude of different contract law regimes throughout Europe and, in the case of commercial contracts (to which his study is confined), market participants have 'almost unlimited' freedom of choice between these regimes, by virtue of the Rome I and Brussels I Regulations.

238 Vogenuaer's mention of competition between dispute resolution mechanisms (in state courts) as well as competition between contract laws can be explained by the fact that 'choices of contract law and choices of forum frequently go hand in hand' (Vogenauer 2013, p. 237).

239 Vogenauer 2013, p. 231.

discovering, analysing and assessing the benefits and drawbacks would be very high,[240] and would therefore overshadow any potential gains the parties may expect to make from choosing the most appropriate regime to govern their contract. Hence, according to Vogenauer, there is 'a classic market failure caused by customers suffering from imperfect information about the costs and benefits of the products available in the marketplace'.[241] And even if one were to assume that contracting parties have 'bounded' rather than 'full' rationality, he argues, it could at any rate be expected that the preferences of contracting parties will at any rate be 'guided by factors other than the substantive merits of the contract laws and fora on offer'.[242] These factors include familiarity with the given regime (that is, what behavioural economists call 'status quo bias'), the fact that there are many other parties who use the regime (what is known in economic literature as the 'network effect'), or even the 'reputation' of the regime, which, as Vogenauer points out, 'does not necessarily correspond to its real performance'.[243] So, for such reasons, there is little apparent incentive for contracting parties to predicate their choices of law and forum on the actual substantive quality of the various regimes available to them, as the model of regulatory competition advanced by the 'law market' theorists requires.

As for the supply side, Vogenauer asserts that manifest incentives are also largely absent here, for two main reasons. First, because it is clear that there are additional costs involved in introducing reforms aimed at making the law more attractive, including both direct costs attached to drafting legislative reforms and developing new case law, as well as indirect costs resulting from the provision of court services to the additional number of litigants that are eventually attracted to the newly-reformed system.[244] And second, because, conversely, it is far from clear what benefits a legislator might derive from attracting individuals to opt into its contract law system. It is not evident that a legislator would derive any direct benefits from this, since 'there are no taxes or fees arising from an agreement to have a transaction governed by a particular contract law or litigated in a particular forum'.[245] In the case of horizontal competition between states, there may be indirect financial benefits to be gained from more individuals engaging legal service providers in a given jurisdiction, including the state's legal profession and court system.[246] Yet, even in this case, Vogenauer retains that such benefits are for the most part intangible and insusceptible to quantification.[247] He therefore concludes that '[m]arket behaviour on the part of the "producers" of law cannot be predicted

240 See Vogenauer 2013, p. 232. By way of clarification, Vogenauer does actually accept that there is a 'wealth of information' on contract law regimes in various jurisdictions. However, he contends that it is not viable for parties to carry out a cost-benefit analysis of all these different regimes, which would be necessary in order for them to make a properly informed choice. On this see also Kieninger 2002.

241 Vogenauer 2013, p. 232.

242 Vogenauer 2013, p. 234.

243 Vogenauer 2013, p. 236.

244 See Vogenauer 2013, p. 237.

245 Vogenauer 2013, p. 238.

246 Smits 2013, p. 53.

247 Vogenauer 2013, p. 238.

with greater confidence than on the part of the "customers"',[248] since there is also no obvious incentive for legislators to ameliorate the substantive quality of their contract law regimes in order to render them more attractive to contracting parties, as the law market view of regulatory competition also requires.[249]

In turn, on the empirical level, Vogenauer claims that '[t]he evidence supports the prediction that regulatory competition in the areas under consideration will not emerge because there is insufficient incentive to invest the necessary resources for improvements of the law'.[250] While he begins his overview of the empirical evidence by noting the difficulty of finding data on the matter of and motivations behind party choice of law and forum,[251] Vogenauer goes on to undertake an extensive examination of the 'available evidence', consisting of a variety of data relating (in one way or another) to choices of contract law and forum, gathered in a total of eleven studies conducted by different individuals and organizations.[252] And, on the back of this assessment, he finds that there are 'no indications whatsoever of European legislatures and courts actually improving their "products" in the area of contract law with a view to acquiring new "customers"'.[253]

Equally, similar reservations to the idea of regulatory competition in the area of contract law have also been expressed by other academics. Michaels, for instance, shares the normative and empirical doubts surrounding the idea of a market for contract laws, adding that '[a] market would require a price mechanism: consumers would have to pay for the laws they choose, and producers of laws would have to benefit. But the choice of one law over the other does not create any direct costs to consumers, and no direct benefits to producers'.[254] In addition, as Michaels indicates, such misgivings had previously been voiced by Kieninger,[255] followed also by Peters.[256] In fact, as Vogenauer observes, even some of those who support the law market model as a general approach accept that its applicability in the field of contract law is dubitable. Parisi and Ribstein, for example, have conceded that, 'in the absence of a residual claim on the supplied legislation (e.g., the ability to charge a hypothetical price for the adoption of the supplied law by foreign parties)', and also 'absent a revenue effect of the parties' choice of law ... nothing explains the legislative incentive to enter the competitive race and improve the quality of the laws that they supply'.[257]

To summarize, then, these doubts go to the root of the law market thesis, insofar as they call into question the extent to which additional requirements needed for full regulatory competition to emerge within the EU are and can be

248 Vogenauer 2013, p. 237.
249 It will be recalled that this necessity for 'incentives to compete' was already mentioned above in a quotation of O'Hara & Ribstein, *supra*, footnote 116.
250 Vogenauer 2013, p. 272.
251 See Vogenauer 2013, p. 243.
252 See Vogenauer 2013, p. 244-256.
253 Vogenauer 2013, p. 272.
254 Michaels 2013, p. 27.
255 See Kieninger 2002.
256 See Peters 2010.
257 Parisi & Ribstein 1998, p. 241.

satisfied in the area of contract law. In other words, the possibility to choose between distinct yet co-existing regimes is, as Rühl acknowledges, a necessary but not sufficient condition for regulatory competition, since the law market model also 'requires that businesses and consumers actually exercise their freedom of choice and that they do so based on the quality of different legal rules',[258] and that legislators respond to such choices by seeking to create or maintain the best regime available[259] - and it is these added conditions that the aforementioned academics argue are not met in the case of contract law. For this reason, they maintain that the existence of and scope for genuine regulatory competition in this area is extremely limited at best, and therefore caution that the idea of a law market leading to legislative experimentation must be 'treated with care'.[260]

Of course, this is not to say that these authors are necessarily correct. Certainly many law market theorists dismiss the doubts they raise on both the conceptual and the empirical level. Conceptually, they contend that the possibility of regulatory competition in the area of contract law cannot be ruled on the basis of the arguments just noted. On the demand side, Rühl, for example, retorts that for regulatory competition to come into existence it is sufficient if a significant number of businesses and consumers are responsive to divergences in laws according to their quality[261] and, likewise, for such parties the quality of laws need not be the only or even the main factor in their choice of law; it just needs to be of sufficient importance.[262] A similar stance is also adopted by Ackermann, who states that, provided there are also incentives on the supply side, '[e]ven if there is only a small group of sophisticated parties who make a deliberate choice-of-law decision depending on the quality of the contract law, they are sufficient to induce a market process ...'.[263] And as regards information costs, while Rühl accepts that these will always be present, she also notes that advances in technology, and particularly the Internet, have led to reductions in such costs.[264] Whereas, on the supply side, these theorists insist that, as far as horizontal regulatory competition is concerned, the increased revenues that a more 'successful' contract law can bring for the providers of legal services in particular can be an influential incentive for the development of contract law, because '[e]ven if these services are not offered by the state itself, the state benefits from them as they generally generate taxable income (and higher voter satisfaction)'.[265] Furthermore, in response to Michaels' concern regarding the fact that private parties do not pay a price for the choice of a given contract law regime, Ackermann (interestingly, citing Google by way of analogy) points out that the 'assumption that competition always requires an exchange of goods for a price paid by the recipients of the goods is false'.[266]

258 Rühl 2013a, p. 66.
259 See also Vogenauer 2013, p. 274.
260 Vogenauer 2013, p. 274.
261 Rühl 2013a, p. 68.
262 Rühl 2013b, p. 288.
263 Ackermann 2013, p. 144.
264 See Rühl 2013a, p. 67.
265 Ackermann 2013, p. 144.
266 Ackermann 2013, p. 143.

As for the empirical level, adherents to the law market view hold that the available evidence demonstrates that the idea of regulatory competition in the field of contract law between national jurisdictions in Europe is actually borne out in practice. In fact, Rühl concludes on the basis of the very same studies examined by Vogenauer that what all of these studies demonstrate is actually that a significant proportion of businesses and consumers do choose the applicable law.[267] And a more recent empirical study on the international market for contracts by Cuniberti has also lent support to this conclusion.[268] Furthermore, Rühl claims that 'there is empirical evidence that states actually have an interest in the application of their contract laws and that they are actually willing to adjust their laws to the perceived needs of businesses and consumers'.[269] In particular, she points to the fact that in recent years European governments have actively sought to attract legal business from contracting parties, as is most clearly exemplified in the now infamous (and ongoing) case of the 'battle of the brochures' between the British, French and German jurisdictions, each of which have issued publications promoting their respective legal systems in an attempt to entice private parties to use their own regimes of contract law and dispute resolution.[270] These contentions are also supported by Engert, for instance, who affirms that '[t]here can be little doubt that we observe, at least in certain fields, conscious party choice of the applicable contract law. Jurisdictions also seem to care about how their contract laws fare in the law market'.[271]

Nevertheless, the point remains that, as Rühl attests to herself, the existence, or possible existence, of regulatory competition in contract law is very much contested.[272] Admittedly, as far as vertical regulatory competition is concerned, Vogenauer does concede that 'the introduction of an optional European contract law instrument might eventually lead to (vertical) regulatory competition between this instrument and the contract laws of the Member States',[273] especially because it offers parties 'the added benefit of providing a neutral regime',[274] and also because, '[g]iven the unique position of the EU to promote and enforce its law, parties are bound to become familiar with the new instrument over time'.[275] This concords with Smits' point (noted previously) that vertical competition can avert a number of the problems associated with traditional jurisdictional competition, and particularly those relating to the lack of information about available legal options in different national jurisdictions, since it will in any event be easier to provide information on optional European regimes in more languages than is possible in case of national

267 Rühl 2013a, p. 68-69.
268 Cuniberti 2014.
269 Rühl 2013b, p. 288.
270 On this 'battle' see in more detail Kötz 2010, and also Smits 2011.
271 Engert 2013, p. 304.
272 Rühl 2013a, p. 63.
273 Vogenauer 2013, p. 274. As Vogenauer also notes, however, others doubt even the possibility of vertical regulatory competition in the area of contract law (cf. Leible 2012).
274 Vogenauer 2013, p. 275.
275 Vogenauer 2013, p. 274. On this point see also Smits 2013, p. 54.

jurisdictions.[276] However, as Vogenauer also indicates, the issue of status quo bias represents an obstacle to vertical regulatory competition as much as it does to traditional jurisdictional competition.[277] What is more, it is arguably even less clear what incentives the EU legislator might have to attract parties to opt into a Union contract law regime, given that it has no 'jurisdiction' (and particularly no dispute resolution system or legal services sector) of its own in this area. And, in turn, this suggests that Member States would not necessarily suffer financial losses as a result of parties opting into an optional European contract law instrument, which could mean that, if anything, there is less incentive still for national legislators to introduce domestic reforms if parties are afforded the possibility of choosing a legal regime that better satisfies their preferences.[278] Therefore Vogenauer still questions 'whether such an exodus from national contract laws will ever happen and, if so, whether it will put competitive pressure on national law makers to improve their own contract laws'.[279]

Furthermore, similar doubts have also been expressed (and refuted)[280] by academics in the context of European company law. That is, like in the field of contract law, it is possible to identify *two* central questions arising out of the European debate, namely whether regulatory competition exists *and* whether it is desirable.[281] And, also in line with the contract law discussion, the former question has been debated at both the conceptual and the empirical levels (particularly, but not only, in relation to horizontal regulatory competition). At the conceptual level, the concern is again that there are inadequate incentives on both the supply and the demand side for functioning regulatory competition to emerge. On the supply side, some commentators point out that European states are not in a position to earn a comparable proportion of fiscal revenues through franchise tax as the US state of Delaware.[282] Additionally, there is also the fact that incorporation fees are not permitted within the EU.[283] Whereas, on the demand side, 'many authors stress that companies do not have the same choice as in the United States, at least in those states that follow the real seat theory. Moreover, choice is felt to be more difficult because at least continental company law seems to be more complex ...'.[284] Plus, of course, other factors such as that of status quo bias can be expected to play a role in the choice of company law too.[285] While, at the empirical level, it has again been

276 Smits 2013, p. 54.

277 On the other hand, as Smits rightly indicates, 'the marketing of an optional instrument as a European system may pre-empt lock in-effects among parties who are active on the European market: they may be better prepared to opt out of the law they use at present ...' (Smits 2013, p. 57).

278 See Vogenauer 2013, p. 275.

279 Vogenauer 2013, p. 275.

280 See, for example, Grundmann 2002; Rühl 2013a; and even Vogenauer 2013.

281 See Grundmann 2002, p. 567.

282 See Grundmann 2002, p. 565, referring specifically to Charny 1991.

283 Cf. Vogenauer 2013, p. 230. On the lack of incentives for national lawmakers in Europe in the area of company law, see also McCahery & Vermeulen 2005, p. 797.

284 Grundmann 2002, p. 565, referring especially to Habersack 1999.

285 Cf. McCahery & Vermeulen 2005, p. 791.

argued that there is scant evidence of meaningful regulatory competition between company law regimes in Europe.[286]

As far as regards vertical regulatory competition, the question of whether there is (or can be) something special about EU OIs that makes them more likely to induce an 'exodus' of private actors from national regimes (and, thereby, to eventually exert 'competitive pressure' on national legislators) has been discussed in more concrete terms in the context of European company law, due to the fact that EU OIs have already been adopted in this area. That is, there has been deeper debate as to the features of OIs that could enhance their attractiveness to potential users, and specifically whether OIs like the European Company (SE) possess such features.[287] In particular, apart from the benefit of providing a neutral regime (which the SE is also said to do),[288] the degree of uniformity of EU OIs has been mooted as another factor that could influence attractiveness to private actors.[289] Indeed, there are many commentators who claim that this is another element that may influence the attractiveness of Union regimes.[290] Yet, for this exact reason, many of them argue that the SE, being an optional instrument that lacks uniformity,[291] is therefore unlikely to attract the number of individuals needed for (vertical) regulatory competition to possibly emerge. According to McCahery and Vermeulen, for instance, 'the failure of the European Statute to address the problem of taxation will clearly undermine the number of firms incorporating as European companies'.[292] More precisely, these authors 'expect that the absence of a specific tax regime, particularly with regard to cross-border real seat transfers, will be a significant impediment to its use by a *majority* of firms'.[293] And this has arguably proven to be the case (at least so far). Certainly, as we have seen,[294] many consider that the number of companies that have selected the SE since its entry into force is relatively low. On the other hand, Siems, for example, contends that the SE could yet prove an attractive instrument for private actors and thereby lead to regulatory competition, even with (or rather, precisely because of) its lack of uniformity. That is, according to Siems, the SE will still prove to be popular with eligible companies 'interested in "shopping around" for the best company law',[295] because its extensive

286 See, for example, Vermeulen *et al.* 2009.

287 This issue is also discussed in greater detail as part of the explanatory theory of EU OIs and the case study on the SE elaborated in Chapter 5.

288 See further Chapter 5, section C.2.

289 In fact, this aspect has also been raised in the discussion on the 2011 proposal for a Common European Sales Law. See, for example, Smits 2013, and also further Chapter 6, section 2(b).

290 See also Chapter 5.

291 On the lack of uniformity of the SE and other EU OIs see, *supra* section A.3(a)(i). This also demonstrates that the criticism that EU OIs lack uniformity is linked not only to the EU regimes for EU activities rationale but also to other arguments put forward in relation to EU OIs.

292 McCahery & Vermeulen 2005, p. 799, citing also Bolkestein 2003. See also Edwards 2003, p. 463, referred to already above, and Cerioni 2007, p. 124-125.

293 McCahery & Vermeulen 2005, p. 799 (italics added), referring also to Thommes 2004.

294 See *supra*, section A.2(c).

295 Siems 2005, p. 438.

reliance on the laws of the Member States[296] actually facilitates *national* company law shopping within the EU, by virtue of the fact that companies have a degree of freedom in selecting the Member State in which they incorporate as an SE. In other words, 'the very lack of a uniform regime may prove to be a key factor for the success of the SE'. The SE is said to have no specific features of its own which make it particularly attractive, 'but its attractive feature is the choice it allows between elements of national company law'.[297] He therefore arrives at the conclusion (also previously reached by Winter)[298] that at any rate one can expect some competition for the best company law as a result of the SE, meaning national legislators are still likely to face greater pressure to offer attractive company laws themselves.[299] Although, in his view, this pressure would be the result of the SE effectively *increasing horizontal* regulatory competition between the company laws of the Member States, rather than *instigating vertical* regulatory competition between itself and corresponding national regimes.

Thus, in sum, it is fair to say that the question whether functional regulatory competition is (or even can be) present in these areas of European law, to name but two, remains unsettled.

At the same time, there are others who accept the law market theorists' premise that regulatory competition (both horizontal and vertical) can and does exist in different areas of European law such as those just discussed, but who dispute the verdict that such competition gives rise to a race to the top. Instead, they maintain that regulatory competition leads to a 'race to the bottom'.

The concept of a race to the bottom - that is, the notion that regulatory competition could give rise to a *reduction* in standards - was first introduced in the context of the US company law debate by Berle and Means, who, as noted above, were opposed to the emergence of such competition.[300] Decades later, the concept was rejuvenated by Cary,[301] who argued that the reason why regulatory competition had resulted in Delaware becoming the leading incorporation state was 'because this state offered management the solution which best favoured her interests at the expense of the interests of the investors, solving the inherent principal agent conflict in favour of the agent'.[302] As a result, this idea of a reduction in standards, whereby states reform their substantive corporate laws in order to make them more beneficial only or mainly for certain parties (i.e. 'those parties who make - or at least strongly influence - the decision of where to incorporate'),[303] became known alternatively as the *Delaware* effect. So although, unlike in the case of European company law, the existence of regulatory competition in US company law

296 On this point, Siems notes that the number of references the SE Regulation makes to the laws of the Member States has been found to total 84.
297 Siems 2005, p. 437.
298 Winter 2003. The statement cited by Siems in the next quotation is made by Winter 2003, p. 122.
299 Siems 2005, p. 439.
300 Berle & Means 1932.
301 Cary 1974.
302 Grundmann 2002, p. 563.
303 Rühl 2013a, p. 80.

has not been the subject of any serious doubt, the notion that such competition is desirable because it engenders a race to the top certainly has.

And this is also the case in Europe, where, as indicated previously, the prevailing view at the outset was that regulatory competition constituted an unsound mechanism for lawmaking in the field of company law.[304] In fact, even the European legislator was apparently of the opinion that such competition should be discouraged, as the company law harmonization efforts of the EC were aimed partly, or even mainly, at preventing a Delaware effect in the Community.[305] More precisely, as McCahery and Vermeulen explain, 'the aim of the EU was to limit the right of establishment of pseudo-foreign companies and create barriers to the introduction of charter competition',[306] by enacting approximating measures that 'avoided intervention into the national legislation of Member States that has limited cross-border mobility of firms'[307] (such as tax and other national law barriers). Importantly, this approach was supported by the founding Member States and France and West Germany in particular, who were afraid of the possibility of a 'race to the bottom'.[308] It was for this reason that the European legislator limited the scope for competition between national company law regimes by allowing Member States to maintain barriers to the mobility of companies within the EU (or, as McCahery and Vermeulen put it, to preserve 'a stable, long-run non-competitive equilibrium').[309] It is true that this situation was later altered by the judgments of the European Court of Justice in *Centros*, *Überseering* and *Inspire Art*,[310] which recognized the right of companies to incorporate in any Member State no matter whether they have a further link to the State of incorporation,[311] thereby potentially opening the door to a more market-based approach to company lawmaking in Europe.[312] But the point is that the emergence of a 'European Delaware' in the area of company law has long been opposed by academics and legislators alike on the ground that it would induce lawmakers in Europe to adopt company law codes that impose lower and fewer standards on firms - and many continue to oppose it on this basis. Indeed, as Grundmann observes, 'even recent textbooks on European company law take this view'.[313]

304 See, for example, Schmitthoff 1973; Wiedemann 1980. For a detailed account of the debate on the desirability of regulatory competition in European company law (and particularly the question whether it induces a race to the top or a race to the bottom), see Sachdeva 2010, p. 137 *et seq*.

305 See Grundmann 2002, p. 565.

306 McCahery & Vermeulen 2005, p. 788.

307 McCahery & Vermeulen 2005, p. 787.

308 See McCahery & Vermeulen 2005, p. 791.

309 Indeed, it could be argued that this is at least part of the reason why there has arguably been only limited regulatory competition taking place in the field of European company law.

310 Case C-212/97, *Centros Ltd* v *Erhvervs- og Selskabsstyrelsen* [1999] ECR I-1459; Case 208/00, *Überseering BV* v *Nordic Construction Company Baumanagement GmbH* [2002] ECR I-9919; Case C-167/01, *Kamer van Koophandel en Fabrieken voor Amsterdam* v *Inspire Art Ltd* [2003] ECR I-10155.

311 Vogenauer 2013, p. 242.

312 On this point see e.g. McCahery & Vermeulen 2001, p. 857.

313 Grundmann 2002, p. 565.

Likewise, concerns that regulatory competition sparks a race to the bottom rather than a race to the top have also been voiced in the domain of European contract law. Admittedly, it is not immediately obvious how the race to the bottom argument could apply in this field because, as Rühl points out, 'a choice of the applicable contract law - at least as a matter of principle - only affects the immediate parties of the contract, i.e. the parties that actually agree on the choice of law'.[314] Therefore, provided that this choice is a free and informed one, it could be expected that 'states do not have an incentive to skew their contract laws one-sidedly towards one party. Rather they have an incentive to account for the interests of all parties involved'.[315] However, this is not necessarily the case, because some contractual choice of law clauses are negotiated by parties with unequal bargaining power (in the context of consumer contracts, for instance), while others affect individuals who are not party to the contract. Hence a race to the bottom scenario has also been predicted in the area of contract law, insofar as legislators may 'compete to attract parties to contracts that impose costs on third parties, or that benefit powerful contract drafters at the expense of weaker contracting parties',[316] by making their laws skewed in favour of these former parties. Eidenmüller, for example, has argued that inequality in bargaining power or exclusion from the drafting process could result in a race to the bottom between contract laws in Europe.[317] As a matter of fact, even Rühl has conceded that these 'are cases that are more likely to trigger a race to the bottom than a race to the top'.[318] For this reason, as we have seen, her argument, like Grundmann's, is that regulatory competition can *usually* be expected to induce a race to the top, although this may be dependent on such competition being regulated in such a way as to curtail market failures such as these.[319]

Once again, then, there is not yet a clear-cut answer at the normative level to the question whether regulatory competition (to the extent that it exists) spawns a race to the top or the race to the bottom.[320] Nor is there any definitive support for a particular answer at the empirical level, because, in certain areas of law, such as contract law, '[j]ust as in other areas of law, notably corporate law, there is no empirical evidence available that would point into one or the other direction'.[321] Thus, as authors such as Sun and Pelkmans and also Hornuf[322] have found, the benefits of regulatory competition are uncertain (too), and must at any rate be assessed on a case-by-case basis.

In conclusion, it is difficult to form a judgment on both the possibility and the desirability of regulatory competition in Europe, especially from an abstract perspective. Fortunately, however, the aim of this study is not to provide an answer

314 Rühl 2013a, p. 81.
315 Rühl 2013a, p. 81.
316 O'Hara & Ribstein 2009, p. 33.
317 See Eidenmüller 2009. See also Kieninger 2002.
318 Rühl 2013a, p. 84.
319 The possible need for regulation is also acknowledged by O'Hara & Ribstein 2009, p. 33 *et seq.*
320 See Rühl 2013a, p. 80.
321 Rühl 2013a, p. 80-81.
322 Sun & Pelkman 1995; Hornuf 2012. See also Reich 1992.

to such questions. Rather, the issue for present purposes is what significance the doubts raised by these discussions have for the overall case for EU OIs. Now, viewed from this angle, it is submitted that the uncertainty surrounding the plausibility of regulatory competition does not strike one as a particularly strong argument against the OI method. It is at most a qualification, in the sense that it obliges one to say that EU OIs preserve *the possibility of* horizontal regulatory competition while at the same creating *the possibility of* vertical regulatory competition (i.e. to the extent that such competition can and does exist in a given area of European law). On the other hand, the misgivings over the desirability of regulatory competition are potentially more damaging to the case for EU OIs, of course, as they suggest that regulatory competition should not be encouraged and, therefore, that the OI method should not be used, *precisely because* it accommodates the possibility of such competition. Still, it is arguable that these reservations should not be seen as fatal to the case for the OI method either, bearing in mind the point made by law market theorists that the race to the bottom scenario can be averted if regulatory competition is itself regulated in such a way as to curtail market failure. In particular, as far as vertical regulatory competition is concerned, this entails that a Union OI can be expected to lead to a race to the top, provided it is not designed to attract private actors (particularly companies) through a reduction in the legal standards to which they would otherwise be subject, but instead establishes a legal regime that also reflects the needs of other parties (particularly weaker ones). And one can certainly expect the EU legislator to give due consideration to the interests of such parties: Indeed as far as regards the area of contract law, for example, the European legislator is legally bound to promote the interests of consumers and to ensure a high level of consumer protection.[323] So it seems more fitting to characterize the concern of a race to the bottom also as a qualification, particularly when it comes to vertical regulatory competition.

(ii) The Social Justice Perspective

In any event, whether or not the OI method fosters regulatory competition, and whether or not this is 'a good thing', what remains beyond doubt is that EU legislation establishing OIs does enlarge the scope for private actors to choose between different legal regimes. And, as we saw, this was said to be beneficial in and of itself, because the availability of additional legal options for private actors can enable them to better satisfy their needs. Indeed for Smits, for example, it is this freedom for parties to choose between diverse legal regimes that provides the main justification for adopting a law market-based approach, over and above the possibility of regulatory competition and any resulting improvement in standards.[324]

323 Art. 169 of the Treaty on the Functioning of the European Union.
324 On the importance of party choice for Smits, see notably Smits 2012c, Smits 2010c.

Yet, the overall desirability of greater party choice[325] has also been called into question by numerous commentators, on the ground that there exist other values than private autonomy, such as social justice and fairness, which rather point in the direction of *restricting* party choice. Again this has been a bone of contention especially (but not only) in the area of European contract law, the principal concern here being that the availability of additional options for contracting parties is in reality a licence for 'sophisticated' parties with strong bargaining power (such as large multinational corporations) to escape mandatory domestic rules designed to protect weaker parties, such as consumers.[326] This concern centres on the proposed Common European Sales law (CESL), as currently under the rules of private international law (specifically Art. 6 of the Rome I Regulation),[327] choices of law in consumer contracts cannot have the effect of depriving consumers of protection accorded to them by the law applicable in their habitual Member State of residence (or 'home State'). By contrast, the CESL inevitably would have had this effect in some cases, because 'even if the optional instrument will contain consumer protection of a very high level it is unlikely that the 28th regime, compared to all other 27, will consistently provide the highest level protection [sic] on all subjects'.[328] Hence, to one degree or another (depending on the law of the given Member State), 'for some consumers a choice for an optional instrument will inevitably lead to some loss of protection on at least some subjects'.[329] For this reason, many argue that, while the introduction of more legal options may be desirable from the perspective of party autonomy, it may not be from the perspective of social justice.

The call for greater attention to social justice in European contract law has been led by the Study Group on Social Justice in European Private Law chaired by Martijn Hesselink. According to the Study Group's *Manifesto*, given that '[t]he rules of contract law shape the distribution of wealth and power in modern societies…[a] modern statement of the principles of the private law of contract needs to recognise its increasingly pivotal role in establishing distributive fairness in society'.[330] Put differently, it should be recognized that the function of contract law - as demonstrated by national contract law regimes - is not only to promote free trade and market efficiency, but it is also to achieve fairness in the distribution of contract gains, particularly by protecting weaker parties (like consumers, but also others with (potentially) weak bargaining power, such as small businesses, employees, etc.) against large enterprises. Therefore, the Study Group contends that:

> 'A unified law will … have to strike a balance between, on the one hand, the weight attached to individual private autonomy as expressed in the idea of freedom of

325 This issue is discussed in greater detail from the perspective of private actors below, section C.

326 See further below, section C.

327 Regulation 593/2008 of the European Parliament and the Council of 17 June 2008 on the law applicable to contractual obligations (Rome I).

328 Hesselink 2010, p. 16.

329 Hesselink 2010, p. 16.

330 Study Group on Social Justice in European Private Law 2004, p. 665.

> contract, and on the other hand, principles which respect other equally important demands for social solidarity, which prohibit individuals from taking advantage of superior economic strength ...'[331]

So, in short, these authors maintain that national contract law regimes must offset the interests of private autonomy against those of social justice in order to prevent unfairness arising from imbalances in the positions of parties to certain contracts, and ergo the same should be true of a Union optional regime. Accordingly, this entails that a Union optional instrument in the field of contract law should not allow certain individuals to circumvent mandatory national laws intended to protect other individuals by making available an alternative regime that provides for less protection (a circumstance that may be referred to as 'social dumping').[332]

This need to balance the interests of party autonomy with those of social justice has been asserted by others as well, though. Storme, for instance, argues that:

> 'Unlimited choice of law is often simply imposing the law chosen by the offeror ... It is justified to limit the choice of law in certain relationships, or at least to limit its effects by applying the mandatory rules of (for example) the country of the consumer, the tenant, the employee, etc. When we take the protective function of law seriously, when we believe that there are other values than private autonomy to be balanced, then we need a Market Law rather than a Law Market; and then we cannot simply throw this rule of law away simply because a relationship is cross-border. There is no justification between a domestic regime on the one hand and 'anything goes' in transnational contracts.'[333]

Also in the opinion of the European Economic and Social Committee, a contract law OI 'should not be used to bypass mandatory provisions of national law',[334] and therefore the Commission 'must assess the risk of it being used to bypass national mandatory rules to the detriment of weaker parties'.[335] And the concern that EU OIs can result in social injustice if the EU legislator fails to take into account these 'other values' has been expressed in relation to other areas of European law, too. For example, Rutgers (a member of the Study Group on Social Justice in European Private Law) claims that this has actually already happened in the area of European Company law with the introduction of the SE, insofar as this OI has enabled companies to evade national rules on worker participation. More precisely, after examining available empirical research, Rutgers affirms that '[f]rom the surveys

331 Study Group on Social Justice in European Private Law 2004, p. 656.

332 On this see notably Rutgers 2006, and Rutgers 2011. In fact, in the way Rutgers and others use this term, it is largely synonymous with that of the 'race to the bottom'; see also Hesselink 2010. However, for present purposes it is employed specifically to denote the use of optional regimes by some private actors to circumvent mandatory rules to the detriment of others.

333 Storme 2010, p. 429.

334 Follow-up of the European Commission on the EESC opinion on 'The 28th regime - an alternative allowing less lawmaking at Community level', p. 2.

335 Opinion of the European Economic and Social Committee on 'The 28th regime - an alternative allowing less lawmaking at Community level' (own-initiative opinion) CESE 758/2010, 1.14.

with respect to the SE it follows that one of the main reasons to establish a SE is to avoid the rules on employee involvement under the national rules'.[336]

In fact, even some law market theorists have conceded that it can be necessary to impose limits on private autonomy. O'Hara & Ribstein, for instance, acknowledge that individuals 'clearly should not always be able to circumvent mandatory rules ...' by choosing between different regimes, and therefore that it is also necessary to 'acknowledge a role for regulating states to attempt to protect their regulations against the eroding effects of choice of law'.[337] Having said that, these authors do not accept that there is necessarily a need for legislative intervention in all cases of inequality in bargaining power. In particular, as far as consumer contracts are concerned, they contend that there might not be any need for legislators to intervene in more competitive markets, since businesses active in such markets may incur 'some reputational or other market penalty for unreasonably enforcing one-sided terms ...'.[338] Similarly, Smits also recognizes the need for national legislators to uphold rules that may be considered essential to their domestic legal orders in certain cases; although in his view this only covers so-called 'super-mandatory laws', in the sense of fundamental rules of public policy that cannot be rendered inapplicable by a (horizontal) choice of law.[339]

Thus, it is generally accepted that there is a need to place constraints on party choice. The question, though, is *to what extent* party choice should be restricted. Clearly if one were to follow the line of those who plead for greater social justice in economic relations between private parties, the answer would be to a relatively large extent, as the social justice perspective dictates that the freedom for parties to choose must stop at most (if not all) mandatory rules of national law. Hence, this would lead one to conclude that the fact that EU OIs make additional legal regimes available for such parties to choose is not a point that stands in their favour. On the contrary, it is a detrimental aspect of the OI method that speaks against its use, unless the EU legislator ensures that the availability of a Union optional regime cannot free those who opt into it from being governed by mandatory domestic rules in the Member States in which they operate. If, however, one attaches greater importance to private autonomy, the answer would be that the limits set on party choice should not go beyond what is strictly necessary, and, in particular, should be confined to only the more (if not the most) essential mandatory rules of national law (i.e. super-mandatory rules). Therefore, from this perspective, it is not a problem if a Union optional instrument enables individuals to opt out of not only default but also mandatory national laws, provided that the mandatory laws in question are not of a fundamental nature. So, on this view, the need to take into account the interests

336 Rutgers 2011, p. 359.

337 O'Hara & Ribstein 2009, p. 36.

338 O'Hara & Ribstein 2009, p. 34.

339 See Smits 2012c, p. 170 *et seq*. Such rules are referred to in the Rome I Regulation as 'overriding mandatory provisions', which are defined in Art. 9 as 'provisions the respect for which is regarded as crucial by a country for safeguarding its public interests, such as its political, social or economic organisation, to such an extent that they are applicable to any situation falling within their scope, irrespective of the law otherwise applicable to the contract ...'.

of social justice would constitute nothing more than a caveat to the case for EU OIs, since the provision of additional options to private actors remains for the most part something to be encouraged.

To conclude, the issue of where the line should be drawn between private autonomy and social justice is another fiercely debated one that will doubtless continue to be discussed for years to come. Nevertheless, focusing again specifically on the significance of the concerns brought up in this debate for the discussion on the desirability of EU OIs as a legislative method, it is submitted that the latter appreciation of such concerns - i.e. as amounting to another qualification at most - again appears to be the more appropriate one. Recalling once more the point that the EU legislator is required to ensure a high level of protection for weaker parties such as consumers, it does seem reasonable to expect that it will have sufficient regard to the interests of such parties in promulgating its OIs. As a matter of fact, as far as regards the area of contract law, one of the explicit aims of the CESL proposal was exactly to provide mandatory consumer protection rules that would 'guarantee a high level of consumer protection with a view to enhancing consumer confidence in the Common European Sales Law and thus provide consumers with an incentive to enter into cross-border contracts on that basis'.[340] And indeed the CESL as proposed was widely considered to provide this high level of protection - or at least a level that 'is about as high under the CESL as it is under any national law' - even if it 'does not contain every rule of consumer protection found anywhere in the EU Member States'.[341] So there are good reasons for thinking that the EU legislator does take the values of social justice sufficiently into account in its design of optional regimes.

(c) The Lack of Converging Effect of EU OIs

The third (counter-) argument that is to be mentioned in our discussion of the case against EU OIs is that Union optional regimes are unlikely to have a converging effect on national laws, and even if they do, it will be a very limited one.[342]

It will be recalled from our account of the case for EU OIs that the two principal reasons that have been adduced for thinking that EU OIs can have an indirect 'converging effect' are, first, that the process of regulatory competition said to be fostered by OIs can result in national legal convergence; and, second, that OIs perform the added roles of a 'model law' (in the sense that they can serve as a source of inspiration and point of reference for domestic reforms in the different Member States) and 'vehicle for communication between Member States' (that is, a mechanism to encourage national legislators to draw inspiration from each other).

340 Proposal for a Regulation on a Common European Sales Law, COM(2011) 635 final., consideration 11.

341 Beale 2012, p. 134-135.

342 In fact, one might even go as far as to argue that, by creating additional regimes, EU OIs actually serve to *increase* legal diversity in Europe; cf. Low 2012a, 142. See also *infra*, section C.1(b).

Now, as regards the first of these reasons, it was already indicated[343] that the weakness of this point is that it relies on the assumption that the conditions necessary for regulatory competition to exist are present in the various areas of European law in which EU optional regimes have been adopted (or proposed); yet, as was observed in the preceding section,[344] the existence of and scope for meaningful regulatory competition in Europe is very much disputed. And even those who affirm such competition exists within the EU do accept that a range of cumulative requirements need to be satisfied in order for it to arise. These include not least the requirement that a substantial number of businesses and consumers actually exercise their freedom to choose between distinct legal regimes, which, in the specific context of vertical regulatory competition, entails that any competitive pressure a given EU optional regime may ultimately exert on the European law market is contingent on a significant proportion of eligible private actors opting into it. Hence, it follows that if relatively few private actors select a Union optional regime as the regime to govern their activities, it is unlikely to stimulate regulatory competition and, accordingly, unlikely to bring about the national legal convergence that may ensue from such competition. In other words, 'the answer is dependent on whether and the extent to which private parties consider and opt for it …'.[345] So, in sum, the production of a converging effect by EU OIs through the inducement of regulatory competition is conditional on the requirements for regulatory competition being satisfied; and, to the extent that regulatory competition does not exist, then such an effect cannot materialize either. That is, 'this entire argument rests on the proper functioning of regulatory competition'.[346]

Moving then to the second reason, the conception of EU OIs as a model law and vehicle for communication between Member States appears to be a less controversial one, as there is little doubt that legislation establishing EU OIs can also serve these functions. What may be questioned, however, is the extent to which this can have a converging effect (or at least a significant converging effect) on the laws of the Member States.

Beginning with the former, it is true that sets of model rules such as the Principles of European Contract Law (PECL) have had a noteworthy influence on legal reforms in certain EU Member States. Most notably, Member States in Central and Eastern Europe have used the PECL as a reference for legal inspiration. For instance, the PECL has served as one of the principal sources for the Estonian Law of Obligations Act.[347] Yet, it is also true that most national legislators have not done so, which denotes that, while it may have led to some convergence between domestic rules of private law in Europe, the converging effect of the PECL has been limited. In fact, the European Commission itself has expressly acknowledged this drawback of 'soft' model law. Referring specifically to the possibility of adopting a Recommendation inviting Member States to assimilate the recommended European

343 *Supra*, section A.2(c).
344 *Supra*, section A.3(b)(i).
345 Low 2012a, p. 143.
346 Low 2012a, p. 144.
347 Cf. Varul 2008.

instrument into their national laws as one of the legislative options available in the area of European contract law - incidentally, in the same Green Paper that put forward the option of an optional instrument which was ultimately selected - the Commission states that, since a recommended instrument would not be binding on Member States and 'would allow them discretion in how and when to implement the instrument into their national laws ... this solution bears the risk of an incoherent and incomplete approach between the Member States, which might enact the Recommendation differently and at different moments in time or not at all'. This is important because it entails that even the European legislator would subscribe to the view that the converging effect an optional instrument might have as a form of model law is at any rate a limited one.

As for the latter, it is worth noting that the Court of Justice of the EU has also cast doubt on the idea that a Union optional instrument can have a more than remote approximating effect on national laws, even in the case of an optional instrument that makes numerous references to the laws of the Member States. More precisely, the Court of Justice raised such doubts in its ruling on the action for annulment brought by the European Parliament against the Regulation on the Statute for a European Cooperative Society (SCE);[348] an optional instrument that, as we have seen, is comparable to the SE not least because it too leaves many matters to be determined by national law.[349] In this ruling, as we saw previously,[350] the Court found that the SCE Regulation could not be said to 'approximate' the laws of the Member States within the meaning of the then Article 95 TEC (i.e. the alternative legal basis for the measure advocated by the European Parliament, as well as the Commission) - and this was notwithstanding 'the fact that the contested regulation does not lay down exhaustively all of the rules applicable to European cooperative societies and that, for certain matters, it refers to the law of the Member State in the territory of which the European cooperative society has its registered office ...'.[351] To recall the exact wording of the Court, it held that the SCE Regulation, 'which leaves unchanged the different national laws already in existence, cannot be regarded as aiming to approximate the laws of the Member States applicable to cooperative societies ...'.[352] This is also pertinent, as it will be remembered that Siems mentions precisely a European company form that refers extensively to existing domestic laws (namely the comparable SE) as an example of an OI that, in his view, can lead to national legal convergence by increasing communication between national legislators regarding their respective regimes. However, this ruling suggests that the Court of Justice for one considers this to be a negligible possibility. And indeed, as Low points out, 'there is no evidence linking the introduction of optional instruments in company ... law to the convergence of the relevant Member States' laws'.[353]

348 Case C-436/03 *European Parliament* v *Council* (*European Cooperative Society*) [2006] ECR I-3733.

349 See Chapter 3, SCE description.

350 Chapter 2, section B.3.

351 Case C-436/03, *European Cooperative Society*, para. 45.

352 *Ibid.*, para. 44.

353 Low 2012a, p. 142.

Suffice it to say, then, that just as there may be reasons to believe that EU OIs do have the potential to produce a converging effect at national level in some way, so there are also reasons to suppose that this effect of EU OIs is insufficient, if not inexistent.

(d) The Economic Case against EU OIs

The last key point in the case against EU OIs calls for a reconsideration of the economic arguments behind the OI method, particularly in the light of the points noted so far.

It will be remembered that three main arguments were advanced in the economic case for EU OIs, all of which were founded on normative arguments that preceded them. First, it was argued that EU OIs reduce the costs faced by private actors arising from national legal divergence, by making available to such actors a Union legal regime that is uniform across the Member States; which means that EU OIs can offer actual or aspiring cross-border operators the same cost savings as similarization measures (if not even greater savings, as uniformity is sought in a single, common regime, rather than in multiple domestic regimes). At the same time, it was claimed that EU OIs do not give rise to as many costs as similarization measures do, mainly because they preserve (if not even increase) the possibility for national legislators to engage in legal experimentation, as well as the legal options available to private actors. Finally, it was contended that, unlike similarization measures, EU OIs are generally also intended to allow private actors to avoid costs attached to the territorial limitations of Member State laws, by creating regimes the applicability of which extends throughout the (usually entire) territory of the European Union.

Now we will see that, in a similar vein, the counter-arguments in the economic case against EU OIs flow principally from the previous normative arguments against the OI method.

Thus, the first economic argument against EU OIs is that many of them do not allow private actors to evade the costs of national legal diversity, or at least not to the degree that has been suggested, because they are significantly lacking in uniformity. That is to say, to the extent that a given EU OI lacks uniformity, it will not serve to diminish transaction costs caused by national legal diversity. This reflects the point made previously[354] that the less uniform a Union optional regime is, the less likely it will be to enable private actors to overcome the barrier of national legal diversity. Once again, then, this argument holds most weight in respect of those EU OIs that make numerous references to the laws of the Member States, such as the Regulation establishing the SE. Indeed, as we have seen, although the SE Regulation was (like most EU OIs) expressly intended to liberate companies with a European dimension from obstacles arising from *both* 'the disparity and the limited territorial application of national company law',[355] the former aim is arguably undermined by the fact that the SE defers to national law in a number of

354 *Supra*, section A.3(a)(i).
355 SE Regulation, consideration 7.

areas, not least that of corporate taxation. Whereas, conversely, the same argument would have less force when it comes to EU OIs that appear to be considerably more uniform in character, such as those in the area of IP law. So, in short, just as the uniformity of EU OIs varies significantly from one OI to another, so too do the cost savings that can be expected to result from their creation.

Furthermore, the second economic argument against EU OIs follows from the alternative view of regulatory competition and the law market. For, if one subscribes to the view that, by fostering experimentation by legislators and enhancing party choice, the law market-based approach ultimately results (or at least could result) in a race to the bottom and social dumping, this implies that such an approach imports other costs, which could overshadow the costs of constraining regulatory competition through the similarization method. In other words, as Reich puts it, 'where social values like consumer ... or worker protection are subject to competition between legal orders, this may result in a downgrading of standards *and in the long run eliminate competitive advantages*'.[356] Hence one may pose the question, as Reich does, whether competition between legal orders will 'result in more efficient and workable competition, or will it distort competition within the EC?'[357] Admittedly, as we have already observed - and as Reich also recognizes - it is not possible to provide a simple answer to this question.[358] But the point is that enabling regulatory competition can give rise to costs of its own, which must also be taken into account in order for a proper cost-benefit analysis of the law market approach to be carried out. So '[i]n every case a detailed analysis is required to decide upon whether competition increases public choice and welfare...or whether it leads to unjustified competitive advantages ...'.[359]

Finally, as we have also noted already,[360] the complexity of analyses such as these entails that any financial valuations derived from them are at any rate largely uncertain, even in specific cases. And this also goes for the cost savings EU OIs are estimated to offer private actors by enabling them to surmount the barrier of territoriality. In the case of the Unitary Patent, for instance, we have seen the Commission's estimates of the cost savings the UP can be expected to offer private actors by providing them with an 'EU regime' may be doubted. It is therefore also important to remember this significant limitation of the economic arguments that are made in support of EU OIs.

4. *Overall Evaluation of EU OIs*

At this stage it is necessary to conclude our examination of the principal arguments for and against the use of optional instruments by the EU legislator (which, as we have seen, centre on the advantages and disadvantages of the OI method as compared to similarization). Our account began by elucidating the two motivations

356 Reich 1992, p. 868 (italics added), referring to Porter 1990.
357 Reich 1992, p. 863.
358 See Reich 1992, p. 863.
359 Reich 1992, p. 896.
360 *Supra*, section A.2(d).

that have been expressly put forward by the legislator itself to explain the use of OIs - namely the desire to create EU regimes for EU activities and that of leaving national legal orders unaffected. It then proceeded to explore other arguments supporting the OI method, which have not been advanced (or at least not explicitly) by the European legislator. These were, first, that EU OIs can be introduced in areas where similarization measures are politically impracticable; second, that EU OIs allow for a law market-based approach (thereby fostering legal experimentation by national legislators and increasing legal options for private actors); third, that EU OIs can also have some converging effect at national level; and, fourth, that EU OIs are more cost-effective than EU similarization measures. Finally, this brought us to the case against EU OIs, and particularly to arguments countering those made in the case for.

As regards the express motivations of the EU legislator, the rationale of EU regimes for EU activities was challenged, at least in part, on the ground that EU OIs may lack the degree of uniformity necessary for them to enable private actors to overcome the barrier of legal diversity, even if these optional regimes do in most cases allow such actors to surmount barriers of territoriality. On the other hand, the rationale of leaving national legal orders unaffected has not been the subject of any serious criticism; although, from a Member State perspective, it could still be questioned to what extent Union optional regimes do actually leave national legal systems 'unaffected'.[361]

As for the other arguments advanced in favour of the OI method, the first of these - i.e. the greater political acceptability of OIs in certain fields where similarization is impracticable - also appears to be generally uncontested, although this too remains to be examined further[362] (and it was also pointed out that there are many areas in which the introduction of optional instruments could be considered impracticable).[363] By contrast, however, the remaining arguments are very much disputed. To start with the law market-based approach, both the possibility and desirability of stimulating national legal experimentation have been called into question, as has the desirability of providing additional legal options to private actors. Furthermore, considerable doubt has been cast upon the idea that EU OIs can have a converging effect on the domestic laws of the Member States. And, last but not least, the economic benefits of Union optional regimes have also been impugned.

So the question at this point is what conclusions should be drawn from this? More particularly, can it be said that, as a legislative method, OIs are preferable to similarization?

Overall, on the back of the foregoing analysis, it can be posited that the general assessment of EU OIs must be favourable, insofar as their use is supported by some important arguments that are difficult to negate. In particular, the broadly undisputed claims that Regulations establishing optional instruments are less disruptive of national legal orders than similarization measures - and therefore also

361 On this question see further *infra*, section B.

362 See section B.

363 On this point see further *infra*, section D.

more politically acceptable to the Member States - are clearly consequential ones, as they suggest that the OI method could have a vital role to play for future EU lawmaking in especially 'sensitive' areas of European (private) law. In addition, the idea that EU optional regimes can enable private actors to transcend barriers of territoriality - which is also unchallenged, at least in general terms - is patently significant too, for it entails that the OI method can achieve something that similarization by definition cannot. And, to the extent that the arguments sustaining the OI method are contested, most of the criticisms that have been levelled at it appear to amount to little more than qualifications, from which one may conclude that EU OIs may be ineffective at worst. Admittedly, this is not the case with the arguments that EU OIs might encourage a race to the bottom and lead to social injustice, as these suggest that a proliferation of optional instruments could have distinctly negative consequences. But even these concerns do not appear to be of such a fundamental nature that they cannot be satisfactorily addressed.

Having said that, it has also emerged from our analysis that the endeavour to arrive at solid normative conclusions regarding EU optional instruments in the abstract appears troublesome, not least because the validity or strength of a number of the arguments supporting the OI method seems to vary depending on the optional regime in question. In other words, the answer to the question of whether OIs are a 'better', or 'more effective', or 'more efficient' way for the EU legislator to achieve its objectives than other legislative methods it has at its disposal (and particularly the similarization method) looks uncertain, and it may only be possible to provide such an answer (if at all) in relation to specific optional regimes. This issue is discussed further below, in section D.

Furthermore, another reason why the answer to this question may be unclear is that it could also depend on the perspective one takes. Thus far our discussion has concentrated on the European perspective, but it should also be considered from the standpoint of Member States and of private actors. And so it is to these perspectives that we now turn, starting with the former, in section B, and then moving to the latter, in section C.

B. EU OIs from the Perspective of Member States

1. *EU OIs versus Similarization: a Less Disruptive and More Acceptable Method?*

Having reviewed both the official and the wider academic discourse regarding EU OIs at the European level, it becomes necessary at this juncture to contemplate the issue from the perspective of other key actors concerned, namely the EU Member States and private actors. It is particularly important to do so for the present study, because this could yield alternative insights and viewpoints on some of the arguments and claims made in the preceding discourse to sustain the desirability of the OI method.

Beginning with the perspective of the Member States (or, more precisely, national legislators of the Member States), this is an especially compelling one to consider, as it opens the door to a deeper examination of the rationale expressed by the European legislator of leaving national legal orders 'unaffected'. In addition, or rather, in turn, it also invites a closer inspection of the argument that EU OIs are more politically acceptable to the Member State legislators than similarization measures in certain areas of European law, which, as we have seen, departs from the premise that Union optional regimes are less disruptive of domestic legal systems. Given that, as was just observed in our overall evaluation, this seems to be one of the strongest and potentially most consequential lines of argumentation supporting EU OIs as a legislative method (alongside the rationale of EU regimes for EU activities), any reappraisal of its foundations could have serious implications for the general case for EU OIs.

Accordingly, in what follows, two fundamental questions are addressed: First, is the claim that the OI method is not so disruptive of national legal orders really correct? And, second, even if so, is it really the case that national legislators (therefore) have less reason to resist EU legislation establishing OIs?

(a) Are EU OIs Less Disruptive of Member State Legal Orders?

Recalling momentarily the rationale of leaving national legal orders unaffected, it will be remembered that this corresponds to the argument that EU OIs are considerably less disruptive of domestic legal systems than similarization measures, since they do not require the Member States to modify their existing laws, nor restrict the Member States' right to continue applying these laws. Of course, the European legislator does not claim that Member State legal orders are completely unaffected by Regulations creating optional regimes that are directly applicable within those legal orders, but it does affirm that the effect on pre-existing national law is minimal. Yet, speaking from the perspective of the Member States themselves, it can be argued that this proposition is not as incontrovertible as it might appear, for two main reasons.

Firstly, even though EU OIs do not require the Member States to amend existing domestic legislation, it has been contended that they may nevertheless lead to a diminution in the *importance* of national legal orders. That is, some argue that the relevance of national law could be diminished where an alternative Union regime is made available for private actors to opt into. For example, in discussing the Common European Sales Law (CESL) proposal, Hesselink observes that 'parties who opt into a European contract law instrument insofar opt out of the national law that would otherwise be applicable. This makes the original national law *pro tanto* less relevant. And in the long run massive opting out of national law may affect the prestige of a national system'.[364] Admittedly, as Hesselink also acknowledges, on a law market view this is actually considered an essential ingredient for the emergence of regulatory competition, as it is the fear of 'losing out' to other legal regimes that is said to create the competitive pressure on legislators to engage in legal experimentation. In other words, 'one could also say that the presence of the alternative of an optional instrument would provide national legislators with

[364] Hesselink 2010, p. 15.

incentives for keeping their law attractive'.[365] But then, even if this were true, on this view EU OIs would still have a notable impact on national legal systems, as they *would* ultimately give rise to modifications in existing domestic regimes. To be sure, in the opinion of law market theorists such modifications would be 'positive', in the sense that they would follow a 'race to the top'. However, as we have seen, this is far from certain, and many take the opposite view. Besides, as we shall see shortly,[366] it could be argued that the very prospect of greater regulatory competition provides Member States with a reason to oppose EU legislation establishing OIs, regardless of whether it engenders a race to the top or to the bottom. At any rate, the point remains that EU OIs could eventually result in a devaluation of corresponding domestic regimes, unless national legislators adopt reforms to prevent this.

Secondly, apart from the prestige of a national system, EU OIs may also have an effect on the applicability of the *core values* to which a national system adheres, insofar as they could enable private actors to escape national mandatory laws. Evidently, this is connected to the argument already noted in the social justice perspective,[367] according to which EU OIs may be used by parties with strong bargaining power (again, for instance, in the area of contract law) to circumvent domestic legal safeguards designed to protect weaker counterparts. Still, it is worth reiterating as a point in its own right that national legislators have a vested interest in such laws being upheld. After all, it was already mentioned that, in regulating areas such as contract law, or company law, etc., Member State legislators seek to strike a balance between values of private autonomy and social justice. So it should be recognized that, accordingly, national legislators have a stake in the maintenance of this balance. Indeed, one very recent indication of this was provided by the European Affairs Committee of the French *Assemblée Nationale* during deliberations on the proposed CESL in 2011, where the rapporteur affirmed that the existence of two bodies of (contract) rules on the French territory would not be acceptable under any circumstances.[368]

For these reasons, looking at the matter from the standpoint of the Member States, it can be maintained that the influence of EU legislation creating OIs on existing national regimes may not be quite as minimal as the European legislator suggests. This does not mean to say that the legislator's argument that EU OIs are less disruptive of national legal orders than approximating measures is necessarily incorrect, bearing in mind that EU OIs still do not legally obligate Member States to amend existing national laws. But it does signify that Member State legal systems may be affected by Union optional regimes to a somewhat greater extent than has been intimated until now.

365 Hesselink 2010, p. 15.

366 *Infra*, section B.1(b).

367 *Supra*, section A.3(b)(ii).

368 (*En aucun cas nous ne pouvons accepter d'avoir concomitamment deux corps de règles sur le meme territoire*). See Commission des Affaires Européennes, Compte rendu 231, 7 December 2011, available at: <www.assemblee-nationale.fr/13/europe/c-rendus/c0231.asp>.

(b) Are EU OIs More Acceptable to Member States?

It will also be recalled from our previous discussion that, on the basis that EU OIs interfere substantially less with existing domestic regimes, it has been argued the OI method is more readily acceptable to Member State legislators than the similarization method, particularly in areas of law where the requisite political agreement on approximating measures is impracticable. More precisely, the contention is that in such areas the OI method not only increases the chances of a binding Union instrument being adopted in the first place, but also allows the Union 'to adopt a body of *coherent* rules, which form a *complete* set'.[369] However, looking again from the perspective of the Member States themselves, one can also question the accuracy of this portrayal, and again on two principal grounds.

For one thing, Member States could conceivably have a number of reasons to resist EU legislation introducing OIs, even if Union optional regimes are ultimately 'less disruptive' than similarization measures. In particular, following on from the previous point, Member State legislators might see the need to oppose EU OIs in order to preserve the importance and uphold the fundamental values of their domestic legal systems, or eventually also to avoid the increased competitive pressure to introduce reforms that could arise as a result. Of course, this could be because the national legislator is wary of regulatory competition giving rise to a race to the bottom;[370] but it could also simply be that the national legislator wishes to insulate itself from the possibility of greater regulatory competition due to protectionist considerations. Indeed, given the tendencies of Member States towards protectionism in relation to various aspects of the 'European project', one might even expect as much. Alternatively, following on from this last point, it may be that a Member State is actually against the introduction of any EU legislation in a certain field, regardless of the form the proposed instrument takes. As Hesselink puts it, '[f]rom such an essentially nationalist point of view an optional instrument, whatever its specific nature or content, would be bad simply because it represents more Europe'.[371]

Furthermore, if one looks at the legislative processes pertaining to existing and proposed EU OIs to date, it is far from clear that Member States have actually shown themselves more inclined to agree to EU legislation creating OIs as a legislative method. If anything, experiences so far seem to substantiate the point that Member States can have reasons to object to a Union legislative instrument even if it is an optional one. The most glaring illustration of this is provided by EU OIs in the field of European company law, starting with the SE Regulation, which, as we have already seen, was finally adopted over 30 years after the Commission's first proposal, and underwent a series of drastic alterations (or rather, dilutions) in the process. Although the European legislator 'initially pursued an exhaustive and

369 Fauvarque-Cosson & Behar-Touchais, p. 34.

370 On this, cf., for example, the discussion regarding the possibility of a race to the bottom in the area of European company law, and particularly the fears expressed by France and Germany, *supra*, section A.3(b)(i).

371 Hesselink 2010, p. 15.

comprehensive legislative measure for the creation of a European Company ...', this approach 'was ultimately shelved in the 1980s, when the European Community replaced the draft with framework legislation that referred extensively to national legislation'.[372] Equally, the SCE Regulation adopted shortly thereafter also contained numerous references to national law, as did the EEIG Regulation before it. And while the Commission did attempt to revive its original approach to the European Company in the proposal for a Regulation on a European Private Company (SPE),[373] this proposal was retracted six years later.[374] Thus, as McCahery and Vermeulen explain, due to the Member States' continued desire to maintain legislative control over company law, 'federal intervention through supranational provisions for truly European company forms faced severe objections and has, until now, not been very successful'.[375]

Still another example of this would be the CESL proposal of 2011 in the area of European contract law. It will be remembered that the EESC identified the field of contract law in particular as one in which the OI method could offer a solution to political impasse over approximating measures. Yet, the CESL proposal ran into serious difficulties in the decision-making process, and was withdrawn by the Commission in the face of opposition from a majority of Member States. In fact, there are only a few examples of existing OIs that have been adopted without encountering any significant objections from the Member States along the way. One could point to the Community Design, for instance, as a Union OI that did not face major political difficulties during its passage through the legislative process. But then, as we have also noted already, this OI was preceded by 'matching' EU legislation approximating national design laws, which did not face formidable adversity from the Member States either. Therefore, it can hardly be taken as evidence of the relative 'palatability' of the OI method. If this experience serves to demonstrate anything, it is that the Member State legislators are more inclined to agree to binding EU legislation in the field of design law than they are in areas like company or contract law, be it in the form of an approximating measure or an optional instrument.

So, in summary, the OI method may not be as acceptable to national legislators as one might think, and arguably does not greatly increase the possibility of a complete and comprehensive piece of Union legislation being adopted in a given area of European law.

372 McCahery & Vermeulen 2005, p. 797.

373 Proposal for a Council Regulation on the Statute for a European private company, COM(2008) 396/3.

374 Although, as was already mentioned, the SPE proposal was replaced by the Proposal for a Directive of the European Parliament and of the Council on single-member private limited liability companies, COM(2014) 212 final. See *supra*, Chapter 3, SUP description.

375 McCahery & Vermeulen 2005, p. 801.

2. *Evaluation of EU OIs from the Perspective of Member States*

Seen from the perspective of Member States, then, some of the key arguments in favour of EU OIs as an alternative legislative method to approximation (in particular) appear to lose some of their force. It may well be that, from the perspective of the EU legislator, optional instruments are unequivocally less disruptive of Member State legal orders - and, as such, likely to be more politically practicable - than approximating measures, especially in more 'sensitive' areas of law. However, taking into account the national viewpoint, there are in fact good reasons to dispute even these seemingly indisputable propositions. Firstly, although EU legislation introducing OIs does not oblige Member States to modify existing domestic laws, it can still affect the prestige and the application of core values of national legal systems (if not even domestic laws themselves). And secondly, following on from this, Member States can have, and have had, strong grounds for opposing EU legislation in certain areas even if it does take the form of an optional instrument. This is particularly significant because it calls into question the idea that the OI method could provide a far-reaching 'solution' in fields of European (private) law where agreement on legislation similarizing national laws is not achievable. Admittedly, as we have seen, this is not the only (or even the main) fundamental conviction supporting the European legislator's employment of the OI method, but it is nevertheless an important one. So the reassessment of this notion does somewhat weaken the overall case for EU OIs.

On the other hand, this is not necessarily to say that the Member States have *as much* reason to object to EU legislation creating OIs as they could do to oppose EU legislation similarizing domestic laws. It is still arguable that, all in all, EU OIs are at least marginally less disruptive of Member State legal systems, and hence that the likelihood of attaining political consensus on an optional instrument is in principle higher than in the case of approximating legislation. It may be that it is just a question of how much the chances of adopting a comprehensive EU measure are improved by proposing it in the form of an OI. Certainly, there is nothing to indicate that the EU OIs should be any more undesirable for Member States than approximating measures might be in a given area. Therefore this again seems to be a caveat at most, as the assertion is not that the OI method is particularly problematic from the Member State perspective, but rather that it may not be much less problematic than the similarization method. And there still remains the possibility of agreement being reached on a Union OI in a situation where approximating measures have proven unacceptable to the Member States. It is true that, as in the case of the SE Regulation, the result may be the adoption of an uncomprehensive instrument, but this could still be useful.

C. EU OIs from the Perspective of Private Actors

1. *EU OIs versus Similarization: an Empowerment of the Individual?*

In addition to the Member State perspective, it is useful to reflect upon EU optional instruments from the perspective of private actors, as this also paves the way for closer scrutiny of some of the arguments made in the case for EU OIs. Specifically, it calls for further discussion of the claim that the creation of additional EU legal options for natural and legal persons operating in the internal market allows such actors to better satisfy their own individual preferences, thereby empowering them to derive greater benefit from this market. To be sure, we have already seen a contrasting view of the increased party choice offered by EU OIs in our discussion of the social justice perspective,[376] which essentially holds that the value of individual private autonomy must be counterbalanced with those of distributive fairness and social solidarity. However, this plea for a balance does not directly controvert the argument that greater party choice confers benefits on businesses and citizens in the EU. Hence, until this point, the claim that EU OIs empower individuals by providing them with more legal options has not been challenged head-on.

Now, looking at it from the perspective of private actors, there are a number of grounds on which this claim could itself be disputed. In particular, as has been alluded to already, the very idea that natural and legal persons operating in the EU can be grouped together under a single heading of 'private actors' is dubious, since the individuals in question are different, and their preferences diverse.[377] Also, on a related point, when it comes to an optional instrument that would be selected by agreement between two or more individuals (such as the Common European Sales Law proposal of 2011),[378] one may wonder whether the instrument would truly be 'the choice' of all parties to the agreement, especially in cases where there is some inequality in bargaining power. Furthermore, it could be argued that the introduction of additional EU legal options actually has a negative effect for private actors active in the internal market, inasmuch as it renders the European legal environment in which they must operate more complicated.

So this penultimate part of our normative framework also tackles two main questions. Firstly, do the alleged advantages of the enhanced party choice instigated by (EU) OIs vary depending on the kind of private actor in question; and, in the case of an OI being selected by parties in a bi- or multi-lateral relationship, can it really be said that all of the private actors involved exercise a choice? Secondly, and at any rate, is the availability of more legal options (within the EU) really beneficial for private actors?

376 *Supra*, section A.3(b)(ii).

377 Of course, the same can be said about the heading of 'Member States', even if this is used specifically to denote Member State executives, since these too have diverse preferences. However, this criticism is even more acute when it comes to 'private actors' because the differences between them are especially pronounced (as we shall now see), and hence it is discussed here in this context. Still, it is important to recognize that the same criticism could also be levelled at the arguments noted previously concerning the preferences of Member States.

378 See Chapter 3, CESL Description.

(a) Which Individual and Whose Choice?

As was just mentioned, one difficulty faced by those who argue that EU OIs are advantageous for 'private actors' and the satisfaction of 'their preferences', is that the members of this group are anything but homogenous. Obviously, some are natural persons while others are legal persons, but even within these sub-categories there are various other differences that can be identified. As far as the sub-group of legal persons is concerned, this comprises *different types* of companies, including both large businesses as well as small and medium-sized enterprises (SMEs), which (depending on the EU OI in question) may even be based in a third country. While, in the case of natural persons, these may be economically active in *different capacities*, be it as consumers, self-employed natural persons, etc.

And, of course, all of these private actors have *different preferences*, particularly in the context of the internal market. As regards legal persons, for instance, 'some may have pan-European or even global ambitions; others, perhaps, may geographically limit their desires to neighbouring countries; still others may prefer to concentrate on their home market'.[379] As Low observes, this will depend on 'whether conducting cross-border trade is (or is a means to) a goal of the firm ...',[380] not to mention the size of the firm and the market sector in which it operates. Equally, the aspirations of natural persons in the capacity of, say, consumers, vary in a similar way. Whereas some consumers are desirous to (and indeed do) enter into transactions with traders located in Member States other than that in which the reside, others 'have no need or desire to shop across borders'.[381] It therefore follows that, to the extent that EU OIs are targeted at providing EU regimes for intra-EU activities,[382] the additional legal options they create could in any case enable only *certain* private actors (i.e. those engaged in cross-border operations, but not those active purely in a domestic context) to better satisfy their preferences.

Furthermore, the preferences of private actors may even be incompatible with one another. Indeed, it was already indicated when recounting the social justice perspective that an additional legal option created via the OI method could be preferred by private actors with strong bargaining power (such as large enterprises), because it allows them to avoid mandatory rules designed to protect conflicting interests of weaker parties (such as consumers or employees, or even SMEs). The concern about incompatible preferences is primarily of relevance to a 'multiple-party' optional instrument such as the CESL proposal of 2011, however, where the issue is whether the choice exercised would truly be that of both (or all) contracting parties. Of course, the CESL would need to have been *selected* by both parties through agreement in order for it to become applicable to their contract, so

379 Low 2011, p. 285. This echoes the point made by Vogenauer (noted previously) that there are no preferences of 'business' as such. Furthermore, it should also be recalled that according to Vogenauer (among others), parties may not even be certain as to what their preferences are, let alone which legal regime of those on offer would come closest to satisfying them. See *supra*, section A.3(b)(i).

380 Low 2011, p. 285. See also Low 2012a, p. 143.

381 Low 2011, p. 270.

382 *Supra*, section A.1(a).

one might assume that, if it were selected - even in, say, a business-to-consumer contract - it must be because 'the optional instrument will be for the benefit of businesses and consumers in the sense that it is preferable to national law for both of them'.[383] However, Sefton-Green for one argues that this is improbable, since 'the question of whether the optional instrument is preferable for consumers will depend on the content of the rule, the level of consumer protection contained therein, and whether the level offered is higher or lower than their national law',[384] and traders may well have opposing preferences on these points. Thus, when a choice for the CESL would have been made, this would probably have reflected more the preferences of only one of the parties. More specifically, it would likely have reflected primarily those of the trader (particularly if it is a large business), for two reasons.

Firstly, it would essentially have been up to the trader to decide whether to offer a contract governed by the CESL in the first place. This is even acknowledged in the preamble to the proposed CESL Regulation, where it states that, when it comes to business-to-consumer transactions, 'in practice, it will usually be the trader who proposes the use of the Common European Sales Law'.[385] Therefore if a trader did not wish use the CESL, they could simply have refrained from making the option available to the consumer at all. Having said that, as the preamble also points out, this is why the Regulation requires the consent of the consumer to be given explicitly in a statement separate to the statement indicating the consumer's agreement to the contract itself in order for it to be admissible.[386] So at least in those cases where the possibility of opting into the CESL *were* offered by the trader, the consumer would be 'fully aware of the fact that they are agreeing to the use of rules which are different from those of their pre-existing national law'.[387] However, even in such cases it could be argued that, as the party with stronger bargaining power, the trader could have been in a position to pressurize the consumer into assenting to the use of the CESL, even if this was not in the consumer's best interests. Hence, for this reason also, one might have expected a choice for the CESL to reflect mainly the preferences of the trader rather those of the consumer.

In fact, as Cartwright adds, 'the "choice" is hardly a real choice in many business-to-business contracts, any more than in business-to-consumer contracts where one party in effect can dictate the core terms of the contract'.[388] As has already been alluded to, this could be the case especially in transactions between large businesses and SMEs, where there is also potentially some notable disparity in bargaining power.[389] Therefore, even in business-to-business contracts, 'a large

383 Sefton-Green 2011, p. 142.
384 Sefton-Green 2011, p. 142.
385 COM(2011) 635 final, consideration 22.
386 *Ibid.* As noted previously, this requirement is contained in Article 8(2) of the proposed CESL Regulation.
387 COM(2011) 635 final, consideration 22.
388 Cartwright 2011, p. 342.
389 Indeed (as Cartwright also points out), the Commission itself concedes that 'large companies with strong bargaining power can ensure that their contracts are subject to a particular national law', and that this 'may be more difficult for SMEs ...' in its Green Paper on policy →

company with strong bargaining power could equally well ensure that it has the benefits, or avoids the disbenefits, of the Optional Instrument (depending on its own assessment of the relative merits of the Instrument as against domestic law)'.[390] Indeed, according to Cartwright, it is only really in 'business-to-business contracts where the parties meet on equal terms' that there is 'a real "choice"',[391] and hence it is only in such cases of equality of bargaining power that a choice for the CESL could have been expected to fully reflect the 'autonomous will' of both contracting parties.

So, in short, whether the availability of more legal options in the EU has the potential to confer a benefit on private actors in terms of 'market optimization' will very much depend on the (kind of) individual in question, and it may even be to the detriment of others.

(b) Is More Choice a Good thing?

Another criticism that may be levelled at the claim that the introduction of more legal options in the European Union is advantageous for private actors, is that, even for those actors who are engaged in cross-border activities (and who therefore could potentially derive some benefit from the availability of an additional EU optional regime), this could also be disadvantageous because it may serve to over-complicate the European legal environment, by providing them with too many possibilities from which to choose. In other words, adding to the number of legal options for private actors will make it too difficult for such actors to discover and decide between the legal regimes available to them. Employing the terminology of behavioural psychology, this may lead to 'choice overload' or 'hyperchoice', which refers to 'the situation where the number of alternatives available to us increases to a point where it seems to us a tidal wave of choice'.[392] In such a situation, arriving at a reasoned choice becomes an excessively onerous task, and may even reduce a private actor's motivation to choose at all.[393]

Indeed, many have argued that more choice is not a 'good thing' for these private actors (or at least not necessarily), on the basis that more choice leads to less legal certainty.[394] Sefton-Green, for example, takes the view that an optional instrument 'will exacerbate the status quo, as legal diversity, with the addition of a 28th regime, and legal uncertainty, will increase respectively'.[395] And a similar view has also been expressed by a number of the respondents to the 2012 study on optional instruments produced for the European Parliament's Legal Affairs

options for progress towards a European Contract Law for consumers and businesses of 2010 (COM(2010) 348, p. 7).

390 Cartwright 2011, p. 342.

391 Cartwright 2011, p. 346.

392 Low 2011, p. 227.

393 See Low 2011, p. 230.

394 See, notably, Schwarz 2004. For a more recent contribution expressing this view, see Sefton-Green 2011.

395 Sefton-Green 2011, p. 147.

Committee.[396] For instance, both the Luxembourgish and Swedish responses assert that 'an increase in the number of optional instruments could generate a feeling of great insecurity by making the law more complex ...'.[397] In fact, the response of Luxembourg is even more explicit on this point, where it states that 'increasing the number of instruments does nothing to simplify a legal scene overrun by different rules governing the same type of situation, which can be confusing to professionals and people seeking justice alike'.[398]

Having said this, it must also be clarified that more choice does not necessarily give rise to a choice overload. Rather, as indicated above, there is a certain threshold that must be reached for this to occur, and one could argue that the addition of common European regimes in each of the legal systems of the Member States would not exceed this threshold. Thus, even if one accepts that increasing the number of legal options in Europe might make it (even) more difficult for private actors to choose between available legal regimes, the point at which this becomes excessive is far from clear.

2. *Evaluation of EU OIs from the Perspective of Private Actors*

The perspective of private actors also calls for a re-evaluation of certain perceived notions in the case for EU OIs. It has been argued that EU OIs enable private actors active in the internal market to better satisfy their needs by offering more legal options, but these needs may differ widely from one private actor to another, and could even come into conflict with each other (like for example in a business-to-consumer contract). As Sefton-Green points out, '[t]he Commission has a tendency to assume that this issue is one-dimensional and that consumers' and businesses' choices will necessarily converge in order to optimize the market. But this is surely an over-simplification: the identical correlation between different stakeholders' interests is far from being obvious ...'.[399] And, in addition, some contend that the creation of EU OIs may actually lead to greater complexity and uncertainty for private actors, by leaving them with too many legal options from which to choose. So, from this perspective, there are reasons to doubt that the increased party choice instigated by EU OIs is necessarily beneficial for private actors. In fact, there are even reasons to believe that it could be detrimental.

Having said that, arguably these contentions can still be satisfactorily addressed. For one thing, as we noted when discussing the social justice perspective, in promulgating an OI such as the CESL the EU legislator can be expected to have due regard to the divergent and conflicting interests of different private actors, and to strike an appropriate balance between them. Therefore even if a choice for the CESL could somehow have been 'imposed' in some cases by stronger parties on weaker ones, the mandatory protections provided therein would still have safeguarded the interests of the latter (at least for the most part).

396 Fauvarque-Cosson & Behar-Touchais 2012.
397 Fauvarque-Cosson & Behar-Touchais 2012, p. 349.
398 Fauvarque-Cosson & Behar-Touchais 2012, p. 352.
399 Sefton-Green 2011, p. 141.

Furthermore, the European legislator could also take steps to limit any uncertainty resulting from the introduction of additional legal regimes, for instance by providing clear and accessible information on the nature of the new legal option being offered, and how it compares to existing alternatives.[400] This could go some way towards facilitating private actors in their task of making a choice, and possibly even increase their motivation to do so. Although, admittedly, one could still question to what extent private actors would be in a position to make informed choices between different legal regimes, for the reasons already noted during our discussion of regulatory competition.[401]

D. Variations in Concreto?

1. *The Peculiarities of OIs in Differing EU Policy Fields*

Having considered the case for optional instruments in the European Union through the lenses of Member States and private actors, we now come to the final part of our normative evaluation which, in general terms, is dedicated to the issue of differences between EU OIs and policy areas and its implications for the theoretical arguments supporting the OI method. More precisely, this final part seeks to address the second set of questions posed at the start of the present chapter, which, while being distinct, are all related to the matter of variations between particular EU OIs and policy fields.

First and foremost, we will focus on the existing EU OIs that have been discussed up to this point, and specifically on the question whether peculiarities of these OIs in differing EU policy fields are such that the general case in favour of the OI method cannot be said to hold true *in concreto*. In particular, this will require us to consider the extent to which the effectiveness of the OI method may depend on the EU OI in question. But we shall then also reflect upon suggestions for EU OIs in other policy fields, and specifically on the question of policy areas in which EU OIs may or may not be (more or less) feasible. In doing so we will be expanding on a point already noted in the case against EU OIs, but as part of a broader argument concerning variations between policy areas. And finally, bringing these two aspects together, we will conclude by discussing possible criteria or factors of relevance in assessing whether - in those areas of European law where it is plausible - the use of the OI method as an alternative is desirable.

(a) Divergences from the General Case for EU OIs

As was indicated in our overall evaluation of EU OIs,[402] the discussion and analysis of the various arguments advanced in support of the OI method has signalled that they are seemingly less well-founded or convincing in the case of some OIs than they are in the case of others, and hence that it may be difficult to reach sound

400 On the importance of such information see further Chapter 5, section A.3(b).

401 See *supra*, section A.3(b)(i).

402 *Supra*, section A.4.

conclusions on the OI method in the abstract. Now, in order to illustrate this issue of divergences from the general case for EU OIs, it is useful to recapitulate some of the peculiarities of EU optional regimes, and to make plain how these may affect arguments made in favour the OI method.

First, there is the fact that the relation with similarization varies between different EU OIs. Although most Regulations establishing OIs can be seen as having been adopted *in lieu of* (or 'as an alternative to') approximating legislation, two of them - namely the Community Trade Mark and Community Design Regulations - were introduced *on top of* (or 'as a complement to') corresponding Directives approximating the core trade mark and design laws of the Member States. This peculiarity of the CTM and CD was already mentioned as one of the limits to the conception of EU OIs as an alternative to similarization measures,[403] but clearly it also has implications for other arguments concerning EU OIs. For one thing, given that the trade mark and design Directives and the CTM and CD Regulations, respectively, were envisaged as matching parts of single overarching legislative initiatives,[404] the argument that EU OIs leave national legal orders unaffected is surely less persuasive when it comes to these optional regimes. Indeed, it will be recalled from our account of the EU legislator's express motivations[405] that this likely explains why the rationale of leaving domestic legal systems unaffected does not feature explicitly in the preamble of either the CTM or the CD Regulation. And, of course, this peculiarity affects the argument that EU OIs allow for legal experimentation too.[406] For, while the Member States are still able to maintain their domestic trade mark and design regimes (and private actors therefore still have a choice between these and the EU optional regimes), the main substantive rules governing national trade mark and design rights cannot deviate from the corresponding EU Directives. So, bearing in mind that the notion of regulatory competition is founded on the premise that states are able to offer private actors different legal solutions for identical activities, the extent to which the legislative action taken in these fields of European law is consistent with a law-market based approach is equally questionable.

Secondly, there is the other peculiar characteristic of the CTM and CD (and also the CPVR and UP) that is not shared by other existing EU OIs, which is that their availability is not subject to any formal cross-border requirement. Admittedly, as we have already acknowledged, these IP law OIs are still patently targeted at private actors engaged in cross-border activities, and it is hard to conceive of situations in which a private actor active in a purely domestic setting would wish to obtain a CTM or CD (at least as long as there is an equivalent national regime available for them to make use of). Nevertheless, it is worth highlighting this idiosyncrasy, as it should also be remembered that other existing OIs, i.e. the EOP and ESCP in the area of European procedural law, did not foresee a cross-border requirement either at the time they were originally proposed. In fact, the

403 See *supra*, section A.3(a)(ii).
404 See descriptions of CTM and CD in Chapter 3.
405 *Supra*, section A.1(b).
406 *Supra*, section A.2(b)(i).

Commission believed these OIs *should* be available for selection in purely domestic cases too, but this approach was subsequently reversed during the decision-making process. So this is a peculiarity that one may eventually find in certain other Union optional regimes, and which, at least in some cases, could have implications for the argument that EU OIs provide EU regimes for EU activities. Because obviously, if a Union optional instrument is also designed to be available for purely domestic activities, it becomes harder to maintain that it adheres to a rationale focused on the needs of cross-border operators.

These peculiarities alone therefore serve to demonstrate that the general case for EU OIs (or at least certain aspects of it) may be inapplicable (or at least less applicable) to certain OIs in existence. But there is also another important reason why the strength of the case for EU OIs can depend on the specific OI in question, as we shall now recall.

(b) Varying Degrees of Effectiveness

A further peculiarity that we have encountered is the fact that certain EU optional regimes in existence appear to be lacking in uniformity to a strikingly large extent. In particular, company law OIs such as the SE stand out as optional regimes that make extensive references to pre-existing Member State laws. This was already mentioned in setting out the contention that all EU OIs lack uniformity to one degree or another,[407] but it is important to note this again here as a point in its own right, that also explains why the strength of the general case for the OI method might depend on the given OI. Since, as we observed, the usefulness of a Union optional regime could be severely constrained by a significant lack of uniformity – particularly in terms of its ability to enable private actors to overcome barriers of legal diversity – it should be clear that also the effectiveness of the OI-based approach in achieving the stated aim of providing EU regimes for EU activities may vary from one EU OI to another. It is true that, as we have also seen, many argue that EU OIs may in any event be effective in reducing legal diversity through some indirect converging effect.[408] However, even if this is the case, one may also argue that the more an OI lacks uniformity, the less converging effect it could potentially have in the first place.

Thus, regardless of whether there are not actually different types of EU OIs,[409] the fact that there exist notable differences between them entails that some of the conclusions resulting from a general evaluation of this legislative method may not hold true *in concreto*. In and of themselves, these variations perhaps cannot be taken as an invalidation of the overall case supporting the OI method; but certainly they do indicate that the validity of some of its tenets can differ from one Union optional regime to another. For this reason, it is difficult to arrive at abstract conclusions on the overall case for EU OIs.

407 *Supra*, section A.3(a)(i).

408 *Supra*, section A.2(c).

409 On this question see Chapter 2, section B.3.

2. *The Feasibility of OIs in Other EU Policy Fields*

Another variation alluded to previously that should be spelled out at this stage is the fact that the use of the OI method is not so feasible in some EU policy fields as it is in others. Once again, this point was already raised in our discussion of the case against EU OIs, as another limitation to the idea of EU OIs providing an alternative to similarization;[410] however, it should be made clear now that the observation that the OI method is less viable in some areas of European law also has broader implications, in terms of variations between policy areas.

Specifically, the customs union and the four fundamental freedoms were already indicated as areas in which the employment of the OI method by the European legislator is not practically feasible, because it would not allow the legislator to attain its primary goal of creating a properly functioning internal market. In order for the customs union and the core system of the four freedoms to function, the applicable rules need to be not only uniformly but also exclusively applicable throughout the Union. Hence these are fields where it is considered necessary to enact similarization measures. However, the use of EU OIs may also be less feasible in some fields of private law for another reason, namely that they contain a large proportion of essential rules of public policy, which individuals are not allowed to deviate from. This is arguably the case with property law, for example, and also, to a large degree, tort law.[411] That is not to say that the EU OIs could not be introduced at all in such fields: In fact the Commission has also previously suggested using the OI legislative method in other fields of private law such as property law.[412] For instance, in a Green Paper of 2005 the Commission mentioned the idea of a so-called 'Euromortgage' in the specific area of surety law, which would correspond to 'an EU-wide instrument for securing loans on property'.[413] But the scope for doing so may be more limited in such areas than in other fields that embody fewer fundamental elements of public policy, such as contract law, for example, as these essential public policy elements are likely to pose obstacles to the introduction of regimes offering private actors 'a choice'. In other words, it is not that there is necessarily something about the subject-matter per se of some fields of private law that does not lend itself to the OI method, but the extent

410 See *supra*, section A.3(a)(ii).

411 Although, in the case of tort law, there is also one very practical reason why an OI would be less feasible, which is that, unlike parties in a contractual relationship, parties in a tortious relationship typically cannot foresee the relationship coming into existence. In such circumstances, it is hard to see how the parties could select an optional instrument as the regime governing their relationship prior to its coming into being.

412 One could argue that a European Union OI has actually already been created in this field, in the form of the European Certificate of Succession. However, as was mentioned in the introductory chapter (Chapter 1), this is as an instrument regulating succession procedures, and therefore may also be described as pertaining to succession law (if not even procedural law).

413 Commission Green Paper Mortgage Credit in the EU, COM(2005) 327 final, paras. 47 & 48 (p. 12). On the possibility (and possible advantages) of the OI method in the field of European property law see further Ramaekers 2013, p. 220 *et seq*.

to which this legislative method could be deployed may well depend on the importance of overriding public policy concerns in the given area of law.

For these reasons, it should be recognized that the very feasibility of the OI method in different EU policy fields varies from one field to another; and, accordingly, that the validity of the case for EU OIs *in concreto* can also be said to depend on the specific *policy field* in question.

3. *The Desirability of OIs Across EU Policy Fields*

(a) General Criteria for Assessing Desirability

Having made the point that the strength of the general case for EU OIs varies not only from one optional instrument to another, but also from one area of law to another, this brings us to a concluding question. Is it possible to propound some *general criteria* to decide whether the OI method is a desirable alternative form of EU legislation, particularly in those EU policy fields where it is (or could be) used as an alternative to the similarization method?

Now, in response to this question, while our discussion of the overall case for EU OIs has certainly shown that the strength of the case varies in specific instances, it has also shown that it *is* possible to identify pertinent criteria on the basis of which to evaluate whether the OI method is a desirable alternative in general terms. Indeed, the reason why it was useful to examine a range of arguments concerning EU OIs, and from different perspectives, is precisely because this can provide indications of potentially relevant criteria for determining the desirability of the OI method in general. And our in-depth account of these contrasting viewpoints has demonstrated that the desirability of EU OIs as an alternative legislative method could actually be determined according to a variety of criteria. Thus, for example, one could do so according to political criteria, economic criteria and/or social criteria, and these could even vary depending on whether one adopts the perspective of the EU legislator or that of Member States or private actors. This way, one could arrive at a conclusion on the desirability of the OI method in the abstract, rather than just reserving one's judgement for concrete cases.

Although, in fact, the foregoing analysis leads me to propose a single general criterion to determine the desirability of OIs as an alternative EU legislative method among other possible methods (and especially similarization). In my view, whether one looks at it from the perspective of the EU legislator, Member States or private actors, the guiding consideration should be which legislative method offers the optimal mix between legal uniformity, on the one hand, and legal diversity, on the other. In other words, the method that strikes the most equal balance between preserving national legal diversity and achieving uniformity at European level should be preferred. The reason I propose this criterion is that it takes into account interests of all the aforementioned stakeholders, meaning it would be appropriate from the perspective of each of them. The European legislator obviously has an interest in achieving more legal uniformity in the EU for the better functioning of the internal market, but it also has an interest in respecting the different traditions (including legal traditions) of the Member States,[414] and particularly in acting in accordance with the principle of subsidiarity.[415] Similarly, Member States obviously have an interest in being able to maintain their own preferred domestic law but, having joined the European Union, they must also have an interest in the proper functioning of the internal market, and therefore in allowing private actors to overcome barriers caused by legal diversity. And, last but not least, private actors themselves can have an interest in legal diversity, as greater choice can allow them to better satisfy their individual preferences, but they can also have an interest in greater legal uniformity, since this can enable them to take better advantage of the internal market. Hence, an optimal mix between diversity and uniformity would satisfy contrasting desires held by all of these stakeholders.

So, applying this criterion, I would argue that generally speaking EU OIs are a desirable alternative, particularly to the similarization method, because they ensure a more balanced mix between national legal diversity and European legal uniformity. As we have seen, by definition, similarization measures seek to increase legal uniformity in the EU by reducing diversity between national laws. Therefore, while the similarization method can serve to establish greater legal uniformity, it does so at the expense of national legal diversity. And when it comes to soft law measures, the scales are tipped in the other direction, because while such measures are not (or at least less) binding on the Member States and, as such, likely to better respect national legal diversity, they are also unlikely to bring about as much uniformity. By contrast, EU OIs, as 'soft hard law', seek to attain greater uniformity by introducing additional European regimes into the legal systems of the Member States, without requiring modifications to existing national regimes. Therefore the OI method has the potential to enhance legal uniformity in the EU to an extent that is comparable with similarization,[416] while at the same time respecting national legal diversity to an extent comparable with soft law instruments of the EU. Indeed, this is arguably the most crucial advantage of EU Optional Instruments. They create more uniform legal regimes in the EU, while also preserving existing legal options available in the Member States. Accordingly, they can satisfy more preferences.

(b) Usage as a Key Ingredient

In any event, regardless of the criteria one chooses to assess the desirability of the OI method, our analysis of the overall case for EU OIs has also revealed another important point, which is that usage is a key ingredient in many of the arguments that have been advanced in support of this alternative method. Notably, whether

414 On this see notably Treaty on European Union, Recital 6.

415 See Art. 5(3) of the Treaty on European Union.

416 As was noted above (section C.1(b)), some, like Sefton-Green, have argued that optional instruments actually serve to increase legal *diversity*, by adding more legal regimes to the already existing ones. However, bearing in mind that these additional regimes are uniform across the Member States (or at least intended to be), they are considered in the present study rather as another form of uniformity that exists at European level; see *supra*, section A.2(c).

EU OIs can be expected to stimulate regulatory competition, have an indirect converging effect, and/or bring about the kind of economic gains that they are predicted to, appears to be dependent at least to some degree on their being selected by a sufficient number of private actors on a sufficiently regular basis. In fact, even the express rationale of enabling private actors to overcome barriers of legal diversity could be considered to depend on the extent to which an OI is opted into, if 'enable' is interpreted in a de facto sense, rather than merely in the sense of offering a possibility. Indeed, the European Commission itself has acknowledged as much. In its response to the EESC own-initiative opinion on the 28th regime of 2010, where it discusses specifically the area of European contract law, the Commission states that '[b]y its very nature, an optional instrument could only constitute a sensible solution to the problems stemming from regulatory divergences if it is chosen by the contracting parties in the first place'.[417]

Therefore, the level of usage of EU OIs by private actors could potentially play a significant role in any assessment of their desirability. And, in turn, this makes the question of what factors determine the attractiveness of EU OIs to end-users an especially important one to address. Of course, we have already touched upon this issue in our discussion of (vertical) regulatory competition,[418] and we mentioned for example the degree of uniformity of an OI as one factor that may affect its attractiveness to private actors (i.e. its level of usage). But the question still remains to be analysed in detail, by examining not only this factor but also other relevant factors that have been or could be suggested.

And so it is to the issue of usage of EU OIs by private actors – and the factors that may influence such usage – that we next turn.

Conclusion

In conclusion, this normative analysis has revealed that the overall case for EU Optional Instruments is a strong one, but also that the validity of many arguments advanced in support of the EU OIs can vary *in concreto*, and according to the perspective one takes. Of course, ultimately, any assessment of the desirability of the OI method depends on the criteria one selects to determine what is desirable – and the normative framework constructed in this chapter has indicated various possible criteria that could eventually be used to evaluate EU OIs in general. In my opinion, OIs are a desirable alternative form of EU legislation because they offer an optimal mix between European legal uniformity and national legal diversity, but others may well come to a different conclusion, on the basis of different criteria. So, in the end, the answer to the question whether the OI method is a 'better' way for

417 Follow-up of the European Commission on the EESC opinion on 'The 28th regime – an alternative allowing less lawmaking at Community level', p. 2. While Smits goes even further, asserting that whether the proposed CESL would facilitate cross-border trade for contracting parties was 'entirely dependent on how attractive it will be for parties to opt-in to the CESL': Smits 2013, p. 55.

418 See *supra*, section A.3(b)(i).

the EU legislator to reach its goals than other means it has available to it is still an uncertain one.

Equally, though, the same could obviously be said about the desirability of any of these other methods the EU legislator has at its disposal, including the similarization method. Whether measures that approximate existing national laws in order to make domestic legal regimes more similar should be the preferred means for the EU legislator to achieve its aims is just as uncertain (if not more so). And, of course, that is assuming that Union intervention in the different areas of law discussed in this thesis is even desirable in the first place. For the purposes of our analysis we have taken this as a given, but it is a debatable issue in and of itself. Still, it is worth adding that this has actually been put forward as another argument in favour of the OI method, insofar as it could be used to 'test' whether a European regime is desirable, particularly for private actors as end-users of the rules. According to Smits, for example, optional law has the additional advantage that it makes clear in a bottom up way whether parties are in need of a European regime at all.[419] Although, as we will see in the next chapter, if relatively few private actors choose to make use of a particular Union OI, the reason might not necessarily be that they do not require *any* European regime in the relevant area of law.

[419] See Smits 2013.

Chapter 5

EXPLANATORY FRAMEWORK

INTRODUCTION

Whereas the first and second set of questions outlined at the start of (and addressed in) the previous chapter are essentially normative in character, the third set - to be discussed in this chapter - are best categorized as explanatory, since they enquire about the apparent divergences in the levels of usage or 'attractiveness' of different EU optional instruments and the factors behind this. It is true that, as we noted towards the end of the preceding chapter, this issue also has normative implications, as many of the arguments that make up the case for EU OIs depend in one way or another on private actors using the OIs that are enacted. But this is nonetheless a distinct type of question, which requires the elaboration of an explanatory rather than a normative framework, in order to explain why it might be that some EU OIs have apparently proved less attractive to eligible private actors (i.e. been opted into less) than others. So - for both of these reasons, in fact - the issue of usage of EU OIs is an especially important one that merits a separate analysis.

Certainly, it can be argued that some EU OIs have proven more attractive to eligible private actors than others, taking the number of 'opt-ins' by private actors as an indicator of attractiveness. For example, a brief comparison between the Community Trade Mark (CTM) and the European Company (SE) shows that the total number of CTMs registered with the Office for Harmonization in the Internal Market (OHIM) in its first five years of operation amounted to around 100,000,[1] while in the first five years or so of operation of the European Company Regulation a total of 595 SEs had been registered in the whole of the EU (not to mention the EEA);[2] and whereas the total number of CTM registrations surpassed one million in

1 OHIM Statistics of Community Trade Marks 2015 (SSC009), last updated on 7 July 2015, available at <https://oami.europa.eu/ohimportal/en/the-office>.

2 Report from the Commission to the European Parliament and the Council on the application of Council Regulation 2157/2001 of 8 October 2001 on the Statute for a European Company (SE), COM(2010) 676 final.

2014,[3] the number of SEs (albeit over a shorter period) had reached a total of 2,125 by 2014.[4] Of course, there is no reason to expect the number of registrations of a new company form to match those of a new intellectual property right (and particularly not one suitable mainly for large businesses), but, even with this in mind, these figures do hint at a notable difference in the respective popularity of the CTM and the SE. Moreover, while most in the European IP law world would agree with the assertion that the CTM has proved relatively popular with eligible individuals,[5] the same cannot be said of their European company law counterparts and the SE. As we have seen, Rutgers, for instance, is of the view that '[t]he number of SEs is not that great if it is compared to the number of other corporate entities'.[6] And a similar view has also been expressed by Fauvarque-Cosson & Behar-Touchais, who concluded in 2012 that the number of SEs is still very small.[7] On the other hand, there are also those who have interpreted the SE's reception more positively. According to Eidenmüller *et al.*, for instance, '[f]ollowing a slow start, the European Company … has become a popular legal form amongst European firms'.[8]

So the attractiveness of some EU OIs is at least more questionable than that of others. The question, therefore, is why is this the case. Obviously, one explanation could be that the relative lack of demand for a given EU OI reflects a lack of need on the part of private actors for *any* Union regime in the area of law or activity with which it deals. Indeed, as we observed at the conclusion of the previous chapter, this has actually been put forward as one of the advantages of EU OIs as a legislative method, on the ground that, in this way, a Union OI may serve to demonstrate whether a European regime is needed at all. However, the fact that a certain EU OI is not particularly popular with eligible private actors does not necessarily go to show that there is no (or at any rate insufficient) need for any such instrument. Instead, it could just as well be that there is something about the particular OI that has been adopted that renders it less attractive to private actors, even though there is in principle demand for a Union regime of its kind in the area of law in question. In fact, as we will see, there are various factors that could affect the attractiveness of a certain EU OI; some general (like, for example, the need for a European regime at all), and others related to particular aspects or features of the OI itself. And, of the factors relating to an OI's specific characteristics, some are peculiar to individual EU OIs and/or areas of law, while others are common among different EU OIs in distinct fields.

3 *Supra* note 1.

4 European Trade Union Institute European Company Database statistics, available at: <www.worker-participation.eu/europa-ag-se/facts-figures/total-number-of-registered-european-companies-ses>.

5 See further the case study on the CTM below, section C.1.

6 Rutgers 2011, p. 356. It should be noted at the outset that because this chapter discusses the 'attractiveness' of EU OIs, making reference also to qualitative as well as quantitative data (as is explained below), in many instances statements made by commentators and in reports are cited verbatim, so as to ensure that they are accurately represented and not misinterpreted.

7 See Fauvarque-Cosson & Behar-Touchais 2012, p. 159.

8 Eidenmüller, Hornuf & Reps 2013, p. 155.

Thus, this chapter aims to investigate the various factors that may have an influence on the attractiveness of EU OIs to private actors, and to see whether or not this could lead to some guidelines for the development of future Union optional regimes. The chapter begins by distinguishing different possible factors that could affect the attractiveness of EU OIs, with a view to determining particularly whether (and if so, to what extent) there could be factors common to EU OIs in general (section A). It is necessary to do so before elaborating on the research questions to be addressed in this chapter, as these will centre on only some of the factors identified, for reasons that will become clear. Then, after laying out the main questions to be considered, the particular methodology to be followed, and the hypotheses (section B), a number of specific Union optional regimes are examined as examples (section C). Finally, the chapter identifies and analyses relevant findings from these examples, before arriving at a conclusion on the validity and utility of the suggested explanatory theory (section D).

A. Sector-Specific, Instrument-Specific and General Factors

1. *Sector-Specific Factors*

To begin with factors that are related to a Union OI's specific features, it should be clear that any given EU OI will contain specific substantive provisions that could influence its attractiveness to eligible private actors. That is to say, the specific content of the Regulation establishing a certain Union optional regime is likely to play a significant role in the decision of private actors whether or not to opt into that regime.

In particular, it should be apparent that Regulations introducing EU OIs contain *sector-specific* provisions that may affect the level of usage of the optional regimes they create. In other words, in the case of any given optional regime there will be a number of applicable rules specific to the particular field of law that it deals with, which, depending on their content, could affect how attractive that regime is to private actors. Returning to the case of the European Company, for example, it was mentioned in our description of this EU OI that the Regulation establishing the SE prescribes various rules governing not only the formation but also the operation of SEs; including, for instance, a minimum capital requirement. To be precise, according to Article 4(2) of the SE Regulation, '[t]he subscribed capital shall not be less than EUR 120 000'.[9] Now, in its report on the application of the SE Regulation submitted to the Council and the European Parliament five years after the entry into force of the Regulation[10] (as required by Art. 69 thereof), the Commission identified this minimum capital requirement as one of a number of

9 Council Regulation 2157/2001 of 8 October 2001 on the Statute for a European Company, Art. 4(2).

10 Report from the Commission to the European Parliament and the Council on the application of Council Regulation 2157/2001 of 8 October 2001 on the Statute for a European Company (SE), COM(2010) 676.

practical problems related to the setting up and running of an SE.[11] That is, many respondents to the public consultation on which the Commission's report was based[12] (comprising companies, including SEs, legal advisers and business associations) cited this provision as a 'considerable obstacle' (or, as the Commission calls it, a 'negative driver') discouraging businesses from establishing a European Company. In particular, the Commission affirmed that the 'high level of the minimum capital requirement (€120,000) is a disincentive for SMEs to adopt the SE ...'.[13] Evidently, then, this suggests that if the Regulation had provided a lower capital requirement (or even perhaps no capital requirement at all), it would have made the SE more attractive to eligible private actors.

To give another example, we can also look again at the case of the Community Trade Mark. As was indicated in our description of this OI, the CTM Regulation (like the Trade Mark Directive that came before it) contains provisions regulating matters such as the criteria for registrability of trade-marks and the actual rights conferred by a trade mark. Among these, for instance, is a provision regarding the fees to be paid for CTMs (Art. 139 of the original CTM Regulation),[14] which provides the basis for more detailed fees regulations to be adopted. Now, some years after the entry into force of the CTM, the Commission (again, in accordance with its obligations under that Regulation)[15] commissioned a study on the overall functioning of the European trade mark system, as part of which the opinions of various 'users' of the system (including trade mark proprietors and applicants, as well as their agents) were canvassed.[16] And this study pinpointed the level and structure of fees payable for CTMs as one of a few particular features of the regime that could deter end-users from opting into it. More precisely, the study found that 'users express little acceptance of OHIM's application and renewal fees. 38 percent of the proprietors consider the application fee as "a bit too high" and 21 percent as "far too high", and 74 percent of the proprietors say that the application fees influence their decisions to file a CTM ...'.[17] Hence this evidently implies that if the fees set under the CTM Regulation were reduced, it would make the CTM more attractive to private actors than it is already.

So it is clear that these provisions and the content of them may have an effect on the attractiveness of the optional regimes to which they apply - and it is also

11 *Ibid.*, p. 6 *et seq*. See also the Commission Staff Working Document accompanying this Report, SEC(2010) 1391 final, p. 7 *et seq*.

12 See Ernst & Young 2009.

13 Commission Accompanying document to the Report from the Commission to the European Parliament and the Council on the application of Council Regulation 2157/2001, p. 7. Indeed, it was already mentioned in our description of the SUP proposal that the minimum capital requirement is one of the reasons why the Commission considers the SE to be inappropriate for many small businesses, and hence why it has proposed the creation of other private European forms of company; see *supra*, Chapter 3, SUP description.

14 Council Regulation 40/94 of 20 December 1993 on the Community trade mark. The provision in the amended Regulation on the Community trade mark (Council Regulation 207/2009 of 26 February 2009) is Art. 144.

15 See in particular Art. 25(4).

16 Max Planck Institute for Intellectual Property and Competition Law 2011.

17 Max Planck Institute for Intellectual Property and Competition Law 2011, p. 40 and 41.

clear that these provisions are specific to the particular area of law in question. As far as the minimum capital requirement for the SE is concerned, this is a provision specific to the sector of company law. A similar rule could be provided in another OI in the area of company law (in fact, we have seen that the European Cooperative Society (SCE) Regulation and the proposed European single-member private limited liability company (SUP) Directive do also contain minimum capital requirements),[18] but EU OIs in other fields of law (such as IP law, or contract law, etc.) would never contain any such provision. Equally, as far as regards the fees for obtaining a Community Trade Mark right, this is a matter specific to the area of intellectual property law. There are also rules on fees in the Regulations establishing the Community Design (CD) and the Community Plant Variety Right (CPVR), as well as the Unitary Patent (UP) Regulation, but one would not expect to encounter provisions on fees payable for the registration of a right in an optional instrument in the area of, say, procedural law.

For this reason, while it is important to take such provisions into account, as they patently can have an effect on the attractiveness of EU OIs, they are at the same time of limited interest for present purposes, since, being peculiar to a certain policy area, they are unlikely to be instructive for future EU OIs in other policy areas.[19] In other words, sector-specific factors correspond to rules that are applicable only to particular optional regimes in particular fields of law and, as such, rules that cannot be meaningfully compared as between different OIs in distinct fields of law. Thus, even if a lowering of the minimum capital requirement may well enhance the attractiveness of the SE, this would be a micro-level observation, which could not inform the substantive design of the CTM; just as the need to reduce the fees for registering a CTM in order to improve its attractiveness could tell us little if anything about the ideal design of the SE Regulation. Perhaps one could still attempt to arrive at macro-level conclusions, such as a statement to the effect that the less expensive or costly an OI is for private actors, the more attractive it will be as a legal product. But this level of abstraction would not be much more informative. Leaving aside the fact that such assertions would amount to little more than common sense, they could be considered as general propositions of application beyond the realm of OIs. Therefore, a comparative analysis of EU optional instruments (or at least OIs in distinct areas of EU law) on the basis of sector-specific provisions would be a rather futile exercise.

2. *Instrument-Specific Factors*

Having made plain that sector-specific rules may have a considerable impact on the attractiveness of a Union optional regime, but also that such sector-specific factors can provide little guidance (if any) for the design of EU OIs in general, the question becomes whether Regulations establishing OIs contain any other kinds of substantive rules that could influence the attractiveness of the regimes they create,

18 See *supra* Chapter 3, SCE description and SUP description.

19 Although they may, of course, be instructive for subsequent OIs in the same policy area.

which are more generalizable, in the sense that they concern matters that are common to most if not all EU OIs.

Now, while it might not be quite as readily apparent, a close inspection of Regulations introducing EU OIs reveals that it is indeed possible to distinguish a second category of substantive provisions contained therein, which may be more aptly described as *instrument-specific*. That is, in the case of any given Regulation creating an optional regime there are also a number of particular features that are specific not to the field of law in question, but to EU OIs as a form of legislation, because they pertain to their very nature as optional instruments. Rather than addressing sector-specific issues of the kind just outlined, these provisions deal with such matters as how the OI is to be administered and (where appropriate) adjudicated upon; in which sub-fields and on which points the OI is to rely on pre-existing national law; and the comparative advantage(s) the OI is designed to offer with respect to existing regimes in the legal systems of the Member States - which are all issues inherent in the design of a Union OI. Accordingly, these are issues that *any* Regulation introducing an OI must address. And, as we shall see, the content of these provisions may also have an influence on the attractiveness of the optional regimes to which they apply.

In order to illustrate such instrument-specific factors, it is useful to elaborate on each of the aforementioned kinds of provision in turn, with reference to different EU OIs as concrete examples.

(a) Institutional Autonomy

The first kind of instrument-specific rules mentioned above concern the system of administration and adjudication of the EU optional regime. In other words, these provisions determine the institutional setup for the EU OI, in the sense of the institution(s) responsible for deciding on applications to opt into the OI, and (where necessary) also the courts competent to judge upon disputes or claims based on the selected OI.

Starting first and foremost with the system of administration of the optional regime, any Regulation introducing an OI must specify the body or bodies that are competent to decide on *requests to opt into the regime*, since, by definition, the regime needs to be validly 'selected' in order for it to apply.[20] In the case of some Union optional regimes, the establishing Regulations provide for a decentralized system of administration. For example, the Regulation on the European Cooperative Society provides that SCEs are to be registered with national registries. Under Article 11(1) of the SCE Regulation, '[e]very SCE shall be registered in the Member State in which it has its registered office in a register designated by the law of that Member State in accordance with the law applicable to public limited-liability companies'.[21] There is

20 See Chapter 2, section B.1(b).

21 Council Regulation 1435/2003 of 22 July 2003 on the Statute for a European Cooperative Society, Art. 11(1).

no such thing as a European registry of SCEs.[22] In the case of other Union optional regimes, however, the establishing Regulations institute a centralized system of administration. For instance, as was mentioned in our description of the CPVR, the Regulation on Community plant variety rights founded a new EU body (namely the Community Plant Variety Office (CPVO)) to which it accorded the exclusive competence of examining CPVR applications and granting CPVRs. This is summed up in Article 4, which states that '[f]or the purpose of the implementation of this Regulation a Community Plant Variety Office ... is hereby established'.[23] Conceivably, the Regulation could - like the SCE Regulation - have accorded this competence to existing bodies in the Member State (e.g. national plant variety or intellectual property offices), but instead the decision was made to create a Union agency for this purpose. In fact applications for CPVRs may be filed with national agencies, but these must then 'take all steps to forward the application to the Office within two weeks after filing'.[24]

It is true that certain existing and proposed EU OIs are somewhat anomalous in this respect. In the case of the procedural law OIs, for example, the institutions to whom private actors must address requests to opt into the regime are in fact the same institutions responsible for adjudicating on actions founded on the regime (i.e. competent national courts - see below). In other words, there is not a separate system of administration provided for these EU OIs. And in the case of the 2011 proposal for a Common European Sales Law (CESL) in the area of contract law, not only was the system of administration envisaged for the regime the same as the system of adjudication, but also, as explained previously,[25] private actors would not actually have had to undergo any form of application procedure in order to opt into the CESL. Rather, the selection would have been made by way of inclusion by the parties of a provision in their contract designating the CESL as the applicable regime, the validity of which could *eventually* (but not necessarily) have been scrutinized by a competent national court, should a dispute over the contract arise.[26] So while the proposed CESL Regulation did also specify the institutions ultimately responsible for deciding on the validity of requests to opt into the regime, such 'requests' would only have been scrutinized *ex post*, if at all.

At any rate, the point remains that, whether they set up a centralized or a decentralized system, all Regulations establishing OIs will contain provisions specifying who is responsible for administering the OI. And, similarly, the establishing Regulations of most (though not necessarily all) EU OIs will also

22 Even though such a registry is certainly conceivable. In fact, as we saw in our description of the SE, a European company registry was actually envisaged in the original proposal for this OI (See Chapter 3, SE Description).

23 Council Regulation 2100/94 of 27 July 1994 on Community plant variety rights, Art. 4.

24 CPVR Regulation, Art. 49.

25 See Chapter 3, CESL Description.

26 Similarly, another anomalous case in this respect is the Community Design, of which, as we have seen, there also exists an unregistered version (see Chapter 3, CD Description). Once again, though, while there is no requirement to register such a design right, the validity of an asserted Unregistered Community Design right could still potentially be scrutinized by a competent (in fact specialized) national court (as we have also seen).

contain provisions on the system of adjudication of the optional regime, as it is also necessary to specify the courts before which private actors may eventually bring *actions founded on the regime*. In the case of the Community Design, for example, the establishing Regulation provides for a system of 'Community design courts', which correspond to national courts that are specialized in hearing disputes concerning the infringement and validity of Community designs.[27] For this reason, Article 80(1) of the CD Regulation imposed on Member States the obligation to 'designate in their territories as limited a number as possible of national courts and tribunals of first and second instance (Community design courts) which shall perform the functions assigned to them by this Regulation'.[28] As for the Unitary Patent Regulation, as we saw this goes even further, in that it foresees the creation of a European-level specialized patent court - albeit through a separate international agreement - with exclusive jurisdiction over disputes regarding the UP.[29] Hence the affirmation in the preamble of the Regulation that '[e]stablishing a Unified Patent Court to hear cases concerning the European patent with unitary effect is essential in order to ensure the proper functioning of that patent ...'.[30] By contrast, in the case of the European Order for Payment Procedure (EOP), the establishing Regulation is stated to be applicable 'to civil and commercial matters in cross-border cases, *whatever the nature of the court or tribunal*'.[31] That is, the system of adjudication (which in fact is also the system of administration)[32] of the EOP consists of any competent national courts, the jurisdiction of which is determined especially in accordance with the Brussels I Regulation.[33] The EOP Regulation does not create some kind of 'Community order for payment courts', in the sense of national courts specialized in hearing cases based on the EOP.

In the case of the OIs in the area of European company law, however, the establishing Regulations do not specify the courts competent to adjudicate on the regimes they enact. Perhaps one might assume, returning to the SCE, for example, that courts in the Member State where the SCE's registered office is located would have jurisdiction over any legal proceedings arising out of the SCE Regulation (between, say, different organs of the SCE), but then one could also imagine a choice of forum being included in the SCE's articles of association. In any event, it appears that no such proceedings have arisen in relation to any of the company law OIs, and to date not a single preliminary question has been referred to the CJEU regarding

27 See Council Regulation 6/2002 of 12 December 2001 on Community designs, Title IX, Section 2.

28 CD Regulation, Art. 80(1).

29 I.e. The Unified Patent Court (UPC). See Chapter 3, Unitary Patent description.

30 Regulation 1257/2012 of the European Parliament and of the Council of 17 December 2012 implementing enhanced cooperation in the area of the creation of unitary patent protection, consideration 25.

31 Regulation 1896/2006 of the European Parliament and of the Council of 12 December 2006 creating a European order for payment procedure, Art. 2(1) (italics added).

32 That is to say, applications to initiate the European Order for Payment procedure are also made before national courts. Indeed it is important to remember that the institution(s) responsible for administering and adjudicating upon a Union OI can be the same.

33 See EOP Regulation, Art. 6.

their interpretation.[34] So while the system of administration is laid down in the Regulations establishing these OIs, the system of adjudication remains unsettled.

Taken together, then, the system of administration and adjudication provided for a Union optional regime may be summarized as the issue of *institutional autonomy* of EU OIs. In other words, this is essentially a question of how far the institutions empowered to administer and - where appropriate - adjudicate upon a given optional regime (which may or may not be the same, depending on the OI in question) are centralized or decentralized and specialized or unspecialized. And it is a question that is intrinsic to EU OIs, because it is prompted by the creation of an *optional* Union regime that constitutes an *alternative* to existing national regimes.

(b) Substantive Autonomy

The second kind of instrument-specific rules that can be identified concern the areas in which, and points on which, the OI refers to pre-existing national laws. That is, these are provisions that determine to what extent the EU optional regime relies on the laws of the Member States for its operation.[35]

Again, the matter of which sub-fields and on which points the optional regime relies on pre-existing national law is one that any Regulation introducing an OI inevitably needs to address, due to the nature of EU OIs as optional alternatives. For while Union optional regimes are designed to subsist in parallel with existing regimes in the domestic legal system of the Member States, at the same time they are not entirely separate from these systems, but rather take effect within them. Therefore any EU OI must ultimately place some degree of residual reliance on pre-existing domestic rules in order for it to be able to function as a legal regime. And such reliance can take the concrete form of references to whole areas of national law, as well as references to individual rules. Take the European Economic Interest Grouping (EEIG), for example. As was indicated in our description of the EEIG Regulation, this makes a number of references to entire areas of pre-existing national (including approximated national) law. In particular, as is stated in the preamble, 'in matters not covered by this Regulation the laws of the Member States and Community law are applicable, for example with regard to: social and labour laws, competition law, [and] intellectual property law'.[36] But it also relies on existing rules in the Member States on some more restricted points. For instance,

34 This may be largely explained by the fact that any dispute that does arise is unlikely to reach the stage of legal proceedings, as this could be detrimental to on-going business activities.

35 It should be noted that this essentially equates to the notion of the 'degree of uniformity' of EU OIs discussed in our normative framework, which we have already seen has been put forward by a number of commentators as a factor influencing the attractiveness of EU OIs; see *supra*, Normative Framework, section A.3(b)(i). However, here we will refer to the 'degree of substantive autonomy' instead, to reflect the fact that we are now looking at this issue particularly in terms of an OI's *reliance* on national law for its operation, rather than from the perspective of how far it overcomes national legal diversity, which was our focus when examining the normative implications of this issue.

36 Council Regulation 2137/85 of 25 July 1985 on the European Economic Interest Grouping (EEIG), consideration 15.

while the Regulation stipulates that '[t]he members of a grouping shall have unlimited joint and several liability for its debts and other liabilities of whatever nature', it leaves it to national law to 'determine the consequences of such liability'.[37] To give another example, the Regulation establishing the European Enforcement Order (EEO) also makes a number - if a smaller number - of references to national law. Perhaps most notably, as was mentioned in our description of this OI, the procedures for execution of an EEO are governed for the most part by national law. At the beginning of the EEO Regulation's Chapter IV regarding enforcement, Article 20(1) states: 'Without prejudice to the provisions of this Chapter, the enforcement procedures shall be governed by the law of the Member State of enforcement'.[38] But the Regulation defers to national law on more specific points too. For instance, Article 10 provides for the rectification of an inaccurate European Enforcement Order certificate or the withdrawal of an incorrectly granted one 'upon application to the court of origin', but then goes on to state in its second paragraph that '[t]he law of the Member State of origin shall apply to the rectification or withdrawal of the European Enforcement Order certificate'.[39]

So, in short, the degree to which a Union optional regime is dependent on pre-existing national law can be characterized as the issue of *substantive autonomy* of EU OIs. Unlike the previous kind of instrument-specific issue labelled 'institutional autonomy', which is concerned with how far a certain optional regime relies on existing Member State systems of administration and adjudication, substantive autonomy corresponds to the question of how far the regime relies on pre-existing Member State laws.[40]

(c) Added Value

The third and final kind of instrument-specific features of EU OIs mentioned above regard the comparative advantage(s) the OI offers to private actors over existing national regimes. Like the issues of institutional and substantive autonomy, this issue of comparative advantage is one that is common to Regulations establishing OIs, because it is integral to the creation of an optional European regime that can be chosen by private actors as an alternative to existing domestic regimes. Since these domestic regimes remain in force alongside Union optional regimes, the question arises as to what additional benefits are conferred on individuals who opt into the latter rather than choosing to make use of the former. And these benefits, of course, can take different forms.

37 EEIG Regulation, Art. 24(1).

38 Regulation 805/2004 of the European Parliament and of the Council of 21 April 2004 creating a European Enforcement Order for uncontested claims, Art. 20(1).

39 EEO Regulation, Art. 10.

40 To this one could also add interpretative autonomy, in the sense of how far the optional regime relies on domestic rules for its interpretation, and how far it provides its own autonomous guiding principles. However in order to avoid over-complication (considering also that interpretative and substantive autonomy are very much interlinked), the issue of interpretative autonomy is left out of the present study.

Perhaps the most obvious form of comparative advantage that may be offered by a Regulation establishing a Union optional regime is the conferral of a legal right or entitlement that, unlike its domestic equivalents, is not subject to national territorial limitations, as it is valid or recognized throughout the whole of the EU. Returning to the CPVR, for example, we saw when describing this EU OI that it enables private actors to obtain a single plant variety right with equal effect in all of the Member States. This is encapsulated in Article 2 of the CPVR Regulation, which affirms that 'Community plant variety rights shall have uniform effect within the territory of the Community and may not be granted, transferred or terminated in respect of the abovementioned territory otherwise than on a uniform basis'.[41] By contrast, national plant variety rights can only ever take effect within the territory of the Member State jurisdictions to which they apply. Therefore, this is a clear form of added value that the CPVR Regulation offers those who select it, as an implication of provisions contained therein. However, it might also be that a Union OI has other, less tangible benefits, such as that of offering a neutral, European regime. For instance, recalling again the SCE, the Commission's report on the application of the SCE Regulation[42] found that, in the opinion of cooperatives and professional organizations, 'the most important benefit of setting up an SCE is to have a European image. This image may help the founders of a cooperative to penetrate markets where a European brand is more marketable than a national one'.[43] And again, this European image results from specific provisions of the Regulation establishing the SCE; particularly Article 5(4), which provides that '[t]he statutes of the SCE shall include ... the name of the SCE, preceded or followed by the abbreviation "SCE" ...'.[44]

In sum, then, the comparative advantage(s) of a Union optional regime over equivalent national regimes can be described as the question of *added value* of EU OIs: That is, how far does a particular optional regime offer added value to private actors who opt into it?

So it is visible that Regulations establishing OIs also comprise certain kinds of substantive rules or features that address issues familiar to EU OIs across different policy areas, due to the fact that they are instrument-specific. And, like sector-specific features of EU OIs, these instrument-specific features can affect the attractiveness of Union optional regimes. To give one example,[45] the same Commission report on the application of the SCE Regulation also found that among the 'most important negative drivers' against setting up an SCE were 'the complex

41 CPVR Regulation, Art. 2.

42 Report from the Commission to the European Parliament, the Council, the European Economic and Social Committee and the Committee of the Regions on the application of Council Regulation 1435/2003 of 22 July 2003 on the Statute for a European Cooperative Society (SCE), COM(2012) 72.

43 Report on the application of the SCE Regulation, COM(2012) 72, p. 6.

44 SCE Regulation, Art. 5(4).

45 The effect instrument-specific features of OIs can have on their attractiveness (and particularly *how* such features affect their attractiveness) is discussed further in sections C and D.

procedures to be followed (because of the numerous references to national law)'.[46] This therefore indicates that the degree of substantive autonomy of the SCE Regulation (which, like the EEIG Regulation, is relatively low, since it relies extensively on pre-existing national rules) is a factor that has impacted upon the popularity of the SCE. In fact, we have already seen that the degree of uniformity of EU OIs has been suggested by European company law experts as an element affecting the attractiveness of Union optional regimes.[47] Furthermore, it is also worth noting at (and on) this point that other scholars have actually already proposed all of the instrument-specific aspects of EU OIs explained here as factors that play a role in the 'success' of Union optional regimes. According to the study on the implementation of optional instruments within European civil law carried out for the Legal Affairs Committee of the European Parliament by Fauvarque-Cosson & Behar-Touchais[48] – which examines various EU OIs and gathers feedback on them in each of the Member States – 'added value', 'autonomy and completeness' (by which the authors mean substantive autonomy)[49] and 'legal certainty' (which corresponds roughly to adjudicative autonomy)[50] are all determining factors in how successful a Union OI is.[51]

Thus, it makes sense to compare optional instruments in diverse fields of European law on the basis of their instrument-specific features, as they concern issues that may affect an optional regime's attractiveness which are common to all EU OIs, irrespective of the policy area in which they are found; and this therefore has the potential to yield some useful conclusions of relevance for the attractiveness of EU OIs in general.

3. *General Factors*

In addition to sector-specific and instrument-specific factors, which are both *internal*, in the sense that they are connected with an OI's specific features, it should be recognized that there are also a number of general factors that could potentially have an impact on the attractiveness of a Union optional regime. Like instrument-specific factors, these general factors are common to different EU OIs in distinct policy fields; but unlike instrument-specific factors, this is not because they are

46 Report on the application of the SCE Regulation, COM(2012) 72, p. 7, para. 4.4.

47 See *supra*, Normative Framework, section A.3(b)(i).

48 Fauvarque-Cosson & Behar-Touchais 2012.

49 As is demonstrated by the fact that the authors discuss the issue of references to national law under their heading of 'autonomy and completeness'; see Fauvarque-Cosson & Behar-Touchais 2012, p. 387-388.

50 In the sense that the authors refer to the degree of specialization of Member State judges under this heading, among other related issues (such as the preliminary ruling procedure). The system of administration, however, is not mentioned at all. See Fauvarque-Cosson & Behar-Touchais 2012, p. 388-389.

51 See Fauvarque-Cosson & Behar-Touchais 2012, p. 385 *et seq*. Along with these the study also puts forward a fourth factor, which the authors call 'communication'. In the present study, however, this is discussed below as a general rather than an instrument-specific factor; see *infra*, section A.3(c).

inherent in the creation of an optional regime. Rather, it is because what are categorized here as 'general factors' are *external* issues that could affect the popularity of any EU OI, regardless of the (sector- and instrument-) specific content of the Regulation that establishes it.

There are a number of issues one could potentially identify under this category, but for present purposes we will mention two such general factors; namely the need for a European regime, and awareness. In other words, to employ the language of the law market, we will now consider the issues of the market for, and the marketing of, the product (having looked before at issues concerning the product itself).

(a) The Need for a European Regime

As was indicated at the outset of this chapter, one general factor that could impact upon the attractiveness of a particular EU OI is the *need* for a European regime – optional or otherwise – in the first place. That is to say, the level of demand on the part of private actors for a European regime in a given area of law *in principle* may well affect the popularity of any Union OI that is eventually introduced in that area, regardless of its particular characteristics. Hence, if the demand (or 'market') for a European regime in a certain field is limited, one could expect the popularity of an OI adopted in that field to be inherently constrained (and vice versa). Or, to put it another way, if the needs of private actors in a given area of law are already largely satisfied by existing regimes in the legal systems of the Member States, and the benefits a European regime could *possibly* offer them are therefore negligible, the uptake of an OI in that area is likely to be limited, no matter how well it is designed. To give an example, notably in the European contract law debate some have put forward the argument that 'a European optional instrument may not be as useful or widely considered as its proponents would like to believe',[52] particularly because the problems of legal diversity which the proposals for EU legislation in this area have focused on addressing 'may be restricted in magnitude'.[53] In other words, the contention is that the potential solutions a European contract law OI could offer as against existing national regimes may be of limited significance from the perspective of private actors (and especially legal persons), and therefore that the eventual uptake of an OI in this area could be circumscribed, irrespective of the OI's specific design.[54] For, as Low points out, '[w]hile an optional instrument [in the area of contract law] may make a contribution in those instances where it does exist, its utility is framed by the limits of how firms perceive that selfsame problem (i.e. the extent of legal diversity)'.[55]

Thus, the need for a European regime is clearly a factor that could play a role in the degree of popularity of a Union OI. But it is also clear that the question of

52 Low 2012b, p. 521.

53 Low 2012b, p. 539.

54 See also e.g. Wulf 2014, and for an alternative view, Ganuza & Gomez 2013, and further Smits 2005a; Van Schagen 2012.

55 Low 2012b, p. 539.

whether there is a market for an OI in a certain field of law is a general one, which is not related to an OI's specific design.

(b) Awareness

Another general factor that could influence the popularity of a given Union OI is the issue of *awareness*. Given that private actors obviously need to be aware of the existence of a European Union OI in order for them to possibly opt into it, the extent to which eligible individuals are informed about a particular Union regime is arguably a crucial element determining its level of usage. For this reason, as Fauvarque-Cosson & Behar-Touchais observe, '[a] great deal of communication, even "advertising", is needed, as ignorance is one of the main causes of failure for some optional instruments'.[56] Indeed, this point is alluded to in a number of the country responses in the *Fauvarque-Cosson* Study. According to the Dutch response, for example, sufficient information on the possibility of using an optional instrument is a 'prerequisite'.[57] If there is a lack of awareness of a Union optional regime among potential users, it is hardly likely to be chosen. Furthermore, as Smits notes, 'the marketing of an optional instrument as a European system may pre-empt lock in-effects among parties who are active on the European market'.[58] Therefore, it is important for the popularity of a Union OI that an appropriate amount of information on its availability (not to mention its substance)[59] is provided to eligible private actors, through appropriate channels. Again, though, while this may well be true, the question of marketing is nevertheless a separate issue from the actual design of the OI.

So, in summary, it is evident that such general factors could also have an effect on the attractiveness of any Union OI, irrespective of the policy area in question. However, because these factors are extraneous to the design of EU OIs, they are of lesser interest for present purposes. Again, it is useful to take note of them, in order to have a better appreciation of the range of influences that could impact upon the usage of EU OIs. But in the remainder of this chapter our focus will be on the product, and more particularly on the impact of instrument-specific factors, as internal issues that are common to EU OIs across policy areas.

56 Fauvarque-Cosson & Behar-Touchais 2012, p. 386. See also p. 201. The term 'communication' here should not be confused with Siems' concept of communication mentioned in the previous chapter (*supra* Chapter 4, section A.2(c)(ii)), which refers to the dialogue between national lawmakers. Instead, this concerns communication from lawmakers to eligible private actors.

57 Fauvarque-Cosson & Behar-Touchais 2012, p. 333.

58 Smits 2013, p. 54.

59 On this point, it is worth adding that it is of course also important that eligible private actors are actually made aware of features such as the added value of the Union OI if such features are to play a significant role in their attractiveness. For present purposes, however, the issue of awareness will not be dealt with in conjunction with the matter of added value, precisely because the former is a general factor.

B. Questions, Methodology and Hypotheses

1. *Questions*

The importance of the foregoing observations should not be underestimated. Apart from giving an overall picture of the factors that may influence the attractiveness of a European Union optional regime, the preceding account also signalled where the focus of our attention should lie. We are especially interested in issues of design – and hence we are not so much concerned about external influences of the kind categorized above as general factors – but the problem is that many aspects of Regulations creating OIs which could have an impact on the attractiveness of the regimes they establish – i.e. sector-specific factors – cannot be meaningfully compared across distinct policy fields. Therefore, the present chapter shall henceforth concentrate on instrument-specific factors; since, conversely, a comparative analysis of the instrument-specific provisions of such Regulations and their effects on the attractiveness of Union optional regimes has the potential to lead to some valuable lessons for the ideal design (at least from a 'market' perspective) of *any* EU OI.

Thus, the main questions we will seek to address are the following:

(a) what impact do the instrument-specific provisions of EU optional instruments have on their attractiveness to eligible private actors?, and;
(b) to what extent could this inform the design of future EU optional regimes by the European legislator?

Regarding the first of these questions, two points of clarification are immediately required.

First of all, it should be recalled that the term *eligible* private actors as it is used in this study refers to those individuals who could in principle opt into a given EU OI, because they fall within its scope of application. Given that individuals who do not meet one or more of the conditions of scope (be it material, personal, territorial or geographical) prescribed by a Regulation creating an OI would not be entitled to select it even if they wanted to,[60] the fact that such individuals do not opt in to the regime obviously cannot provide any indication whatsoever of its 'success'. Therefore, it should be understood that we are concerned purely with eligible private actors, as determined by the particular provisions on scope contained in the Regulation that introduces the OI in question. This is not necessarily to say, however, that the scope provisions of Regulations establishing EU OIs can *only* be relevant in demarcating which (and under which circumstances) private actors are eligible to opt in. In particular, it is not excluded that such provisions could also have an influence on the attractiveness of a Union optional regime. For instance, one could again point to the CESL in this regard, as the precise scope that was envisaged for the CESL is one aspect of the formerly proposed Regulation

[60] See *supra* Chapter 4, section B.2(c)(i).

introducing this OI that has been debated in terms of its likely influence on the popularity of the regime.[61] Although this may be largely explained by the fact that, as previously noted,[62] the CESL constitutes something of an anomaly, among other things because it is an optional instrument that would have had to be opted into jointly by two or more parties; for, in this situation, it follows that the potential group of private actors with whom (and circumstances in which) a certain contracting party may eventually use the OI could have an effect on the party's decision whether or not use it themselves (i.e. even for transactions that would have fallen within the scope of the CESL). But, in any event, the point remains that provisions on scope are primarily of relevance in determining eligibility.

And, secondly, it should also be remembered that the term *attractiveness* is used in the present context to denote the extent to which an optional instrument is opted into by private actors. As will be spelled out shortly, taking the number of opt-ins by private actors as one's measure of attractiveness is not without its drawbacks, and indeed it could be seen as a rather crude measure. But, for reasons that will also be made clear, this is the best indicator for present purposes and, as such, the one that is employed herein.

Now, in addressing these questions, we will first examine the instrument-specific provisions of different EU OIs in existence, and consider what effect (if any) they may have had on the popularity of these optional regimes. Then, we shall proceed to compare these provisions and their effects in each of these cases, with a view to analysing how instrument-specific factors might affect the attractiveness of EU OIs in general. Finally, we will reflect on the significance of this analysis for the design of future Union OIs, and its usefulness for the European legislator. Before doing so, however, it is necessary to further explain the methodology we will follow, as well as to outline some working hypotheses.

2. *Methodology*

In order to answer the questions posed above, a case study-based approach is followed. That is to say, a selection of existing EU OIs in different areas of European law are examined as case studies; namely, the Community Trade Mark (CTM) in the area of IP law, the *Societas Europaea* (SE) in the field of company law, and the European Small Claims Procedure (ESCP) in the area of procedural law. It is useful to take such an approach, partly because it is beyond the scope of the present study to carry out a comparative survey of all EU OIs currently in force, but also because some EU OIs that have been adopted have not been in existence long enough for data to be gathered on their usage. By contrast, these three EU OIs have been in existence for some time already, and (at least some) relevant data concerning their usage is already available.

In terms of the rationale for choosing these EU OIs in particular as case studies, this can be explained as follows. Firstly, the SE has been chosen because this

61 On this point see further Chapter 6, section 2(b).

62 See Chapter 3, CESL description.

is the most important of the existing optional instruments in the field of European company law, which for its part is an especially prolific area as far as OIs are concerned. Furthermore, as was already mentioned in the introduction to the present chapter, the SE has arguably seen a relatively low degree of uptake by eligible private actors since its adoption. Therefore, the SE could be of especial interest for our analysis of the effect of instrument-specific provisions on the popularity of EU OIs. Similarly, the CTM has been selected due to the fact that it is the most notable of the optional instruments (or at least those already in operation) in the field of European IP law, which is again a field comprising a number of existing EU OIs. And (as was also indicated already in the introduction to this chapter), in contrast to the SE, the CTM appears to have proved relatively popular with eligible individuals, so it could serve as a revealing counter to the experience of the SE. Finally, the main reason for choosing the ESCP is once again that it can be considered as the most noteworthy OI to have been adopted in the area of procedural law, which is the third area of European law in which several EU OIs have already been introduced. Admittedly, unlike the SE and CTM Regulations, the ESCP Regulation is at the same time the most recent of the OIs that have been adopted in the field to which it pertains; but still, as we will see, like the SE and CTM, the ESCP has been in existence long enough for information to be compiled on its reception among eligible private actors.

So, in short, this case study-based approach will be used as a means of comparing different EU OIs that can be considered as representative of the respective policy fields to which they pertain.

As regards the empirical data on which this comparative analysis will be based, this is drawn from a number of existing studies, which are both qualitative and quantitative in nature. First and foremost, where possible, reference is made to 'official' sources, in the sense of European Commission progress reports. This is the case with the SE[63] (indeed this report has already been mentioned), and also the ESCP,[64] both reports having been produced by the Commission a few years after their introduction, as required by the Regulations that created them.[65] On the other hand, in the case of the CTM, the primary study of relevance (which has also been cited already) is rather 'semi-official', for while it too was 'arranged' by the Commission pursuant to its obligations under the founding Regulation, it was produced by an external institute (i.e. the Max Planck Institute for Intellectual Property and Competition Law).[66] Then, in addition, use is also made of another

63 Report from the Commission to the European Parliament and the Council on the application of Council Regulation 2157/2001 of 8 October 2001 on the Statute for a European Company (SE), COM(2010) 676.

64 Report from the Commission to the European Parliament, the Council and the European Economic and Social Committee on the application of Regulation (EC) 861/2007 of the European Parliament and of the Council establishing a European Small Claims Procedure, COM(2013) 795.

65 As regards the ESCP, this obligation is contained in Art. 28 of the ESCP Regulation.

66 Max Planck Institute for Intellectual Property and Competition Law 2011. It is also worth noting (or in the case of the SE, reminding), though, that the Commission reports on the SE and the ESCP were themselves actually based on external studies that it had previously →

(still less official) study that was mentioned before, namely the study on the implementation of optional instruments within European civil law produced by Fauvarque-Cosson & Behar-Touchais for the Legal Affairs Committee of the European Parliament.[67] Being a more general study, this contains empirical data on a range of EU OIs (not to mention other kinds of optional instrument), including all three of the OIs under examination.

Of course, the methodology proposed here is not unproblematic. For one thing, the reliance on the number of opt-ins as a gauge of attractiveness of EU OIs could be criticized on the basis that this only includes 'successful' opt-ins, and thereby completely excludes all instances where private actors attempt to opt into a certain EU OI but fail in their application. Take, for example, the CTM. An application to register a CTM may be refused by OHIM, say, on an absolute ground (e.g. the sign applied for is devoid of distinctive character),[68] in which case it would not be included in the statistics on the number of CTM registrations; and yet, it would be apparent in such a case that the individual in question desired to select the OI and was eligible to do so. Thus, it may be contended that the number of opt-ins constitutes an excessively narrow operationalization of the concept of 'attractiveness', and that the number of applications would be a better indicator of the attractiveness of EU OIs, since the success of an OI should not depend on applications to opt into it being successful. However, using the number of applications would also be problematic, not least because, in some cases, applications to opt into an OI will be refused on the ground that the applicant does not fall within the scope of the Regulation establishing the OI, meaning that they are not eligible. And since we are concerned with attractiveness to *eligible* private actors, it is therefore more certain to look at the number of opt-ins, as obviously only eligible private actors can successfully opt in to EU OIs. Furthermore in the case of some OIs, detailed statistics on the number of applications are less widely available than data on the number of opt-ins, so it is also easier to take the latter as our measure, even if it is a rather simplistic one.

Also, regarding the data on which the analysis will be based, apart from the fact that not all of these data are official, another problem is that the main studies to be used (i.e. the Commission progress reports on the SE and ESCP and the *Max-Planck* Study on the CTM) were not all produced after the same period of the OI's existence. Whereas the reports on the SE and the ESCP were both compiled roughly five years after the entry into force of the optional regime, the study on the CTM was published over ten years after the Community trade mark system was introduced. Therefore, being snapshots of EU OIs at different stages in their respective lifetimes, a comparison based on these studies is destined to be an imperfect one. Nevertheless, since these are the most authoritative reports that have been produced on the usage of these EU OIs, it still makes sense to rely on them as the principal sources, albeit keeping drawbacks such as these in mind.

commissioned. Indeed, for this reason, reference will also be made to these 'semi-official' studies as regards the SE and ESCP where necessary.

67 Fauvarque-Cosson & Behar-Touchais 2012.

68 See CTM Regulation 2009, Art. 7(1)(b).

In addition, the idea of employing a case study-based approach could be criticized on the basis that any conclusions drawn from only a few case studies would lack force, and that a greater number of EU OIs should be examined in order to provide a more reliable picture. Still, while this may well be true, for the reasons already stated it is expedient for us to focus on three EU OIs, which can be seen as representative of OIs in their respective areas of law.

3. *Hypotheses*

Before proceeding to explore the case studies, it is helpful to first outline our working hypotheses regarding the two main questions posed.

As far as regards the first question ('what impact do the instrument-specific provisions of EU optional instruments have on their attractiveness to eligible private actors?'), not only is it foreseen that the instrument-specific provisions of the EU OIs under examination will have had a considerable influence on their attractiveness, but it is envisaged that they will have impacted on their attractiveness in a certain way. More specifically, the hypothesis is that the less institutionally and substantively autonomous the EU OI is, and the less added value it offers, the less attractive it will have proved to eligible private actors. Or, to phrase it in positive terms, the more a Union OI has institutional autonomy (in the sense of a centralized and/or specialized system of administration and/or adjudication), substantive autonomy (i.e. relying to a limited extent on pre-existing national law) and added value (that is, comparative advantage(s) over existing national alternatives), the more attractive it will be as a legal product on the European law market. Indeed, it is worth noting in this respect that the aforementioned study on EU optional instruments by Fauvarque-Cosson & Behar-Touchais actually describes the instrument-specific factors it identifies (which correspond in our analysis to adjudicative autonomy, substantive autonomy and added value) as '*rules* for creating a successful optional instrument ...'.[69] That is to say, these authors also postulate that optional instruments must be autonomous as well as advantageous in order to be more attractive to private actors. Hence on the matter of substantive autonomy, for example, the authors maintain that '[i]f an optional instrument has to refer to the national law, it is a sign of failure'.[70] So it makes sense for us to take these proposed 'rules' as the starting point for a deeper investigation into the impact of instrument-specific provisions on the attractiveness of EU OIs.

In turn, concerning the second, connected, question ('to what extent could this inform the design of future EU optional regimes by the European legislator?'), it is expected that the answers to the first question could provide the European legislator with valuable indications for the design of optional regimes in future, by demonstrating how a Union OI's instrument-specific provisions should be designed in order to maximize its attractiveness to eligible private actors. However, the extent

69 Fauvarque-Cosson & Behar-Touchais 2012, p. 386 (italics added). This is also how the authors describe the factor of communication, which we have distinguished as a general factor.

70 Fauvarque-Cosson & Behar-Touchais 2012, p. 387.

to which this could inform the design of future EU OIs is likely to be constrained, due to the difficulty of accurately measuring the (institutional and substantive) autonomy and added value of EU OIs, as well as the impact these instrument-specific features have on their attractiveness. In other words, while it may be possible to form a visceral impression of the effect of instrument-specific factors on the attractiveness of EU OIs, it will be harder to demonstrate this with precision. And, in addition, it should not be forgotten that, apart from instrument-specific factors, there also exist sector-specific and general factors that play a role in the attractiveness of EU OIs. So it will be more difficult still to ascertain the *relative* impact of instrument-specific factors (i.e. relative to these other factors). Thus, while the conclusions that result from this analysis could be of value to the European legislator, by pointing to certain instrument-specific principles that should be followed when creating future EU OIs, it will be troublesome to offer more precise indications than this.

C. Case Studies

1. *The Community Trade Mark (CTM)*

To begin with the Community Trade Mark, the instrument-specific features of the CTM Regulation are as follows. Firstly, as far as regards institutional autonomy, the CTM Regulation (like the CPVR Regulation) created a new EU agency, i.e. OHIM, with the exclusive competence to decide on applications for CTMs.[71] The Member State IP offices have no such competence, although CTM applications may be filed via national trade mark offices. And (like the CD Regulation), the CTM Regulation enacted a system of *designated* national courts within the Member States, i.e. 'Community trade mark courts',[72] with the competence to decide on legal actions involving CTMs (albeit in cooperation with the CJEU via the preliminary reference mechanism). So, in other words, the CTM Regulation provides for a centralized system of administration, and a decentralized, but specialized, system of adjudication. Secondly, in terms of substantive autonomy, as was already recalled in the previous chapter[73] the CTM Regulation makes a couple of references to entire areas of pre-existing national law, particularly civil liability and unfair competition,[74] as well as a more restricted reference to Member State rules relating to (national) trade-marks as objects of property, subject to the rules that are provided by the Regulation to govern this matter.[75] In addition, it also refers to national law on infringement of trade marks to govern the effects of CTMs in respects other than those dealt with in the Regulation[76] (including, for instance,

71 See notably Art. 2 of Regulation 40/94 of 20 December 1993 on the Community trade mark.
72 CTM Regulation, Art. 91.
73 Chapter 4, section A.3(a)(i).
74 See CTM Regulation, Art. 14(2). See also Art. 106(2) regarding administrative and criminal law.
75 CTM Regulation, Art. 16(1).
76 See CTM Regulation, Art. 14(1).

effects *vis-à-vis* third parties[77] and sanctions for infringement),[78] not to mention national procedural law governing actions relating to trade marks, again unless otherwise provided in the Regulation.[79] All in all, though, one does not encounter numerous references to national law, as the CTM Regulation contains extensive provisions regulating various aspects of CTMs and the CTM system. Therefore, it can be said that the CTM Regulation relies on pre-existing national law only to a limited extent. Last but not least, as far as the comparative advantage provided by the CTM Regulation is concerned, the CTM (like both the CPVR and the CD) constitutes a unitary right with uniform effect throughout the whole territory of the EU,[80] whereas national trade marks can only ever be valid in the territory of the Member States to which they pertain. Thus, the CTM Regulation offers a clear-cut advantage over equivalent regimes in the legal systems of the Member States, in the form of a new intellectual property right that is not constrained by national territorial limitations.

As for the popularity of the CTM, it was already mentioned in the introduction to this chapter that the statistics on CTM registrations suggest that the CTM has proved to be an attractive optional instrument with eligible private actors, and indeed that many consider it to be so. This is made especially clear by the *Fauvarque-Cosson* Study on European optional instruments, which affirms that these official statistics 'show that the Community trademark is a big success', if not 'perhaps the most successful optional instrument', as '[o]verall, the OHIM statistics show a favourable growth in the use of the Community trademark'.[81] Also, many of the country responses to the questionnaire on which the *Fauvarque-Cosson* Study was based attest to the popularity of the CTM. According to the German country report, for example, the CTM is seen as 'an "exceptional success" and is justly considered "one of the most widely accepted tools" by operators'.[82] Similarly, the French response states '[a] quick look at...statistics shows that national operators increasingly choose to use the Community trademark, which has achieved significant success'.[83] As regards the *Max-Planck* Study on the overall functioning of the European trade mark system produced for the Commission, admittedly this does not declare the 'success' of CTMs in quite so explicit terms. But it too asserts that, just as demand for trade mark protection has been on the rise since 1996, when OHIM started its operations, so '[d]emand for CTMs has also been increasing since then. It was particularly high during the dot-com boom, but has continued to grow since then'.[84] And one certainly does not find any statements calling into question the popularity of the CTM in the *Max-Planck* Study (which, as we shall see, is more than can be said for the Commission reports on the SE and the ESCP). So, in short,

77 CTM Regulation, Art. 23.
78 CTM Regulation, Art. 98.
79 See CTM Regulation, Art. 97(3). See also Art. 101 regarding appeals.
80 See in particular CTM Regulation, Art. 1(2).
81 Fauvarque-Cosson & Behar-Touchais 2012, p. 116.
82 Fauvarque-Cosson & Behar-Touchais 2012, p. 123.
83 Fauvarque-Cosson & Behar-Touchais 2012, p. 127.
84 Max Planck Institute for Intellectual Property and Competition Law 2011, p. 39.

the available evidence does generally lend support to the view that the CTM has proven to be a popular EU OI.

Now, looking at the findings of these studies in more detail, it can be observed that they also both offer indications as to particular aspects of the CTM that eligible individuals find attractive, as well as, conversely, aspects that may deter such individuals from opting into this optional regime. In fact, we have already seen that the *Max-Planck* Study identified the fees level and structure for CTMs as one (sector-specific) characteristic of the CTM that had a negative influence on the decisions of many of the users surveyed to file a Community trade mark.[85] But it also indicated a number of other features influencing the attractiveness of the CTM. Most notably, the study found that '[a]s regards users' general attitudes towards the CTM system, a broad majority of 76 percent of proprietors and 84 percent of agents recognize that the CTM system offers trade mark owners substantial simplifications and expanded possibilities compared with national trade mark systems'.[86] This is of particular interest to us, as it suggests that the comparative advantage offered by the CTM Regulation (an instrument-specific feature) has also had a significant influence - and in this case a positive influence - on the popularity of the CTM regime. And indeed this is also supported by many of the country responses in the *Fauvarque-Cosson* Study. The German response, for instance, asserts that the trend towards registering Community trade-marks appears to be due to the fact that it 'allows for protection - through a single registration with OHIM - in 27 different States, an advantage that outweighs the financial aspect given that the costs of registering a Community trademark are much higher than the costs of a national application in Germany'.[87] Likewise, according to the French response, 'the advantages of the Community trademark, which gives companies the right to use a single procedure for acquiring Community trademarks that are uniformly protected throughout all EU countries, are attracting more and more French applicants who choose to use it to protect their signs'.[88] Hence it appears from these studies that the comparative advantage of the CTM has been a driving force behind its popularity with eligible private actors.

On the other hand, as far as the CTM's other instrument-specific features are concerned, the influence these have had on the CTMs' popularity is less apparent from these studies. Still, on the point of the CTM's system of administration, the *Max-Planck* Study does also find that 'OHIM's performance in terms of quality is predominantly rated as "average" or "high"', and that '[a] clear majority rates OHIM's performance in terms of consistency as either "fairly consistent" or "very

85 See *supra*, section A.1.

86 Max Planck Institute for Intellectual Property and Competition Law 2011, p. 39.

87 Fauvarque-Cosson & Behar-Touchais 2012, p. 123-124.

88 Fauvarque-Cosson & Behar-Touchais 2012, p. 126. While the Greek country report states: 'The Community Trademark (CTM) has proved to be a very effective tool, in particular because the centralized registration of trademarks has legal effects in all Member States, which reduces costs and human resources since it is no longer necessary to file trademark applications in each Member State. In general, the Community trademark system allows for resolving many problems and legal complexities caused by the principle of territoriality' (p. 124).

consistent"';[89] which could be taken as an intimation that the centralized system of administration provided by the CTM Regulation is seen by users as another alluring aspect of this Union OI. However, there is no clear statement to this effect in the *Max-Planck* Study - nor, for that matter, in the *Fauvarque-Cosson* Study. Similarly, there is not a clear indication of the influence of the CTM's decentralized but specialized system of adjudication on the regime's attractiveness, although the *Max-Planck* Study does note that it 'seems unsatisfactory that the number of CTM courts in the Member States varies widely'.[90] And the same goes for the effect of the CTM Regulation's limited reliance on pre-existing national law, which, apart from the observation in the *Max-Planck* Study that the Regulation 'provides a fully autonomous and complete system where all issues of substantive and procedural law are provided for',[91] is not really discussed.

Thus, while the comparative advantage provided by the CTM Regulation evidently has had a noteworthy effect on the attractiveness of the CTM, the existing empirical research sheds less light on the impact of the other instrument-specific characteristics of the CTM in this respect. Perhaps the fact that they are not identified as features having a negative effect on the CTM's popularity might in and of itself be seen as an indication that these other instrument-specific characteristics have also contributed to the attractiveness of the CTM, but the studies examined offer nothing more than hints such as this.

2. *The European Company (SE)*

Moving on to the European Company, the SE Regulation has the following instrument-specific features. Firstly, the SE Regulation (like the SCE Regulation, not to mention also the EEIG Regulation) specifies that SEs must be registered with competent national registries in the Member States.[92] It did not establish a Union-level authority to administer the registration of European Companies. Hence the SE Regulation provides for a decentralized system of administration. And, as in the case of these other company law OIs, the SE Regulation does not specify a system of adjudication. Secondly, the SE Regulation (again, similarly to the other existing company law OIs) makes many references to pre-existing national law, both in entire areas such as those of taxation and insolvency,[93] as well as on various other more specific points.[94] Indeed, it was already recalled in the previous chapter that many of the requirements of the SE Regulation are made subject to requirements of national law relating to public companies of the Member State where the SE's registered office is located. In fact, according to Siems, '[i]t has been counted that the

89 Max Planck Institute for Intellectual Property and Competition Law 2011, p. 39.
90 Max Planck Institute for Intellectual Property and Competition Law 2011, p. 156.
91 Max Planck Institute for Intellectual Property and Competition Law 2011, p. 223.
92 Council Regulation 2157/2001 of 8 October 2001 on the Statute for a European Company (SE), Art. 12(1).
93 SE Regulation, Art. 16.
94 See Chapter 4, section A.3(a)(i).

SE Regulation refers 84 times to the law of the Member States'.[95] So it is fair to say that the SE Regulation relies on the domestic laws of the Member States to a large extent. Finally, on the point of the comparative advantage of the SE, the SE actually has a range of potential advantages over equivalent domestic company forms. For one thing, as with the SCE, a possible benefit of setting up a European company is that it is a neutral company form with a European image.[96] But there are also various others. In particular, as we saw when describing the SE, the SE Regulation enabled the European company to transfer its registered office to another Member State without the need to dissolve and re-establish the company, unlike public limited-liability companies formed under the laws of a Member State. This possibility is provided for in Article 8(1) of the SE Regulation, which states that '[t]he registered office of an SE may be transferred to another Member State in accordance with paragraphs 2 to 13. Such a transfer shall not result in the winding up of the SE or in the creation of a new legal person'.[97] Also, as was alluded to in the previous chapter,[98] the SE can enable companies to avoid national mandatory rules on worker participation, by virtue of its accompanying Directive on the involvement of employees.[99] Thus, depending on the given case, the SE could potentially offer any number of comparative advantages to eligible legal persons.

As far as regards the popularity of the SE, we have already seen at the beginning of this chapter (as well as in the previous one)[100] that the figures on SE registrations suggest that it has not proved to be a particularly popular optional instrument, and that its attractiveness is very much disputed. This is also reflected in the *Fauvarque-Cosson* Study, which, while recognizing that 'the number of SEs has increased exponentially since 2004',[101] concludes that the figures 'remain very low'.[102] By way of illustration, Fauvarque-Cosson & Behar-Touchais point out that the number of SEs registered in France, for example, amounted to 21 as of 24 February 2011, compared with 60,000 public limited liability companies and 120,000 simplified joint stock companies.[103] In fact, the Commission itself acknowledges in

95 Siems 2005, p. 432, referring to Brandt & Scheifele 2002.

96 For the relevant provision of the SE Regulation in this respect, see notably Art. 11, which specifies that '[t]he name of an SE shall be preceded or followed by the abbreviation SE' (Art. 11(1)), and that '[o]nly SEs may include the abbreviation SE in their name' (Art. 11(2)).

97 SE Regulation, Art. 8(1).

98 Chapter 4, section A.3(b)(ii).

99 Council Directive 2001/86/EC of 8 October 2001 supplementing the Statute for a European company with regard to the involvement of employees. See also SE Regulation Art. 1(4). While our previous discussion of this possibility centred on criticisms that have been made of it from the perspective of social justice, however, we are now looking at this purely from the perspective of the advantage it can represent for private actors eligible to opt in to the SE (i.e. businesses).

100 See Chapter 4, section A.2(c)(ii).

101 Fauvarque-Cosson & Behar-Touchais 2012, p. 158.

102 Fauvarque-Cosson & Behar-Touchais 2012, p. 159.

103 See Fauvarque-Cosson & Behar-Touchais 2012, p. 159. The authors also give the example of Luxembourg, where the 15 SEs registered in the country as of December 2009 'must be viewed in light of the 73 838 public limited companies established in Luxembourg during the same period'.

its report on the application of the SE Regulation that the conclusion from the external study on which the report was based is that 'the original objectives of the SE Statute have been achieved to some extent, but the situation could still be improved'.[104] More precisely, this external study, produced by Ernst & Young, concluded that '[f]rom a practical point of view, the SE legal form has not yet encountered the success anticipated: the overall number of SEs as of 15 April 2009 is lower than initially expected, with 369 SEs created up to that date', although '[t]he number of SEs created has however accelerated considerably from year to year'.[105] Therefore it can be seen from the relevant studies that, at best, the SE has proved to be less attractive than the European legislator had hoped - if not even downright unattractive.

Now, a closer inspection of these studies reveals that they provide several indications of factors affecting the SEs popularity, which the Commission in its report (following the *Ernst & Young* Study) calls 'positive and negative drivers to set up an SE'.[106] Again, one such factor has already been mentioned, namely the (sector-specific) minimum capital requirement for the SE, which the Commission identified as a negative driver discouraging eligible private actors from setting up a European Company.[107] But the Commission's report - not to mention the other studies - also adduces various others.

In terms of negative drivers, the Commission finds that '[t]he set-up costs, time-consuming and complex procedures, and legal uncertainty of the SE formation process, mostly stemming from the lack of uniformity of the SE Statute and the many references to national law, are amongst the most important obstacles discouraging businesses from establishing an SE'.[108] This concords with the finding in the *Ernst & Young* Study that uncertainty 'results from the fact that behind the unified image of the SE, many different national legislations apply ...'.[109] Hence the Commission's conclusion that '[t]he SE Statute does not provide for a uniform SE form across the European Union, but 27 different types of SEs. The Statute contains many references to national law and there is uncertainty about the legal effect of directly applicable law and its interface with national law'.[110] This is particularly interesting for present purposes, because it indicates that the SE Regulation's extensive reliance on national law has had an especially significant detrimental

104 Report from the Commission to the European Parliament and the Council on the application of Council Regulation 2157/2001 of 8 October 2001 on the Statute for a European Company (SE), p. 9.

105 Ernst & Young 2009, p. 271.

106 See report from the Commission to the European Parliament and the Council on the application of Council Regulation 2157/2001 of 8 October 2001 on the Statute for a European Company (SE), p. 10.

107 See *supra*, section A.1.

108 Report from the Commission to the European Parliament and the Council on the application of Council Regulation 2157/2001 of 8 October 2001 on the Statute for a European Company (SE), p. 6.

109 Ernst & Young 2009, p. 14.

110 Report from the Commission to the European Parliament and the Council on the application of Council Regulation 2157/2001 of 8 October 2001 on the Statute for a European Company (SE), p. 9.

effect on the attractiveness of the SE. And this is corroborated by a number of the country reports in the *Fauvarque-Cosson* Study too. According to the UK response, for example:

> 'The European Company system is not a uniform legal system in the European Union. The European Regulation also contains references to national law and this uncertainty originates from the cross-over and interrelations between the rules that apply directly to the Regulation and national law.'[111]

Similarly, the Belgian report notes that 'operators prefer other types of companies', among other things because 'SEs must juggle different legislations'.[112]

Furthermore, the *Ernst & Young* Study (though not the subsequent Commission report) also found that the provision of the SE Regulation according to which an SE must be registered in the Member State in which it has its registered office in a register designated by the law of that State[113] was another important reason for not setting up SEs, because 'the commercial registrars are less familiar with the administrative formalities of incorporating an SE (in comparison with a national public limited-liability company); this lack of practical experience results in an increased administrative burden'.[114] In other words, another obstacle discouraging the establishment of SEs is the additional administrative burden resulting from the fact that SEs are registered by national registrars who lack knowledge of the European Company regime. Therefore, this suggests that the SE Regulation's provision of a decentralized rather than a centralized system of administration has also had a notable - and negative - impact on the attractiveness of the SE as a company form.

So it is can be seen from these studies that the extent to which the SE Regulation relies on national law is a prominent factor driving the unpopularity of the SE, and there is also some evidence that the system of administration provided by the SE Regulation acts as a negative driver as well.

On the other hand, with respect to positive drivers, the Commission also pinpoints in its report on the SE several features identified by companies as positive drivers. The first one mentioned in the Commission report is the European image of the SE, which is 'reported to be one of the most important positive drivers ...' and is 'particularly attractive for companies who seek to stress their European affiliation or want to benefit from a European legal form, which is better known than their national forms, to penetrate other Member States' markets without having to set up foreign subsidiaries'.[115] Then, in addition, the Commission affirms that the possibility for an SE to transfer its registered office to another Member State 'is considered an essential driver and a real comparative advantage of the SE

111 Fauvarque-Cosson & Behar-Touchais 2012, p. 167.

112 Fauvarque-Cosson & Behar-Touchais 2012, p. 161.

113 SE Regulation, Art. 12(1).

114 Ernst & Young 2009, p. 239.

115 Report from the Commission to the European Parliament and the Council on the application of Council Regulation 2157/2001 of 8 October 2001 on the Statute for a European Company (SE), p. 3.

compared to national companies'.[116] Furthermore, the report states that respondents to the public consultation indicated also 'advantages of the SE form in terms of ... the SE's flexible rules on employee involvement in Member States where these matters are regulated by mandatory rules'.[117] And these findings are also supported by the *Ernst & Young* Study. The first positive driver mentioned in this study is again the 'value of the "European" image connected to being an SE', which, according to the authors, 'obtained a high ranking in the positive drivers for the choice of the SE corporate from among the existing SEs (3/5)'.[118] That is, according to this study one notable motive for establishing an SE is the European identity it gives to a business, which is 'enhanced by the fact that "the name of an SE shall be preceded or followed by the abbreviation SE" and that "only SEs may include the abbreviation SE in this name", thus clearly labelling the European identity of these selected companies'.[119] Secondly, and moreover, the *Ernst & Young* Study finds that '[t]he possibility of transfer of the registered office provided by Article 8 of the SE Regulation appears to be a major advantage of the SE and hence a strong incentive for choosing this corporate form'.[120] Further, the study also cites 'considerations linked to the labour law regime', noting that 'the SE corporate form can be used to loosen the grip of national co-determination laws or reduce their influence, thus leading to a "perverse incentive"'.[121]

Thus, it also appears from these studies that the various comparative advantages offered by the SE Regulation have had an influence on its popularity too, as positive drivers that have encouraged the setting up of SEs.

Additionally, it is worth noting that both the Commission report and the *Ernst & Young* Study also highlight (on top of various other sector-specific factors) the issue of awareness and knowledge about the SE form in the business and legal community as another factor that seems to have impacted upon its popularity. According to the Commission, '[t]estimonies suggest that in Member States where the SE form has been actively promoted, for instance, in the Czech Republic and Germany, there are more SEs, whereas in Member States such as Italy or Spain, where information and advice on the SE form is not easily available, very few or no SEs have been set up'.[122] While the *Ernst & Young* Study asserts that '[a]n increased awareness and knowledge of the SE form amongst companies and their legal

116 *Ibid.*

117 Report from the Commission to the European Parliament and the Council on the application of Council Regulation 2157/2001 of 8 October 2001 on the Statute for a European Company (SE), p. 4. More precisely, according to the Commission, 'both companies and unions report that the SE Statute offers the possibility to ... negotiate an employee involvement model, thereby tailoring it to the specific needs of the company or group, instead of having to comply with mandatory national rules.

118 Ernst & Young 2009, p. 210.

119 Ernst & Young 2009, p. 210.

120 Ernst & Young 2009, p. 212.

121 Ernst & Young 2009, p. 238.

122 Report from the Commission to the European Parliament and the Council on the application of Council Regulation 2157/2001 of 8 October 2001 on the Statute for a European Company (SE), p. 5.

advisors' might partially explain the acceleration in the number of SEs being registered.[123] Therefore it seems that the general factor of awareness has had a considerable influence on the level of usage of the SE as well.

3. *The European Small Claims Procedure (ESCP)*

Finally, let us examine the European Small Claims Procedure. The instrument-specific characteristics of the ESCP Regulation are as follows. First, the ESCP Regulation (as in the case of the EOP Regulation, and also the EEO Regulation) states that it is applicable in civil and commercial matters, 'whatever the nature of the court or tribunal'.[124] To be more precise, the institutions that both decide on applications to initiate the procedure and judge upon actions based on the procedure are any national courts and tribunals in the Member States 'with jurisdiction' (as determined by the Brussels I Regulation). There is not a closed list of national courts that have competence to hear cases founded on the ESCP. Therefore, the system of administration and adjudication provided for the European Small Claims Procedure is both decentralized and non-specialized. Second, the ESCP Regulation (again, like both the EEO and EOP Regulations) makes a number - though arguably not a particularly large number - of references to pre-existing rules in the legal systems of the Member States. For one thing, as was explained in the description of this OI, the ESCP Regulation defers to the procedural rules of the Member States of enforcement for the purpose of cross-border execution of judgments obtained pursuant to the procedure, subject to the few rules on this matter provided by the Regulation itself (and notably the rule requiring such judgments to be executed 'under the same conditions as a judgment given in the Member State of enforcement').[125] Also, the Regulation relies on the law of the State in which the procedure is commenced (that is, the State where the competent court is located) to govern the review of judgments given in the European Small Claims Procedure, subject to the 'minimum standards for review' that it prescribes.[126] And one can find other more specific references to national law as well. To give but one example, while it is stated in Article 4(4) regarding the commencement of the procedure that where a claim 'appears to be clearly unfounded or the application inadmissible ... the application shall be dismissed',[127] it is made clear in the preamble to the Regulation that '[t]he concepts of "clearly unfounded" ... and of "inadmissible" ... should be determined in accordance with national law'.[128] So, all in all, it may be said that the ESCP Regulation relies considerably, but not necessarily extensively, on the domestic laws of the Member States.[129] Third, in

123 Ernst & Young 2009, p. 12.
124 Regulation 861/ 2007 of the European Parliament and of the Council of 11 July 2007 establishing a European Small Claims Procedure, Art. 2(1).
125 ESCP Regulation, Art. 21.
126 ESCP Regulation, Art. 18.
127 ESCP Regulation, Art. 4(4).
128 ESCP Regulation, consideration 13.
129 Cf. Kramer 2008, p. 368-369.

terms of the comparative advantage of the ESCP, the ESCP's particular advantage lay (until the entry into force of the recast Brussels I Regulation in 2015) in the fact that a judgment rendered by a competent court under the European Small Claims Procedure must be recognized in another Member State 'without the need for a declaration of enforceability',[130] and enforcement of such a judgment can only be refused by a court of enforcement in certain exceptional circumstances (where there has been an earlier judgment given on the same cause of action between the same parties).[131] In other words, there is no need for an intermediary procedure in the Member State of enforcement in order for a judgment handed down in the Member State of origin under the ESCP to be enforceable. In contrast, a foreign judgment delivered under a domestic small claims procedure was until recently subject to an *exequatur* procedure, as regulated by the original Brussels I Regulation.[132] Hence the ESCP has for many years offered a distinct advantage to claimants in cross-border cases, by eliminating an obstacle that these individuals would otherwise have faced in seeking to have their claims enforced in another Member State.

As far as the popularity of the ESCP is concerned, the picture when it comes to this OI appears to be somewhat gloomy. According to the Commission in its report on the application of the ESCP Regulation of November 2013, 'the use of the European Small Claims Procedure is still rather limited compared to the number of potential cases'.[133] This accords with the external study on which the Commission report was based, produced by Deloitte, which concluded that '[t[he figures show that the use of the ESCP has been rather limited'.[134] More precisely, the *Deloitte* Study estimated that the total number of ESCP applications filed in the European Union in 2012 amounted to around 3,500 applications,[135] which as the study notes is 'far behind the target of 5 million claims set out in the 2005 Impact Assessment' on the ESCP.[136] Admittedly, this is just an estimate, which is derived from information

130 ESCP Regulation, Art. 20(1).

131 See ESCP Regulation, Art. 22.

132 Council Regulation 44/2001 of 22 December 2000 on jurisdiction and the recognition and enforcement of judgments in civil and commercial matters.

133 Report from the Commission to the European Parliament, the Council and the European Economic and Social Committee on the application of Regulation (EC) 861/2007 of the European Parliament and of the Council establishing a European Small Claims Procedure, COM(2013) 795, p. 2. See also the proposal for a Regulation of the European Parliament and of the Council amending Regulation 861/2007 of the European Parliament and the Council of 11 July 2007 establishing a European Small Claims Procedure and Regulation 1896/2006 of the European Parliament and of the Council of 12 December 2006 creating a European order for payment procedure, COM(2013) 794 final, where the Commission states that the ESCP 'remains under-used several years after the entry into application of the Regulation' (p. 3).

134 Deloitte 2013, p. 63.

135 It should be made clear that this estimate is about the number of *applications received* by the courts of the Member States, rather than instances of the procedure actually being commenced. Although the *Deloitte* Study actually assumes that 'the number of ESCP applications per year is equal to the number of ESCP judgments per year': Deloitte 2013, footnote 172.

136 Deloitte 2013, p. 64, referring to the European Commission's Extended Impact Assessment, Annex to the Proposal for a Regulation of the European Parliament and of the Council establishing a European Small Claims Procedure, COM (2005)87 final. Although, as the →

on the use of procedure in a handful of Member States, due to the fact that '[o]nly limited data concerning the number of claims filed under the ESCP are available'.[137] But, in any case, this does suggest that the ESCP has not proved to be as attractive as could have been expected. Having said that, the Commission does also point out in its report that 'the number of applications under the Regulation has constantly increased since its entry into application in 2009'[138] And this is again supported by the *Deloitte* Study, which found that 'in six out of the seven Member States for which data are available, the number of ESCP applications increased on a yearly basis'.[139] So one can find some more positive signs regarding the use of this OI as well.

Now, examining these studies more closely, it becomes apparent that these too offer indications of factors influencing the popularity of the ESCP. In particular, the Commission report identifies a number of 'obstacles to the application of the Regulation'[140] that it considers to have affected the usage of the ESCP (or 'negative drivers', to borrow the terminology used by the Commission in its report on the application of the SE).

Interestingly, one important negative driver identified by the Commission is a lack of awareness of the existence or operation of the European Small Claims Procedure among national courts and judges, which entails that 'a high number of courts or tribunals are not in a position to ensure efficient assistance to citizens ...'.[141] As evidence of this lack of awareness, the Commission cites a survey carried out by ECC-Net[142] which 'showed that almost half of the courts have never heard about the procedure, while the other half was not fully informed of its details'.[143] This therefore implies that the fact that the ESCP Regulation provides for an unspecialized as well as decentralized system of administration and adjudication has been noticeably detrimental to its popularity. In fact, the Commission report also finds that '[s]ome Member States have established one or a few specialised courts to deal with the European Small Claims Procedure ...', and that '[s]uch

Deloitte study also notes, this target of 5 million claims was made on the assumption that purely domestic cases would fall within the scope of the ESCP Regulation, which is not the case. On the other hand, it is also true that this target was for the EU composed of 15 Member States, whereas the Deloitte estimate relates to the EU27.

137 Deloitte 2013, p. 62. This lack of data is also affirmed in the *Fauvarque-Cosson* Study, which indicates that official statistics on small claims are 'rare'; see Fauvarque-Cosson & Behar-Touchais 2012, p. 101.

138 Report from the Commission to the European Parliament, the Council and the European Economic and Social Committee on the application of Regulation (EC) 861/2007 of the European Parliament and of the Council establishing a European Small Claims Procedure, COM(2013) 795, p. 3.

139 Deloitte 2013, p. 64.

140 See report from the Commission on the application of Regulation 861/2007 establishing a European Small Claims Procedure, p. 7.

141 *Ibid.*, p. 8.

142 European Consumer Centres Network ECC-Net, European Small Claims Procedure Report, September 2012, available at: <http://ec.europa.eu/consumers/ecc/docs/small_claims_210992012_en.pdf>.

143 *Ibid.*

concentration has certain advantages such as concentrating specialised knowledge of courts ...'.[144] So this would seem to lend support to the notion that a more specialized institutional system for the ESCP would increase its popularity considerably.

On the other hand, the ESCP Regulation's reliance on national law is not mentioned in the Commission report, although it does find that 'some problems on the actual enforcement have been reported to the European Consumer Centres, for example concerning ... the lack of information regarding enforcement procedures ...', and also that '[i]mplementation of the review procedure ... has given rise to questions and uncertainties'.[145] Nor is there any mention of the ESCP's main comparative advantage (at the time), save for the statement that '[n]o problems have been reported concerning the abolition of exequatur in the Regulation'.[146] Instead, what the Commission does indicate (again, along with a series of sector-specific factors)[147] is that a lack of awareness about the existence of the procedure also among private actors is another important factor limiting the usage of the ESCP. More precisely, according to the report, 'Eurobarometer 395 shows that 86% of citizens have never heard about the procedure. As a result, potential claimants, in particular consumers, either do not pursue their claims or pursue them using national procedures'.[148] This point is also made in the *Deloitte* Study, which states that 'the limited use of the ESCP may be partly due to the limited awareness of the ESCP'[149] among 'relevant actors' including citizens businesses, and that 'there is a large potential to increase the number of ESCP applications by reaching a much larger base of potential claimants through, for example ... promotional activities in the ESCP'.[150] Therefore it appears that the general factor of awareness has also had a significant impact on the uptake of the ESCP.

Thus, while there are indications in these studies that the system of administration and adjudication provided for the ESCP has had a notable impact on its attractiveness to private actors, there are but a few hints as to the effect of the other instrument-specific provisions of the ESCP Regulation on the OI's popularity. Again, one might argue that the fact that they are not highlighted as negative drivers is indicative in itself, but this is a clue at most

144 Report from the Commission on the application of Regulation 861/2007 establishing a European Small Claims Procedure, p. 4.

145 *Ibid.*, p. 6.

146 *Ibid.*

147 Such as the court fees for the ESCP, which the Commission finds to be disproportionate in some Member States and, where this is the case, 'an important obstacle to the use of the procedure': Report from the Commission on the application of Regulation 861/2007 establishing a European Small Claims Procedure, p. 7.

148 Report from the Commission on the application of Regulation 861/2007 establishing a European Small Claims Procedure, p. 8.

149 Deloitte 2013, p. 68.

150 Deloitte 2013, p. 73.

D. Findings and Analysis

1. *Findings*

Summarizing the findings from the preceding case studies, it can be observed that at least some (if not all) of the instrument-specific provisions of the OIs under scrutiny appear to have had at least some (if not a particularly significant) effect on their popularity with eligible private actors in each and every case.

Starting with the case of the Community Trade Mark, the available evidence suggests that the added value of the CTM has been a major factor in the popularity of this optional regime, with most users of the system recognizing that the CTM offers a substantial comparative advantage over national trade mark regimes. On the other hand, the influence of the CTM's institutional and substantive autonomy on its popularity is less clear, since the relevant studies do not contain any precise indications of the effects these instrument-specific features have had, as they do in respect of the added value of the CTM. Although, turning this observation on its head, it may also be inferred from this that the centralized system of administration and decentralized but specialized system of adjudication provided for the CTM as well as the CTM Regulation's limited reliance on national law have at least not had a negative impact on the popularity of the CTM.

Meanwhile, in the case of European Company, the available studies again indicate that the SE's added value has played an important role in inducing businesses to opt into the regime, citing as they do various comparative advantages of the SE as so-called positive drivers that have encouraged the setting up of SEs. Furthermore, they also contain definite indications that the institutional and substantive autonomy of the SE have had a significant impact on its popularity too, in a negative way. In particular, the SE's lack of substantive autonomy is highlighted as one of the most important negative drivers that have discouraged legal persons from establishing an SE, due to the legal uncertainty that results from the SE Statute's numerous references to pre-existing national law. But the SE's lack of institutional autonomy also appears to have acted as a noteworthy negative driver, inasmuch as the decentralized system of administration provided for the SE has given rise to administrative burdens for companies seeking to establish an SE, resulting from the fact that national registrars are less familiar with this European company form. And, in addition, these studies suggest that the general factor of awareness has had a considerable influence on the popularity of the SE as well.

Finally, in the case of the European Small Claims Procedure, the relevant studies signal that the ESCP's lack of institutional autonomy - with an unspecialized as well as decentralized system of administration and adjudication - has impacted negatively upon the usage of this regime, insofar as many competent courts and tribunals in the Member States appear to lack awareness and knowledge of the procedure, meaning they are not in a position to provide effective assistance to potential litigants. On the other hand, the effect the ESCP's reliance on national law and added value have had on its popularity is not elucidated by these studies. What is also made clear is rather that the general factor of awareness has again had a significant impact on the uptake of the ESCP.

2. *Analysis of Findings*

At this point, it is useful to recall the two principal questions set out before in this chapter,[151] with a view to offering an analysis of the above findings. These were, first, what impact do the instrument-specific provisions of EU optional instruments have on their attractiveness to eligible private actors?; and, second, to what extent could this inform the design of future EU optional regimes by the European legislator?

Now, regarding the first of these questions, the foregoing findings clearly indicate that the instrument-specific provisions of EU OIs can and do have a noteworthy impact on their attractiveness to eligible private actors. Specifically, it appears from the case studies on the CTM and the SE that the added value of a Union OI is a significant factor determining its popularity, meaning the comparative advantages an OI offers greatly influence its attractiveness to eligible individuals. Furthermore, the findings from the case studies on the SE and the ESCP (and arguably also the CTM) demonstrate that the institutional autonomy of a Union OI can be an important factor in its popularity too, and that the provision of a decentralized/unspecialized system of administration/adjudication can render an OI considerably less attractive to private actors. And, in addition, the case study on the SE (though not so much the other case studies) provides definite support for the proposition that the substantive autonomy of a Union OI can have a notable influence on in its popularity as well, and suggests that an OI can also be made less attractive if it relies extensively on the laws (i.e. as well as the institutions) of the Member States. It would seem, therefore, that the hypothesis according to which the instrument-specific provisions of the EU OIs under scrutiny would have a considerable influence on their attractiveness has proven correct; and that there is at least some evidence supporting the hypothesis that the more added value an OI offers, and the more institutional and substantive autonomy it has, the more attractive it will be as a legal product. Having said that, it must also be stressed that the above findings do only sustain the latter hypothesis to a *certain* extent, as we did not encounter a clear indication of the impact of each of these instrument-specific features in relation to each of the EU OIs that were examined. It is true that the case study on the SE shed light on how each of its instrument-specific features affect its attractiveness, but the same cannot be said about the case studies on the CTM and the ESCP, where the effects of only one of these features were illuminated. It is equally true that the available evidence does not disprove the suggested explanatory theory, but the extent to which it serves to validate the (instrument-specific) 'rules for creating a successful optional instrument' proposed by Fauvarque-Cosson & Behar-Touchais is open to discussion.

In any event, proceeding on the understanding that instrument-specific features do or at least can affect the attractiveness of Union OIs in these specific ways, this brings us to the second question, which asks us to consider the usefulness of this analysis for the design of future EU OIs.

151 *Supra*, section B.1.

In this regard, the first observation that should be made is that, apart from illustrating how instrument-factors can impact upon the attractiveness of EU OIs, the above findings also indicate that in some instances such factors appear to play a key or even *decisive role* in determining an OI's popularity. In particular, added value appears to have been a crucial factor driving the popularity the CTM, while in the case of the SE, the substantive autonomy factor seems to have been a fundamental negative driver counteracting the positive influence of its added value. And when it comes to the ESCP, it is arguable that the factor of institutional autonomy has been one of the most important drivers stifling the popularity of this OI. This therefore signals that (as expected) the suggested explanatory theory could indeed be of value to the European legislator, as adherence to the proposed instrument-specific rules when creating EU OIs could be essential in order to ensure that, once adopted, they will be popular with eligible private actors.

However, the question is to what extent this explanatory theory could inform the design of EU OIs. For, while the proposed instrument-specific rules may be clear, they are not detailed. That is to say, they do not offer any guidance as to *how much* added value, or institutional autonomy, or substantive autonomy a Union OI needs to become 'a successful optional instrument.' In order to do so, it would first be necessary to quantify the level of added value and (institutional and substantive) autonomy of EU OIs and, in turn, to measure their impact on usage. Only by comparing instrument-specific features and their effects on this more 'scientific' basis, might one eventually arrive at more precise guidelines concerning the influence of each of these instrument-specific factors on the attractiveness of EU OIs. Yet, it is questionable how far such an exercise would be practicable (or even possible), for two main reasons.

Firstly, it is difficult to see how one could reliably measure the instrument-specific features of a given OI, let alone their effects on uptake by eligible private actors. As regards the former, this is so particularly because the added value and institutional and substantive autonomy of EU OIs are all matters of degree that do not lend themselves to quantification. Measuring the substantive autonomy of an optional instrument, for example, would require one to quantify not only the number of references to national law, but also the significance of each of these references in the context of the given policy area being regulated. Similarly, in the case of added value, this would necessitate not only identifying the different forms of comparative advantage an OI offers, but also placing a value on the importance of these comparative advantages in the context of the relevant policy field. And even when it comes to the institutional autonomy of EU OIs, the question is *how* centralized or decentralized and specialized or unspecialized is an OI's system of administration, as there are various different possible levels of centralization and specialization imaginable.[152] This is not to say that it is not possible to offer a reasonable estimate of the degree of institutional and substantive autonomy and

152 Furthermore, as regards the degree of specialization of an OIs system of administration or adjudication, this could also be said to depend on other factors too, such as the level and quality of training of the persons responsible for administering or adjudicating upon an OI, or indeed even the degree of centralization of the system.

added value of an OI. Perhaps one could seek to develop an analytical model through which to attach numerical values to an OI's instrument-specific features. But, apart from the fact that this would be merely estimation, even this would be an arduous task.

Therefore, the potential for comparing the instrument-specific features of EU OIs more accurately seems limited. For if (or as long as) one does not quantify these features, one cannot hope to compare with a higher degree of precision the extent to which EU OIs (and especially EU OIs in different fields of law) possess (institutional and substantive) autonomy and added value. That is, one would not be in a position to properly demonstrate the degree of reliance on national law and institutions and the degree of advantage offered by one EU OI *relative* to another. Maybe in the case of EU OIs in identical policy fields, a more precise qualitative comparison could still be made.[153] But how could one possibly determine with greater accuracy the degree of autonomy or added value of the SE, as compared to that of, say, the CTM, bearing in mind that these EU OIs pertain to distinct sectors of European law, which are not really comparable?

Then, on top of this, there is the added difficulty of measuring the impact of an OI's instrument-specific features on its level of uptake by eligible individuals. In other words (and leaving aside the problems associated with taking the number of opt-ins as one's indicator of attractiveness mentioned previously),[154] it is also hard to see how one could reliably quantify the effects of instrument-specific provisions on usage, not least because this would involve ascertaining the motivations of various eligible private actors behind their decisions to opt in (or not) to a given OI, which are likely to be as complex and diverse as they are numerous. Again, this does not necessarily mean to say that an attempt at estimation is out of the question. A more comprehensive and deeper inquiry into the motivations of eligible private actors could potentially yield more detailed estimates as to the extent to which instrument-specific features played a role in their decision-making, and such estimates would no doubt be of great use. But the possibilities of comparing more precisely the impact of instrument-specific features of EU OIs on their attractiveness seem even more limited.

Secondly, it must be remembered that, along with instrument-specific factors, sector-specific and general factors can also play an important role in the popularity of EU OIs. Indeed the above findings, particularly those from the case studies on the SE and ESCP, also indicate that the general factor of awareness, for example, has had a significant impact on the popularity of these EU OIs. And in the case of another OI it could well be that, for instance, the sector-specific features of that OI turn out to be among the most influential drivers behind its popularity. Therefore, a reliable appraisal of the impact of instrument-specific factors on the uptake of a given OI would also need to take into account the influence of such other factors, in

153 For example, one might expect it to be more feasible to qualitatively compare the (institutional and substantive) autonomy and added value of the SE with that of the SCE, as each of these optional instruments in the area of European company law cover similar legal ground.

154 See *supra*, section B.2.

order to be able to say something about the 'overall' impact of instrument-specific factors on that OI (that is, *relative to the impact of other factors*). However, this would obviously add yet more complications to what is already an extremely challenging prospect. Thus, the potentiality for accurately comparing the impact of instrument-specific factors on the attractiveness of EU OIs relative to the impact of other factors is arguably more limited still.

For these reasons, while it does seem possible to form a visceral impression of the relative degree of (institutional and substantive) autonomy and added value of different EU OIs, as well as of how (and even how much) these instrument-specific features have influenced their attractiveness - and while this impression may lend support for the instrument-specific rules that have been proposed - demonstrating this with accuracy presents a far greater challenge. So, although the suggested explanatory theory could certainly be useful to the European legislator, by indicating certain instrument-specific principles that should be adhered to when creating EU OIs, the extent to which this explanatory theory could inform the design of future EU OIs appears to be constrained.

Conclusion

To conclude, this explanatory analysis has shown that there is a range of factors that may have an influence on the attractiveness of EU OIs, and that many of these factors are common to EU OIs in diverse fields of European law. These include both general factors that are external to the design of EU OIs, as well as instrument-specific factors, which are inherent in the design of EU Optional Instruments. The available evidence on the existing EU OIs examined in this chapter suggests that such factors have had a significant (and in some cases even momentous) effect on the usage of these OIs. In particular, it appears from the case studies that, along with the general factor of awareness, the instrument-specific factor of added value can play a crucial role in the attractiveness of a Union OI to eligible individuals, although this can also be considerably affected by the (institutional and/or substantive) autonomy of the optional regime. Therefore there are indications that the European legislator should pay close attention to such factors when promulgating EU optional regimes, if it wants to ensure that those regimes will be popular with private actors. For this reason, the proposed explanatory theory we have explored clearly could be useful for the design of EU OIs in future. Having said that, though, we have also seen that the suggested 'rules for creating a successful optional instrument' may only inform the design of future OIs to a certain extent, because the evidence supporting them is not conclusive, and it is hard to see how the relative impact of instrument-specific factors on the uptake of EU OIs could be reliably quantified. So while these instrument-specific principles can offer some guidance to the EU legislator, just how much guidance they can provide is another matter.

PART 3

OUTCOMES OF STUDY AND FUTURE PERSPECTIVES

Chapter 6

OUTCOMES OF STUDY AND FUTURE PERSPECTIVES

INTRODUCTION

With a view to concluding our discussion of EU Optional Instruments, it is useful at this point to recapitulate the main findings of our inquiry, and to reflect on what importance this could have in years to come. Accordingly, this final chapter is dedicated to summarizing the principal outcomes of the present study, as well as to offering some future perspectives on the matter of EU OIs. We shall start with the former, focusing on outcomes of particular relevance to academics, on the one hand, and to policymakers, on the other (section 1). Then we will proceed to consider the implications of this study both for future research on the subject, as well as for prospective Union OIs (section 2). Finally, the chapter ends with some concluding remarks and observations.

1. *Outcomes of Study*

The rise of Optional Instruments of the European Union is a phenomenon that provokes a multitude of profound and far-reaching questions, and the present study offers a response to the most pivotal of them. Of course, there is still much to be said about this important legislative trend happening with the EU, but this study aims to elucidate the main points and evaluate the key arguments and viewpoints on the subject. By way of recollection, three central questions are addressed in this study, from which a discussion of various others has followed.[1] Put simply, they are: What are EU Optional Instruments, what (if anything) makes them desirable, and why are some EU OIs more successful than others?

In answer to the first of these questions, this study has offered a fundamental definition of EU Optional Instruments, and sought to differentiate EU legislation creating OIs from EU approximating measures, which has led to a proposal for a novel distinction between affiliation and similarization. In addition, the idea that EU OIs constitute approximation in the technical sense within the meaning of the

1 See Chapter 1, section 2(a).

EU treaties has also been disputed and, in connection with this, so has the notion of a dichotomy between 28th regimes and 2nd national regimes. Accordingly, the thesis has provided a solid basis for viewing EU OIs as a distinct form of EU legislation, while at the same time rejecting the assertion that there exist different types of EU OIs in this sense.

As regards the second question, it has emerged that, overall, the advantages of EU legislation introducing OIs clearly seem to outweigh the drawbacks, although the strength of the case for the OI method varies from one optional instrument and area of law to another, not to mention depending on the perspective one adopts. Ultimately, a general assessment of whether and why OIs are a desirable alternative form of EU legislation depends on the criteria by which one thinks this should be judged, and the thesis has pointed to various criteria that could be considered relevant. In this study a general criterion has been proposed - the optimal mix between European legal uniformity and national legal diversity - according to which EU OIs should be judged favourably; but in the end the answer to this question cannot be certain, particularly in the abstract.

Finally, concerning the third question, this study has identified various types of factors that could explain why, relatively speaking, some EU OIs have apparently proven more popular with private actors than others - including factors that are common to EU OIs in diverse policy areas. And our analysis of available empirical data has revealed that the instrument-specific factors of added value and autonomy, as well as the general factor of communication, appear to have had a particularly significant on the levels of usage of different EU OIs. Having said that, we have also seen that it may be difficult to arrive at a more definitive conclusion on this question as well.

(a) Outcomes of Relevance to Academics

Of the principal outcomes just recounted, the first and second points are particularly relevant for academia.

The first point is important for the fledgling academic discussion of EU Optional Instruments because a detailed account of what defines such instruments and what distinguishes them from other kinds of legislative regimes or measures has not yet been provided by others. A thorough explanation of the nature of EU OIs is of course essential for a proper understanding of this legislative phenomenon, which in turn is a prerequisite for scholarly debate on the subject. Unless it is made clear what EU OIs are, and what they are not, there is a risk of talking past one another, or of confusing different issues. For, as we have seen, there are various regimes in the law that could be described as 'optional' in some way and, at the same time, there are those (including the Commission) who have described EU OIs as a form of 'harmonization'. Yet, while it no doubt makes sense to view EU OIs within this broader context, there are also a number of fundamental elements of EU OIs that distinguish them as a particular group of legislative instruments. So the account furnished in this study will serve at least as a step towards arriving at such an understanding, by identifying where the main borders between EU OIs and other legal instruments lie.

As for the second point, this is of special academic relevance (but also of relevance for policymakers) because a comprehensive theoretical analysis of the normative issues surrounding the increasing use of the OI method by the European legislator has not yet been produced either. Of course some of these issues have already been discussed in other contexts, or in relation to specific optional instruments, but an all-embracing examination and assessment of the arguments for and against EU OIs as a general legislative method has not been attempted. It is therefore expected that the normative theory put forward in the thesis will serve both to promote and also frame the debate itself, insofar as it offers not only an evaluation but also a framework for the evaluation of EU OIs. In other words, the study will help both to provoke and to steer future discussion and research on the subject of EU OIs. The significance of this framework for scholarship on the matter of optional instruments in European private law (if not also beyond) is elaborated further in the section on future research below.

(b) Outcomes of Relevance to Policymakers

As far as regards the third point, on the other hand, this is especially relevant for policymakers, including most notably the EU legislator. The identification of instrument-specific features of EU OIs that can have a considerable influence on their popularity with eligible private actors could help to inform the design of future Union optional regimes (at least to some extent), by indicating how they can be made more attractive to end users. This was already discussed in the preceding chapter, and is also illustrated in the section below on future EU OIs. In addition, this is of relevance to national policymakers too, insofar as it could inform their positions on future proposals for EU OIs brought forward by the European Commission.

At the same time, it should not be forgotten that this point is also of relevance to the academic debate on the desirability of the OI method, since a number of the arguments supporting this method depend in one way or another on private actors making use of the optional regimes that are enacted. And for this purpose the explanatory theory developed in this study should equally provide a framework for future academic research on the matter, as is also specified below.

2. *Future Perspectives*

Having summarized the main results of the present study, it is interesting to offer some future perspectives on EU OIs, both in terms of future research and also in terms of prospective Union optional regimes.

(a) Future Research

Following directly on from the previous section, arguably the most important outcome of this thesis for academics is that it provides a *framework* for the study and discussion of EU Optional Instruments. That is, it offers a theoretical footing for EU OIs, which could help not only to stimulate but also to guide further debate and research on the subject. Even if the answers to some of the questions addressed herein are unsure, the real value of this thesis lies precisely in the fact that it can serve as a foundation for deeper research into such questions. By elaborating a framework for the normative evaluation of the OI method, as well as to explain the differing levels of uptake of EU OIs, the study has identified a number of potential lines of future research.

In particular, the normative framework constructed in this study has identified a variety of arguments and viewpoints that could be explored more deeply by specialists dealing with specific aspects of law and lawmaking. Whether it is the argument that EU OIs are more politically practicable than approximating measures, or that EU OIs foster regulatory competition, or the economic case for EU OIs (to name but a few), the thesis has indicated many issues that are in need of more academic research. And, of course, these issues could be investigated in relation to EU OIs across different policy areas, or focusing on certain OIs in specific fields of EU law. Therefore this study has significant implications for future research both on (EU) optional instruments in general, as well as on OIs in specific areas of European private law (be they already existing or still to come), insofar as it highlights what such research should concentrate on.

In addition, the (connected) explanatory framework that has been formulated in this thesis could also serve as the basis for future research. For one thing, the proposed explanatory theory itself needs to be tested further (as well as in relation to more EU OIs), as the evidence supporting it is inconclusive. But also, or perhaps better, in conjunction with this, we have seen that it would be necessary to determine the effects of instrument-specific factors (as well as the influence of other factors) on the usage of EU OIs more precisely, in order to provide accurate and detailed guidelines on the ideal design of EU OIs from a 'market' perspective. Admittedly, our preliminary reflection on this point actually suggests that the potential for doing so may not be so high, but this should not be taken as a definitive conclusion on the matter. Hence further research (and especially empirical research) on this issue is required, if not to yield more precise data on the factors affecting the usage of EU OIs, then at least to demonstrate whether this is even feasible.

(b) Future EU OIs

Equally, it is important to spell out the implications the normative and explanatory theories developed in this study could have for future optional instruments. For while these theories may not provide definitive answers to the questions of whether any given EU OI should be introduced and how it should be designed, they can nevertheless inform the debate over, and design of, EU OIs at least to some degree, as was already explained. And this of course applies to specific EU OIs in concrete cases as much as it does to EU OIs in general. This can be illustrated with reference to prospective EU OIs such as the European Patent with unitary effect (UP), or the idea of a Union optional instrument in the area of contract law, for example.

As far as the notion of an OI in the field of European contract law is concerned, it will be recalled that the proposal for a Common European Sales Law (CESL) of

2011 was withdrawn in 2014, so the adoption of this particular OI is no longer a possibility. However, as was also mentioned in our description of the CESL proposal,[2] this is an idea that has been mooted and discussed for several years, which reflects its significance in the context of European private law. So while the Commission has now decided to propose further approximating measures in this area in place of the CESL proposal, it cannot necessarily be discounted that an OI may eventually be (re-)introduced in this area at some point in future. And keeping in mind the general evaluation of the OI method elaborated in this study, it is in my view a pity that the CESL proposal has been replaced with proposals for EU legislation similarizing Member State contract laws. Not only would similarization be more disruptive of national legal orders than legislation introducing an optional instrument, as the Commission itself has acknowledged, but it would also serve to reduce, rather than increase, the possibility for legal experimentation, as well as legal options for private actors. Furthermore, there is arguably less chance of securing political agreement on a Union measure in the area if this measure takes the form of a similarizing Directive or Regulation.

On the other hand, as we have already noted, the experience with adopted and proposed EU OIs so far, including the CESL, seems to indicate that the use of the OI method does not greatly increase the chances of comprehensive EU legislation being adopted (if it does at all). In addition, it must be acknowledged that the rationale of providing EU regimes for EU activities does not provide as much support in the case of an OI like the CESL, since national contract law regimes are not subject to the same territorial limitations as other domestic legal regimes. This does not mean to say that the rationale does not apply, because the provision of EU regimes is also intended to enable private actors to overcome barriers caused by national legal diversity. But obviously, unlike national territorial limitations, differences between the laws of the Member States can equally be addressed by EU legislation that makes national laws more similar. Also this entails in turn that the economic case for introducing an OI is not as strong when it comes to the area of contract law. In fact, it was observed in the previous chapter that the need for a Union optional instrument - or indeed for any EU legislation - in the field of contract law is disputed, since even the problems caused by legal diversity are considered by some to be of limited importance.[3] So it is not clear that Union intervention is required in this area, particularly from the perspective of private actors.

Nevertheless, assuming there is a need for EU legislation addressing (in one way or another) barriers caused by national legal diversity in the field of contract law, I would still maintain that the case for using the OI method is stronger than the case supporting the similarization method, as the former still has significant advantages over the latter. Overall, the OI method strikes a better balance between the achievement of legal uniformity and the preservation of national legal diversity, and for this fundamental reason it is to be preferred in principle. Therefore I believe that, if the European legislator insists on pressing ahead with the contract law project, it should give serious thought to proposing the rules it wishes to introduce

2 Chapter 3, section D.
3 Chapter 5, section A.3(a).

– or may wish to introduce in future – in this area of law in the form of optional instruments, rather than similarizing measures.

Having said this, it is also necessary to recall two significant caveats. The first is that the effectiveness of a Union OI in achieving its aim of enabling private actors to overcome barriers of legal diversity is of course very much dependent on the degree of uniformity that it provides for. In fact a very similar thing can be said about EU similarizing measures, in the sense that the extent to which they reduce such barriers equally depends on the degree of legal uniformity that they establish, but it is nonetheless important to remember that this point also applies to EU OIs. Indeed, as we have seen, some existing EU OIs appear to be constrained by a notable lack of uniformity. So if an OI were to be created in the area of contract law, it would need to provide for a large degree of uniformity. As far as regards the CESL proposal, it was noted in our description of this OI[4] that the CESL envisaged a comprehensive set of legal provisions to govern contracts falling within its scope, including a vast array of consumer protection rules. Therefore, with this in mind, it could be argued that the CESL Regulation would have established a largely uniform EU optional regime. Although it was also observed that, comprehensive as it was, the proposed CESL Regulation still deferred entirely to national law on a range of significant matters, including capacity, illegality, transfer of ownership, etc., so from this perspective it could have gone yet further. In addition, it should not be forgotten that even if the CESL had successfully passed through the legislative process, it might well have been modified considerably along the way (as has occurred with other EU OIs such as the SE).

The second caveat is that for many of the arguments in favour of the use of the OI method to hold true, and particularly the arguments put forward by law market theorists, it is important that any optional instrument that is eventually introduced attracts a sufficient number of private actors to opt into it. In other words, a number of the grounds for favouring the OI method are dependent (at least to some extent) on OIs actually being used by the individuals they are aimed at. For this reason, while I would generally support the use of the OI method over the similarization method in the area of contract law, I also recognize that much rests on how far a given EU OI proves attractive to eligible private actors. And it is on this point that the explanatory theory developed in this study comes in, as it identifies a number of different factors that could play a role in this respect.

Looking once more at the CESL proposal of 2011, for one thing, as was just recalled, the level of demand for a European regime in the area of contract law has been doubted, meaning this is one general factor that could have had a negative influence on the popularity of this optional regime. But the design of the CESL, and more precisely of its sector- and instrument-specific features, would clearly also have influenced its attractiveness. As far as its instrument-specific features are concerned, it was also just reiterated that the Common European Sales Law Regulation as proposed envisaged a largely uniform sales law regime, even if it did still rely on national law for a number of relevant aspects. So, assuming (for the sake

4 Chapter 3, CESL description.

of argument) that the proposal had been adopted without significant amendments, the CESL would have possessed a considerable degree of substantive autonomy. However, the CESL proposal did not provide for a particular court system for actions that would have been founded on the CESL; instead any competent national court would have had jurisdiction. That is, the proposed CESL Regulation envisaged a decentralized and unspecialized system of (administration and) adjudication, rather than providing for, say, a system of designated national courts to hear actions based on the CESL. Therefore the CESL would have lacked institutional autonomy. And, more importantly, the CESL may not have offered sufficient added value. It is true that the CESL would have enabled traders in B2C contracts to make use of a common contract law regime to govern their cross-border dealings with consumers *including with respect to mandatory consumer protection rules*, which is something they are not currently able to do by means of choice of foreign law, pursuant to the Rome I Regulation. However, traders would still not necessarily have been able to use one single set of contract law rules to govern their contracts with consumers across the EU, since the territorial scope of the proposed CESL did not cover purely domestic cases (though Member States would have had the option to extend it to such cases). Nor for that matter would businesses have necessarily been able to use the CESL for all of their B2B contracts, not only because the proposed CESL Regulation did not cover purely domestic cases, but also because the personal scope of the Regulation did not extend to contracts between large companies. Similarly, one may question whether other potential advantages of the CESL, such as the idea that it would have provided a 'neutral' contract law regime, would have been enough to entice contracting parties to opt into the instrument. For reasons such as these, it is doubtful whether the proposed CESL Regulation would have proven especially attractive to eligible private actors, even if it had been adopted as proposed.

By contrast, the outlook in the case of the European Patent with unitary effect is quite different. The rationale of creating EU regimes for EU activities holds more weight in the area of patent law, because Member State patent regimes *are* territorially limited (and existing European patents do not have unitary effect). This means that the UP Regulation offers a valuable solution to cross-border operators, by making available to such operators a European patent that has the clear advantage of being a unitary right that enjoys uniform protection in all of the participating Member States. In addition, the correlated agreement on a Unified Patent Court to which the UP Regulation refers, and which at the time of writing is awaiting ratification, envisages the creation of a new centralized system of patent adjudication. This would make the Unitary Patent the first Union OI to be adjudicated upon by a new European-level court established for this purpose, which is potentially an extremely significant development in the evolution of Optional Instruments of the European Union. This Unified Patent Court, which will be common to all of the participating Member States, is to have exclusive jurisdiction over actions concerning the validity and infringement of (among other things) European patents with unitary effect, in place of existing national court systems. It will therefore be very interesting to see how this influences the application of the Unitary Patent, and particularly whether the availability of a centralized and not only specialized system of adjudication for users of the UP system (which is not the case for users of the Community Trade Mark and the Community Design systems) will prove to be an important 'positive driver' for private actors to make use of this optional instrument. The explanatory theory elaborated in this study suggests that it would, though this remains to be seen. Also the institution competent to administer the UP will be an already established European, though not EU, body, namely the European Patent Office. Therefore the unitary patent regime will have a centralized and specialized system of administration as well as adjudication and, as such, a high degree of institutional autonomy. In terms of its substantive autonomy, it is true that certain key provisions concerning the scope of protection conferred on UP proprietors were removed from the UP Regulation as one of the final compromises to be made during the decision-making process, which could be seen as a serious omission. But given that these provisions were transferred to the UPC agreement, and that existing rules contained in the European Patent Convention will also be applicable to European patents with unitary effect, it is arguable that the UP system as a whole will have a large degree of substantive autonomy too. Accordingly, there are good reasons for thinking the UP will be an attractive instrument for private actors, just as the IP law OIs that preceded it.

Conclusion

The trend of creating optional legal regimes that is currently occurring in EU legislation is an intriguing phenomenon that cannot go unnoticed. As part of a broader strive for new governance and better EU lawmaking, the European legislator is increasingly looking to optional instruments as an alternative way of regulating various areas of (private) law with a view to attaining its internal market-related goals. Optional Instruments of the European Union are a distinct form of legislation, which could be described as a kind of soft hard law. As in the case of other hard law instruments such as approximating measures, EU OIs are binding on Member States, meaning they are not optional for national legislators. However, they also have soft law elements, as Member States are able to retain the domestic regimes in their respective legal systems, and private actors have the choice as to whether to use a Union optional regime or an existing national legal regime.

As well as being its key component, the 'optionality' of this form of EU legislative instrument is arguably also its greatest advantage. By allowing Member States to maintain their own laws and leaving individuals with a choice, rather than modifying these national laws directly, optional instruments provide the European legislator with a means to establish uniform European rules while at the same time respecting legal pluralism and national legal identity, not to mention the principles of subsidiarity and proportionality. In other words, by providing additional pan-European legal options, OIs constitute an optimal way for the EU to operationalize the ideal of unity in diversity in the European integration process, thereby satisfying more preferences of the European legislator, the Member States and private actors. Furthermore, it can be argued that this also makes the European Union Optional Instrument a more politically practicable form of legislation than other forms of hard law, in the sense that, because OIs are less disruptive of Member State legal orders, they are in principle more acceptable to national legislators. This implies that OIs could be an essential tool for future EU lawmaking, in different (and especially sensitive) policy areas, as a less controversial solution than similarizing measures. Although, on this point, experience thus far actually suggests that EU OIs are not proving as politically acceptable as the European legislator might have hoped. Instead, national legislators have shown that they can nevertheless have various reasons to oppose the introduction of optional regimes, either completely or at least as they are originally proposed. This could be partly due to a desire on the part of national legislators to insulate themselves from regulatory competition, for example, or to uphold fundamental values embodied in their respective legal systems, or even to preserve the importance of these systems. On the other hand, the fact that the OI-based approach is consistent with law market theory is also another reason why the optional nature of EU OIs can be seen as advantageous, insofar as it promotes legal experimentation and party choice, which may offer various benefits for cross-border activities within the EU.

Yet, while the optionality of the OI method may well be a significant advantage, for EU OIs to produce many of the benefits attributed to them it is critical that private actors opt into them in practice. In this sense, the fact that EU OIs are only applicable if they are chosen is also their Achilles' heel. For if a Union OI is not opted into by eligible individuals, the EU regime it provides cannot really be said to facilitate the cross-border activities of private actors, or reasonably be expected to stimulate regulatory competition. This is not necessarily to say that an OI is of no benefit at all if it does not prove popular with private actors, but clearly its impact on both the internal market and the law market will be limited if this is the case. And the popularity of a European Union optional regime may depend on a range of different factors, including (but not limited to) both the design as well as the marketing of and market for the legal product. As regards the former, EU OIs possess not only sector-specific but also instrument-specific features that can play a pivotal role in their attractiveness as a product on the law market. These instrument-specific factors correspond to the added value an OI offers, coupled with the degree of institutional and substantive autonomy it enjoys. If an OI is designed in such a way that it offers little value and also if it relies to a large extent on pre-existing national laws and institutions, it is likely to be considerably less attractive to private actors. As for the latter, there are also general factors that can play a role in the attractiveness of EU OIs, such as how far eligible private actors are actually informed of the existence - not to mention the added value and degree of autonomy - of EU OIs, or to what extent there is demand for a European regime in the first place. Because obviously even if a legal product is well designed, it also needs to be well founded and well communicated.

In addition, it must be recognized that the matter of design is not only a legal but also ultimately a political discussion. That is, whether an optional instrument is well designed also depends on the extent to which Member States agree with its content. And as was just mentioned, Member States could have a number of reasons if not to oppose an optional regime entirely, then at least to object to part of its substance - one such reason being the desire to constrain potential competition with their existing domestic regimes. Therefore, one might say that the Commission has to walk a tightrope between proposing EU OIs that are uniform, autonomous and most importantly advantageous, on the one hand, but also politically realistic, on the other. An optional instrument has to be popular in order to function properly, but the more attractive it would be to private actors, the more Member States could have grounds to view it with suspicion. To the Member States, the optional instrument might represent something of a Pandora's box, which, if opened, could have unintended consequences for national law. Unfortunately for the Commission, the mere fact that optional instruments leave national laws 'untouched' does not seem to have made them or their content much more palatable to national legislators.

At any rate, just how useful the optional instrument tool turns out to be in the context of the Europeanization process remains to be seen. In theory, there are solid grounds for believing that the OI method has the potential to transform European Union lawmaking and revolutionize the legislative approach to dealing with obstacles to the internal market. In practice, though, the EU Member States may have other ideas.

SUMMARY

This thesis is about a particular kind of European Union legislation known as the 'optional instrument'. The thesis examines and discusses existing and proposed EU Optional Instruments (OIs) in different fields of European law, including company law, intellectual property law and procedural law (such as the European Company, the Community Trade Mark and the European Small Claims Procedure, respectively), as well as contract law.

In general terms, the principal aims of this research are fourfold. First and foremost, the thesis aims to identify the core elements that define this kind of EU legislation, and that distinguish it from other kinds of EU legislation, notably 'harmonization'. The second main objective is then to describe in detail and ultimately 'map' a number of EU OIs that have been adopted or proposed in the various EU policy areas mentioned above, charting their development, characteristics and (where appropriate) usage in practice. Thirdly, the thesis seeks to assess and evaluate EU OIs by investigating the advantages and disadvantages of creating optional private law instruments at European level as an alternative to harmonization. And, last but not least, the research aims to explain the apparently varied degree of 'success' of EU OIs already in existence, by identifying and analysing possible factors that could play a role in this respect.

While there does already exist considerable literature on optional instruments as a distinct form of legislation in specific areas of European law, a general account of Optional Instruments as a distinct kind of EU legislative method that transcends individual policy areas is much harder to come by, and to date no research project has conducted an in-depth theoretical study of the nature, object, advantages, drawbacks and usage of EU OIs. Such a study is therefore needed in order to build upon the existing academic research into this fast-evolving phenomenon.

Chapter 2 concerns the question of what defines EU Optional Instruments. More specifically, it is focused primarily on identifying the grounds or core elements on the basis of which the various legislative measures under examination in this study can be classified as EU OIs. In addition, this chapter seeks to place EU OIs in the wider context of optional instruments in general, as well as contrasting EU OIs with other kinds of EU legislation, and particularly EU 'approximation', both in a conceptual and in a technical, legal sense. Furthermore, the question of whether there are actually different types of EU OIs (and particularly if a distinction should be drawn between the so-called '28th regime' and '2nd national regime) is also addressed.

This chapter begins by looking at optional regimes in general, before defining the fundamental nature and essential character of Optional Instruments of the European Union. In this regard, two core elements of EU OIs are identified, namely the element of 'selection' and that of 'choice'. EU OIs are then distinguished from EU approximation in a conceptual sense, which leads to the point that EU OIs would better be described as 'affiliation'. Subsequently, EU OIs are distinguished from EU approximation in a legal sense also, which, in turn, leads to the issue of whether there exist different types of EU OIs. Ultimately, the distinction between 'the 28th regime' and 'the 2nd national regime' is disputed, and it is argued that EU OIs are all fundamentally the same type of legislative instrument. Accordingly, just as it is maintained that there are good reasons not to blur the conceptual difference between EU OIs and EU approximation, so it is concluded that the technical meaning of the term approximation should not be stretched to cover EU OIs.

Chapter 3 provides a detailed overview of the various EU OIs under examination in the study. A total of twelve existing and proposed EU Optional Instruments in four diverse policy areas are presented and described in this chapter, starting with the very first EU OI to have been formally adopted. The overview of EU OIs systematically addresses a range of aspects, including the nature of, background to and legal base for the optional instrument; the aims and objectives behind the optional instrument; the legal and institutional framework, substantive content and scope of the optional instrument, and the advantages of the optional instrument, as well as (where appropriate) relevant statistics on its application. In doing so, some pertinent similarities and differences between particular EU OIs are also brought to the fore.

What soon becomes apparent from this overview is that while there are a number of interesting parallels between different EU OIs, and even OIs in different policy fields, there are also a number of anomalies and points of divergence between them. In other words, while EU OIs may all be said to conform to a basic definition, they certainly do not give the impression of being a homogenous group of legislative instruments. This is a significant point that resurfaces - and is revisited - in Chapters 4 and 5.

Having defined and described EU Optional Instruments, the thesis moves on in Chapter 4 to analyse their advantages and disadvantages and to assess their desirability from different perspectives in this chapter, taking into account the heterogeneity of this family of legislative instruments. This chapter commences with an examination of the EU legislator's rationale behind the use of optional instruments, before undertaking a broader evaluation of EU OIs, considering not only the 'European' perspective but also the perspective of Member States and that of private actors. From each of these perspectives, the appraisal concentrates in particular on the issue of utility of EU OIs relative to EU approximating measures.

Then the issue of divergences between EU OIs is also discussed, which ultimately leads to the question of whether it is possible to identify pertinent criteria on the basis of which the desirability of EU OIs in general may be assessed.

This normative analysis reveals that the overall case in favour of EU Optional Instruments is a strong one, but also that the validity of many of the arguments supporting EU OIs can vary *in concreto*, and according to the perspective one takes. The normative framework constructed in this chapter indicates various possible criteria that could eventually be employed in order to evaluate EU OIs in general, but ultimately it also shows that the answer to the question whether the OI method is a 'better' way for the EU legislator to reach its goals than other means available to it is an uncertain one, particularly in the abstract.

Following directly on from the analysis set out in Chapter 4, Chapter 5 is dedicated to investigating the apparent divergences in the level of usage or 'attractiveness' of different EU OIs and the possible explanations for this. While this issue certainly has normative implications, the question of what drives the usage (or lack of usage) of EU OIs by end users is a distinct type of question, which requires the elaboration of an explanatory rather than a normative framework, in order to explain why it is that some EU OIs have been opted into by eligible private actors less than others.

So this chapter identifies and analyses various factors that may have an influence on the attractiveness of EU OIs to private actors (general, sector-specific and instrument-specific), with a view to seeing whether this could lead to some guidelines for the development of future Union optional regimes. The chapter begins by distinguishing different possible factors that could affect the attractiveness of EU OIs, before considering whether (and if so, to what extent) there could be factors common to EU OIs in general. Then, after laying out the specific questions to be addressed, the particular methodology to be followed, and the hypotheses, a number of specific Union optional regimes are examined as case studies. Finally, the chapter identifies and analyses relevant findings from these examples, before arriving at a conclusion on the validity and utility of the suggested explanatory theory.

Chapter 6 summarizes the outcomes of Chapters 2, 3, 4 and 5 and offers some future perspectives and insights on the matter of EU OIs, with a view to reflecting further on the importance this study could have in years to come. In particular, it discusses the likely or potential implications of the study not only for future academic research, but also for the promulgation of future EU OIs that have been proposed.

VALORIZATION ADDENDUM

1. *The Societal Relevance of this Thesis*

The rise of Optional Instruments of the European Union is a phenomenon that provokes a multitude of profound and far-reaching questions, and this thesis offers a response to the most pivotal of them. The phenomenon of EU OIs is connected with a number of highly relevant issues in current legal research. These include (but are by no means limited to) the new governance debate and the exploration of alternative ways of lawmaking in the Europeanization process; the issue of how to find solutions for problems that cannot be solved at the national level while at the same time preserving Member State sovereignty; the question of whether to encourage the transnational application and enforcement of law amidst fears of 'forum shopping' and a 'race to the bottom'; and how to reconcile pleas for greater choice of law for private actors with concerns of social justice. All of these issues constitute central themes in the academic discussion of EU Optional Instruments.

There is, however, a conspicuous paucity of academic literature on Optional Instruments of the European Union as a general legislative method, and the need for an innovative and profound inquiry into the phenomenon of EU OIs is therefore indubitable. Of course, there is still much to be said about this important legislative trend happening with the EU, but this study serves to elucidate the main points and evaluate the key arguments and viewpoints on the subject, thereby addressing the definitional, normative and explanatory gaps in the existing literature. Accordingly, the present study is of great relevance to an academic discussion that is still in its infancy. By defining, mapping and analysing in detail existing and proposed optional instruments in the EU, as well as identifying pertinent similarities and differences between them, the research serves to advance knowledge of this novel legislative trend in academia. In particular, the study's analysis and evaluation of the normative issues surrounding EU OIs is of especial academic relevance, as this is intended not only to provoke but also to provide a framework for further academic debate on the subject of OIs, primarily (though not necessarily only) in the field of European private law. Hence, it is expected that the results of the research could both inspire and serve as the basis for further exploration into the topic.

In addition, alongside its academic relevance, this thesis also has a strong practical relevance. The research is able to promote greater awareness and understanding of EU OIs in wider society, and particularly among actual and potential 'users' of these optional instruments (i.e. eligible natural and legal persons). Bearing in mind the proliferation of existing and proposed optional instruments of the EU in recent years, the importance of informing private actors about them should not be underestimated. Furthermore, by individuating and comparing certain common provisions of different EU OIs with a view to assessing the influence such provisions (can) have on the 'popularity' of a Union optional instrument with end users, the research has a valuable practical relevance for policymakers (and particularly the EU legislator) too, insofar as it can help to inform the design of future EU OIs.

2. *The Innovative Character of the Research Results*

By way of recollection, three central questions are addressed in this study (from which a discussion of various others then follows). Put simply, they are: What are EU Optional Instruments, what (if anything) makes them desirable, and why are some EU OIs more successful than others?

In answer to the first of these questions, this study has offered a fundamental definition of EU Optional Instruments, and sought to differentiate EU legislation creating OIs from EU approximating measures, which has led to a proposal for a novel distinction between affiliation and similarization. In addition, the idea that EU OIs constitute approximation in the technical sense within the meaning of the EU treaties has also been disputed and, in connection with this, so has the notion of a dichotomy between 28th regimes and 2nd national regimes. Accordingly, the thesis has provided a solid conceptual and technical basis for viewing EU OIs as a distinct form of EU legislation, while at the same time rejecting the assertion that there exist different types of EU OIs in this sense.

As regards the second question, this thesis has not only provided a general assessment of whether and why OIs are a desirable form of EU legislation, but it has also pointed out a range of criteria that could be considered relevant in this respect. It has emerged from this study that, overall, the advantages of EU legislation introducing OIs clearly seem to outweigh the drawbacks, but it has also become clear that the strength of the case for the OI method varies from one optional instrument and area of law to another, not to mention depending on the perspective one adopts. In this study a general criterion has been proposed - the optimal mix between European legal uniformity and national legal diversity - according to which EU OIs should be judged favourably, but in the end the answer to this question cannot be certain, particularly in the abstract.

Finally, concerning the third question, this thesis has identified and categorized various types of factors that could explain why, relatively speaking, some EU OIs have apparently proven more popular with private actors than others - including factors that are common to EU OIs in diverse policy areas. And the innovative analysis of available empirical data has revealed that the instrument-specific factors of added value and autonomy, as well as the general factor of communication, appear to have had a particularly significant on the levels of usage of different EU OIs. Having said that, it has also demonstrated how and why it may be difficult to arrive at a more definitive conclusion on this question as well.

3. *Target Groups for the Research Results*

As already indicated, the results of this research may be of relevance to various target groups, for a variety of reasons.

Of the principal outcomes just recounted, the first and second points are particularly important for academics. The first point is important for the fledgling academic discussion of EU Optional Instruments because a detailed account of what defines such instruments and what distinguishes them from other kinds of legislative regimes or measures has not yet been provided by others. A thorough explanation of the nature of EU OIs is of course essential for a proper understanding of this legislative phenomenon, which in turn is a prerequisite for scholarly debate on the subject. Unless it is made clear what EU OIs are, and what they are not, there is a risk of talking past one another, or of confusing different issues. So the account furnished in this study will serve at least as a step towards arriving at such an understanding, by identifying where the main borders between EU OIs and other legal instruments lie. As for the second point, this is targeted especially at academics because a comprehensive theoretical analysis of the normative issues surrounding the increasing use of the OI method by the European legislator has not yet been produced either. Of course some of these issues have already been discussed in other contexts, or in relation to specific optional instruments, but an all-embracing examination and assessment of the arguments for and against EU OIs as a general legislative method has not been attempted. The normative theory put forward in the thesis will therefore serve both to promote and also frame the academic debate itself, insofar as it offers not only an evaluation but also a framework for the evaluation of EU OIs. In other words, the study will help both to provoke and to steer future discussion and research on the subject of EU OIs.

As far as regards the third outcome, on the other hand, this is targeted especially at policymakers, including most notably the EU legislator. The identification of instrument-specific features of EU OIs that can have a considerable influence on their popularity with eligible private actors could help to inform the design of future Union optional regimes (at least to some extent), by indicating how they can be made more attractive to end users. In addition, this is of relevance to national policymakers too, insofar as it could inform their positions on future proposals for EU OIs brought forward by the European Commission. At the same time, though, this point is also intended to inform the academic debate on the desirability of the OI method, since a number of the arguments supporting this method depend in one way or another on private actors making use of the optional regimes that are enacted. For this purpose, the explanatory theory developed in this study should equally provide a framework for future academic research on the matter. And, in addition, this is of importance to private actors themselves of course, as, apart from informing such actors about the existence of EU optional regimes, the thesis will therefore also serve to increase awareness of salient differences between EU OIs from the perspective of end users.

4. *Concrete Products, Services, Processes and Activities into which the Research Results will be Translated and Shaped*

The research results may be offered to European policymakers and, in particular, to the European Commission, in order for the EU legislator to gain a better understanding of the factors influencing the attractiveness or 'success' of Union optional instruments, and ultimately to inform the design of future EU OIs. Equally, this research may be made available to national policymakers to inform their approach to and positions on future proposals for EU OIs put forward by the Commission.

The findings of the study will also be made available to actual and potential end users of optional instruments (i.e. individuals, companies and their legal representatives), as the thesis provides a uniquely detailed overview of existing and proposed EU optional regimes, including not only the similarities but also noteworthy differences between them, which could be of great practical interest to such parties.

In addition, the analysis provides a basis for future academic research into the subject of EU OIs. More specifically, the thesis identifies a range of normative issues and arguments surrounding EU OIs that are in need of deeper exploration by specialists dealing with specific aspects of law and lawmaking, as well as possible future lines of empirical research into the question of usage of EU OIs and the factors influencing this.

The research will be presented at conferences and seminars organized or attended for this purpose and dealing with such themes as new governance, regulatory competition and European harmonization. In addition, the results of this study will be disseminated through articles and discussion papers, with a view to ensuring that it features prominently in the academic and social debate.

BIBLIOGRAPHY

LITERATURE

Ackermann 2013
Ackermann, T.,'Private Production of Transnational Regulation through Standard Form Contracts', in: H. Eidenmüller (ed.), *Regulatory Competition in Contract Law and Dispute Resolution*, Munich: Beck 2013, p. 142-146.

Alpa *et al.* 2013
Alpa, G., Conte, G., Perfetti, U. & Graf van Westphalen, F. (eds.), *The Proposed Common European Sales Law - the Lawyers' View*, Munich: Sellier 2013.

Anderson 1990
Anderson, M., *European Economic Interest Groupings: Current EC Legal Developments*, Lincoln: Butterworths 1990.

Arnold 2013
Arnold, R., 'An Overview of European Harmonization Measures in Intellectual Property Law', in: A. Ohly & J. Pila (eds.), *The Europeanization of Intellectual Property Law: Towards a European Legal Methodology*, Oxford: Oxford University Press 2013, p. 25-35.

Ashiagbor 2004
Ashiagbor, D., 'Soft Harmonisation: The Open Method of Coordination in the European Employment Strategy', 10(2) *European Public Law*, 2004, p. 305-332.

Barnard 2007
Barnard, C., *The Substantive Law of the EU: The Four Freedoms* (2nd edition), Oxford: Oxford University Press 2007.

Basedow 2012
Basedow, J., *The Law of Open Societies: Private Ordering and Public Regulation in the Conflict of Laws*, Leiden: Martinus Nijhoff 2012.

Basedow 2015
Basedow, J., *The Law of Open Societies: Private Ordering and Public Regulation in the Conflict of Laws* (2nd edition), Leiden: Brill 2015.

Beale 2010
Beale, H., 'European contract law: The Common Frame of Reference and Beyond', in: C. Twigg-Flesner (ed.), *European Union Private Law*, Cambridge: Cambridge University Press 2010, p. 116-130.

Beale 2012
Beale, H., 'A Common European Sales Law (CESL) for Business-to-Business Contracts: Pros and Cons', 53 *Annales Universitatis Scientiarum Budapestinensis de Rolando*, (2012), p. 133-151.

Berle & Means 1932
Berle, A.A. & Means, G.C., *The Modern Corporation and Private Property*, Buffalo: Transaction Publishers 1932.

Bolkestein 2003
Bolkestein, F., 'The New European Company: Opportunity in Diversity', in: J. Rickford (ed.), *The European Company, Developing a Community Law of Corporations*, Antwerp: Intersentia 2003, p. 41-45.

Brandt & Scheifele 2002
Brandt, U. & Scheifele, M., 'Die Europäische Aktiengesellschaft und das anwendbare Recht', *Deutsches Steuerrecht*, 2002, p. 547-558.

Bratton, McCahery & Vermeulen 2009
Bratton, W.W., McCahery, J.A. & Vermeulen, E.P.M., 'How Does Corporate Mobility Affect Lawmaking: A Comparative Analysis', 57(2) *The American Journal of Comparative Law*, 2009, p. 347-386.

Burrows 2013
Burrows, A., *English Private Law* (3rd edition), Oxford: Oxford University Press 2013.

Cartwright 2011
Cartwright, J., 'Choice is Good. Really?', 7 *European Review of Contract Law*, 2011, p. 335-349.

Cary 1974
Cary, W.L., 'Federalism and Corporate Law: Reflexions upon Delaware', 83(4) *Yale Law Journal*, 1974, p. 663-701.

Cerioni 2004
Cerioni, L., 'The European Company Statute (SE) and the Statute for a European Cooperative Society (SCE): a Comparison between the Two New Supranational Vehicles', *The European Legal Forum*, 2004, p. 296-302.

Cerioni 2007
Cerioni, L., *EU Corporate Law and EU Company Tax Law*, Cheltenham: Edward Elgar 2007.

Charny 1991
Charny, D., 'Competition among Jurisdictions in Formulating Corporate Law Rules: an American Perspective on the Race to the Bottom in the European Communities', 32(2) *Harvard International Law Journal*, 1991, p. 423-456.

Chirico 2010
Chirico, F., 'The Function of European Contract Law: An Economic Analysis', in: P. Larouche & F. Chirico (eds.), *Economic Analysis of the DCFR: The Work of the Economic Impact Group within CoPECL*, Munich: Sellier 2010, p. 1-30.

Colombi Ciacchi 2005
Colombi Ciacchi, A., 'Non-Legislative Harmonisation of Private Law under the European Constitution: The Case of Unfair Suretyships', 13(3) *European Review of Private Law*, 2005, p. 285–308.

Craig & De Búrca 2015
Craig, P. & De Búrca, G., *EU Law: Text, Cases and Materials* (6th edition), Oxford: Oxford University Press 2015.

Crifò 2005
Crifò, C., 'First Steps towards the Harmonisation of Civil Procedure: The Regulation Creating a European Enforcement Order for Uncontested Claims', 24(2) *Civil Justice Quarterly*, 2005, p. 200-223.

Crifò 2009
Crifò, C., *Cross-Border Enforcement of Debts in the European Union: Default Judgments, Summary Judgments and Orders for Payment*, Austin: Kluwer 2009.

Crifò 2011
Crifò, C., 'Europeanisation, Harmonisation and Unspoken Premises: the Case of Service Rules in the Regulation on a European Small Claims Procedure', 30 *Civil Justice Quarterly*, 2011, p. 283-303.

Cuniberti 2008
Cuniberti, G., 'The First Stage of Abolition of the Exequatur in the European Union' 14 *Columbia Journal of European Law*, 2008, p. 371-376.

Cuniberti 2014
Cuniberti, G., 'The International Market for Contracts: The Most Attractive Contract Laws', 34 *Northwestern Journal of International Law & Business*, 2014, p. 455-517.

Currall 1984
Currall, J., 'Some Aspects of the Relation between Articles 30-36 and Article 100 of the EEC Treaty with a Closer Look to Optional Harmonisation', 4(1) *Yearbook of European Law*, 1984, p. 169-205.

Dannemann 2013
Dannemann, G., 'Choice of CESL and Conflict of Laws', in: G. Dannemann & S. Vogenauer (eds.), *The Common European Sales Law in Context: Interactions with English and German Law*, Oxford: Oxford University Press 2013, p. 21-81.

Dannemann & Vogenauer 2013
Dannemann, D. & Vogenauer, S. (eds.), *The Common European Sales Law in Context: Interactions with English and German Law*, Oxford: Oxford University Press 2013.

Dashwood 1996
Dashwood, A., 'The Limits of European Community Powers', *European Law Review*, 1996, p. 113–128.

Dawson 2011
Dawson, M., 'Three Waves of New Governance in the European Union', 36(2) *European Law Review*, 2011, p. 208-226.

De Bruycker 1991
De Bruycker, J., 'EC Company Law-The European Company v. The European Economic Interest Grouping and the Harmonization of the National Company Laws', 21 *Georgia Journal of International and Comparative Law*, 1991, p. 191-216.

De la Oliva Santos & Calderón Cuadrado 2011
De la Oliva Santos, A. & Calderón Cuadrado, M., *European Civil Procedure*, Cizur Menor: Aranzadi 2011.

Deloitte 2013
Deloitte, *Assessment of the Socio-Economic Impacts of the Policy Options for the Future of the European Small Claims Regulation*, Report for the European Commission - Directorate-General for Justice, Brussels: European Union 2013, available at: <www.ec.europa.eu/justice/civil/files/small_claims_report_ia_en.pdf>.

Demeyere 2008
Demeyere, L., 'Commercial Litigating in the European Union: a Changing Landscape', *International Business Law Journal*, 2008, p. 481-508.

Dimopoulos 2015
Dimopoulos, A., 'An Institutional Perspective II: The Role of the CJEU in the Unitary (EU) Patent System', in: J. Pila & C. Wadlow (eds.), *The Unitary EU Patent System*, Oxford: Hart Publishing 2015, p. 57-76.

Drury 2008
Drury, R., 'The European Private Company', *European Business Organization Law Review*, 2008, p. 125-136.

Edwards 2003
Edwards, V., 'The European Company - Essential Tool or Eviscerated Dream?', 40(2) *Common Market Law Review*, 2003, p. 443-464.

Eidenmüller 2009
Eidenmüller, H., 'Recht als Produkt', *JuristenZeitung*, 2009, p. 641-653.

Eidenmüller 2013a
Eidenmüller, H. (ed.), *Regulatory Competition in Contract Law and Dispute Resolution*, Oxford: Hart Publishing 2013.

Eidenmüller 2013b
Eidenmüller, H., 'Regulatory Competition in Contract Law and Dispute Resolution', in: H. Eidenmüller (ed.), *Regulatory Competition in Contract Law and Dispute Resolution*, Oxford: Hart Publishing, 2013, p. 1-11.

Eidenmüller *et al.* 2012
Eidenmüller, H., Jansen, N., Kieninger, E.-M., Wagner, G. & Zimmermann, R., 'The Proposal for a Regulation on a Common European Sales Law: Deficits of the Most Recent Textual Layer of European Contract Law', 16(3) *Edinburgh Law Review*, 2012, p. 301-357.

Eidenmüller, Hornuf & Reps 2013
Eidenmüller, H., Hornuf, L. & Reps, M., 'Contracting Employee Involvement: An Analysis of Bargaining over Employee Involvement Rules for a Societas Europaea', in: H. Eidenmüller (ed.), *Regulatory Competition in Contract Law and Dispute Resolution*, Oxford: Hart Publishing 2013, p. 155-186.

Engert 2013
Engert, A., 'Network and Lemons in the Market for Contract Law', in: H. Eidenmüller (ed.), *Regulatory Competition in Contract Law and Dispute Resolution*, Munich: Beck 2013, p. 304-312.

Ernst & Young 2009
Ernst & Young, *Study on the Operation and the Impacts of the Statute for a European Company (SE)*, Report for the European Commission, 9 December 2009, available at: <http://ec.europa.eu/internal_market/consultations/docs/2010/se/study_se_912 2009_en.pdf>.

European Commission 1989
European Commission, *The European Economic Interest Grouping (EEIG): A New Instrument for Economic Cooperation in the Community*, The European File, Brussels 1989.

European Commission 1999
European Commission, *The EEIG: an instrument for transnational cooperation: A practical handbook for SMEs'* (2nd edition), Brussels: Office for Official Publications of the European Communities 1999.

Fauvarque-Cosson & Behar-Touchais 2012
Fauvarque-Cosson, B. & Behar-Touchais, M., *Implementation of Optional Instruments within European Civil Law*, Study for European Parliament Legal Affairs Committee, PE 462.425, Brussels 2012, available at: <www.europarl.europa.eu/commit tees/en/juri/studiesdownload.html?languagedocument=en&file=72928>.

Fiorine 2008
Fiorini, A., 'Facilitating Cross-Border Debt Recovery: The European Payment Order and Small Claims Regulations', 57(2) *International & Comparative Law Quarterly*, 2008, p. 449-465.

Fleischer 2010
Fleischer, H., 'Supranational Corporate Forms in the European Union: Prolegomena to a Theory on Supranational Forms of Association', *Common Market Law Review*, 2010, p. 1671-1717.

Fleischer 2012
Fleischer, H., 'Optionales europäisches Privatrecht ("28. Modell")', 76(2) *Rabels Zeitschrift für ausländisches und internationales Privatrecht*, 2012, p. 235-252.

Fornasier 2012
Fornasier, M., '"28." Versus "2. Regime": Kollisionsrechtliche Aspekte eines optionalen europäischen Vertragsrechts', 76(02) *Rabels Zeitschrift für ausländisches und internationales Privatrecht*, 2012, p. 401-442.

Funder 1999
Funder, J.V., 'Rethinking Patents for Plant Innovation', 21 *European Intellectual Property Review*, 1999, p. 551-577.

Ganuza & Gomez 2013
Ganuza, J.J. & Gomez, F., 'Optional Law for Firms and Consumers: An Economic Analysis of Opting into the Common European Sales Law', 50(1/2) *Common Market Law Review*, 2013, p. 29-50.

Gar-Gill & Ben-Shahar 2013
Gar-Gill, O. & Ben-Shahar, O., 'Regulatory Techniques in Consumer Protection: A Critique of European Consumer Contract Law', 50(1/2) *Common Market Law Review*, 2013, p. 109-125.

Grundmann 2002
Grundmann, S., 'Regulatory Competition in European Company Law - Some Different Genius?', in: G. Ferrarini, K.J. Hopt & E. Wymeersch (eds.), *Capital Markets in the Age of the Euro*, The Hague: Kluwer Law International 2002, p. 561-595.

Habersack 1999
Habersack, M., *Europäisches Gesellschaftrecht: Einführung für Studium und Praxis*, Munich: Beck 1999.

Hertel 2014
Hertel, C., 'European Certificate of Succession - Content, Issue and Effects', 15(3) *Europäische Rechtsakademie Forum*, 2014, p. 393-407.

Hesselink 2010
Hesselink, M.W., *An Optional Instrument on EU Contract Law: Could it Increase Legal Certainty and Foster Cross-Border Trade?*, Study for European Parliament Legal Affairs Committee, PE 425.642, Brussels: European Parliament 2010.

Hesselink, Rutgers & De Booys 2008
Hesselink, M.W., Rutgers, J.W., De Booys, T.Q., *The Legal Basis for an Optional Instrument on European Contract Law*, Short study for European Parliament Legal Affairs Committee, PE 393.280, Brussels: European Parliament 2008.

Hirte & Teichmann 2012
Hirte, H. & Teichmann, C. (eds.), *The European Private Company – Societas Privata Europaea (SPE)*, Berlin: de Gruyter 2012.

Hommelhoff & Teichmann 2012
Hommelhoff, P. & Teichmann, C., 'Societas Privata Europaea (SPE) - General Report', in: H. Hirte & C. Teichmann (eds.), *The European Private Company - Societas Privata Europaea (SPE)*, Berlin: de Gruyter, 2012, p. 1-32.

Hornuf 2012
Hornuf, L., *Regulatory Competition in European Corporate and Capital Market Law: An Empirical Analysis*, Antwerp: Intersentia 2012.

Hubbard 2012
Hubbard, W.H.J., 'Another Look at the Eurobarometer Surveys', 50(1/2) *Common Market Law Review*, 2013, p. 187-206.

Ilarda 2015
Ilardi, A., *The New European Patent*, Oxford: Hart 2015.

Izquierdo Peris 2006
Izquierdo Peris, J.J., 'Registered Community Design: First Two-Year Balance from an Insider's Perspective', 28(3) *European Intellectual Property Review*, 2006, p. 146-158.

Jehoram, Van Nispen & Huydecoper 2010
Jehoram, T.C., Van Nispen, C. & Huydecoper, T., *European Trademark Law: Community Trademark Law and Harmonized National Trademark Law*, Austin: Wolters Kluwer Law & Business 2010.

Jung 2015
Jung, S., 'Societas Unius Personae (SUP) - The New Corporate Element in Company Groups', 26(5) *European Business Law Review*, 2015, p. 645-692.

Kamba 1974
Kamba, W.J., 'Comparative Law - A Theoretical Framework', 23(485) *International and Comparative Law Quarterly*, 1974, p. 490-505.

Kerber & Grundmann 2006
Kerber, W. & Grundmann, S., 'An Optional European Contract Law Code: Advantages and Disadvantages', *Marburger volkswirtschaftliche Beiträge*, 2006, p. 215-526.

Kieninger 2002
Kieninger, E., *Wettbewerb der Privatrechtsordnungen im Europäischen Binnenmarkt*, Tübingen: Mohr Siebeck 2002.

Kiewit 2003
Kiewiet, B., *Relations between Plant Variety Protection and Patents on Biotechnology*, Community Plant Variety Office Publications Archive, 2003, available at: <www.cpvo.europa.eu/documents/articles/bk%20bangkok%20november%202003.pdf>.

Kiewit 2005
Kiewiet, B., 'Plant Variety Protection in the European Community', 27 *World Patent Information*, 2005, p. 319-327.

Kilpatrick 2006
Kilpatrick, C., 'New EU Employment Governance and Constitutionalism', in: G. de Búrca & J. Scott (eds.), *Law and New Governance in the EU and the US*, Oxford: Hart Publishing 2006, p. 121-152.

Kötz 2010
Kötz, H., 'The Jurisdiction of Choice: England and Wales or Germany?', 18(6) *European Review of Contract Law*, 2010, p. 1243-1257.

Kramer 2008
Kramer, X.E., 'The European Small Claims Procedure: Striking the Balance between Simplicity and Fairness in European Litigation', 2 *Zeitschrift für europäisches Privatrecht*, 2008, p. 355-373.

Kramer 2010
Kramer, X.E., 'Enhancing Enforcement in the European Union. The European Order for Payment Procedure and Its Implementation in the Member States, Particularly in Germany, the Netherlands, and England', in: C.H. van Rhee & A. Uzelac (eds.), *Enforcement and Enforceability. Tradition and Reform* (Ius Commune Europaeum, 84), Antwerp/Cambridge: Intersentia 2010, p. 17-36.

Kuipers 2011
Kuipers, J.J., 'The Legal Basis for a European Optional Instrument, 19(5) *European Review of Private Law*, 2011, p. 545–564.

Lando & Beale 1995-2003
Lando, O. & Beale, H., *Principles of European Contract Law*, prepared by the Commission on European Contract Law, The Hague: Kluwer Law International 1995-2003.

Law Society 2012
Law Society, *Preliminary Comments on the Relationship between the Proposal for a Common European Sales Law and the Law Applicable to Contractual Obligations* (Rome I), 2012, available at: http://international.lawsociety.org.uk/files/lsew_preliminary%20comments%20on%20relationship%20between%20cesl%20and%20rome%20I.pdf.

Leible 2012
Leible, S., 'Kollisionsrecht und vertikaler Regulierungswettbewerb', 76(2) *Rabels Zeitschrift für ausländisches und internationals Privatrecht*, 2012, p. 374-400.

Lefebvre 1992
Lefebvre, F. (ed.), *Bureau d'études fiscales et juridiques Francis Lefebvre*, Deventer: Kluwer 1992.

Lenoir 2008
Lenoir, N., 'The Societas Europaea (SE) in Europe: A Promising Start and an Option with Good Prospects', 4(1) *Utrecht Law Review*, 2008, p. 13-21.

Levin & Richman 2003
Levin, K.A. & Richman, M.B., 'A Survey of Industrial Design Protection in the European Union and the United States', 25 *European Intellectual Property Review*, 2003, p. 111-124.

Lilleholt 2011
Lilleholt, K., 'European Private Law: Unification, Harmonisation or Coordination?', in: R. Brownsword, H.-W. Micklitz, L. Niglia & S. Weatherill (eds.), *The Foundations of European Private Law*, Oxford: Hart Publishing 2011, p. 293-308.

Llewelyn & Adcock 2006
Llewelyn, M. & Adcock, M., *European Plant Intellectual Property*, Oxford: Hart 2006.

Loos 2011
Loos, M., 'Individual Private Enforcement of Consumer Rights in Civil Courts in Europe', in: R. Brownsword, H.-W. Micklitz, L. Niglia & S. Weatherill (eds.), *The Foundations of European Private Law*, Oxford: Hart Publishing 2011, p. 487-512.

Low 2011
Low, G., *European Contract Law between the Single Market and the Law Market – a Behavioural Perspective*, Nijmegen: Wolf 2011.

Low 2012a
Low, G., 'Unitas via Diversitas: Can the Common European Sales Law Harmonise through Diversity?' 19(1) *Maastricht Journal of European and Comparative Law*, 2012, p. 132-147.

Low 2012b
Low, G., 'Will Firms consider a European Optional Instrument in Contract Law?', 33 *European Journal of Law and Economics*, 2012, p. 521-540.

Luginbuehl 2011
Luginbuehl, S., *European Patent Law: Towards a Uniform Interpretation*, Cheltenham: Edward Elgar 2011.

Luginbuehl 2015
Luginbuehl, S., 'An Institutional Perspective I: The Role of the EPO in the Unitary (EU) Patent System', in: J. Pila & C. Wadlow (eds.), *The Unitary EU Patent System*, Oxford: Hart Publishing 2015, p. 45-56.

Luhmann 2004
Luhmann, N., *Law as a Social System*, Oxford: Oxford University Press 2004.

Lutter & Kock 2015
Lutter, M. & Kock, J. (eds.), *Societas Unius Personae (SUP): Beiträge aus Wissenschaft und Praxis*: Berlin: de Gruyter 2015.

MacCormick 2008
MacCormick, N., *Institutions of Law: An Essay in Legal Theory*, Oxford: Oxford University Press 2008.

MacQueen *et al.* 2010
MacQueen, H., Waelde, C., Laurie, G. & Brown, A., *Contemporary Intellectual Property: Law and Policy* (2nd edition), Oxford: Oxford University Press 2010.

Mahne 2012
Mahne, K.P., 'A Unitary and Unified Patent Court for the European Union: An Analysis of Europe's Long Standing Attempt to Create a Supranational Patent System', 94 *Journal of the Patent and Trademark Office Society*, 2012, p. 162-191.

Malberti 2015
Malberti, C., 'The Relationship between the Societas Unius Personae Proposal and the Acquis: Creeping toward an Abrogation of EU Company Law?', 12 *European Company and Financial Law Review*, 2015, p. 238-279.

Max Planck Institute for Intellectual Property and Competition Law 2011
Max Planck Institute for Intellectual Property and Competition Law, *Study on the Overall Functioning of the European Trade Mark System*, Munich, 15 February 2011, available at: <http://ec.europa.eu/internal_market/indprop/docs/tm/20110308_allensbach-study_en.pdf>.

McCahery & Vermeulen 2001
McCahery, J.A. & Vermeulen, E.P.M., 'The Evolution of Closely Held Business Forms in Europe, *Journal of Corporation Law*, 2001, p. 855-878.

McCahery & Vermeulen 2005
McCahery, J.A. & Vermeulen, E.P.M., 'Does the European Company Prevent the "Delaware Effect"?', 11(6) *European Law Journal*, 2005, p. 785–801.

McConville & Chui 2007
McConville, M. & Chui, W.H. (eds.), *Research Methods for Law*, Edinburgh: Edinburgh University Press 2007.

Michaels 2013
Michaels, R., 'Make or Buy – A Public Market for Legal Transplants?', in: H. Eidenmüller (ed.), *Regulatory Competition in Contract Law and Dispute Resolution*, Munich: Beck 2013, p. 39-54.

Micklitz 2012
Micklitz, H.W., 'A Self-Sufficient European Private Law – A Viable Concept?', in: H.W. Micklitz & Y. Svetiev (eds.), *A Self-Sufficient European Private Law – A Viable Concept?* (EUI Law, 2012/31), Florence: European University Institute 2012, p. 5-25.

Micklitz & Cafaggi 2010
Micklitz, H.W. & Cafaggi, F. (eds.), *European Private Law After the Common Frame of Reference*, Cheltenham: Edward Elgar 2010.

Micklitz & Svetiev 2012
Micklitz, H.W. & Svetiev, Y. (eds.), A Self-Sufficient European Private Law – A Viable Concept? (EUI Law, 2012/31), Florence: European University Institute 2012.

Millett 1999
Millett, T., 'The Community System of Plant Variety Rights', 24(3) *European Law Review*, 1999, p. 231-258.

Monti 2010
Monti, M., *A New Strategy for the Single Market: At the Service of Europe's Economy and Society*, Report to the President of the European Commission, May 2010, available at: <http://ec.europa.eu/internal_market/strategy/docs/monti_report_final_10_05_2010_en.pdf>.

Möslein 2010
Möslein, F., 'Legal Innovation in European Contract Law: Within and Beyond the (Draft) Common Frame of Reference', in: H.W. Micklitz & F. Cafaggi (eds.), *European Private Law After the Common Frame of Reference*, Cheltenham: Edward Elgar 2010, p. 173-199.

Mourre & Lahlou 2004
Mourre, A. & Lahlou, Y., 'The Construction of the European Judicial Space: the Enforcement of Uncontested Claims and the Prohibition of Anti-Suit Injunctions', 4 *International Business Law Journal*, 2004, p. 538-563.

Murray & DeSanctis 2009
Murray, M.D. & DeSanctis, C.H., *Legal Research Methods*, New York: Foundation Press 2009.

O'Hara & Ribstein 2009
O'Hara, E. & Ribstein, L.E., *The Law Market*, Oxford: Oxford University Press 2009.

Parisi & Ribstein 1998
Parisi, P. & Ribstein, L.E., 'Choice of Law', in: P. Newman (ed.), *The New Palgrave Dictionary of Economics and the Law* (Volume 1), London: Macmillan 1998, p. 236-241.

Peters 2010
Peters, A., 'Competition of Legal Orders', 69 *Veröffentlichungen der Vereinigung der Deutschen Staatsrechtslehrer*, 2010, p. 7-56.

Pila 2013
Pila, J., 'The European Patent: An Old and Vexing Problem', 62(4) *International and Comparative Law Quarterly*, 2013, p. 917-940.

Pila 2015
Pila, J., 'An Historical Perspective I: The Unitary Patent Package', in: J. Pila & C. Wadlow (eds.), *The Unitary EU Patent System*, Oxford: Hart 2015, p. 9-32.

Pila & Wadlow 2015
Pila, J. & Wadlow, C. (eds.), *The Unitary EU Patent System*, Oxford: Hart 2015.

Porter 1990
Porter, M., *The Competitive Advantage of Nations*, London: Macmillan 1990.

Ramaekers 2013
Ramaekers, E., *European Union Property Law: From Fragments to a System* (Ius Commune Europaeum, 117), Antwerp: Intersentia 2013.

Reich 1992
Reich, N., 'Competition between Legal Orders: A New Paradigm of EC Law?', 29(5) *Common Market Law Review*, 1992, p. 861–896.

Ribstein & Kobayashi 1996
Ribstein, L.E. & Kobayashi, B.H., 'An Economic Analysis of Uniform State Laws', 25(1) *Journal of Legal Studies*, 1996, p. 131-199.

Rickford 2002
Rickford, J. (ed.), *The European Company: Developing a Community Law of Corporations: Collected Papers from the Leiden University Unilever Programme*, Antwerp: Intersentia 2002.

Romano 1985
Romano, R., 'Law as a Product: Some Pieces of the Incorporation Puzzle', 1(2) *The Journal of Law, Economics and Organization*, 1985, p. 225-283.

Rühl 2012
Rühl, G., 'The Common European Sales Law: 28th Regime, 2nd Regime or 1st Regime?', 19(1) *Maastricht Journal of European and Comparative Law*, 2012, p. 148-163.

Rühl 2013a
Rühl, G., 'Regulatory Competition in Contract Law: Empirical Evidence and Normative Implications', 9 *European Review of Contract Law*, 2013, p. 61-89.

Rühl 2013b
Rühl, G., 'The Choice of Law Framework for Efficient Regulatory Competition in Contract Law', in: H. Eidenmüller (ed.), Regulatory Competition in Contract Law and Dispute Resolution, Munich: Beck 2013, p. 287-303.

Rutgers 2006
Rutgers, J.W., 'An Optional Instrument and Social Dumping', 2(2) *European Review of Contract Law*, 2006, p. 199-212.

Rutgers 2011
Rutgers, J.W., 'An Optional Instrument and Social Dumping Revisited', 7(2) *European Review of Contract Law*, 2011, p. 350-359.

Sachdeva 2010
Sachdeva, A., 'Regulatory competition in European Company law', *European Journal of Law and Economics*, 2010, p. 137-170.

Santa Maria 2009
Santa Maria, A., *European Economic Law*, The Hague: Kluwer Law International 2009.

Schmidt 2006
Schmidt, J., 'SE and SCE: Two New European Company Forms - and More to Come!', 27 *Company Lawyer*, 2006, p. 99-109.

Schmitthoff 1973
Schmitthoff, C.M. (ed.), *The Harmonization of European Company Law* (UK National Committee of Comparative Law), London: National Committee of Comparative Law 1973.

Schoordijk 2008
Schoordijk, H.C.F., 'Het recht moeten wij niet denken als een systeem vooraleer wij er systeem in gebracht hebben' (translated as 'We should not View the Law as a System, before Systematising it'), 1387 *Nederlands Juristenblad*, 2008, p. 1720-1723.

Schulte-Nölke 2011
Schulte-Nölke, H., 'How to Realise the "Blue Button"? - Reflections on an Optional Instrument in the Area of Contract Law', in: R. Schulze & H. Schulte-Nölke (eds.), *European Private Law - Current Statues and Perspectives*, Munich: Sellier 2011, p. 89-106.

Schulze 2012
Schulze, R. (ed.), *Common European Sales Law (CESL): Commentary*, Baden-Baden: Nomos, Hart and Beck 2012.

Schulze & Schulte-Nölke 2011
Schulze, R. & Schulte-Nölke, H. (eds.), *European Private Law - Current Statuses and Perspectives*, Munich: Sellier 2011.

Schwarz 2004
Schwarz, B., *The Paradox of Choice. Why More is Less*, New York: Harper Collins 2004.

Sefton-Green 2011
Sefton-Green, R., 'Choice, Certainty and Diversity: Why More is Less', *European Review of Contract Law*, 2011, p. 134-150.

Senden 2012
Senden, L., 'Changes in the Relative Importance of Sources of Law - The Case of EU Soft Law', in: U. Neergaard & R. Nielsen (eds.), *European Legal Method*, Copenhagen: DJØF 2012, p. 225-260.

Seville 2009
Seville, C., *EU Intellectual Property Law and Policy*, Cheltenham: Edward Elgar 2009.

Siebert 1990a
Siebert, H. (ed.), *The Completion of the Internal Market*, Tübingen: Siebeck 1990.

Siebert 1990b
Siebert, H., 'The Harmonization Issue in Europe: Prior Agreement or a Competitive Process?', in: H. Siebert (ed.), *The Completion of the Internal Market*, Tübingen: Siebeck 1990, p. 53-75.

Siems 2005
Siems, M.M., 'The Impact of the European Company (SE) on Legal Culture', 30 *European Law Review*, 2005, p. 431-442.

Smits 1998
Smits, J.M., 'A European Private Law as a Mixed Legal System', 5(4) *Maastricht Journal of European and Comparative Law*, 1998, p. 328-340.

Smits 2002a
Smits, J.M., 'Towards a Multi-Layered Contract Law for Europe', in: Grundmann, S. & Stuyck, J. (eds.), *An Academic Green Paper on European Contract Law*, The Hague: Kluwer Law Interational 2002, p. 387-398.

Smits 2002b
Smits, J.M., 'The Harmonisation of Private Law in Europe: Some Insights from Evolutionary Theory', 31 *Georgia Journal of International and Comparative Law*, 2002, p. 79-99.

Smits 2005a
Smits, J.M., (ed.), *The Need for a European Contract Law: Empirical and Legal Perspectives*, Groningen: Europa Law Publishing 2005.

Smits 2005b
Smits, J.M., 'Diversity of Contract Law and the European Internal Market', in: J.M. Smits (ed.), *The Need for a European Contract Law: Empirical and Legal Perspectives*, Groningen: Europa Law Publishing 2005, p. 153-186.

Smits 2006
Smits, J.M., 'European Private Law: A Plea for a Spontaneous Legal Order', in: *European Integration and Law*, (Ius Commune Europaeum, 56) Antwerp: Intersentia 2006, p. 55.105.

Smits 2008
Smits, J.M., 'Mixed Jurisdictions: Lessons for European Harmonisation?', 12 *Electronic Journal of Comparative Law*, 2008, p. 1-8.

Smits 2009
Smits, J.M., 'Democracy and (European) Private Law: A Functional Approach', 2 *European Journal of Legal Studies*, 2009, p. 26-40.

Smits 2010a
Smits, J.M., 'Full Harmonization of Consumer Law? A Critique of the Draft Directive on Consumer Rights', 18 *European Review of Private Law*, 2010, p. 5-15.

Smits 2010b
Smits, J.M., 'Optional Law: A Plea for Multiple Choice in Private Law', 17(4) *Maastricht Journal of European and Comparative Law*, 2010, p. 347-352.

Smits 2010c
Smits, J.M., 'Beyond Euroscepticism: On the Choice of Legal Regimes as Empowerment of Citizens', 6(3) *Utrecht Law Review*, 2010, p. 68-74.

Smits 2011
Smits, J.M., *Private Law 2.0: On the Role of Private Actors in a Post-National Society*, The Hague: Hague Institute for the Internationalisation of Law and Eleven International Publishing 2011.

Smits 2012a
Smits, J.M., *The Mind and Method of the Legal Academic*, Cheltenham: Edward Elgar 2012.

Smits 2012b
Smits, J.M., 'The Common European Sales Law (CESL) Beyond Party Choice', Zeitschrift für Europäisches Privatrecht, 2012, p. 904-923.

Smits 2012c
Smits, J.M., 'A Radical View of Legal Pluralism', in: L. Niglia (ed.), *Pluralism and European Private Law*, Oxford: Hart Publishing 2012, p. 161-172.

Smits 2013b
Smits, J.M., 'Party Choice and the Common European Sales Law, or: How to Prevent the CESL from Becoming a Lemon on the Law Market', 50(1/2) *Common Market Law Review*, 2013, p. 51-68.

Smits 2016
Smits, J.M., 'New European Union Proposals for Distance Sales and Digital Contents Contracts: Fit for Purpose?', *Zeitschrift für europäisches Privatrecht*, 2016 (forthcoming).

Smits & Bull 2013
Smits, J.M. & Bull, W.A., 'The Europeanization of Patent Law: Towards a Competitive Model', in: A. Ohly and J. Pila (eds.), *The Europeanization of Intellectual Property Law: Towards a European Legal Methodology*, Oxford: Oxford University Press 2013, p. 39-55.

Spencer 1959
Spencer, R., 'A European Patent: An Old and Vexing Problem', *American Bar Association Journal*, 1959, p. 1157-1159.

Storme 2010
Storme, M.E., 'The Foundations of Private Law in a Multi-Level Structure: Balancing, Distribution of Lawmaking Power and other Constitutional Issues', in: R. Brownsword, H.-W. Micklitz, L. Niglia & S. Weatherill (eds.), *The Foundations of European Private Law*, Oxford: Hart 2010, p. 417-430.

Study Group on Social Justice in European Private Law 2004
Study Group on Social Justice in European Private Law, 'Social Justice in European Contract Law: a Manifesto', 10 *European Law Journal*, 2004, p. 653-674.

Sun & Pelkmans 1995
Sun, J.-M. & Pelkmans, J., 'Regulatory Competition in the Single Market', 1(33) *Journal of Common Market Studies*, 1995, p. 67-89.

Teichmann & Fröhlich 2014
Teichmann, C. & Fröhlich, A., 'Societas Unius Personae (SUP): Facilitating Cross-Border Establishment', 21 *Maastricht Journal of European and Comparative Law*, 2014, p. 536-544.

Teubner 1987
Teubner, G. (ed.), *Autopoietic Law: A New Approach to Law and Society*, Berlin: de Gruyter 1987.

Thommes 2004
Thommes, C., 'EC Law Aspects of the Transfer of Seat of an SE', *European Taxation*, 2004, p. 22-27.

Tiebout 1956
Tiebout, C.M., 'A Pure Theory of Local Expenditures', 64(5) *The Journal of Political Economy*, p. 416-424.

Tritton *et al.* 2007
Tritton, G., Quintin, T.St., Longstaff, B. & Roughton, A., *Intellectual Property in Europe* (3rd edition), London: Sweet and Maxwell 2007.

Trubek & Trubek 2006
Trubek, D. & Trubek, L., 'New Governance & Legal Regulation: Complementarity, Rivalry and Transformation', 13 *Columbia Journal of European Law*, 2006, p. 539-564.

Twigg-Flesner 2015
Twigg-Flesner, C. (ed.), *Elgar Research Handbook on EU Consumer and Contract Law*, Cheltenham: Edward Elgar 2015.

Ullrich 2012
Ullrich, H., *Select From Within the System: The European Patent with Unitary Effect*, Max Planck Institute for Intellectual Property and Competition Law Research Paper No. 12-11, 2012.

Van der Grinten 2006
Van der Grinten, P.M.M., 'Abolishing Exequatur in the European Union: An Alternative', in: P.M.M. van der Grinten & T. Heukels (eds.), *Crossing Borders; Essays in European and Private International Law, Nationality Law and Islamic Law in Honour of Frans van der Velden*, Deventer: Kluwer 2006, p. 71-83.

Van der Grinten & Heukels 2006
Van der Grinten, P.M.M. & Heukels, T. (eds.), *Crossing Borders; Essays in European and Private International Law, Nationality Law and Islamic Law in Honour of Frans van der Velden*, Deventer: Kluwer 2006.

Van der Kooij 1997
Van der Kooij, P.A.C.E., *Introduction to the EC Regulation on Plant Variety Protection* (2nd edition), London: Kluwer 1997.

Van Gerven & Aalders 1990
Van Gerven, D. & Aalders, C.A.V., *European Economic Interest Groupings: The EEC Regulation and its Application in the Member States of the European Community*, The Hague: Kluwer Law International 1990.

Van Schagen 2012
Van Schagen, E., 'The Proposal for a Common European Sales Law: How its Drafting Process Might Affect the Optional Instrument's Added Value for Contract Parties and its Success', in: A.L.M. Keirse & M.B.M. Loos (eds.), *Alternative Ways to Ius Commune: The Europeanisation of Private Law* (Ius Commune Europaeum, 105), Antwerp: Intersentia 2012, p. 85-110.

Varul 2008
Varul, P., 'Performance and Remedies for Non-performance: Comparative Analysis of the PECL and DCFR', *Juridica International*, 2008, p. 104-110.

Vogenauer 2013
Vogenauer, S., 'Regulatory Competition Through Choice of Contract Law and Choice of Forum in Europe: Theory and Evidence', in: H. Eidenmüller (ed.), *Regulatory Competition in Contract Law and Dispute Resolution*, Munich: Beck 2013, p. 227-284.

Von Bar & Clive 2009
Von Bar, C. & Clive, E. (eds.), *Principles, Definitions and Model Rules of European Private Law: Draft Common Frame of Reference*, Munich: Sellier 2009.

Wadlow 2015
Wadlow, C., 'An Historical Perspective II: The Unified Patent Court', in: J. Pila & C. Wadlow (eds.), *The Unitary EU Patent System*, Oxford: Hart Publishing 2015, p. 9-32.

Wagner 2002
Wagner, G., 'The Economics of Harmonization: The Case of Contract Law', 39 *Common Market Law Review*, 2002, p. 995-1023.

Wagner 2009
Wagner, H., *Legal Uncertainty – Is Harmonization of Law the Right Answer?*, Hagen: Fernuniversität Hagen 2009.

Watkins & Burton 2013
Watkins, D. & Burton, M. (eds.), *Research Methods in Law*, Abingdon: Routledge 2013.

Whittaker 2012
Whittaker, S., 'The Proposed "Common European Sales Law": Legal Framework and the Agreement of the Parties', 75 *Modern Law Review*, 2012, p. 578-605.

Wiedemann 1980
Wiedemann, H., *Gesellschaftsrecht I*, Munich: Beck 1980.

Winter 2003
Winter, J.,'Thalassa! Thalassa! – The SE as a Glimpse of the Future?', in: J. Rickford (ed.), *The European Company: Developing a Community Law of Corporations*, Antwerp: Intersentia 2003, p. 113-122.

Winter 1977
Winter, R.K. jr., 'State Law, Shareholder Protection and the Theory of the Corporation', 6(2) *The Journal of Legal Studies*, 1977, p. 251-292.

Wuisman 2015
Wuisman, I., 'The Societas Unius Personae (SUP)', 12(1) *European Company Law*, 2015, p. 34–44.

Wulf 2014
Wulf, A.J., *Institutional Competition between Optional Codes in European Contract Law: A Theoretical and Empirical Analysis*, Wiesbaden: Springer 2014.

Würtenberger *et al.* 2006
Würtenberger, G., Van der Kooij, P., Kiewiet, B. & Ekvad, M., *European Community Plant Variety Protection*, New York: Oxford University Press 2006.

Yablon 2007
Yablon, C.M., 'The Historical Race Competition for Corporate Charters and the Rise and Decline of New Jersey: 1880-1910', 32 *The Journal of Corporation Law*, 2007, p. 323-380.

Zilinsky 2006
Zilinsky, M., 'Abolishing Exequatur in the European Union: The European Enforcement Order', 53(3) *Netherlands International Law Review*, 2006, p. 471-492.

EUROPEAN UNION - DIRECTIVES, REGULATIONS AND DECISIONS

First Council Directive 68/151/EEC of 9 March 1968 on co-ordination of safeguards which, for the protection of the interests of members and others, are required by Member States of companies within the meaning of the second paragraph of Article 58 of the Treaty, with a view to making such safeguards equivalent throughout the Community [1968] OJ L65/8

Second Council Directive 77/91/EEC of 13 December 1976 on coordination of safeguards which, for the protection of the interests of members and others, are required by Member States of companies within the meaning of the second paragraph of Article 58 of the Treaty, in respect of the formation of public limited liability companies and the maintenance and alteration of their capital, with a view to making such safeguards equivalent [1977] OJ L26/1

Fourth Council Directive 78/660/EEC of 25 July 1978 based on Article 54 (3) (g) of the Treaty on the annual accounts of certain types of companies [1978] OJ L222/11

Third Council Directive 78/855/EEC of 9 October 1978 based on Article 54 (3) (g) of the Treaty concerning mergers of public limited liability companies [1978] OJ L295/36

Sixth Council Directive 82/891/EEC of 17 December 1982 based on Article 54 (3) (g) of the Treaty, concerning the division of public limited liability companies [1982] OJ L378/47

Seventh Council Directive 83/349/EEC of 13 June 1983 based on the Article 54 (3) (g) of the Treaty on consolidated accounts [1983] OJ L193/1

Eighth Council Directive 84/253/EEC of 10 April 1984 based on Article 54 (3) (g) of the Treaty on the approval of persons responsible for carrying out the statutory audits of accounting documents [1984] OJ L126/20

Council Regulation 2137/85 of 25 July 1985 on the European Economic Interest Grouping [1985] OJ L199/1

Council Directive 85/577/EEC of 20 December 1985 to protect the consumer in respect of contracts negotiated away from business premises [1985] OJ L372/31

Council Directive 87/54/EEC of 16 December 1986 on the legal protection of topographies of semiconductor products [1987] OJ L24/36

First Council Directive 89/104/EEC of 21 December 1988 to approximate the laws of the Member States relating to trade marks [1989] OJ L40/1

Council Regulation 2100/94 of 27 July 1994 on Community plant variety rights [1994] OJ L227/1

Council Regulation 40/94 of 20 December 1993 on the Community trade mark [1994] OJ L11/1

Directive 98/44 of 6 July 1998 on the legal protection of biotechnological inventions [1998] OJ L213/13

Directive 98/71/EC of the European Parliament and of the Council of 13 October 1998 on the legal protection of designs [1998] OJ L289/28

Directive 1999/44/EC of the European Parliament and of the Council of 25 May 1999 on certain aspects of the sale of consumer goods and associated guarantees [1999] OJ L171/12

Council Regulation 44/2001 of 22 December 2000 on jurisdiction and the recognition and enforcement of judgments in civil and commercial matters [2001] OJ L12/1

Council Directive 2001/86/EC of 8 October 2001 supplementing the Statute for a European company with regard to the involvement of employees [2001] OJ L294/22

Council Regulation 2157/2001 of 8 October 2001 on the Statute for a European company (SE) [2001] OJ L294/1

Council Regulation 6/2002 of 12 December 2001 on Community designs [2001] OJ L3/1

Council Regulation 1435/2003 of 22 July 2003 on the Statute for a European Cooperative Society (SCE) [2003] OJ L207/1

Council Directive 2003/72/EC of 22 July 2003 supplementing the Statute for a European Cooperative Society with regard to the involvement of employees [2003] OJ L207/25

Regulation 805/2004 of the European Parliament and of the Council of 21 April 2004 creating a European Enforcement Order for uncontested claims [2004] OJ L143/15

Regulation 1896/2006 of the European Parliament and of the Council of 12 December 2006 creating a European order for payment procedure [2006] OJ L399/1

Regulation 861/2007 of the European Parliament and of the Council of 11 July 2007 establishing a European Small Claims Procedure [2007] OJ L199/1

Council Regulation 15/2008 of 20 December 2007 amending Regulation 2100/94 as regards the entitlement to file an application for a Community plant variety right [2008] OJ L8/2

Regulation 593/2008 of the European Parliament and of the Council of 17 June 2008 on the law applicable to contractual obligations (Rome I) [2008] OJ L177/6

Regulation 207/2009 of 26 February 2009 on the Community trade mark [2009] OJ L78/1

Council Decision 2011/167/EU of 10 March 2011 authorising enhanced cooperation in the area of the creation of unitary patent protection [2011] OJ L76/53

Regulation 650/2012 of the European Parliament and of the Council of 4 July 2012 on jurisdiction, applicable law, recognition and enforcement of decisions and acceptance and enforcement of authentic instruments in matters of succession and on the creation of a European Certificate of Succession [2012] OJ L201/107

Regulation 1215/2012 of the European Parliament and of the Council of 12 December 2012 on jurisdiction and the recognition and enforcement of judgments in civil and commercial matters [2012] OJ L351/1

Regulation 1257/2012 of the European Parliament and of the Council of 17 December 2012 implementing enhanced cooperation in the area of the creation of unitary patent protection [2012] OJ L361/1

Regulation 1260/2012 of 17 December 2012 implementing enhanced cooperation in the area of the creation of unitary patent protection with regard to the applicable translation arrangements [2012] OJ L361/89

Regulation 655/2014 of the European Parliament and of the Council of 15 May 2014 establishing a European Account Preservation Order procedure to facilitate cross-border debt recovery in civil and commercial matters [2014] OJ L189

EUROPEAN UNION – COMMISSION AND COUNCIL DOCUMENTS

Commission, 'Proposal for a Council Regulation Embodying a Statute for the European Company' COM(70) 600 final

Commission, 'Proposal for a regulation of the Council on the European cooperation grouping' COM(73) 2046

Commission, 'White Paper from the Commission to the European Council' COM(85) 310 final

Commission, 'Green Paper on the Legal Protection of Industrial Design' III/F/5131/91

Commission, 'Memorandum to Parliament, Council and the two sides of industry on the Statute for the European Company of 8 June 1988' COM(88) 320 final

Commission, 'Proposal for a Council Directive on the Legal Protection of Biotechnological Inventions' COM(88) 496 final

Commission, 'Proposal for a Council Regulation on the Statute for a European company' COM(89) 268

Commission, 'Proposal for a Regulation on Community plant variety rights' COM(90) 347 final

Commission, 'Proposal for a Council Regulation on the statute for a European cooperative society' COM(91) 273 final

Commission, 'Proposal for a European Parliament and Council Regulation on the Community Design' COM(93) 342 final

Commission, 'Towards greater efficiency in obtaining and enforcing judgments in the European Union' (Communication) COM(97) 609 final

Council, 'Tampere European Council 15 and 16 October 1999 Presidency conclusions' [1999]

Commission, 'Proposal for a Council Regulation on the Community Patent' COM(2000) 412 final

Council, 'Draft programme of measures for implementation of the principle of mutual recognition of decisions in civil and commercial matters' [2001] OJ C12/1

Commission, 'Communication from the Commission to the Council and the European Parliament on European Contract Law' COM(2001) 398 final

Commission, 'Green Paper on a European order for payment procedure and on measures to simplify and speed up small claims litigation' COM(2002) 746 final

Commission, 'A more coherent European contract law: An action plan' (Communication) COM(2003) 68 final

Commission, 'Proposal for a Regulation creating a European order for payment procedure' COM(2004) 173 final

Commission, 'European Contract Law and the revision of the acquis: the way forward' (Communication) COM(2004) 651 final

Commission, 'Proposal for a Regulation establishing a European Small Claims Procedure' COM(2005) 87 final

Commission, 'Green Paper Mortgage Credit in the EU' COM(2005) 327 final

Commission, 'Green Paper on improving the efficiency of the enforcement of judgments in the European Union: the attachment of bank accounts' COM(2006) 618 final

Commission, 'Proposal for a Council Regulation on the Statute for a European private company' COM(2008) 396/3

Council, Interinstitutional File 2000/0177 (CNS) [2008] 9465/08

Council, Draft Agreement on the European and Community Patents Court and Draft Statue [2009] 5072/09

Commission, 'Green Paper on European Contract Law for consumers and businesses' COM(2010) 348 final

Commission, 'Report from the Commission to the European Parliament and the Council on the application of Council Regulation 2157/2001 of 8 October 2001 on the Statute for a European Company' COM(2010) 676 final

Commission, 'Staff Working Document accompanying document to the Report from the Commission to the European Parliament and the Council on the application of Council Regulation 2157/2001 of 8 October 2001 on the Statute for a European Company (SE)' SEC(2010) 1391

Commission, 'Proposal for a Regulation of the European Parliament and of the Council implementing enhanced cooperation in the area of the creation of unitary patent protection' COM(2011) 215

Commission, 'Accompanying document to the Proposal for a Regulation of the European Parliament and the Council implementing enhanced cooperation in the area of the creation of unitary patent protection and Proposal for a Council Regulation implementing enhanced cooperation in the area of the creation of unitary patent protection with regard to the applicable translation arrangements' SEC(2011) 482 final

Commission, 'Proposal for a Regulation of the European Parliament and of the Council on a Common European Sales Law' COM(2011) 635 final

Council, Interinstitutional File 2008/0130 (CNS) [2011] 10611/11

Commission, 'Proposal for a Council Regulation on the Statute for a European Foundation (FE)' COM(2012) 35 final

Commission, 'Report from the Commission to the European Parliament, the Council, the European Economic and Social Committee and the Committee of the Regions on the application of Council Regulation 1435/2003 of 22 July 2003 on the Statute for a European Cooperative Society' COM(2012) 72 final

Commission, 'Report from the Commission to the European Parliament, the Council and the European Economic and Social Committee on the application of Regulation (EC) No 861/2007 of the European Parliament and of the Council establishing a European Small Claims Procedure' COM(2013) 795

Council, Agreement on a Unified Patent Court [2013] 16351/12

Commission, 'Proposal for a Directive of the European Parliament and of the Council on single-member private limited liability companies' COM(2014) 212 final

Commission, 'Commission Work Programme 2015: A New Start' COM(2014) 910 final

Commission, 'A Digital Single Market Strategy for Europe' COM(2015) 192 final

Commission, 'Proposal for a Directive of the European Parliament and of the Council on certain aspects concerning contracts for the supply of digital content' COM(2015) 634 final

Commission, 'Proposal for a Directive of the European Parliament and of the Council on certain aspects concerning contracts for the online and other distance sales of goods' COM(2015) 635 final

European Union – Protocols, Conventions and Agreements

Brussels Convention on jurisdiction, recognition and enforcement of judgments in civil and commercial matters, Convention adopted on 27 September 1968 [1972] OJ L 299

Convention 76/76/EEC for the European Patent for the Common Market (Community Patent Convention) [1976] OJ L17/1

Protocol on the Settlement of Litigation Concerning the Infringement and Validity of Community Patents [1989] OJ L401/34

Agreement 89/695/EEC relating to Community patents [1989] OJ L401/1

Brussels Convention on jurisdiction, recognition and enforcement of judgments in civil and commercial matters [2001] OJ L 12

European Union – ECJ Case Law

Case C-212/97, *Centros Ltd* v *Erhvervs- og Selskabsstyrelsen* [1999] ECR I-1459

Case 208/00, *Überseering BV* v *Nordic Construction Company Baumanagement GmbH* [2002] ECR I-9919

C-305/00, *Schulin* v *Saatgut-Treuhandverwaltung* [2002] ECR I-03525

C-305/00, *Schulin* v *Saatgut-Treuhandverwaltung* [2002] ECR I-03525, Opinion of AG Jarabo-Colomer

Case C-167/01, *Kamer van Koophandel en Fabrieken voor Amsterdam* v *Inspire Art Ltd* [2003] ECR I-10155

Case C-66/04, *United Kingdom* v *Parliament and Council* [2005] ECR I-10553

Case C-436/03, *European Parliament* v *Council* [2006] ECR I-3733

Case C-436/03, European Parliament v Council [2006] ECR I-3733, Opinion of AG Stix-Hackl

Case C-217/04, *United Kingdom* v *Parliament and Council* [2006] ECR I-3771

Opinion 1/94 of the Court of Justice [1994] ECR I-5276

Joined Cases C-274/11 and C-295/11 *Spain and Italy* v *Council* [2013] ECR I-0000, not yet reported.

International Treaties

Paris Convention for the Protection of Industrial Property 1883

Hague Agreement Concerning the International Registration of Industrial Designs 1925

International Convention for the Protection of New Varieties of Plants 1961

European Patent Convention 1973

United Nations Convention on Contracts for the International Sale of Goods 1980

Madrid Agreement Concerning the International Registration of Marks 1981

Protocol Relating to the Madrid Agreement 1989

Agreement on Trade-Related Aspects of Intellectual Property Rights 1994

Consolidated versions of the Treaty on European Union and the Treaty on the Functioning of the European Union [2010] OJ C 83/01

INTERNET SOURCES

Assemblée Nationale, 'En aucun cas nous ne pouvons accepter d'avoir concomitamment deux corps de règles sur le meme territoire' (Commission des affaires européennes, Compte rendu 231, 7, 2011) <www.assemblee-nationale.fr/13/ europe/c-rendus/c0231.asp>

Commission, 'Civil Justice' <http://ec.europa.eu/justice/civil/index_en.htm>

Commission, 'A European contract law for consumers and businesses: Publication of the results of the feasibility study carried out by the Expert Group on European contract law for stakeholders' and legal practitioners' feedback' (2011) <http://ec.europa.eu/justice/contract/files/feasibility_study_final.pdf>

Commission, 'Flash Eurobarometer 320: European contract law in business-to-business transactions - Analytical Report' (2011) <http://ec.europa.eu/public_opinion/flash/fl_320_en.pdf>

Commission, 'Flash Eurobarometer 321: European contract law in consumer transactions – Analytic Report' (2011) <http://ec.europa.eu/public_opinion/flash/fl_321_en.pdf>

European Commission, 'Commission proposes unitary patent protection in 25 Member States – Frequently Asked Questions' (Memo/11/240, 2011) <http://europa.eu/rapid/press-release_MEMO-11-240_en.htm?locale=en>

Commission, 'Practice guide for the application of the European Small Claims Procedure' (2014) <http://ec.europa.eu/justice/civil/files/small_claims_practice_guide_en.pdf>

Community Plant Variety Office, Annual Report 2014 (2014) <www.cpvo.europa.eu/main/en/home/documents-and-publications/annual-reports>

Community Plant Variety Office, statistics of 31st December 2014 <www.cpvo.europa.eu/main/en/home/about-the-cpvo/statistics>

ESCOOP - The first European Social Cooperative, <www.escoop.eu>

European Consumer Centre Finland, 'European small claims procedure' <www.ecc.fi/en/about-us/court-proceedings-in-cross-border-trade-consumer-disputes/european-small-claims-procedure/>

European Consumer Centre Ireland, 'European Small Claims Procedure' <www.eccireland.ie/popular-consumer-topics/european-small-claims-procedure/>

European Consumer Centres Network ECC-Net, 'European Small Claims Procedure Report' (2012) <http://ec.europa.eu/consumers/ecc/docs/small_claims_210992012_en.pdf>

European Economic and Social Committee, 'The 28th regime - an alternative allowing less lawmaking at Community level' (own-initiative opinion, CESE 758/2010, 2010) <www.eesc.europa.eu/?i=portal.en.int-opinions.10007>

European Parliament, 'Go-Ahead for the European Payment Order' (press release 20061002ipr11283, 2006) <www.europarl.europa.eu/sides/getdoc.do?language=mt&type=im-press& reference=20061002ipr11283>

European Trade Union Institute, European Company Database statistics <www.worker-participation.eu/europa-ag-se/facts-figures/total-number-of-registered-european-companies-ses>

Institut für Demoskopie Allensbach, 'Survey of Market Participants Who Use the CTM System: The Findings of a Survey Among CTM Applicants/Owners and their Professional Representatives in All EU Member States' (2010) <www.ip.mpg.de/fileadmin/user_upload/ctm-systema.h.jan.2011.pdf>

Law Society, 'Common European Sales Law' (paper, 2013) <http://international.lawsociety.org.uk/files/Law%20society%20and%20bar%20council_cesl%20briefing%20for%20meps%20april%202013.pdf>

LIBERTAS - European Institute GmbH, 'List of European Cooperatives (SCE)' <www.libertas-institut.com/de/ewiv/List_sce.pdf>

LIBERTAS - European Institute GmbH, EEIG Statistics from the European EEIG Information Centre <www.libertas-institut.com>

LIBERTAS - European Institute GmbH, SE statistics, available at: <www.libertas-institut.com/de/se/se_statistics.pdf>

OHIM, 'Statistics of Community Trade Marks 2011' (SSC009, last updated on 11 July 2014) <https://oami.europa.eu/tunnel-web/secure/webdav/guest/document_library/contentPdfs/about_ohim/the_office/SSC009-Statistics_of_Community_Trade_Marks-2014_en.pdf>

OHIM, 'Statistics of Community Designs 2015' (SSC007, last updated on 6 July 2015) <https://oami.europa.eu/ohimportal/en/the-office>

OHIM, 'Statistics of Community Trade Marks 2015' (SSC009, last updated on 7 July 2015) <https://oami.europa.eu/ohimportal/en/the-office>

Reding V, 'Making the Most of the Internal Market: Concrete EU Solutions to Cut Red Tape and to Boost the Economy' (Commission press release, Speech/10/42, 2012) <http://europa.eu/rapid/press-release_speech-10-42_en.htm>

CURRICULUM VITAE

William Bull was born on the 1st March 1981 in Milan, Italy. He attended school and obtained his 'A' Levels in Bath, England.

William has a Bachelor of Laws in English law with Italian law (University College London and the University of Genoa) and a Master of Laws from Maastricht University. During his Master studies, he worked as a student assistant at the METRO Institute for Transnational Legal Research, assisting the editor of the Maastricht Journal of European and Comparative Law, as well as with the Ius Commune Europaeum casebook series.

William began his career as a researcher in 2008 for the European Institute of Public Administration, an independent institute providing technical assistance and capacity building services to officials of the EU institutions and civil servants in national and regional administrations of Member States and applicant countries. His field of specialization at EIPA was intellectual property law, though he also gained experience in a range of other areas of European law. William commenced his doctoral research at Maastricht University in 2011, specializing in European private law and particularly contract law, in addition to intellectual property law.

Alongside his academic research, William has taught undergraduate and graduate courses in the fields of European contract law and IP law. He has also published and lectured consistently on various aspects of his research interests and fields of expertise, both in the academic context and for officials of the EU institutions.

William Bull is a member of the Maastricht European Private Law Institute and the Ius Commune Research School. The research that culminated in this book was funded by a subsidy from the Dutch Ministry of Education, Culture and Science that was granted to the Hague Institute for the Internationalisation of Law (HiiL) and Maastricht University as part of the UM-HiiL Chair on the Internationalisation of Law 2009/2010.

IUS COMMUNE EUROPAEUM

A peer-reviewed book series in which the common foundations of the legal systems of the Member States of the European Union are the central focus.

The *Ius Commune Europaeum* series includes horizontal comparative legal studies as well as studies on the effect of treaties within the national legal systems. All the classic fields of law are covered. The books are published in various European languages under the auspices of METRO, the Institute for Transnational Legal Research at the Maastricht University.

Recently published:

Volume 136: *Common Core, PECL and DCFR: Could They Change Shipping and Transport Law?*, W. VERHEYEN, F.G.M. SMEELE and M.A.I.H. HOEKS
Volume 137: *Who does What? On the Allocation of Competences in European Private Law*, B. AKKERMANS, J. HAGE, N. KORNET and J.M. SMITS
Volume 138: *The Nature of Mutual Recognition in European Law. Re-examining the Notion from an Individual Rights Perspective with a View to Its Further Development in the Criminal Justice Area*, W. VAN BALLEGOOIJ
Volume 139: *Evidence in Contemporary Civil Procedure. Fundamental Issues in a Comparative Perspective*, C.H. VAN RHEE and A. UZELAC (eds.)
Volume 140: *The Effect of D&O Insurance on Managerial Risk Taking*, M. GABER
Volume 141: *Information and Notification Duties*, I. SAMOY and M.B. LOOS (eds.)
Volume 142: *The Application of the Theory of Efficient Breach in Contract Law. A Comparative Law and Economics Perspective*, W. LIAO
Volume 143: *A European Legal Framework for Nuclear Liability. Rethinking Current Approaches*, T. HELDT
Volume 144: *The Development of European Private Law in a Multilevel Legal Order*, E.A.G. VAN SCHAGEN
Volume 145: *Property Law Perspectives IV*, D. GRUYAERT, E. RAMAEKERS and L. ROSTILL (eds.)
Volume 146: *The Citizen in European Private Law: Norm-setting, Enforcement and Choice*, C. CAUFFMAN and J. SMITS (eds.)
Volume 147: *Legal Certainty in Real Estate Transactions: A Comparison of England and France*, B. DU MARAIS and D. MARRANI (eds.)
Volume 148: *Scarcity and the State I. The Allocation of Limited Rights by the Administration*, P. ADRIAANSE, F. VAN OMMEREN, W. DEN OUDEN and J. WOLSWINKEL (eds.)

www.ingramcontent.com/pod-product-compliance
Ingram Content Group UK Ltd.
Pitfield, Milton Keynes, MK11 3LW, UK
UKHW051926100926
8556IPUK00022B/1394

9 781780 684109